Network Design Template

1. Use this portion of the tearcard to create a handy reference for your network configuration. (Photocopy it as necessary.)

2. In the "Network Address Information" section, record the Network ID and Subnet Mask for the network.

3. In the "Network Computer Information" section, record the computer name, IP address and operating system type for each network computer. If a computer uses dynamic IP addressing, use the word "dynamic" in place of its IP address.

4. In the Services Installed fields, record all services or resources made available by each computer on the network. For example, a computer may share a folder or a printer, provide shared modem access to the Internet or act as a dial-up server.

5. In the Provided Protocols field, record all protocols installed on the computer.

Network Address Information

Network ID: _____

Subnet Mask: _____ . _____ . _____ . _____

Network Computer Information

Computer Name	IP Address	OS Type	Services Installed	Provided Protocols
1. _____	_____	_____	_____	_____
2. _____	_____	_____	_____	_____
3. _____	_____	_____	_____	_____
4. _____	_____	_____	_____	_____
5. _____	_____	_____	_____	_____
6. _____	_____	_____	_____	_____
7. _____	_____	_____	_____	_____
8. _____	_____	_____	_____	_____
9. _____	_____	_____	_____	_____
10. _____	_____	_____	_____	_____

Workstation Configuration Template

1. Use this portion of the tearcard to create a handy reference for your computer configuration (photocopy as necessary).
2. In the "Computer Information" section, record the IP address, subnet mask, default gateway, and applicable DNS servers for the computer. If the computer dynamically assigns itself IP address information or receives its IP settings from another computer, list these fields as "dynamic."
3. In the "Computer Information" section, record the computer's name, operating system type, any installed protocols, clients or services, and any shared printers, drivers, or folders.
4. In the "Location of Useful Network Resources" section, record any drive mappings and include information about the data in the location that is mapped. Record the location of network file servers or printers that may be useful and include information about them. For example, you might identify a shared laser printer and include its location.

Computer Information

IP Address: _____ . _____ . _____ . _____

Subnet Mask: _____ . _____ . _____ . _____

Default Gateway: _____ . _____ . _____ .

Primary DNS: _____ . _____ . _____ . _____

Secondary DNS: _____ . _____ . _____ . _____

Computer Name: _____

Operating System: _____

Installed Protocols: _____ _____

_____ _____

Installed Clients: _____ _____

Installed Services: _____ _____

Shared Printers: _____ _____

Shared Drivers/Folders: _____ _____

_____ _____

_____ _____

Location of Useful Network Resources

Mapped Drives: _____ _____

_____ _____

File Servers: _____ _____

_____ _____

_____ _____

Network Printers: _____ _____

_____ _____

Other: _____ _____

Practical Microsoft® Windows Peer Networking

Jerry Lee Ford, Jr.

Contents at a Glance

A Division of Macmillan USA
201 W. 103rd Street
Indianapolis, Indiana 46290

Practical Microsoft® Windows Peer Networking

International Standard Book Number: 0-7897-2233-x

Library of Congress Catalog Card Number: 99-65444

Printed in the United States of America

First Printing: November 1999

01 00 99   4 3 2 1

Trademarks

Warning and Disclaimer

Associate Publisher
Jim Minatel

Acquisitions Editor
Jenny Watson

Development Editors
Rick Kughen
Steve Schafer
Jill Hayden

Managing Editor
Lisa Wilson

Project Editor
Linda Seifert

Copy Editor
Cheri Clark

Indexer
Bill Meyers

Proofreaders
Bob LaRoche
Rachel Lopez Bell

Technical Editor
Ariel Silverstone

Team Coordinator
Vicki Harding

Interior Design
Anne Jones

Cover Design
Rader Design

Layout Technicians
Stacey DeRome
Ayanna Lacey
Heather Hiatt Miller

Contents

About the Author

Jerry Lee Ford, Jr. is an author, instructor, and automation engineer with over 11 years' experience in the information technology field. He holds a Masters in Business Administration from Virginia Commonwealth University in Richmond, Virginia. Jerry is a Microsoft Certified Systems Engineer (MCSE). He serves as an adjunct instructor at John Tyler Community College in the Information Services Technology department, where he teaches in the networking program. He lives in Richmond, Virginia, with his wife, Mary, and their sons, Alexander and William.

Dedication

To Alexander and William.

Daddy loves you.

Acknowledgments

This book is the culmination of many efforts by a team of dedicated professionals. I would like to thank my mother, Martha Ford, for lending me her considerable literary skills as she proofread, more than once, every word in this book. I would also like to recognize Jim Minatel, associate publisher, and Jenny Watson, my acquisitions editor, who worked to get this book off the ground.

I also want to acknowledge Jill Hayden, Steve Schafer, and Rick Kughen for their hard work as development editors and for all their suggestions and improvements. Many thanks to Ariel Silverstone, who as technical editor made sure that everything was technically accurate.

Finally, I wish to thank my wife, Mary, for carrying more of the workload at home so that I could find the time to write this book.

Tell Us What You Think!

As the reader of this book, *you* are our most important critic and commentator. We value your opinion and want to know what we're doing right, what we could do better, what areas you'd like to see us publish in, and any other words of wisdom you're willing to pass our way.

As a publisher for Que, I welcome your comments. You can fax, email, or write me directly to let me know what you did or didn't like about this book—as well as what we can do to make our books stronger.

Please note that I cannot help you with technical problems related to the topic of this book, and that due to the high volume of mail I receive, I might not be able to reply to every message.

When you write, please be sure to include this book's title and author as well as your name and phone or fax number. I will carefully review your comments and share them with the author and editors who worked on the book.

Fax: 317–581–4666

Email: opsys@mcp.com

Mail: Publisher
Que
201 West 103rd Street
Indianapolis, IN 46290 USA

introduction

Computer networks have been around since the late 1960s, when the U.S. Department of Defense first began the development of a network that would later become the Internet. In the 1980s, a company called Novell brought the networking of the personal computer to the forefront of business computing. Since then, computer networks have pretty much been the exclusive property of large companies and government agencies that could afford the cost of expensive hardware and software resources and the salaries of teams of highly paid network administrators.

These times are changing. Two driving forces are pushing networking into the home and small company. The first force is the continued reduction in the cost of computer hardware, resulting in millions of small companies and homes now owning more than one computer. The second is the continued efforts of companies like Microsoft to bring the benefits of networking into our everyday lives. With the introduction of its Windows 98 and Windows 2000 Professional operating systems, Microsoft has made network technology available to everybody.

The capability to share files and printers, create and share a network connection to the Internet, connect to other computers over the Internet using Virtual Private Networking technology, and support remote access are but a few of the many network features Microsoft has seamlessly integrated into these operating systems. This book will help you master these topics and more. And the best part is that you don't have to be a computer genius to make it work, nor do you have to invest in expensive servers and even more expensive training to run them.

This book will show you what you need to know to take advantage of this technology and create your own peer network, whether you want to share one printer among a few computers at your small business or you are setting up a network at home so that you can smoke your friends in a rousing game of Quake.

About This Book

This book provides a practical, concise, step-by-step approach to building and administering a small computer network using Windows 2000 Pro and other Microsoft operating systems. This book focuses on how to get a network up and running from scratch. The chapters provide enough technical material to make sure that the reader understands what is happening during the process of building the network. The appendixes contain additional technical discussions that build on the concepts found in the chapters. Where appropriate, technical notes, providing related but not necessarily essential material to the current topic, are presented to ensure a thorough examination of the material.

This book focuses on Windows 2000 Pro as the primary operating system for peer networking. Although Windows 2000 Pro boasts many improvements over Windows NT 4.0, most of these improvements occurred in areas of the base operating system rather than in the networking components. Graphic examples displayed throughout most of this book show Windows 2000 Pro screen shots. A chapter on Windows NT 4.0 outlines the differences between the two operating systems. Additional chapters have been set aside in the latter portion of the book to address the unique features of Windows for Workgroups, Windows 95, and Windows 98.

How This Book Is Organized

This book is organized into five parts. It is recommended that Parts I and II be read in sequence. Parts III and IV are independent of one another and can be read in any order. Part V is a series of appendixes, which provide a technical reference as needed and can be read in sequence when all the chapters have been read.

Part I: Getting Started

This section provides everything you need to know about how to get a peer network up and running from the ground up. You will get detailed information about the hardware required to put it all together. This includes how to design your network layout and install network interface cards, hubs, and cabling. The section ends by providing you with detailed step-by-step instructions on how to install all the basic network software components you'll need.

Part II: Network Configuration

This section takes the basic network built in Part I and carries it a step further. You'll learn how to perform the administrative tasks required to configure networked computers to share resources and optimize computer performance. Before you know it, you will be sharing disk and printer resources with other network computers. You will learn network administration in detail as you establish logon management and remote administration. This section ends with a strong understanding of network security, password maintenance, and user management.

Part III: Network Utilities

In this section, you'll find out how to connect to the Internet and how to share that connection with the entire network. You will learn everything you need to know to set up a Virtual Private Network over the Internet so that your network can grow to span the globe. You will discover the secrets of remote access and then apply security to ensure that remote users can safely connect to the network. This section ends with a complete discussion of applications and utilities you will learn to use to make your network run as efficiently as possible.

Part IV: Operating Systems

Although this book presents examples using Windows 2000 Pro, this section ensures that you'll have all the information you'll need to set up peer networking in the Windows for Workgroups, Windows 95, Windows 98, and Windows NT Workstation 4.0 operating systems. Finally, we'll take a look at how to expand the network if it should outgrow the peer-networking model by discussing the steps required to convert to a client-server model.

Part V: Appendixes

This section is a series of appendixes that provide a technical reference. If you did not find what you were looking for in the chapters, you'll probably find it here. Although not required to get your network running, the information presented in this section provides an additional level of detail that covers advanced information on topics such as network protocols, networking modems, and standards.

How to Use This Book

Most of the information and examples presented in this book depend on the readers possessing the appropriate authority on the computer at which they will be working. For Windows for Workgroups, Windows 95, and Windows 98, this is not an issue. However, for Windows NT 4.0 and Windows 2000, the reader will require an account that is a member of the Administrators group. Membership in this group provides the required set of access permissions needed to install and configure components on these two operating systems.

Who Should Use This Book?

This book is for anyone interested in or charged with the responsibility of building and administering a peer network. A Windows-based peer network typically provides services for two to ten computers. For the small business, this book provides everything required to build a network that can connect office computers and printers, and provide security to protect against unauthorized use of those devices. For the home user, this book demonstrates how to build a quick two-computer network that allows the family to share a single printer and hard drives, and to play network games. For the student studying for Microsoft certification exams, this book provides information directly relevant to the Windows 2000, NT, 95, and 98 exams. It also provides a foundation for the MCSE Networking Essentials exam, as well as providing a test network from which to practice what is learned. Simply put, this book is for anyone who has at least two computers and wants to network them to share resources between them.

Conventions Used in This Book

Commands, directions, and explanations in this book are presented in the clearest format possible. The following items are some of the features that will make this book easier for you to use:

- *Menu and dialog-box commands and options:* You can easily find the onscreen menu and dialog-box commands that you're supposed to select or click by looking for bold text like you see in this direction: Open the **File** menu and click **Save**.

- *Commands you must enter:* Commands you'll need to type are easily identified by a special monospace typeface. For example, to view IP configuration information (IP address, subnet mask, and default gateway), I'll display the command like this: `ipconfig`. This tells you that you'll need to enter this command exactly as it is shown.

- *Hotkeys for commands:* The underlined keys onscreen that activate commands and options are also underlined in the book, as shown in the earlier example.

- *Cross-references:* If there's a related topic that is a prerequisite to the section or steps you are reading, or a topic that builds further on what you are reading, you'll find the cross-reference to it after the steps or at the end of the section, like this:

SEE ALSO
➤ *To see how to access a network printer, see page 420.*

- *Glossary terms:* For all the terms that appear in the glossary, you'll find the first appearance of that term in the text in *italic*, along with its definition.

- *Sidenotes:* Information related to the task at hand, or "inside" information from the author, is offset in sidebars so as not to interfere with the task at hand and to make it easy to find this valuable information. Each of these sidenotes has a short title to help you quickly identify the information you'll find there. You'll find the same kind of information in these sidenotes that you might find in notes, tips, or warnings in other books, but here the titles should be more informative.

part

1

GETTING STARTED

chapter

1

What Networks Can Do for You

Defining Networking

From the pony express to the first telegraph system to the public phone network, people have continually worked to provide better means of communicating and sharing information.

The basic purpose of a network is to share. Networks increase human efficiency by providing tools that make getting work done easier. Networks allow users to focus on doing a job without having to be concerned with many of the mechanics of finding or sharing information. Before computers were first grouped into networks, they existed as standalone systems. For users to work together, they had to be concerned with more than working with data. They had to provide data packaging, transport, and sharing. In the early days of the personal computer, people quickly found that they could share data very effectively, albeit slowly, using *sneakernet*. Sneakernet is a "network" based on the idea that people copy their data onto floppy disks and run them down the hall or corridor to a coworker's desk. In the past 5 to 10 years, sneakernet has given way to a new form of communications, the computer network.

Computer networking is the interconnection of computer equipment that allows for communication, data exchange, and device sharing. A network is a communications tool. Computer networks, like their telephone counterpart, are a communication medium for sending and receiving information. A computer network can transmit text, audio, and video from device to device at enormous speeds.

A network is a medium for data exchange. *Email* systems allow electronic messages to travel across the network, *databases* allow easy access to data stored on a central network database server, and *file servers* allow users to store files and share them with other users on the network.

A network is a means of saving money. Certain pieces of computer equipment such as laser printers and color printers can be very expensive. When these devices are connected to a network, they can be shared by all users of the network. This results in a considerable savings because duplicate pieces of equipment do not have to be purchased for each computer, and users do not have to expend time and company dollars running a sneakernet instead of working.

In simplest terms, a network is the interconnection of devices that can communicate and share data. One particularly well-known network is the Internet, which provides a global-based network that serves as an excellent model for data sharing. A person connected to the Internet has access to data on virtually every subject known to man.

Building a personal network from two computers results in a new system that is literally greater than the sum of its parts. Network users can access and utilize the total storage capacity of the entire network and not just their local system. For the home network, this means that if the kids' computer has a small hard drive, and the children need someplace to store all their games and homework, mom and dad can make a portion of their large hard drive available over the home network for supplemental storage.

The Parts of a Network

A network is composed of two distinct parts: hardware and software. *Hardware* includes such things as computers, network adapter cards to connect the computers to the network, cables for connecting everything, and other equipment.

Computers can be interconnected so that they can send and receive data, as well as share common pieces of hardware such as disk drives, CD-ROMs, and printers.

Software includes the operating system that runs each computer, the network operating system that runs the network, protocols that allow computers to communicate over the network, and client and server software to allow computers to share and access resources over the network.

SEE ALSO

➤ *To learn more about the software that supports Windows networks, see page 66.*

Windows 2000 Pro is both a network operating system, or NOS, and an operating system, or OS. Windows 2000 Pro includes multiple types of client software that allows a Windows 2000 Pro computer to connect to many types of networks in addition to Microsoft networks. A client is a computer on the network that uses services provided by other computers on the network known as servers.

Windows 2000 Pro also supports multiple types of protocols. *Protocols* are sets of communications standards. Protocols are also the languages that all devices on the network will use to speak, or communicate, with one another. Windows 2000 Pro makes an excellent client for use on large server-based networks such as a Novell NetWare network or a Windows 2000 domain. A *domain* is a collection of clients and servers that are managed as an organizational unit with centralized security database.

SEE ALSO

➤ *To learn more about which network protocols are supported by Windows networks, see page 66.*

➤ *For a complete review of network protocols, see page 524.*

In addition, Windows 2000 Pro, like Windows NT 4.0 and other Windows operating systems, has integrated NOS functionality, which makes it a great tool for building peer networks. This means that Windows 2000 Pro is the only software required to build a small network of 2 to 10 computers that can provide all the features expected of larger server-based networks.

Types of Networks

There are many types of networks. A network can be identified by its physical size or location. Using these two criteria, three types of networks can be identified:

- LAN
- MAN
- WAN

A *local area network*, or *LAN*, is a network that occupies an area the size of a small office, floor, or building. This is the type of network this book addresses. A *metropolitan area network*, or *MAN*, is a network that spans a city or other similar metropolitan area. A *wide area network*, or *WAN*, is created by interconnecting smaller local area networks over a large geographic area. WAN links are usually made over telephone lines leased from various long-distance carriers. The Internet is the largest WAN in existence today.

Examining Networking Benefits

Networks provide increased productivity by speeding up communication and the flow of data. Businesses realize substantial savings because networks allow for the pooling of limited hardware resources that otherwise would have to be duplicated. When combined with applications such as databases, networks can provide unprecedented access to shared information by multiple users while protecting against unauthorized access.

Reduced Cost of Doing Business

Allowing multiple computers to share printers, hard drives, and CD-ROMs provides a direct cost savings. One expensive color printer or large-capacity disk drive can be purchased and made available to other computers on the network instead of having to buy redundant pieces of hardware and attach them locally to each computer. The only other alternative is sneakernet, whereby users copy data onto floppy disks and walk it over to the computer where the required hardware is available. Sneakernet results in lost time; slows processes; and exposes the possibility of lost, stolen, or misdirected data.

These are some of the resources that can be shared over a network:

Hardware

Printers

CD-ROMs

Hard drives

Fax modems

Scanners

Floppy disks

Tape backup systems

Plotters

Data

Files

Databases

Software

Email

Scheduling

Project planning

Faster System Processes

Eliminating sneakernet and transmitting data at rates of 10Mbps to 100Mbps increases access time to data. Data from one process can be made available to another instantly without the added dimension of physical transport.

Tightened Control over Data

Networks make it easy to store data in a single place that can be accessed from multiple locations. This centralized approach makes knowing where to find data easier. Having multiple copies of data in different locations exposes the possibility that things might get out of sync when one copy of the data receives an update that another copy might not get. In addition to higher data integrity, data is also made more secure because a single system backup can capture and archive all the data.

Secured Access to Data

Networks provide controlled access to data and network resources by authenticating network users during the login process and limiting their access based on their preassigned permissions. When combined with an audit policy, the network can not only prevent unauthorized access but also record any attempts to access data and resources.

Higher Productivity

When data is made available to different users at the same time and resources are made available that otherwise might not exist or be convenient, user productivity increases. The capability to access shared data via systems such as email means better communication and further reduces the possibility of error.

Examining the Roles of Computers on Networks

Computers can play three general roles on a network:

- Client
- Peer
- Server

A network computer acting as a *client* uses services provided by network servers but does not offer any services of its own. A networked computer acting as a *peer* performs as a client when a user is working at the computer while accessing network resources but also acts as a *server* by making a local resource available over the network to other computers. Examples of operating systems that provide network client as well as peer functionality are OS/2 Warp, Windows for Workgroups, Windows 95, Windows 98, and Windows NT Workstations. A computer acting as a server on the network is typically a high-performance machine with more hardware resources than other computers. It provides services to other computers. Operating systems that provide a client-service operating system are OS/2 Warp Server, Novell NetWare, Windows NT Server 4.0, and Windows 2000 Server.

Just as there are three general roles a computer can play on a network, there are many specific roles computers can carry out. The role of a computer is often determined by its use. For example, a computer running Windows 2000 Server can be set up to serve as a *dedicated* print server. This means that the server has been configured and optimized to provide print services to other client computers on the network. On a peer network, a computer with a locally attached printer that has been shared on the network becomes a *peer* printer server. If the computer that shares its printer on a peer network is not used as a user workstation but is used exclusively as a printer server, then the computer is a dedicated printer server.

There are many types of servers on a network, as outlined in Table 1.1. These roles are the same for all servers whether they reside on a client-server or peer network.

Table 1.1 Types of Services Supported by Peer Computers

Server Type	Description
File	Shares files across the network.
Print	Shares one or more printers with other computers on the network.
Application	Provides shared applications to computers on the network.
Database	Stores large amounts of managed data and allows client computers to access the database and retrieve individual records of information.
Message/mail	Provides an electronic post office to manage the sending and receiving of email between network clients.
Fax	Provides faxing services that allow other network computers to send and receive fax messages using that computer's modem.
Proxy	Provides a service that allows other network computers to access the Internet using that computer's modem.

Comparing Peer Networks to Server-Based Networks

As just explained, there are two kinds of Windows networks: peer and server. On Windows peer networks, all computers can act as both peers and clients. When a computer is sharing a resource with another computer on a peer network, it is acting as a server, and when it accesses a resource provided by another computer on the network, it is performing the role of a network client.

Windows 2000 Server is Microsoft's client-server networking solution. Windows 2000 Server provides the networking operating system and all network services. Clients for the server include other Windows 2000 Servers; Windows 2000 Workstations; Windows NT 4.0 Workstations; and Windows 98, Windows 95, and Windows for Workgroups computers. There is a clear distinction between the role of server machines and that of client machines. Windows 2000 Server computers provide all server roles, and other Windows operating systems function as clients that use the services provided by the server computers.

Peer Network Features

Peer networks have many features that differentiate them from their server-based network counterparts. On a peer network, all users log on to the computer where they will work. There is no central account server to validate user identity or determine whether the user has permission to access the network. As long as the computer has the proper hardware and software installed, the user can at least view network resources.

Every computer on a peer network, therefore, maintains its own information about the users who log on to that computer. On a peer network with five computers, all five computers maintain separate and distinct user account information. Windows 2000 Pro provides user-level security, which means that users are assigned individual user accounts with a logon ID and a password, and perhaps group memberships. Individual resources, such as a folder or printer, are then made secure by the assignment or denial of specific permissions such as Read or Write to individual users or groups of users. In this way, resources can be tightly locked down so that only authorized users can access them.

Advantages

Windows 2000 Pro security is decentralized. Security information is defined and stored locally on each computer. If one primary person is responsible for administration of the network, that person must physically or remotely visit every computer on the network to administer security, define new users, and perform other types of network administration. On server-based networks, all this work can be performed on a single centralized network computer.

One big advantage of peer networks is that no extra costs in terms of software are required to set up a peer network, and the cost of hardware is limited to cabling, network adapter cards, and an optional hub. Setting up a client-server network requires the purchase of additional networking software and dedicated server computers as well. Peer networks are relatively easy to set up compared to server networks.

Other Microsoft Operating System Security Models

Operating systems such as Windows for Workgroups, Windows 95, and Windows 98 offer much weaker security, providing only share-level security in which passwords are assigned to individual network resources. Any user who knows the password for a resource can access it.

Client-server networks require a dedicated network administrator who is technically knowledgeable and experienced. Peer networks, on the other hand, do not usually have a dedicated administrator.

In a peer network users are generally responsible for managing their own computers. This leaves the responsibility of setting up shared resources and applying security to the individual network user. Therefore, the stability of the network can depend greatly on the cooperative participation of its users. Another option is to appoint a single person to perform most of the network administrative duties so that individual users can be left to utilize the network to get things done.

Overall, the total cost of setting up and maintaining a peer network of two to ten workstations is considerably less than that for setting up a client-server network of the same size. You can set up a peer network to emulate a client-server network by using powerful peer computers that are dedicated to providing services to other computers on the network. For example, a company might set aside one computer on the peer network that no one uses to act as a workstation; the computer is dedicated exclusively to providing a service to the network. Using a computer in this manner on a peer network results in the creation of a dedicated server.

Disadvantages

Peer networks have some disadvantages compared to client-server networks. Additional load is placed on peer computers that share their resources over the network. The size of the network is typically limited to ten computers. And because peer networks have no central administration, the possibility of disorganization and confusion is higher for peer networks.

Peer networks have decentralized security and usually depend on trusted users and good physical security to keep data safe. When responsibility is placed in the hands of users, it becomes more difficult to enforce standards and policies. On a client-server network, the network administrator can enforce operating-system policies and standards as part of the network security model.

Client-Server Network Features

In contrast to peer networks, client-server networks are almost always more reliable, better performing, and more secure. But all these advantages come at a price, which includes dedicated high-end hardware, additional software purchases, and compensation for at least one dedicated network administrator.

A client-server network dedicates at least one computer to provide centralized security and user account management. Centralized security allows for single password access to all network resources, as opposed to maintaining multiple user accounts on peer networks. As such, this type of network can prevent user access to the network through logon authentication. Because of dedicated server equipment, individual computers are relieved of the burden of providing network services. This might mean that users' computers can run with lower levels of hardware, such as less memory and smaller hard drives.

As client-server networks grow in size, they are able to more effectively manage large numbers of users. Client-server computers can be configured and optimized for specific functions to provide the best possible service. Removing network administration from users and placing the responsibility in the hands of a few administrators makes enforcement of network policies much easier.

Of course, client-server networks have their drawbacks as well. They are always more expensive than their peer counterparts. They require dedicated hardware, software, and at least one network administrator.

Table 1.2 outlines many of the key differences between peer and client-server networks.

Protecting Important Data on the Network

If Windows 95, Windows 98, or Windows for Workgroups computers are on the network, network security becomes weaker. None of these operating systems implements user-level security, and a user can penetrate them by selecting Cancel when prompted to log on to the network. To tighten security of a peer network with mixed operating systems, store any data on computers running either Windows 2000 Pro or Windows NT Workstation 4.0.

Table 1.2   A Comparison Between Peer and Client-Server Networks

Windows Peer Networks	Windows Client-Server Networks
Lack central security	Maintain centralized security
Are suitable for 2 to 10 computers	Are suitable for any-sized network
Depend on distributed user-level security or share-level security, which uses individual passwords to protect resources	Provide both share-level and user-level security to protect network resources
Are not optimized for sharing resources; user workstations that share resources can take performance hits	Have dedicated hardware that supports client-server resources and can be configured to provide optimal network performance
Are less expensive—no extra cost in server hardware or software	Are more expensive—require dedicated hardware and additional software
Have no central administrator	Require at least one dedicated administrator
Depend heavily on physical security	Have excellent built-in security

Reviewing Different Types of Peer Networks

Many types of peer networks are on the market today. It is important to be aware that these competing networks provide services similar to those provided by a Microsoft Windows 2000 Pro peer network. These include various Microsoft offerings as well as those from other vendors. Table 1.3 compares the capabilities of these networks to help you decide which is right for you.

Table 1.3   Comparing Network Capabilities in Different Operating Systems

Network	Characteristics
LANtastic	LANtastic was the first popular peer network offering. LANtastic has taken a back seat since the arrival of Windows 95. However, it still remains as a viable competitor in the peer arena and does a good job of connecting DOS and Windows computers. LANtastic is capable of networking hundreds of computers on a single network. It also offers support for OS/2 computers in the form of an add-on product. LANtastic is a NOS and not an operating system. It provides the NOS and supports multiple-operating-system connectivity.

Network	Characteristics
Personal NetWare	Personal NetWare is Novell's entry in the peer networking market. Personal NetWare connects DOS and Windows computers, and it supports networks of up to 50 computers. It provides the NOS and supports multiple-operating-system connectivity.
OS/2 Warp Connect	OS/2 Warp Connect was IBM's first entry into the peer networking market. Warp Connect supports DOS, Windows, and OS/2 computers and offers all the services of Windows 95. Warp Connect, however, was doing so a full year before Windows 95 was first introduced. It supports peer networks of up to 10 computers. OS/2 Warp Connect is both a NOS and an operating system. As a NOS, it supports multiple operating systems.
OS/2 Warp 4.0	OS/2 Warp is IBM's most current version of its OS/2 network operating system. It streamlines the support provided by the Warp Connect version, making peer network setup and management easier and more convenient. It supports peer networks of up to 10 computers. OS/2 Warp Connect is both a NOS and an operating system. As a NOS, it supports multiple operating systems.
Windows for Workgroups	Windows for Workgroups was Microsoft's first entry into the peer-networking arena. It was essentially an upgrade to Windows 3.1 that added integrated, 32-bit support for networking. It supports peer networks of up to 10 computers. Windows for Workgroups is both a NOS and an operating system. As a NOS, it was intended to support connectivity with other Windows for Workgroup computers. It can exist and cooperate on peer networks with both OS/2 Warp network operating systems and all later versions of Windows network operating systems.
Windows 95	Windows 95 was Microsoft's successor to Windows for Workgroups. Like Windows for Workgroups before it, it featured integrated 32-bit networking. Windows 95 further refined the network components, and it added Plug and Play support for easier configuration and an improved graphical user interface that makes network setup, configuration, and management considerably easier than in Windows for Workgroups. It supports peer networks of up to 10 computers. It can exist and cooperate on peer networks with both OS/2 Warp network operating systems and all versions of Windows network operating systems.

continues...

Table 1.3 Continued	
Network	Characteristics
Windows 98	Windows 98 is Microsoft's successor to Windows 95. It features improvements in operating-system performance, an integrated Internet shell, support for universal serial bus hardware, faster program execution, more efficient use of disk space, and support for MMX and Virtual Private Networking. With all these improvements, Windows 98 is a more capable and user-friendly network operating system. It supports peer networks of up to 10 computers. It can exist and cooperate on peer networks with both OS/2 Warp network operating systems and all versions of Windows network operating systems.
Windows NT 4.0	Windows NT 4.0 exists in multiple flavors, including Windows NT 4.0 Workstation and Windows NT 4.0 Server. Windows NT has existed for many years. Windows NT and OS/2 have a common ancestry that goes back to the days when Microsoft and IBM were partners. Together they developed OS/2 and OS/2 Version 2. OS/2 was originally intended to replace MS-DOS as the next-generation operating system. Differences between the two companies emerged, and they decided to split. Each company took with it the work that had been shared. IBM retained the OS/2 brand name. Microsoft continued to work and refine its version, which has come to be known as Windows NT. Although the operating systems share a common ancestry, many differences exist between OS/2 and NT. To a large extent, OS/2 is no longer being pushed by IBM as a computer operating system. IBM's Warp Server version still competes on the high end of the client-server market. Windows NT 4.0 does not feature Plug and Play support like the Windows 95 and Windows 98 operating systems do. Nor does it provide support for the universal serial bus architecture. It shares the Windows 95 graphical user interface. It provides a more secure and stable network operating system but requires substantially higher levels of hardware support.

Network	Characteristics
Windows 2000	Windows 2000 is Microsoft's most recent and most powerful operating system, built on NT technology. It represents a combination of core improvement over Windows NT 4.0, features borrowed from Windows 98, and support for modem hardware. It is sold in four different packages, with Windows 2000 Pro representing both desktop and peer networking capabilities. This operating system features support for Plug and Play hardware, advanced power management, and the universal serial bus architecture. It improves on Windows NT 4.0's security model and provides a new set of management tools for better system administration. It also features integration with Internet Explorer 5. The operating system is more stable and flexible than Windows NT 4.0, providing easier maintenance tools and requiring fewer system restarts.

Windows 2000 Pro peer networks lack central security provided by their client-server counterparts. They are suitable for 2 to 10 computers. Windows 2000 Pro offers a cost-effective means of building networks, but because it is not optimized for sharing resources, users' computers that share resources can experience light to moderate performance hits. Perhaps the most important feature of a Windows 2000 Pro peer network is its cost. exception of network adapter cards and cabling, peer networks require little investment in new hardware or software. The weak spot of Windows peer networking resides in its decentralized security. On peer networks that include Windows for Workgroups, Windows 95, and Windows 98, network security is made more complicated by the weak security model provided by these operating systems, and peer networks with these other operating systems must depend heavily on physical security.

Architecting a Network: Hardware

Overviewing Required Hardware

Multiple issues need to be addressed in order to build a computer network.

A *topology* must be selected that will determine how the network will be physically laid out. The two basic choices are the *bus* and the *star* topologies.

The next selection that needs to be made is the *cable type*. In most small networks the cabling is unshielded twisted-pair, though in some situations, coax might be used. A more expensive and less used option is wireless communication, such as a radio-signal–based network.

After the decision is made as to how the network will be designed and what media will be used for connectivity, an *access method* must be chosen that governs *low-level protocol communication*. For a small peer network, Ethernet is usually a safe and correct choice. It is by far the least expensive and most commonly used access method.

A final step is the selection of the type of *network interface card*, or NIC, that will be deployed in each connected device. Although all the other decisions will be applied uniformly through the network, this last option does not have to be. In modern computers, there are typically two choices, ISA or PCI. PCI is the more recent of the two options, and it is the preferred bus card. PCI is a 32-bit architecture, whereas ISA offers only 16-bit performance. However, either bus type will work.

Topology-Specific Hardware

A network can be as small as two connected computers. Depending on the selected topology, each networked computer has one of the following sets of requirements:

Bus Topology

- Two or more computers
- A NIC in each computer
- Coaxial cabling

Ring Topology

There is another topology choice, namely the ring. However, ring topologies are somewhat dated and are not supported by most current hardware. Their coverage has been minimized in this chapter.

- A BNC T connector for each computer
- Two terminators, one for each end of the cable run

Ring Topology

- Two or more computers
- A NIC in each computer
- Coaxial cabling
- A BNC T connector for each computer

Star Topology

- Two or more computers
- A NIC in each computer
- An RJ-45 cable for each computer
- A hub

The amount and type of cabling needed depends on the topology selected for the network. The star topology requires the most cable. A *hub* or *concentrator* provides connectivity, with *twisted-pair* wiring making the connection for each computer. A run of cable is required for each network device; therefore, if the star supports five computers, five cables are required.

A bus network uses less cabling than a star network and does not require a hub, but it requires a *BNC T connector* for each NIC and a pair of *terminators* to provide termination on both ends of the network cable. On a bus topology, a length of cable is required between each connected computer. Therefore, if the bus supports five computers, four cables and five total BNC T connectors are required, as shown in Figure 2.1. Finally, a bus requires a single pair of terminators installed at both ends of the line.

FIGURE 2.1
A bus network with coax cabling, BNC T connections, and two terminators (one at each end of the cable run).

Table 2.1 summarizes the features of both cable options.

Table 2.1 Specifics of Each Network Topology

Topology	Typical Cable Type	Cable Run	Extra Hardware
Bus	Coax	One length between each computer	Two terminators
Star	twisted-pair	One length between each computer and the hub	Network hub

Computer Hardware Required

Which computers should be used as network clients depends on the type of operating system being used and the role that the computer will play on the network. Microsoft peer networks can support any combination of the following operating systems:

- Windows 3.1 with client software
- Windows for Workgroups
- Windows 95
- Windows 98
- OS/2 Warp Connect
- OS/2 Warp 4.0
- Windows NT Workstation 4.0
- Windows NT Server 4.0 (as a standalone server)
- Windows 2000 Pro
- Windows 2000 Server (as a standalone server)

The hardware resources required also depend on the role that a computer will play on a network. A workstation dedicated exclusively to providing print services might require less horsepower than a typical workstation. A computer used as a normal workstation might require less memory than a workstation that has been dedicated to provide services over a network. Likewise, a computer set aside for database services might require a fast NIC, a faster CPU, more memory, and a faster hard drive than a regular workstation.

Recommended minimum hardware requirements for each operating system are listed in Table 2.2.

Table 2.2   Recommended Hardware Requirements for Network Workstations

Operating System	Processor Speed	Hard Drive	Memory
Windows 98	486 66MHz	300MB	16MB
Windows 95	486 33MHz	250MB	8MB
Windows for Workgroups	486 20MHz	120MB	4MB
Windows 3.1	486 20MHz	100MB	4MB
Windows 2000 Pro	Pentium 233MHz	2GB	64MB
Windows 2000 Server	Pentium 300MHz	2GB	64MB
Windows NT Workstation	Pentium 75MHz	400MB	16MB
Windows NT Server	Pentium 100MHz	500MB	32MB
OS/2 Connect	486 33MHz	250MB	8MB
OS/2 Warp 4.0	486 33MHz	400MB	16MB

The requirements in Table 2.2 are not necessarily those listed by the manufacturers of those products. Acquiring computers whose hardware meets the minimum requirements stated by the manufacturers often results in computers that perform at an unacceptable level. It is therefore recommended that the requirements in Table 2.2 be considered as minimum starting points. As stated earlier, some computers might have additional hardware requirements, depending on their role on the network.

Explaining Architectural Options

When designing a peer network, you need to take multiple variables into consideration, including the following:

What kind of physical layout is best suited to the environment?

What kind of distances have to be traversed?

What are the speed and capacity requirements that the network must provide?

What types of data will be transmitted over the network?

All of these questions must be considered as the following three components are considered:

- Topology
- Media access method
- Transmission media

Each of these components provides multiple options, and the selection of any one component affects the selection of the remaining components. These components are covered in detail through the rest of the chapter.

Identifying Topologies

The logical outlay of a network is known as its topology. Topology is determined by the type of location in which the network will operate, any physical barriers that are of concern, and the type of work to be performed on the network.

Three primary types of topologies are used in modern networks: the bus, ring, and star. In addition, there are combinations of these types known as *hybrids*. Windows 2000 Pro integrates well regardless of topology selected. However, peer networks are typically based on either the star or the bus topology.

Bus Topology

On a bus, all computers are connected to a single trunk or line of cabling. The trunk actually consists of a series of smaller cables joined by BNC T connectors to form the line. Both ends of the line must be terminated with terminators to prevent the signal from echoing or bouncing back after reaching the end of the cable.

Bus networks are commonly implemented using thin coax or 10BASE-2 cabling.

A bus network is easy to install, especially in a single room or small office. A bus design is a good choice for a temporary network. For example, for a consultant who rents a hotel room once a month to teach a hands-on computer programming class, a bus network offers the fastest setup. The consultant would simply place computers on tables arranged in rows and connect the computers using a cable, beginning with the first computer on the first table and moving to the next computer until the end of the first table is reached. The cable could then be dropped to the floor and stretched to the next table and from there be connected to the next computer. This example is illustrated in Figure 2.2. In this example, a bus represents the least expensive cabling option. It uses a minimal amount of cable, is simple to configure, and is easy to understand.

Connecting Coax Cable

BNC T connectors are small T-shaped connectors that connect a computer's NIC to the network coax cable. Terminators are small connectors placed at both ends of the network cable to prevent signals from bouncing back when they reach the end of the network.

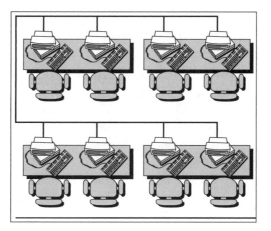

FIGURE 2.2
Temporary bus networks are fast and easy to set up.

A single run of coax cable is limited to 185 meters with a limit of 30 network nodes. Up to five network segments can be joined by a *repeater* for a total distance of 925 meters. A repeater is a device that boots a signal as it passes through the device and is passed on to the next segment. However, only three of these segments can be populated, providing a total limit of 90 nodes on the networks. A node is a networked device that can be a workstation, a network attached printer, or another networked device. For a small peer network, a single cable run should provide all networking needs.

A bus network is a passive network. As a signal passes down the wire, it is not regenerated or amplified to keep it strong. The farther down the wire the signal travels, the weaker the signal becomes. As the signal travels the wire, every network node receives the signal or data packet. If the packet is not addressed to a given computer, that computer discards it. Only the addressed computer accepts the packet.

A bus network is more difficult to troubleshoot than a star network. The network becomes unstable if there is a break anywhere in the cable, if it is not properly terminated on both ends, or if the 185-meter cable length or the 30-node limit is exceeded. As network traffic increases, the effectiveness of a bus decreases. It is a simple design best suited to a network that will not change often.

You can expand bus networks by simply removing a terminator, adding a new stretch of cable, connecting a BNC T connector, connecting the new workstation, and adding the terminator back on the new end of the bus.

To add a workstation in the middle of the bus, locate a portion of the cable nearest the location where you want the new workstation. Disconnect a portion of the cable from one side of the BNC T connection, add a new stretch of cable, place a new BNC T connector at the end, and connect the open end of the cable to the BNC T connector. If there is no BNC T connector nearby that can be opened, you will have to cut into the cable, crimp two new BNC connectors, connect the two pieces of cable with the BNC T connector, and connect the BNC T connector to the NIC of the new workstation.

A bus network offers many advantages and disadvantages, including these:

Bus Advantages

- It offers easy installation and expansion.
- It provides a convenient means of assembling a temporary network.
- It requires the least amount of cable.

Be Careful When Adding a Computer to BUS Networks

Usually, adding a new computer to a BUS network takes only a few moments. For example, to add a computer to the end of a network, an administrator would remove the terminator from the last BNC T connector, replace it with a new segment of cable, attach a BNC T connector to the end of the new cable, and then place the terminator on the end of the BNC T connector. However, if adding a new workstation to the network takes more than a few moments, the LAN might stop operating. Some or all of the computers might lose the network connection. In this case the affected computers must be rebooted.

Bus Disadvantages

- It's difficult to troubleshoot.

- Adding and removing computers to the bus can disrupt network computers.

- A break at any point on the bus will disrupt part or all of the network.

- Improper termination leads to unpredictable network performance.

Ring Topology

The ring topology applies to *Token-Ring* networking. It resembles a bus network except that the ends of the line are connected to each other instead of to terminators. Because of the popularity of Ethernet and the ring topologies' relationship to Token-Ring, it is no longer a common topology—typically found only in older networks. One of the major weaknesses of a ring network is that a break at any point in the cable will disable the entire ring.

The ring topology is especially effective in networks that require heavy processing loads. Because all traffic flows in one direction, traffic collisions are not an issue. As more workstations are added to the network, networks based on the token topology will gracefully support declined performance, whereas a bus network's performance will decline more quickly under the same load. The ring topology is best suited for relatively stable networks that will not require a great deal of reconfiguration after being initially set up (see Figure 2.3).

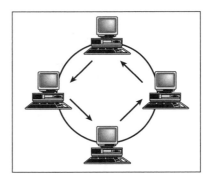

FIGURE 2.3
A sample network with four workstations operating under a Token-Ring topology.

All data is transmitted on the network in the form of packets in one direction. The ring is an active network in which each workstation retransmits what it receives from the previous computer. The ring, therefore, is not subject to a signal loss. A packet or token is passed around the ring until it reaches a computer that wants to transmit. The computer modifies the token, adds the address of the destination computer that will receive the transmitted data, and sends it out on the ring.

As the packet travels down the ring, every computer receives the token and passes it on to the next computer until either the destination computer receives it or the token is returned to the originator. A destination computer returns a message to the originator indicating that it has received the message. The sending computer then creates another token and places it on the network, allowing another computer on the network to capture the token and begin transmitting.

A ring-based network offers many advantages and disadvantages, including these:

Ring Advantages

- Every workstation is given equal access to the network.
- The network degrades gracefully as the workload increases.

Ring Disadvantages

- It's difficult to troubleshoot.
- Adding and removing computers to the ring disrupts the network.
- Failure at any point on the ring can affect the entire network.

Star Topology

On a star-based network, all nodes are connected to a hub or concentrator. Physically, the network is laid out in a star formation with the hub at the center. Locally, however, the network is managed within the hub like a bus in that every node still receives all network traffic that passes through the hub. This *home run cabling* style results in higher costs because significantly more cabling is required to implement a star network.

A star network is typically cabled using twisted-pair cable. Every node communicates directly with the hub. This design offers greater reliability than a bus network because the only single point of failure that can disable the network is the hub itself (see Figure 2.4). A cable break or another problem affects only an individual network node. Therefore, the hub effectively isolates the many individual legs of the star. This makes it easy to modify and add new computers to the network without disturbing the rest of the network.

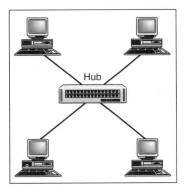

Hub

FIGURE 2.4
The star topology utilizes a central hub to provide network connectivity and route data packets from computer to computer.

A star network is easily expanded. Simply run a twisted-pair cable from the computer to the hub, and plug the cable into the computer's NIC port on the one end and into an open port in the hub on the other end.

A hub also makes a network easier to troubleshoot. Most hubs provide a level of diagnostic information including the status of individual connections, network traffic loads, and the occurrence of collisions. A star network can be expanded to support large networks that go well beyond the node capacity of a bus network. It is well suited for situations in which network growth is anticipated. As long as there are open expansion ports in the hub, you can simply add new network nodes by connecting to an open port. When the hub has no more ports available, you can expand the network by purchasing another hub and daisy-chaining them together to add additional capacity.

A star-based network offers many advantages and disadvantages, including these:

Star Advantages

- It's easy to expand.

- Diagnostic information is usually provided by the hub.

- It's easy to troubleshoot.

- Adding and removing computers does not disrupt the network.

- Cable breaks affect only individual computers.

Star Disadvantages

- The hub represents a single point of failure.

- Costs are increased due to the home run cabling style.

Working with Network Hubs

Hubs can support multiple cable types to unify a network. For example, you might have a network based on coax cabling that also needs to support a single Ethernet device.

Hubs can be either passive or active. Passive hubs simply act as a pass-through, allowing signals to be sent to all other workstations without any strengthening of the original signal. Active hubs amplify the signal as it passes through the hub to all other computers connected to the network. Simple hubs might offer basic connectivity with few other features. Power, collision, and status LED indicators are among the many features that might be present. More expensive hubs might include protection of electric circuitry, error detection, LED indicators showing the channel status of each connection, and internal programming.

A simple hub suitable for a small peer network of 10 or fewer computers might run around $100 to $200 for a 10Mbps Ethernet network. A smaller network of 2 to 4 computers might be able to make do with a four- or five-port hub. If the network grows beyond this size, an additional port can be purchased to support the new computers. The two hubs can then be connected to one another to create a network backbone as shown in Figure 2.5. Connecting a standard RJ-45 cable connection from the uplink port on one hub to the uplink port on the other hub makes the connection.

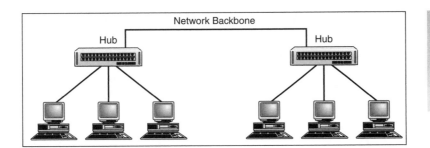

Network Backbone

FIGURE 2.5
Connecting multiple hubs to form a network backbone allows for network expansion.

More expensive hubs (that is, hubs with a microprocessor) can provide a level of intelligence that can, in addition to repeating a signal, provide centralized monitoring and management of the network. An intelligent hub designed to support larger networks can range in cost up to $2,000 or $3,000.

In a simple network in which the computers are close together, hub placement is not complicated. Usually, this involves placing the hub near one of the computers and then running the wires from there to the other workstations. If the workstations are spread out over a wide area, the hub should be located in a central location to minimize the distance of any one cable run from the hub to the farthest workstation. In a new building, wiring is usually run in the walls, floors, or ceilings with outlets placed in walls throughout the office. Short cable runs can be connected from the wall outlets to individual computers.

Examining Network Cabling Options

Cabling connects all the components of a network and provides a communication path for data exchange. Networks support various cabling options, including coaxial, twisted-pair, fiber-optic, and air-based transmission methods. Cabling is the communications media for the networks. It provides the means by which data is transmitted over a network.

The Difference in Cable and Other Media

On small peer networks, coaxial and twisted-pair will be the norm. Coaxial cable—or simply coax—is a common cable type. However, today it is mainly supported in older networks and has been supplanted by twisted-pair cable in most installations.

Fiber-optic is a high-capacity medium typically used in large networks that require high-speed data transmission. It is capable of data transmission rates up to 2Gbps, although 100Mbps is typical. It is often used as a backbone to connect distant networks into a wide area network. It is very expensive and requires expert installation. The core of a fiber-optic cable consists of glass. This makes it somewhat inflexible to work with. Due to its cost, purpose, and complexity, this cabling medium is not used in small peer networks.

Air-based transmission is used in some situations as an alternative to physical cabling. For example, if a preservation society purchased a historical building and needed to set up a small network inside, but did not want to alter the physical environment by installing cabling or leave the cabling exposed on open floors, air-based transmission could provide an alternative. Examples of air-based transmission include infrared and radio. *Infrared* is a point-to-point direct line-of-sight transmission that requires that there be no physical obstruction between the sender and the receiver. It can be used to effectively connect networks in two buildings across the street from one another.

Radio-based transmission is not a point-to-point transmission, meaning that direct line of sight is not required. This allows for more flexible placement of network components. However, radio-based transmissions are subject to interception and support only relatively short distances.

Another type of communications media comprises the use of ISDN lines, T-lines, and regular phone lines. Telecommunications carriers such as local and national phone companies can provide communications lines that allow companies to connect to distant network resources. This normally involves connecting two distant LANs, creating a metropolitan area network (MAN) or wide area network (WAN), which go beyond the scope of this book.

Going Wireless

Many companies offer wireless networking solutions. For example, WebGear at www.webgear.com offers the Aviator wireless networking kit with everything required to set up a network of two computers. This kit is priced under $200. WebGear also sells individual add-on modules for adding more computers to the network.

Getting Started with Networking Kits

Many companies offer different types of networking kits, including 10BASE-T ISA kits, 10BASE-T PCI kits, and 100Mbps Fast Ethernet kits. These kits include network interface cards, a hub if required, and the cabling media required to connect them.

Laying Cable

Installing of physical cable such as twisted-pair or coax can be a time-consuming process. In fact, cabling can represent a large percentage of the cost of installing a network. If the network is small and located within a small area such as a single room or small office, it might be acceptable to run the cable from workstation to workstation along the edges of walls, under tables, and around corners. In this case, it might be feasible for a small business to install the cabling itself. For example, Figure 2.2, shown earlier, presents a small coaxial bus network that could be installed relatively quickly and easily without outside expertise.

However, if running the cabling through walls, floors, and ceilings is a requirement, the cost of installation becomes significant. Usually, this means contracting out the cable installation process. Another concern with running cabling through walls, floors, air ducts, and ceilings in an office environment is local building-code standards. Coax cable used in computer networks is normally made with polyvinyl chloride, or PVC. Fire codes prohibit the use of this type of cable in specific areas where air circulates (in air ducts, under raised floors, and above false ceilings). The problem with PVC is that it produces a poison gas when burned. An alternative to PVC is Plenum-level wiring, which does not produce a poison gas when burned. The disadvantage of Plenum cabling is that it costs more and is less flexible to work with. If the network cabling plan calls for running cable in locations that would require Plenum, it might be best to consider contracting out the task to a company familiar with local building codes.

Coax Cable

Coaxial cable is a copper cable capable of supporting 10Mbps data transmissions. It costs a little more than unshielded twisted-pair. It is also a little less flexible than unshielded twisted-pair or UTP, but this difference is almost negligible. This makes coax an easy cable to work with. Coax cabling is usually associated with a bus network, presenting a 30-node limit per segment. It is susceptible to outside *electromagnetic interference* or EMI, which can interfere with the electric signals traveling over the wire. However, it is more resistant than UTP to EMI.

Coax consists of a solid copper wire surrounded by a plastic insulator, which is wrapped in a wire mesh and then covered by an outer jacket of plastic (see Figure 2.6).

FIGURE 2.6
Coaxial cabling.

The ends of the coax cable are crimped or attached to a BNC connector, as depicted in Figure 2.7. This connector is also referred to as a bayonet or a stab-and-twist connector—named for the method of attaching the connector to its mate.

FIGURE 2.7
A BNC connector.

Although coaxial cable is usually associated with a bus network, it can also be used in conjunction with a star network, in which case it requires a BNC hub to provide connectivity.

Workstations are connected to the coax cable using a BNC T connector, as depicted in Figure 2.8. The BNC connectors are attached to a BNC T connector on both sides. The NIC in a networked device is then attached to the bottom of the BNC T connector.

FIGURE 2.8
A BNC T connector.

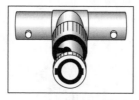

At the ends of the cable run, terminators are placed to prevent signal echoes or bounce-back. The terminators are attached to the end of the last networked device on either end of the bus. It is important that both ends of the bus are terminated; otherwise, the network will not function properly. Figure 2.1 shows a bus network with a group of workstations, cabling, and connectors with terminators at each end of the bus. Figure 2.9 shows a common terminator.

Two types of coax are used in computer networks. These are 10BASE-5 and 10BASE-2. *10BASE-5*, or *ThickNet*, is the older technology and is not commonly found in modern networks. It is much thicker than standard coax and requires special tools and skills to attach it to network devices.

FIGURE 2.9
A terminator.

10BASE-2, or *ThinNet*, is still in use as a network cable media. Physically it resembles standard cable TV coaxial, but they are incompatible because of differing electrical characteristics. There are different grades of coaxial cable, as indicated in Table 2.3. Each of these types of coax is suited for a particular purpose, and various types cannot be intermingled on the same network bus. For example, standard TV-grade cable, or RG-6, has an operations characteristic of 75-ohm. If a new workstation were added in the middle of a bus network using this cable, the network would become unreliable or completely inoperable.

Table 2.3 Coax Cable Types and Their Specifications

Coax Cable Type	Characteristic	Grade
ThickNet/ 10BASE-5	50-ohm	RG-8 and RG-11
ThinNet/10BASE-2	50-ohm	RG-58
Cable TV	75-ohm	RG-6
ARCnet	93-ohm	RG-62

Twisted-Pair

Twisted-pair is the most popular form of network cable media. A twisted-pair cable consists of two or more pairs of copper wire. Because the electric signals of the wires tend to interfere with one another (*crosstalk*) and are susceptible to outside EMI, pairs of wires are twisted around one another. Twisting the pair of wires together reduces this outside interference. Two types of twisted-pair cables are used in modern networks: shielded and unshielded. Each has it own advantages and disadvantages.

41

Shielded Twisted-Pair

Shielded twisted-pair, or STP, is the more expensive of the two types. Both STP and UTP have a layer of insulation around the wires, but each pair of STP has an extra shielding around it. STP is flexible and makes for an easy installation. It can support transmission data rates of up to 155Mbps.

Like all forms of copper-based wiring, STP is moderately vulnerable to EMI, although it offers better resistance than UTP. STP was the first type of twisted-pair cabling used in networks. However, in recent years UTP has become the new standard. Like UTP, an STP cable run is limited to a maximum of 100 meters from hub to workstation.

Unshielded Twisted-Pair

Unshielded twisted-pair, or UTP, is made of multiple pairs of twisted-pair in a simple plastic-covered casing. One type of UTP is commonly found in today's telephone systems. This telephone-system cable consists of one or two pairs of copper wires and can provide one or two communication lines. The ends of the line are connected to an RJ-11 plastic modular phone jack. The twisted-pair cable used in today's network consists of two to four pairs of wires connected to an RJ-45 modular jack, as depicted in Figure 2.10. The RJ-45 jack resembles the RJ-11 jack except that it is larger and has twice the number of wires.

SEE ALSO

➤ *For more specific information on the wiring specifications of the cable types referenced previously, see page 539.*

> **Avoid Nine-Pin D Connectors Whenever Possible**
>
> Another type of cable connector, the D connector, uses a nine-pin connection similar to the pin configuration with serial cables. It can be used with STP cabling. It is an inexpensive option to add onto a NIC, and some cards on the market today still provide this connection option in addition to coax or RJ-45. It is not a very popular option, however, and has been outdated since the arrival of the RJ-45 connector.

FIGURE 2.10
RJ-45 cabling.

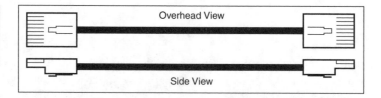

UTP is the least expensive of the available cable choices on the market today. It is very flexible and easy to install. The RJ-45 connectors are plugged into a hub on one end and a NIC on the other. There are seven grades of UTP cable, as shown in Table 2.4. UTP can support transmission speeds up to 100Mbps. Of all the available cable options, UTP is the most susceptible to EMI. Normally, cable is run around any obstacles such as florescent lights or power generators, making this a non-issue and eliminating the need to use STP. UTP is limited to 100-meter runs. UTP is the cabling of choice for most networks.

Table 2.4 Coax Cable Types and Specifications

Twisted-Pair Types	Transmission Rate	Supports
Category 1 or CAT 1	<4Mbps	Voice communications
Category 2 or CAT 2	<4Mbps	Voice communications/TR
Category 3 or CAT 3	16Mbps	Voice communications/ Ethernet
Category 4 or CAT 4	20Mbps	Ethernet
Category 5 or CAT 5	10–100Mbps	Ethernet/Fast Ethernet
Category 6 or CAT 6	1000Mbps	Gigabit Ethernet
Category 7 or CAT 7	1000Mbps	Gigabit Ethernet

CAT 1 and CAT 2 UTP are not used in network cabling. They once were used for supporting low-bandwidth voice communications. CAT 3 is the current standard voice-grade wiring found in many of today's homes and office buildings. CAT 3 can support the common 10Mbps Ethernet standard but does not offer an expansion path to 100Mbps networking.

This type of cable is not typically used in modern networks. However, if a building or an office is already wired with CAT 3 and the networking budget is limited, CAT 3 wiring can be substituted. 100BASE-T4 is a 100Mbps Ethernet specification that can run over CAT 3, 4, or 5 cable. However, this option is very uncommon in peer networks. CAT 4 can support transmission rates up to 20Mbps but has been overshadowed by CAT 5, which is the current standard. CAT 5 supports today's 10Mbps networks and offers support for expansion to 100Mbps networking in the future without requiring replacement. Given the choice of any of the previously mentioned UTP cables, always go with CAT 5.

Can I Use CAT 6 or CAT 7?

CAT 6 and CAT 7 are used primarily for Gigabit Ethernet and are not commonly used for peer networks.

43

Crossover Cabling Gigabit Ethernet

One special type of twisted-pair cabling is known as the *crossover* cable. This cable is used to build a small peer network of two computers by directly connecting the two machines without an intervening hub. Although the cable might cost a few more dollars than a normal twisted-pair cable, it eliminates the need for a hub. This solution is particularly well suited to networking two home computers. The alternatives to using a crossover cable are using coax cabling or two regular UTP cables in conjunction with a hub. An RJ-45 crossover cable is identical to a normal RJ-45 cable except that the send and receive wires are reversed on one end. A two-workstation peer network using a crossover cable is shown in Figure 2.11.

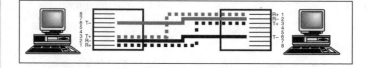

Media Concerns

The choice of cable media depends on several criteria. These criteria include such categories as cost, performance, ease of use, distance requirements, and troubleshooting:

Finding a Crossover Cable

It is unusual to find prepackaged crossover cabling at retail computer stores. That leaves two options: Either crimp the cable yourself or go to a specialty store and have one made for you. Crimping your own cable requires a specialized tool, which might make the cost of creating a simple cable impractical. A custom-made crossover cable will cost a few more dollars than a typical network cable, but because it eliminates the cost of having to purchase a hub, you will save money.

- **Cost**

  Several factors contribute to cost, including the actual length of cable needed (and the cost thereof) and the cost of installing the cable. UTP is the least expensive option. It is also the most common and therefore has the most technical and hardware support. If electrical or mechanical interference is a factor, STP or coaxial offers better performance.

- **Performance**

  If 100Mbps performance is important, only UTP provides that level of transmission. Even if 100Mbps rates are not currently required, the need to plan for future bandwidth demands might require the installation of UTP CAT 5 cabling.

- **Ease of use**

  All these options are easy to work with, but UTP is a little easier than the others.

- **Distance requirements**

  10BASE-2 cable supports a distance of up to 185 meters, whereas STP and UTP top off at 100 meters. However, a properly placed hub can result in a network in which any two computers can be 200 meters apart.

- **Troubleshooting**

  Coax bus networks are more difficult to troubleshoot but can be simpler to assemble. Twisted-pair star networks are easier to troubleshoot but require substantially more cabling and thus are more expensive to deploy.

Media Access Method

There are two primary access methods to choose from on a Windows 2000 Pro peer network: Ethernet and Token-Ring. Ethernet is the obvious choice due to its popularity, its cost, and the availability of resources. Nevertheless, an examination of both methods will be beneficial.

These access methods use different techniques for data transfer, which makes them incompatible with one another. There is one exception in which two different network segments using different access methods can be joined into a single network. This is done using a device known as a *router*, which can translate data packets from one access method to another.

Ethernet Versus Token-Ring

Two different media access methods are available today: Ethernet and Token-Ring. Ethernet is the more widespread and least expensive option, whereas Token-Ring is mainly found on older networks.

Token-Ring   Token-Ring has been around since 1984. These networks operate at either 4Mbps or 16Mbps. On the way are 100Mbps Token-Ring networks, but like their counterparts, they appear to be more expensive than the Ethernet product. Key features of Token-Ring include these:

- All computers on a Token-Ring network must operate at the same speed.
- A single Token-Ring network has a 260-PC limit.
- 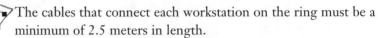The cables that connect each workstation on the ring must be a minimum of 2.5 meters in length.

The IEEE 802.5 standard defines Token-Ring. It operates on a physical ring with all data moving in a single direction down the ring. It performs using a token passing scheme. A token is an electronic message packet that is passed around the network. A computer can use the network only when it possesses the token.

The following steps demonstrate how data is transmitted over a Token-Ring network:

1. When a computer has something to transmit, it waits until it receives a token.

2. The sending computer changes the contents of the token to mark it in use and sends it down the wire followed by whatever data it has to transmit.

3. The computer can continue to transmit its data either until its time runs out or until it is done.

4. The data travels down the network until either the destination computer receives the data or the data makes a complete trip around the ring back to the sender.

5. When the sending computer is done, it changes the token to mark it as available and places it back on the network.

6. The token travels down the wire until a computer with something to transmit receives it; that computer then marks it in use and begins to transmit its data.

This scheme prevents *data collisions* that might occur if multiple computers were allowed to try to transmit simultaneously. This makes the Token-Ring network very reliable. As new workstations are added to the network, overall performance degrades a little but does so in a predictable and graceful manner.

The token-passing scheme is a noncompetitive method in which every computer patiently waits its turn on the network. To ensure fairness, every computer receives a limited amount of time before it is forced to yield the token. Data that is sent out over the ring is broken down into data packets. Compared to Ethernet, Token-Ring packets are small. Token-Ring networks are well suited to support a data entry/database environment in which most transactions are small.

SEE ALSO

➤ *For information on the IEEE network standard, see page 516.*

Ethernet   Ethernet has been around since 1975, when Xerox first introduced it. The original Xerox implementation supported a data transmission rate of 2.94Mbps. Ethernet networking standards are outlined in the IEEE 802.3 specification. Ethernet is supported by twisted-pair, coax, and air-based media.

The Ethernet access method uses a technique called *carrier sense multiple access with collision detection*, or CSMA/CD. This is a competitive method in which every computer with data to send on the network competes for access to the line. In an Ethernet network, only one device can transmit at a time. If two devices attempt to transmit data simultaneously, a data collision occurs and both machines have to wait and retransmit their data later.

When a computer has some data to transmit over the wire, it first listens to find out whether another device is currently transmitting. This is carrier sensing. If no other devices are transmitting data at that moment, the computer assumes that it is free to send its data on the wire. If another network device is currently using the network, the computer waits for a random period before checking the status of the network again. After the computer determines that the network is free, it begins transmitting its data. Because multiple computers can access the network simultaneously, this is a multiple access method. When a computer listens to the wire after transmitting its data, it is performing collision detection.

When the network is small and has relatively few attached devices, the number of collisions is small. As each new device is added, the load on the network increases. Unlike Token-Ring, in which network performance declines gracefully as usage increases, an Ethernet network's performance degrades much faster.

At some point, as new devices are added to an Ethernet network, the attached devices will begin to spend more time recovering from collisions than transmitting actual data. The solution to this problem is to split the network into two segments and use a device called a *router* to connect the segments, as shown in Figure 2.12. Every device on an Ethernet network receives a copy of every data packet whether or not the packet is addressed to that device. With the network split in half, only the devices on the side of the network where a packet originates will view the network. The router will not pass the packet through to the other side unless the destination machine resides on the other side of the router. This greatly minimizes network traffic; however, it increases costs because routers are fairly expensive devices, and it adds to administrative complexity.

FIGURE 2.12
An example of two networks connected by a router.

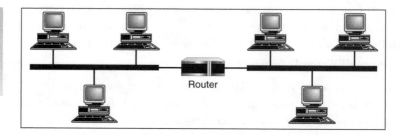

Router

Fortunately, for small peer networks of two to ten networked computers, collision traffic on an Ethernet network is not an issue. This fact, combined with Ethernet's lower cost and popularity, makes it the access method of choice for peer networks.

Compared to Token-Ring, Ethernet packets are large. Ethernet networks are well suited to support a network that handles large file transfers. With its larger-packet-size payload, it can more efficiently transmit data than can a Token-Ring network. This makes Ethernet an excellent choice for supporting software packages such as Microsoft Office in which access to data files tends to be random and data retrieval is large.

Selecting and Working with Network Interface Cards

Selection of a NIC depends on various factors, including

- The selected media access method
- The selected network media (coax or twisted-pair)
- Each computer's bus architecture

NIC Media Access Concerns

Selection of NICs depends on the access method selected for the network. Supporting the Ethernet access method requires an Ethernet-compatible NIC, and supporting a Token-Ring passing access method requires a Token-Ring NIC.

NIC Network Media Concerns

Depending on the features and support offered by the NIC, the card can cost from $20 to $200. Most Ethernet cards support RJ-45 connectivity. Combo cards are NIC cards that offer support for multiple media types such as coax, D connector, and RJ-45. Combo cards are generally a little more expensive.

On initialization, Windows 2000 Pro should be able to auto-detect the type of cable connection and configure the card supporting that media type. However, some older cards might require jumper or pin changes in order to be configured to work with a specific medium. Changing jumper and pin settings is described later in this chapter.

NIC Interface Bus Concerns

Data moves inside a computer from the CPU to other components along a bus. A bus is an electronic pathway that connects the internal components on a computer motherboard to the CPU and memory subsystem. Most computers today support two bus types: PCI and ISA. Older computers might support only the ISA bus standard. The EISA bus is an updated 32-bit version of the ISA bus that is sometimes found in older computers. Laptop computers support a bus architecture known as PCMCIA. Older generations of IBM computers support the MCA bus. However, this architecture never caught on and is seldom seen today. The primary differences between these buses are their supported transmission speed and plug-and-play compatibility. Table 2.5 provides a comparison between the available bus types.

Table 2.5 Characteristics of Computer Bus Architectures

Bus Architecture	Width	Characteristics
ISA	8-bit or 16-bit	Is the oldest technology
EISA	32-bit	Also supports 8-bit and 16-bit cards
MCA	32-bit	Supports only MCA cards
PCI	32-bit	Supports only PCI cards
PCMCIA	32-bit	Is typically found only in laptops

The ISA bus is slow compared to the other buses. However, until the introduction of the PCI bus a few years ago, it was the dominant bus architecture. Most computers made within the past three years support a dual ISA and PCI bus architecture. Generally, this means there is a combination of expansion slots for each bus. For example, a computer might have two ISA and four PCI slots on its motherboard. Other notable facts about bus architectures include the following:

- The ISA bus is the slowest bus but supports many legacy devices.
- The MCA bus is found only in older computers made by IBM and supports relatively few devices.
- The EISA bus is an extension of the ISA bus but has been outdated by the PCI bus.
- PCI cards are better designed to work with the Windows Pro Plug and Play feature.
- Of all the bus architectures, PCI supports the best performance and is preferred for devices that require high bandwidth support.

For computers that support a dual ISA/PCI bus architecture, the selection of which type of bus to use with a given peripheral device is very important. Some computer peripherals, such as the video card and the NIC, require very high bandwidth support. The 32-bit PCI bus best supports these types of devices. Other devices, such as modems, have more modest needs and perform equally well on a PCI bus and an ISA bus.

A final criterion to consider before selecting a NIC is the speed at which the network operates. On an Ethernet network, this is either 10Mbps or 100Mbps. Although 100Mbps networks are becoming the standard in larger organizations, those at the 10Mbps speed are usually satisfactory for smaller networks. A NIC that works with the ISA bus supports only a 10Mbps network connection. To connect to a 100Mbps Ethernet network, a PCI NIC is required.

Many Ethernet NICs provide dual 10Mbps or 100Mbps and are capable of detecting the speed of the network, and thus they can install themselves at the appropriate speed. These cards cost more than other cards but are recommended for use on a 10Mbps Ethernet network. If the network is ever upgraded to a Fast Ethernet 100Mbps network in the future, the computer will automatically change to support the new speeds.

SEE ALSO

➤ *For additional details on converting from an Ethernet 10Mbps to a Fast Ethernet network, see page 64.*

Parallel Interface

If all expansion slots on a computer are full, there is an alternative means of connecting the computer to a network via the parallel port. A parallel port adapter attaches to the 25-pin connection on the back of a computer. However, it performs slowly compared to a normal NIC connection. These devices usually support printer pass-through so that the computer can still use a locally attached printer.

Installing a NIC

Make sure that you have at least one available expansion slot on the computer. Expansion slots on a computer are connected to sets of wires called a bus, along which data is transferred. On a computer with available PCI and ISA expansion slots, it is always preferable to select a PCI slot.

Choices Limited for Laptop Users

For laptop users the problem of bus selection is eliminated because the computer supports only the PCMCIA bus.

Selecting the Right NIC

Not all PCI NICs support 100Mbps transmission speeds. Be sure to verify the speed of any card before purchase. If a computer with a NIC supports only a single transmission rate and the network is operating at a different speed, the computer will not be able to communicate with the network.

The PCI cards are 32-bit cards that offer superior speed and bandwidth support, as well as enhanced plug-and-play support. Devices such as video cards and NICs have benefited more from the PCI architecture than many other devices such as modems or sound cards. Whenever possible, use the PCI bus for your NIC adapter. A PCI NIC might cost a few dollars more than its ISA equivalent but will be well worth the extra dollars.

NIC Installation Steps

Installing a NIC card

1. Shut off the computer and unplug it.
2. Remove the computer case.
3. Remove the metal slot cover from over one of the available expansion slots.
4. Insert the NIC into the slot and screw it in.
5. Start the computer.
6. If the card is a plug-and-play card, Windows 2000 Pro should recognize it and automatically configure.
7. If Windows 2000 Pro does not detect the card, it can be manually added from the Add/Remove Hardware utility in the Control Panel.
8. After making sure that the device has been properly installed, shut down the computer and replace the case.

Modifying NIC Settings

If the card is a non–plug-and-play card, the card's default settings will usually work fine. However, if there is a resource conflict with another device, the card's settings must be manually reconfigured. Typically, three settings might need to be changed:

- **IRQ**

  An *IRQ* is a communications channel that a peripheral address uses to communicate with the CPU. There are only 16 IRQs available, numbered 0 through 15.

- **I/O Port Address**

  The *I/O port address* of the card identifies the location where the data being manipulated by the card will be stored.

Protecting Your Warranty

Computer manufacturers have strict warranties on their systems. If anyone other than an authorized technician opens the computer case or performs any maintenance on the computer, the warranty might be violated, resulting in a refusal to provide technical support or honor the remaining period of the warranty. If you are considering performing your own hardware maintenance while the computer's warranty period is still in effect but do not have the appropriate credentials, you might want to arrange for the retailer who sold you the computer or the card to perform the NIC installation.

■ **Direct Memory Access Channels of DMAs**

DMA assignments provide a NIC with direct-access system memory that it can independently access without relying on the CPU.

Settings are typically set on a card manually using either jumpers or switches. A jumper is a small grouping of pins that stick up on the motherboard and adapter cards. Typical jumpers have one pair of pins, though sometimes they have three or four pins. In the event that jumpers are present on a card, the documentation that came with the card will explain the function and purpose of each jumper.

For example, a card might be a combo card, meaning that it can support both a twisted-pair and a coax-cable connection. By default, the card might be set up to expect a twisted-pair connection. To instruct the card to use the coax connector instead might require physically setting a jumper. A typical jumper is depicted in Figure 2.13.

A jumper has two possible settings that are set either by placing a small metal shorting clip covered in plastic over the pins or by removing the shorting clip. Refer to the documentation that came with the card to determine the appropriate settings for the card.

Open   Closed

FIGURE 2.13
An open and a closed jumper.

Switches are located in a series of rows in a small plastic case located on the surface of the card (see Figure 2.14). The documentation that came with the card explains the function and purpose of each switch. You set switches by moving them to either an Off or an On position.

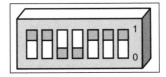

FIGURE 2.14
Dip switches 1, 2, 5, 6, and 7 are in the On position.

Some NICs might be configured using a software program supplied by the manufacturer instead of by manually working with jumpers and switches. Such NICs are typically configured using a supplied DOS disk. Check the manual that came with your NIC for more details on running the configuration program. For example, Figure 2.15 demonstrates the EZSET utility that was supplied with some older-generation ISA NIC cards.

FIGURE 2.15
The EZSET configuration utility provides a tool for configuring and running diagnostics on the NIC.

Follow the instructions that came with the card to set any conflicting settings to alternative configurations. Reinsert the card into the computer and restart the system. If the new settings have removed the conflicted resources, the card should be ready for use. Otherwise, there is still a device conflict, and a different alternative card configuration should be tried.

Determining Resources Already in Use

The process of configuration on a non–plug-and-play card is an iterative process. If you aren't sure which settings are currently available on the computer, use the Device Manager utility. This is a utility Microsoft has transported from Windows 95 and Windows 98.

Starting Device Manager

1. Select **Start**, then **Settings**, and then **Control Panel**. Choose **System** to open the System Properties dialog.

2. Click on the **Hardware** tab.

3. Click the **Device Manager** button. The Device Manager utility appears as shown in Figure 2.16.

FIGURE 2.16
The Windows 2000 Device Manager utility provides a tool for viewing and configuring hardware.

Reviewing Network Kit Options

Network starter kits are available from multiple vendors and contain everything you need to set up a two-station network. Coax-based kits include Network interface cards, a ThinNet cable, two BNC T connectors, and two terminators. Tables 2.6 and 2.7 outline the components normally provided in network starter kits. You can add computers to the network by adding a new stretch of cable to a coax-wired network or plugging a new RJ-45 cable into an open port on the hub of a twisted-pair network.

Table 2.6   10BASE-2 Network Kit Components

Quantity	Description
2	10BASE-2 (ThinNet) network interface cards
2	BNC T connectors
1	RG-58 AU coaxial cable with BNC connectors on each end
2	50-ohm terminators

Table 2.7   10BASE-T Network Kit Components

Quantity	Description
2	10BASE-T network interface cards
2	Category 5 RJ-45 cables
1	Network hub

55

Many companies are offering network starter kits. A partial list of these manufacturers and their web sites is presented in Table 2.8.

Table 2.8 Manufacturers Offering Network Starter Kits

Manufacturer	Web Site
D-Link Systems, Inc.	www.dlink.com
Linksys	www.linksys.com
NDC Communications, Inc.	www.sohoware.com
Bay Networks, Inc.	netgear.baynetworks.com
3COM	www.3com.com

Most of these companies offer several types of kits, including 10BASE-T ISA kits, 10BASE-T PCI kits, and 100Mbps Fast Ethernet kits. Some kits include all the hardware required to set up a network of as many as five or ten computers.

Examining Advanced Hardware Options

A *gateway* is a device or software that provides shared access to other resources. An Internet gateway, then, provides Internet access to multiple users on a network. Various hardware solutions can provide Internet gateway access. Several of these options are outlined in the following sections.

A list of major Internet Gateway hardware options includes

- 56Kbps modems
- ISDN modems
- Cable modems
- ADSL modems
- Analog routers
- Hubs

56Kbps LAN Modems

A *56Kbps LAN modem* is a modem with built-in support for multiple concurrent users. This device is typically connected to the network via its own built-in Ethernet interface. Software provided with the device and installed on a network computer provides Internet Explorer with the capability of configuring Internet access. Some LAN modems feature additional Ethernet ports and provide hub functionality for the network. Features typically include built-in IP routing, a voice pass-through port, and support for the V.90 modem standard.

ISDN LAN Modems

An *ISDN modem* is not really a modem because it does not convert analog and digital signals. But it does provide the same basic services that a modem provides, only at higher transmission rates over special digital high-speed ISDN lines. An ISDN modem requires that an ISDN line be installed. An ISDN line, though, is more expensive than a regular phone line, and not all local phone companies provide this service. An *ISDN LAN modem* is a special type of ISDN modem that also provides gateway Internet services to other computers. Although higher levels of throughput are available, the basic rate for ISDN provides 128Kbps support. An ISDN LAN modem can also be referred to as a *dial-on-demand router*. It also provides many unique features, including limited multiport hub functionality for IP-based networks, which means that it can perform the functions of both a hub and a modem on a small network.

By combining ISDN modem functionality with other advanced features, an ISDN LAN modem can act as a router and provide limited firewall support for the network by managing the types of communications that will be allowed to pass through to the network. It can even control the Internet addresses that are permitted to connect to the network, as well as the Internet addresses that the local network users are permitted to access.

Configuration of ISDN LAN modems is usually performed from Internet Explorer using instructions by the manufacturer. ISDN is a moderate-cost alternative to traditional modems that offer roughly double the throughput with the addition of firewall security and gateway services. The popularity of ISDN LAN modems has waned in the past couple of years with the rise of faster technologies such as cable modems.

Cable Modems

Cable modems provide an alternative to traditional analog modems. Many also provide Internet Gateway capabilities. Cable modems cost more than conventional modems with prices starting in the upper $200s. The capability to use a cable modem depends on the availability of cable modem service from the local cable company. This service has still not yet been installed in many areas. In addition to the cost of the modem, there is a monthly subscription charge for the service.

Cable modems offer multiple advantages, including these:

- Download transmission rates up to 3Mbps
- Upload transmission rates up to 1Mbps
- Superior support of video and audio streaming
- Immediate network access to the Internet because connections are never dropped
- Elimination of the cost of maintaining extra phone lines or Internet accounts

External cable modems often feature multiple connection jacks that allow many computers to directly connect. Another feature offered by both internal and external cable models is an Ethernet connection, which then opens access to the device to every computer on the network.

ADSL LAN Modems

Digital subscriber lines, or DSL, is a technology that provides data transportation over standard telephone lines into digital lines. One particular version of DSL is *Asymmetric Digital Subscriber Line*, or *ADSL*, which is becoming popular. This technology has been designed to work over standard telephone lines without interrupting regular telephone services.

ISP Cable Providers

@Home, the nation's leading cable-modem ISP, does not allow networks to connect through one modem on the standard plan. Up to three individual IP addresses can be purchased to allow multiple machines (up to the three) to connect through the same modem. However, network connectivity and server connectivity require business contracts. Contact your local cable provider to see whether cable-modem access is supported in your area and what plan best suits your intended purpose.

The *A* in *ADSL* stands for "asymmetric," which means that it is a technology that allows greater bandwidth for receiving data than for transmitting it. It originally was developed by the phone companies as a way to provide TV and phone service over normal telephone wiring. ADSL communications are capable of supporting downloading at rates over 6Mbps and upload transmission rates up to 1Mbps. Like cable modems, ADSL modems support continuous connectivity to the Internet. One limitation of ADSL is its lack of general availability.

These devices typically include such support options as Internet Gateway support with firewall protection for IP network. This device is typically connected to the network via its own built-in Ethernet interface. Software provided with the device and installed on a network computer provides Internet Explorer with the capability of configuring Internet access. Other features that might be available include a DHCP service and control over Internet traffic such as FTP or Telnet using firewall capabilities.

Analog Routers

An *analog router* is very similar to a LAN modem. It depends on using conventional 56Kbps modem technology but typically provides multiple modems that it then combines into a single logical bandwidth. For example, a four-port analog router could provide up to 224Kbps data transmission rates. These devices typically provide hub support for the network. Uplinking them to other hubs expands the modem sharing/router capabilities of the device. Another feature included might be multiple modem ports for directly attaching non-networked computers. Configuration of the device is performed through a web-based interface using software provided by the manufacturer. This device requires multiple Internet accounts and phone lines.

Internet Hubs

An *Internet hub* is essentially a device that incorporates the functionality of a network hub with the features of a modem. It requires an external modem or might feature one or more integrated modems built into the unit. A separate ISP account is required for each modem. The Internet hub connects to the modem and provides uplink connectivity to other hubs for network expansion. These devices might include built-in firewall capability.

Better Safe Than Sorry: Power Protection

If your network is required to be up during hours in which it might be unattended, certain workstations will be left powered on for extended periods. Because of the obvious dangers of electrical spikes and *brownouts* (the sudden reduction of power), special care should be taken to protect important stations on the network. A computer is especially sensitive to fluctuations in electrical power. As power from the electrical outlet is brought into the computer, it runs through an internal power supply within the computer, where several things occur:

- It is converted from AC to DC.
- It is cleaned to provide a consistent and steady flow of current.

However, the internal power supply in computers is insufficient to protect against most electrical problems. Several options are on the market to further protect computers on the network:

- *Surge protector*: A device that resembles a power strip with the added feature that it protects the attached devices from sudden occurrences of surges in the electrical current.
- *Line conditioner*: A device that functions in much the same way as a surge protector with the added benefit of protecting attached hardware from spikes. The flow of electrical current is further refined to a higher level of consistency.
- *Uninterruptible power supply (UPS)*: A device that functions in much the same way as a line conditioner with the added benefit that it can supply power to attached devices during lapses in electrical current. Typically, these devices can cost from $100 to several hundred dollars and can support both computers and attached monitors.

More expensive UPS devices are intelligent, meaning that they can be connected to a serial port on the computer and can communicate with the Windows 2000 Pro operating system. An intelligent UPS can inform a computer when the electrical current has failed and the UPS is supplying electricity. Because the typical UPS might supply backup power for only 2 to 10 minutes, an intelligent UPS can warn the computer when its backup power supply is near exhaustion so that the computer can perform a clean shutdown (saving crucial data) before a total power failure occurs.

It is a good idea to purchase UPS protection for other network components in addition to the computers. Hubs, routers, and laser printers are all susceptible to damage from power spikes and brownouts.

Considering the Costs

The cost of networking hardware can vary greatly. Costs vary depending on the size of the network, its topology, and the cable medium. The most common network costs include the costs of the following components:

- Networked computers
- Network interface cards
- Cabling
- Extra equipment

The Cost of Networked Computers

The price of a computer today can range from $250 for used 486 PCs to several thousand dollars for Pentium III–based machines. Higher-end computers provide better resources such as more disk space and faster response time. However, many networks are built using a collection of existing computers that might not be of the latest technology or have an abundance of resources. Purchasing one or two high-end computers offers an alternative to upgrading all network computers. Network applications that create a heavy processing load can be migrated to these machines. In addition, disk storage space on these machines can be shared with other network users. However, low-end machines might still have plenty of life left in them. For example, establishing a computer as a dedicated print server does not usually require a high-end computer. A 486 with moderate memory and disk space should be able to adequately provide printer services on a peer network.

The Cost of Network Interface Cards

NICs can cost anywhere from $20 to several hundred dollars, depending on the type of card and the features it offers.

Ethernet cards tend to cost substantially less than other cards, such as Token-Ring, due mainly to the popularity of Ethernet networks that allows Ethernet card manufacturers to take advantage of mass production for those cards. Ethernet cards also vary in price depending on the speed of data transfer that the cards support. A 10Mbps Ethernet card is significantly less expensive than its 100Mbps counterpart. Cards that feature support for both 10Mbps and 100Mbps speeds also cost more. More expensive cards usually provide more documentation and more software support than less expensive cards.

The Cost of Cabling

Cabling costs vary in several ways. ThinNet coax cabling requires special tools that add to the cost of doing it yourself. ThinNet coax cable costs little more than unshielded twisted-pair cabling. ThinNet cabling, though still popular, is mostly found in older networks. ThinNet cabling is especially good when the network is located in a single room or small area where cable can be run from PC to PC.

Buying prepackaged, off-the-rack cables costs more than crimping (that is, assembling) your own cables when the amount of cabling required is significant. When the network is small, buying already-assembled cabling can be less expensive.

The Cost of Extra Equipment

A hub is required to connect more than one computer on a star-based network. Small hubs provide support for connecting as few as four PCs for a cost as low as $50, whereas larger hubs capable of supporting dozens of computers can cost many hundreds of dollars. UPS devices range from the low $100 upward to several hundreds of dollars. More expensive UPS devices might offer the capability to protect more than a single computer and its monitor. Surge protectors range from $20 to $50. Other devices such as cable modems, ADSL LAN modems, analog routers, and Internet hubs can cost anywhere from $200 to $500 dollars. And 56Kbps LAN modems range from $150 to $200, whereas regular 56Kbps modems tend to cost between $50 and $150.

Many of these devices actually result in significant savings and quickly pay for themselves. For example, a 56Kbps LAN modem that gives a network of five computers access to the Internet using just one Internet account and phone line saves the cost of four additional modems, in addition to the monthly expense of the four additional phone-line and Internet accounts that are no longer required.

Sample Cost-Effective Configurations

A small two-computer network can be assembled for less than $60. This price includes two low-end NIC cards at $20 each and a crossover cable that should cost less than $20.

The two-computer network can be expanded with the purchase of a four-to-five-port hub for $40 to 50 and replacement of the crossover cable with two RJ-45 twisted-pair cables at less than $30 per run. Each new computer added to the network would then require an additional NIC and its own cable.

Assuming that the network administrator is able to install all network equipment and cabling, and excluding the cost of the computers, a small 10Mbps peer network consisting of 10 workstations can be assembled for under $600. This includes the costs of purchasing the required Ethernet NICs, prepackaged twisted-pair cabling, and a 10-port hub. Low-end NICs can be purchased for under $20, and 50-foot RJ-45 twisted-pair cables can be purchased for less than $30 per run. A 10-port hub should cost under $100.

Modems and other optional network equipment will add to the overall cost of the network but are not required and do not have to be purchased to get a basic network up and running. UPS protection is highly recommended and will add $100 to $300 per computer. If the cost of protecting the entire network with UPS is too prohibitive, consider purchasing UPS protection for any critical computer on which important network data resides.

NICs for Home and Small Businesses

Small home and office networks will probably not require high-end NIC cards. However, it's a good idea to make sure that Ethernet 10/100BASE-T cards are purchased. This will allow the network to be upgraded to support 100Mbps Fast Ethernet. Dedicated peer servers or computers that will support high-volume network applications might require more expensive NICs that can range up to $100.

Upgrading to a 100Mbps Fast Ethernet Network

For most small offices and home networks, 10Mbps is sufficient. For LANs that will support high use of multimedia and videoconferencing, a 100Mbps speed is required. It is doubtful that the small office and home user will have such requirements. If the network was wired with Category 5 twisted-pair cable, the upgrade process is relatively simple, as outlined in the following set of steps. If Category 5 cable is not in place, it must be installed before the upgrade continues. Category 3 and coaxial cable used in 10Mbps Ethernet networks will not support 100Mbps networks.

To Install a 10/100Mbps NIC

1. Disconnect the computer from the network by unplugging its cable connection from the NIC.

2. If 10/100Mbps network interface cards were installed, skip steps 3 through 5 and proceed to step 6.

3. Within Windows 2000 Pro, use the Add New Hardware Wizard to remove the 10Mbps Ethernet network interface cards, as well as to add the new 100Mbps network interface card.

4. Replace the 10Mbps Ethernet network interface cards with 100Mbps Fast Ethernet network interface cards.

5. Reconnect the computer to the network.

6. Replace any 10Mbps hubs with 100Mbps Fast Ethernet hubs.

7. Reboot all computers attached to the network.

If the computers have 10/100Mbps network interface cards, they will automatically detect the new 100Mbps network and initialize at that speed. If you installed 100Mbps cards, they will already be prepared to operate on the new network.

chapter

3

Architecting a Network: Software

Understanding Basic Network Software Components

Windows 2000 Professional provides a full suite of networking tools that enables it to perform as both a client on a client-server network and an effective participant in a peer network. Windows 2000 Pro, like the Windows NT Workstation 4.0 before it, is primarily designed to serve as a network client and not a server, although it does maintain qualities of both. Windows 2000 Professional adds to the networking capabilities of Windows NT 4.0 with new features such as support for automatic IP addressing, enhanced support for virtual private networking, and a modem proxy service.

Administrators and users of Windows 98 will find Windows 2000 Pro's network configuration pleasantly familiar. The dialogs and wizards are very similar to those used to configure a Windows 98 computer.

Understanding Security Options

In Windows networking there are two primary types of security: user-level and share-level. Windows 2000 Pro provides for both types of security. Share-level security essentially provides security on a given resource such as a network drive or printer by assigning a password to the device and allowing access only to users who know the password. Share security can become cumbersome as the number of shared devices requiring security increases. Because only two levels of passwords can be applied—read-only and full control—share-level security is not very robust. In addition, it is not very secure because anyone who learns a share password can access the device. Maintaining and remembering the password for a few shared devices is decidedly easier than memorizing dozens of passwords.

User-level security is substantially more powerful and provides Windows 2000 Pro with a superior security model. User-level security uses user IDs and passwords to identify every user who logs on to the computer. It assigns a unique access token to each user that the operating system uses to determine whether the user has permission to access any particular resource on the computer. This approach enables network security to set specific levels of security on computer resources and to dictate very specific permissions such as read or no access on a user-by-user basis.

Windows NT 4.0 also provides for both user- and share-level security.

When Windows 2000 Pro is installed on a computer, two user accounts are automatically created. These are the Administrator and Guest accounts. The Administrator account is a special account that provides full and total control over all resources on the computer. The Administrator account is automatically made a member of the Administrators group. Any account that is a member of this group automatically receives administrative privileges on the computer. The Guest account is an account set up to allow users without an account on the computer to have limited access to computer resources. By default, the Guest account is disabled, thus preventing anyone but the Administrator account from logging on to the computer after Windows 2000 is first installed.

For the exercises in Chapters 3 through 6 of this book, it is assumed that the user is either using the Administrator account or has an account that has been made a member of the Administrators group. If work is being done on a new installation of Windows 2000 Pro, it might be best to complete the setup and configuration presented in Chapters 3 through 6 using the Administrator account before creating and distributing user accounts as described in Chapter 7, "Network Administration and Security."

It is important to thoroughly configure and test each Windows 2000 computer before allowing other users to have access. As soon as initial configuration of each Windows 2000 computer is completed, it is recommended that new accounts be set up for each person designated as a network administrator. It is typical that administrators create for themselves new accounts and then make these accounts members of the Administrators group. The original Administrator account should then be disabled.

User-Level Security Lacking in Other Windows Flavors

Windows 95, Windows 98, and Windows for Workgroups operating systems provide only for share-level security. This is a point of distinction between operating systems built on Windows NT technology and those created on Windows 9X platforms. Lack of user-level security makes these operating systems inherently less secure.

Network Software Prerequisites

After the network topology, cable media, access method, and network adapter cards have been selected and deployed, the process of installing network drivers, protocols, and client software can begin. This chapter begins with the assumption that the workstations to be added to the network will be running Windows 2000 Pro as the operating system, and that physical installation of cabling and network adapters has been completed.

SEE ALSO

➤ *To review network cabling installation, see page 37.*

➤ *To review network interface card installation, see page 49.*

Networking Software

Five basic pieces of software are required to get a Windows peer network up and running:

- The appropriate network operating system on every computer
- A software driver for each installed NIC on every computer
- A common network protocol on all networked computers
- A network client on each computer
- The installation of a service on at least one computer

If PCI network adapters are chosen and physically installed when the Windows 2000 Pro operating system is first installed, plug-and-play support should automatically detect the network adapter and configure it. In addition, Windows will install a default protocol, file and print sharing, and a network client as outlined later in this chapter.

A network *protocol* is an agreed-on set of rules and procedures for communicating and exchanging data over a network. Multiple layers of protocols are required by the network, each of which is discussed in one of the following sections.

Access Methods

The lowest level is the *protocol access method*. The selection of an access method determines the type of network cards that will be

---

Same Goes for NT 4 and Windows 9x

The processes outlined in this chapter are essentially the same for Windows NT 4.0, Windows 95, and Windows 98. Most differences will appear in the form of changes in the various operating systems' graphical user dialogs. For specifics on these operating systems, see their respective chapters later in this book.

required to support the network. Access method protocols specify how data will be passed over the network, when workstations will be allowed to transmit their network data, and how data collisions on the network will be handled. The protocols are loaded when the software drivers are installed for the network adapter card.

The two most appropriate protocols for small networks are Ethernet and Token-Ring. Because Token-Ring is the less popular of the two, it costs more and fewer options are available. Ethernet is the current network access method standard for small networks. Unless there is a pressing need to use Token-Ring, it is recommended that Ethernet be selected.

Transport Protocols

The next layer of protocols involves selection from three primary transport protocols:

- NetBEUI
- IPX/SPX
- TCP/IP

Windows 2000 Pro supports all three of these protocols, as do the other Windows operating systems except for Windows for Workgroups, which out of the box, supports only the NetBEUI and IPX/SPX protocols. However, Microsoft has added support for TCP/IP to Windows for Workgroups, which is available on the www.microsoft.com Web site.

These protocols specify how the computers will communicate by governing data packet size, speed, and format. Unlike the lower-level access method protocols, Windows operating systems support the use of multiple protocols over a single network adapter through a process known as binding. This allows, for example, a computer on a TCP/IP network to also use the NetBEUI protocol to communicate with another computer on the network that is running the NetBEUI protocol.

Clients

The third level of protocols manages how the operating system and its software will communicate. These protocols are provided in the form of network clients such as the Client for Microsoft Networks. These protocols are loaded as part of the network customization process as outlined in Chapter 4, "Configuring the Network."

SEE ALSO

➤ *For more information on working with network clients, see page 89.*

Understanding the Network Interface Card Driver

Check for New Drivers

Hardware vendors are constantly improving their software drivers and making them available for free download from their Web sites. This provides easy access to the most current version of software driver. It is usually best to use the newest available driver for your NIC.

When you purchase your NIC, a disk or CD-ROM will be included that will provide a software driver and other files required to support the card. The driver provides software required for the operating system to control and manage the NIC. Windows operating systems are prepackaged with many software drivers and might already have the driver for your NIC; in this case, Windows won't ask you to supply the driver provided by the vendor.

The relationship of the NIC software driver to the rest of the operating system and the network is demonstrated in Figure 3.1. The driver is installed as part of the NIC installation process. It is then saved to the hard disk and registered in the system *registry* on Windows 9X, Windows NT 4.0, and Windows 2000 Pro operating systems, and in a configuration file on Windows for Workgroups systems. Whenever the operating system requires access to the network, it relies on the instructions provided by the driver software. The driver software becomes a customized extension to the operating system itself.

The Registry Stores Info

The Registry is a special hierarchical database repository for information about a computer's configuration. It contains profiles for every user, configuration information for the operating systems and installed applications, and detailed information on system hardware and its status. Windows operating systems use information stored in the Registry to control and manage computer operations.

SEE ALSO

➤ *For instruction on how to install a driver, see page 82.*

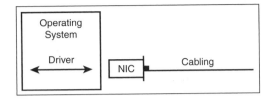

FIGURE 3.1

The network interface card driver extends the operating system's control to include management of the NIC.

Examining Local Area Network Protocols

A network protocol is an agreed-on set of rules and procedures for communicating and exchanging data over a network. Windows protocols can be viewed as a three-layered model, as shown in Figure 3.2. This model parallels the three-layered model demonstrated in Appendix C, "Protocols."

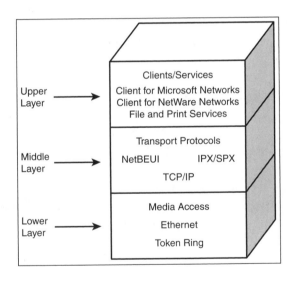

FIGURE 3.2
The three layers of the Windows protocols.

Lower-Level Protocols

- Detail how traffic is managed across the network
- Are hardware protocols
- Specify how two devices will exchange information
- Specify how the network will react if data is improperly transmitted or interrupted

71

Middle-Level Protocols

- Detail how hardware will communicate, specifying packet parameters and their speed
- Are software protocols
- Programs communicate via software protocols
- All computers must have at least one set of common protocols

Upper-Level Protocols

- Detail how the operating system and its software will talk

Binding Protocols

Windows can support multiple protocols at the same time. This is performed through a process called *binding*. For example, the network demonstrated in this book will be based on the TCP/IP protocol. Yet this does not prohibit some of the computers on the network from running the NetBEUI protocol in parallel.

Transport Protocols

All Windows operating systems support three basic transport protocols: NetBEUI, IPX, and TCP/IP.

Each protocol enables the movement of data over the network but has distinct differences that make it incompatible with the other protocols. As discussed in the "Binding Protocols" section, any combination of these protocols can exist and operate in parallel with one another over the same NIC. The important point to remember about transport protocols is that for any computer to communicate over the network, it must have a transport protocol installed that matches the protocol being used by the rest of the computers on the network.

Don't Run Unneeded Protocols

Although peer computers on a Windows network can support multiple protocols, it is best not to run extra protocols, services, or clients on a computer if they are not going to be used. A small amount of overhead is associated with each additional protocol, service, or client; this places an additional burden on the system without any benefit and results in small reductions in performance.

Installing TCP/IP Support for Windows for Workgroups

In addition to being found on the Microsoft Web site, the TCP/IP add-on module for Windows for Workgroups is available on the Windows NT Server 4.0 CD-ROM. It is located in the `\clients\ tcp32wfw\disks\ disk1` folder.

NetBEUI

NetBIOS Extended User Interface, or *NetBEUI*, is relatively small and fast. It is the fastest of the three transport protocols supported by Microsoft networking. IBM and Microsoft created it in the mid-1980s for the purpose of supporting IBM's PC Network. NetBEUI was designed in the days when memory was sparse and programs had to live together in the 640KB lower memory area. When the protocol was designed, it was envisioned that most networks would be small departmental networks. Routing support was not designed into the protocol.

NetBEUI requires no configuration during setup and is completely self-tuning. The only configuration information used by NetBEUI is the computer's name, which is established during the installation of the operating system. The computer's name uniquely identifies the computer on the network. This makes deploying a NetBEUI protocol–based network very attractive on small networks. NetBEUI performance degrades quickly after more users are added on the network and is therefore not well suited for medium and large networks.

For small networks, such as peer networks, NetBEUI is often a good choice for the transport protocol. It is a default protocol on Windows for Workgroups and Windows 95 networks.

IPX/SPX

Novell developed the *IPX/SPX* protocol based on the Xerox *XNS* protocol. IPX/SPX is the default protocol on all NetWare version 4.x and earlier network operating systems. It is a little slower than NetBEUI and might require a little more setup, but it provides routing and high speed when compared with TCP/IP. Microsoft's IPX/SPX-compatible protocol is compatible with the NetWare version. IPX/SPX is often required for Microsoft operating systems to interoperate with NetWare networks running NetWare 4.x or earlier versions. However, by itself, it is a fully functional protocol that can be used as the transport protocol on a peer network. This means that IPX/SPX can be selected as the common transport protocol for the network.

What Is a Router?

A *router* is a device that is used to connect two different networks. There are various reasons to divide a network into multiple sub-networks. The main reason for routing is to divide network traffic to reduce the amount of traffic that goes over each segment. Dividing a network into multiple parts or subnetting the network is usually not an issue on small peer networks. Both IPX/SPX and TCP/IP support the routing of network traffic across multiple network segments. NetBEUI does not.

If All Else Fails, Try NetBEUI

If problems occur when you're trying to add a new computer to a peer network, try loading the NetBEUI protocol on the new computer and on at least one other computer on the network. If, after you install NetBEUI, the new computer can view and communicate with other computers on the network running NetBEUI, then the problem is with the configuration of the protocol on the new computer and not with the new computer's NIC, cable connection, or other hardware component.

IPX/SPX is an acceptable choice for a peer network if direct access to the Internet is not required, or if the network needs to be extended to another network over a router.

TCP/IP

TCP/IP is the protocol of the Internet and is the protocol of choice on larger networks. More and more, it is becoming the protocol of choice on smaller networks as well. It performs very well in a routed environment. TCP/IP was developed in 1969 as part of the Department of Defense's *ARPAnet* network that was designed to survive a nuclear attack. The protocol was therefore designed to operate on a wide area network that could suffer from multiple failures and still continue to provide communications.

TCP/IP is actually a suite of protocols, of which TCP and IP are only two. Other protocols include the following:

FTP	A file transfer protocol used to transport files over IP networks
SMTP	An electronic mail transfer protocol
Telnet	A protocol that supports remote terminal access
DHCP	A protocol designed to automatically assign IP configuration data to network computers
UDP	A protocol similar to TCP except that it does not provide the guaranteed delivery of data
ICMP	A protocol that reports on packed delivery errors
ARP	A protocol that is used to locate hardware addresses of network computers using their IP addresses
RARP	A protocol that is used to locate a network computer's IP address when using its hardware address

Compared to NetBEUI and IPX/SPX, TCP/IP is relatively slow and consumes more of a system's resources. This might make it inappropriate for small peer networks, especially if the peer network is deployed on machines that have a minimum of system memory and slower CPU speeds.

TCP/IP requires the most configuration during setup. TCP/IP is the default protocol of Windows 2000 Pro and Windows 98 and is automatically installed during the NIC installation process. Microsoft has gone to great lengths to ensure that TCP/IP is as easy as possible to implement. A new feature added to Windows 2000 and Windows 98 provides for automatic IP-address assignment of computers on small networks. This enables Windows 2000 and Windows 98 to automatically assign themselves a temporary IP address when they boot up. Windows 2000 Pro and Windows 98 computers will automatically create a Class B network address of 169.254.0.0 with a subnet mask of 255.255.0.0.

Because TCP/IP is installed by default and set to automatically assign itself a dynamic IP address, no additional configuration is required to quickly build a peer network of Windows 2000 and Windows 98 computers.

SEE ALSO

➤ *For more information on installing and configuring the TCP/IP protocol, see page 87.*

SEE ALSO

➤ *For information on working with TCP/IP settings on Windows operating systems other than Windows 2000 Pro, see Chapters 12 through 15.*

Viewing and changing TCP/IP settings

1. From the Windows 2000 Control Panel, double-click on the **Network and Dial-up Connections** icon. The network and Dial-up Connections dialog appears.

2. Select the **Local Area Connection** icon; select **File** and then click on **Properties**. The Local Area Connection Properties dialog appears.

3. Select **Internet Protocol (TCP/IP)** and click on the **Properties** button. The Internet Protocol (TCP/IP) Properties dialog appears.

Dynamic Addressing Not Supported Outside of Windows 98 and 2000

Windows for Workgroups, Windows 95, and Windows NT 4.0 do not support the automatic self-assignment of IP addresses.

If computers on the network are running these operating systems, they will need a static, or permanently assigned, IP address configured for the 169.254.0.0 network, as demonstrated in Figure 3.3. During initialization of the network, computers with a static address should be started before any computer supporting dynamic address assignment. Otherwise, a computer might dynamically assign itself an IP address that belongs to another statically defined computer. On a TCP/IP–based network, no computers are permitted to have the same IP address.

If duplicate addresses occur, the computer that was started second cannot operate on the network and is assigned a new IP address and restarted. The alternative to this is to find the computer that dynamically assigned itself this address and shut it down. This allows the statically defined computer to be restarted and to join the network. The offending computer is started, and automatically assigns itself a different IP address.

4. To configure static IP information, select **Use the Following IP Address** (see Figure 3.3). The **IP Address**, **Subnet Mask**, and **Default Gateway** fields are then enabled. Configure these settings as required. Refer to Appendix C, "Protocols," for more information regarding these settings. Other options presented on this dialog are associated with Windows client-server network operating systems and are beyond the scope of this book. When configuration is complete, click **OK**.

5. Click **OK** on the Local Area Connection Properties dialog.

FIGURE 3.3
Establishing a static IP configuration.

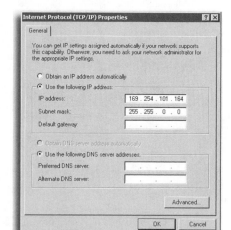

NT and 2000 Server Support DHCP

Windows NT Server and Windows 2000 Server offer the DHCP service, which can be installed and configured to automatically provide dynamic assignment of IP information to network computers including Windows 95 and Windows NT 4.0. Such a service requires a machine capable of being a DHCP server, such as an NT server.

Valid Addresses

The valid range of available IP addresses on a Class B network of 169.254.0.0 is from 169.254.0.1 to 169.254.255.254. Any statically defined IP addresses outside this range will result in the computer's not being able to communicate on the network.

SEE ALSO

➤ *For information on working with TCP/IP, see the book Special Edition Using TCP/IP (ISBN: 0-7897-1897-9), from Que.*

Reviewing Client Software

Client software enables workstations to access and use services provided by other computers on the network. Every installation of a network computer will require at least one network client. For a Windows peer network, the required client is the *Client for Microsoft Networks*. The Client for Microsoft Networks is installed by default when a NIC is detected and installed. A computer that is not connected to a network knows only about its own resources. However, to take advantage of network resources such as shared drives and printer, the computer requires a mechanism for redirecting a call for resources over the network. The client performs this redirection.

When an application makes a call for a resource, the client or *redirector* intercepts the request and determines whether the targeted resource is located on the computer. If it is a request for a local resource, the request is allowed to proceed normally. However, if the resource is not local, the client redirects the request out over the network. Windows can support multiple clients and thus connect to multiple networks simultaneously. However, the Client for Microsoft Networks is required for peer networking Microsoft workstations.

A Windows computer can run clients for multiple networks at the same time. For example, by installing both the Client for Microsoft Networks and the Client for NetWare Networks, a single computer can communicate with both Windows and NetWare computers that might be connected to the same network (see Figure 3.4).

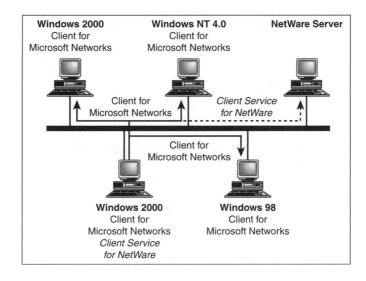

FIGURE 3.4
Adding the client service for NetWare as a second client provides the capability to communicate with a NetWare server.

Reviewing Server Software

For a computer to make its local resources available to other computers on the network, the File and Print service must be installed. Microsoft operating systems provide this capability by supporting two basic services:

- File sharing
- Printer sharing

Unlike computer workstations on a client-server network in which file and print servers manage all sharing functions, computers on a peer network share their own local resources. Because of their dual role, their performance is affected. Care should be taken to make sure that the sharing workload is distributed evenly among network computers to prevent any one workstation from becoming overloaded. Limit the sharing of computer resources to the minimum level necessary in order to reduce processing overhead. If done properly, peer resource sharing can provide a level of performance similar to that provided on larger client-server networks. This allows companies to leverage existing resources and reduce the overall cost of networking.

SEE ALSO

➤ *For instructions on installing the Network File and Print service, see page 92.*

Reviewing Operating-System Defaults

Each Windows operating system has its own unique set of system defaults that are automatically installed when a network adapter is installed on a workstation. The operating systems and their defaults are outlined here:

Windows for Workgroups Installation Defaults

- Client for Microsoft Network
- NIC driver
- NetBEUI
- IPX/SPX (automatically installed only if at least 6MB of RAM is available on the computer)

Windows 95 Installation Defaults

- Client for Microsoft Network
- NIC driver
- NetBEUI

Windows 98 Installation Defaults

- Client for Microsoft Network
- Microsoft Family Client
- NIC driver
- TCP/IP—network card

Windows NT Workstation 4.0 Installation Defaults

- Workstation
- Computer browser
- NIC driver
- RPC
- Server
- NetBIOS interface
- TCP/IP

Windows 2000 Professional Installation Defaults

- Client for Microsoft Network
- File and printer sharing for Microsoft Networks
- NIC driver
- Internet Protocol (TCP/IP)

Understanding Plug and Play (PnP)

Plug and Play is a software/hardware specification that allows the operating system to automatically detect and configure new hardware. It is highly recommended that a plug-and-play–compatible NIC be installed in all computers. For Plug and Play to work, a computer needs to have the following:

Upgrading Versus a Clean Install

If Windows 2000 Pro is being installed over another Windows-based operating system (an upgrade, not a dual-boot installation), any existing configuration settings will be transferred to Windows 2000. For example, if Windows 2000 Pro is being installed as an upgrade on top of a Windows NT Workstation 4.0 installation, the current Windows NT Workstation 4.0 network settings will be transferred into Windows 2000 Professional.

So, if you don't want your old settings cropping back up in Windows 2000, your best bet is to do a clean install of Windows 2000.

- Plug and Play system BIOS
- Plug and Play operating system
- Plug and Play adapter cards
- Plug and Play software drivers

A system *BIOS* is the software instructions stored in read-only memory on the motherboard of the computer. When a computer is booted, the system BIOS performs a power on self-test and checks system resources. A *Plug and Play BIOS* has the capability to detect hardware and manage hardware configuration. The easiest way to determine whether your system has a Plug and Play BIOS is to observe system messages that occur on the monitor as the system boots up. Messages typically include information stating that the BIOS is Plug and Play. For example, you might see statements such as "Initialization of Plug and Play loads" or "PnP Init Complete."

Windows 2000 Pro is a Plug and Play operating system. A Plug and Play operating system interacts with the system BIOS and peripheral devices to manage the plug-and-play process.

As long as new NICs are purchased that are Windows 2000-compatible, Plug and Play should be able to detect and configure the cards, providing that the computer's BIOS is plug-and-play–compatible.

Windows 98 Plug and Play looks for new hardware on three different occasions:

- When Windows 2000 Pro is first installed
- Whenever the computer is started
- Whenever the user initiates the hardware detection processes

Plug and Play NICs are cards that have been designed to support the plug-and-play technology. *PCI* is a specification designed by Intel to specifically interoperate with its Pentium series of CPUs and is designed to be plug-and-play–compatible. *ISA* cards, an older bus architecture, must be modified to support Plug and Play. It is recommended that if possible you purchase only PCI cards. ISA cards support a 16-bit architecture, whereas PCI cards can support either 32-bit or 64-bit capabilities. Modern computer systems usually support a multiple bus architecture that has both ISA and PCI expansion slots. Due to the increased capacity and speed of PCI cards and their

Plug and Play

Windows 95 and Windows 98 are Plug and Play (PnP) operating systems. Windows for Workgroups and Windows NT Workstation 4.0 do not support the Plug and Play feature.

plug-and-play compatibility, it is difficult to go wrong when selecting PCI cards.

Plug and Play NIC cards will make the hardware-installation part of the network installation substantially easier. Just about every PCI card sold today is plug-and-play–compatible. This means that after the card is physically inserted into the computer and the computer is powered on, the operating system will automatically recognize the new card and complete its installation. About the only thing you might have to do is provide either the Windows CD or a vendor-supplied copy of the NIC driver.

Some lower-end ISA NIC cards might not be plug-and-play–compatible. These are known as legacy cards. This does not mean that Windows 2000 Pro installation will be difficult. If the factory default settings do not conflict with other hardware already installed in the computer, you will be able to use the Add New Hardware Wizard to identify the card and supply its driver during NIC setup. However, if there is a hardware conflict, you will have to either physically remove the card or change its settings using either *jumpers* or *dip switches*, or you will have to run a special setup program supplied by the vendor to configure the card.

If Windows 2000 Pro detects legacy cards, it first assigns resources to these cards before attempting to assign the remaining resources to plug-and-play cards. This ensures that legacy cards receive required resources and allows Windows 2000 Pro to try to arbitrate remaining resources among peripherals that have the flexibility of allowing plug-and-play setup.

Adding and Removing Network Access

After a NIC has been physically installed in a computer, several software components need to be installed before the computer can access network resources. These components include a software driver for the NIC, as well as at least one protocol and one network client. If the computer is going to share any local resources, a service must also be installed. A computer can be removed from the network with a simple disconnect of its cable connection. However, to completely uninstall network access, all protocols, clients, services, and NICs should be removed.

Installing a Network Interface Card

Windows 2000 Pro supplies a hardware installation wizard that assists in the installation and configuration of the network interface card. Normally, Windows 2000 auto-detects a newly installed NIC and automatically launches the wizard. However, if it fails to do this, the wizard can be manually started. The wizard can be instructed to attempt to try auto-detecting the NIC or can present a series of steps to allow a NIC card to be manually specified. It is usually easiest to allow Windows to auto-detect the card and configure it. If Windows cannot perform this operation, the card can still be added manually. This process will need to be performed on every Windows computer that will be joined to the network.

Installing a NIC

1. Click the **Start** button on the Windows 2000 Pro taskbar to display the Start menu (see Figure 3.5).

2. Select **Settings** and then click **Control Panel**. The Windows 2000 Pro Control Panel appears, as shown in Figure 3.6.

3. Double-click the **Add/Remove Hardware** icon to initiate the Add/Remove Hardware Wizard.

4. Click the **Next** button to start the hardware setup process.

Installing NICs Under Other Windows Flavors

This installation process applies specifically to Windows 2000 Pro; however, the basic steps presented here are essentially the same for Windows 95 and Windows 98. Windows for Workgroups has a different process for installing a NIC, as outlined in Chapter 12, "Windows for Workgroups."

Launch It from the System Icon

The Add/Remove Hardware Wizard can also be launched via the System icon on the Windows 2000 Control Panel using the following steps:

Double-click on the **System** icon located on the Windows 2000 Control Panel. The System Properties dialog appears.

Select the **Hardware** tab.

Click on the **Hardware Wizard** button. The Welcome dialog for the Add/Remove Hardware Wizard appears.

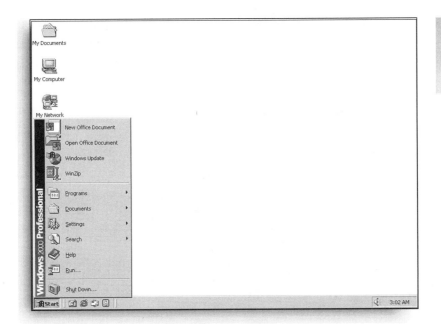

FIGURE 3.5
Windows 2000 Pro desktop.

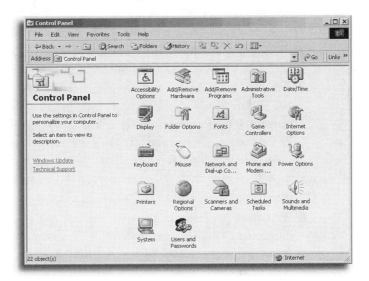

FIGURE 3.6
Windows 2000 Pro Control Panel.

5. The Add/Remove Hardware Wizard presents two options (see Figure 3.7). The default option is to **Add/Troubleshoot a Device**. Make sure that the default option is selected, and click **Next** to continue.

FIGURE 3.7
The default option pro-
vides for adding new
hardware devices to the
computer.

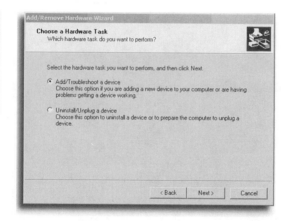

6. Windows displays a dialog informing the user that it is performing a search for new Plug and Play hardware.

7. After a few moments, the Choose a Hardware Device dialog
appears. Windows 2000 Pro displays a list of all currently
installed hardware on the computer (see Figure 3.8). If you
wanted to troubleshoot any currently installed device, you would
select the device and click Next. Windows would then display a
status for the device, and after Finish was clicked, it would automatically start the Hardware Troubleshooter Wizard. To install a
new hardware device, however, select **Add a new device** from
the Devices list, and click **Next**.

8. Windows displays a dialog with two options for finding new
hardware. The first option instructs Windows 2000 Pro to run
an automatic scan for the new hardware (see Figure 3.9). The
second option allows the administrator to specify the new hardware either from a list of known vendors or by supplying
Windows with a disk or CD-ROM that contains a vendor-supplied software driver. If you know that the NIC will not be
detected by the Plug and Play process, select **No, I Want to
Select the Hardware from a List**. Otherwise, leave the default
option of **Yes, Search for New Hardware** and click **Next**.

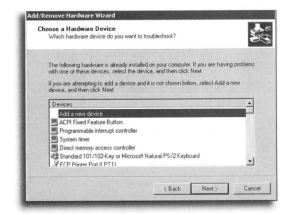

FIGURE 3.8
A list of all installed hardware is presented.

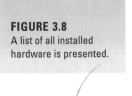

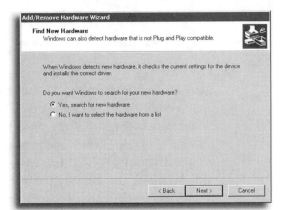

FIGURE 3.9
Windows offers to run an auto-detect scan for new hardware devices.

9. If you selected the default option to have Windows 2000 Pro auto-detect your NIC, a dialog appears that indicates the status of the auto-detect scan. When the Total Detection progress bar is completely full, the detection process is complete.

10. If the wizard fails to detect the new NIC, another dialog appears. Click the **Next** button on this dialog to initiate the process of manually specifying the network adapter card. If, on the other hand, Windows successfully locates the new NIC, the dialog offers a detailed view of its findings. Clicking the **Next** button takes the administrator to step 13, where a dialog very similar to the one displayed in Figure 3.12 is displayed.

11. Windows produces a dialog and prompts for the selection of the type of device that will be installed (see Figure 3.10). Click on **Network Adapters** and then click the **Next** button.

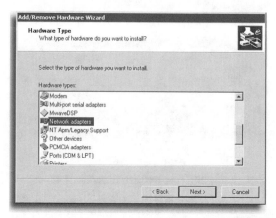

12. From the Select Network Adapter dialog, locate the manufacturer of the NIC from the **Manufacturers** list and then select your specific card from the **Network Adapter** list (see Figure 3.11). Then, click the **Next** button. If the NIC cannot be located, click the **Have Disk** button, and when prompted, supply the disk or CD-ROM that came with the NIC to provide Windows with the software files required for the operating system to manage the device (see Figure 3.12).

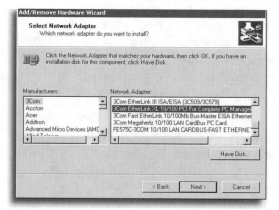

13. Windows displays a confirmation dialog. Click the <u>N</u>ext button to continue.

14. Windows 2000 Pro now begins to install the files required to configure the NIC. When it has completed this process, a dialog appears, summarizing the current status of the new device. Click **Finish**.

The NIC installation is complete, and the administrator is now ready to configure the computer and access the network as described in Chapter 4, "Configuring the Network."

Installing a Network Protocol

By default, TCP/IP is installed when Windows 2000 Pro installs a NIC. Windows supports other major LAN protocols. The process of installing an additional protocol is outlined next.

Installing a protocol

1. From the Control Panel, double-click the **Network and Dial-up Connections** icon. The Network and Dial-up Connections dialog appears.

2. Select the **Local Area Connection icon**; then, select the <u>File</u> menu and click **Properties**. The Local Area Connection Properties dialog appears, as shown in Figure 3.13.

Rebooting No Longer Required

One improvement you might notice during the installation of new hardware is that Windows 2000 Pro no longer requires a reboot of the computer for changes to take effect. Previous versions of Windows NT were notorious for requiring a reboot of the system after configuration changes were made.

FIGURE 3.13
Protocols, clients, and services are all installed from the Local Area Connection Properties dialog.

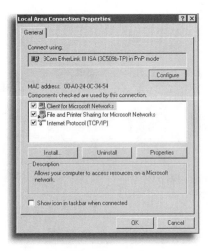

3. Click the **Install** button to display the Select Network Component Type dialog (see Figure 3.14). Three categories are displayed: Client, Service, and Protocol.

FIGURE 3.14
Selecting network components for installation.

4. Select **Protocol** and click the **Add** button to display the Select Network Protocol dialog.

5. Select the desired protocol from the **Network Protocol** list (see Figure 3.15). For example, select **NetBEUI Protocol** and click the **OK** button.

6. After the protocol installation process is complete, you are prompted to restart the computer. Until the computer is restarted, the new protocol will not be available to the system. Click **Yes** to restart the system.

FIGURE 3.15
Selection of a network protocol.

Installing a Network Client

By default, the Client for Microsoft Networks is installed when Windows 2000 Pro installs a NIC. Windows supports clients for other networking models. For peer networking, this client is all that is required. If a NetWare server is added to the network, each Windows 2000 computer will require a client specifically designed to function on NetWare networks before it can communicate with the NetWare server. The process of installing the Client Service for NetWare is outlined next.

Installing a client

1. From the Control Panel, double-click the **Network and Dial-up Connections** icon. The Network and Dial-up Connections dialog appears.

2. Select the **Local Area Connection** icon; then, select the **File** menu and click **Properties**. The Local Area Connection Properties dialog appears, as shown in Figure 3.16.

3. Click the **Install** button to display the Select Network Component Type dialog (see Figure 3.17). Three categories are displayed: Client, Service, and Protocol.

4. Select **Client** and click the **Add** button to display the Select Network Client dialog.

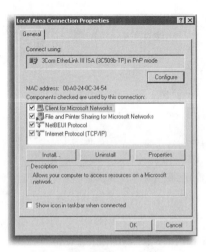

FIGURE 3.16
The Local Area Connection Properties dialog lists all installed network clients.

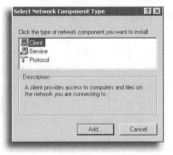

FIGURE 3.17
Selecting network components for installation.

5. Select **Client Service for NetWare** and click on the **OK** button (see Figure 3.18).

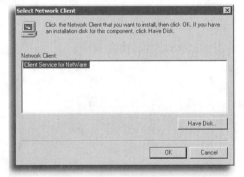

FIGURE 3.18
Selection of a network client.

6. The Select NetWare Logon dialog appears. From here
   you can configure the client for the appropriate NOS version
   supported by your NetWare server. Contact your local
   NetWare administrator for information on how to complete
   this dialog (See Figure 3.19) , and click on the **OK** button
   when done.

FIGURE 3.19
The Select NetWare
Logon dialog provides
for specification of a
NetWare server.

At this point the client installation is complete. Windows 2000
Pro will require a restart of the computer before the client can be
used. Click **yes** when prompted. After the computer restarts, it
will be able to make direct connections to Netware servers running Netware versions 2.x, 3.x, or 4.x. However, the client service
for Netwrae does not provide support for TCP/IP in conjunction
with the Netwrae Version 5.x. Therefore, this client cannot be
used to connect to Netware 5.x servers.

**Only Non-Installed
Clients Appear**

If the client you are looking
for does not appear in the
Select Network Client dialog, it is already installed.
Only non-installed clients
appear on the Network
Client dialog.

Installing a Network Service

NWLink Protocol Required

You might have noticed that entries for *NWLink* were automatically added when the Client Service for NetWare was installed. This is because this service requires the NWLink protocol in order to communicate with the NetWare server. NWLink is simply the term Microsoft uses to refer to its version of IPX/SPX in Windows 2000 and Windows NT 4.0.

By default, File and Printer Sharing for Microsoft Networks is installed when Windows 2000 Pro installs a NIC. The File and Print service is required if the computer is to provide services to other computers on the network. If this service has been uninstalled on a computer, the process of re-installing, as outlined next, can be used.

Installing a service

1. From the Control Panel, double-click on the **Network and Dial-up Connections** icon. The Network and Dial-up Connections dialog appears.

2. Select the **Local Area Connection** icon; then, select the **File** menu and click on **Properties**. The Local Area Connection Properties dialog appears, as shown in Figure 3.20.

FIGURE 3.20
The Local Area Connection Properties dialog lists all installed network services.

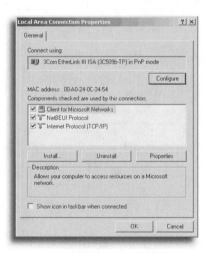

Reinstalling the Client for Microsoft Networks

If the Client for Microsoft Networks should accidentally be uninstalled from a Windows 2000 computer, steps 1 through 6 can be used to reinstall it.

3. Click on the **Install** button to display the Select Network Component Type dialog. Three categories are displayed: Client, Service, and Protocol.

4. Select **Service** and click on the **Add** button to display the Select Network Service dialog (see Figure 3.21).

5. Select **File and Printer Sharing for Microsoft Networks**, and click **OK** (see Figure 3.22).

FIGURE 3.21
Selection of a network component.

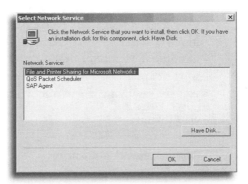

FIGURE 3.22
Selection of a network service.

6. The Local Area Connection Properties dialog reappears (see Figure 3.23). Click on the **Close** button.

FIGURE 3.23
The Local Area Connection Properties dialog shows the newly added service.

SAP Agent Included with Windows 2000 Pro

Windows 2000 Pro provides other services, including the SAP Agent. This agent advertises servers and addresses on networks with NetWare servers and the QoS Packet Scheduler or Quality of Service Packet Scheduler, which provides control over network traffic by automatically prioritizing services and managing flow control.

The computer now can share its files and printers with other computers running on the network.

SEE ALSO

➤ *For details of how to configure the sharing of specific devices, see Chapter 5, "Disk Sharing," and Chapter 6, "Printer Sharing."*

Removing Network Adapters, Protocols, Clients, and Services

The process of removing network adapters, protocols, clients, or services is essentially the reverse of the process used to install them. It is important to note that protocols can be used in conjunction with multiple devices. For example, TCP/IP can be bound to both a network adapter and a dial-up adapter. Always be careful to be sure that you are removing the correct component.

SEE ALSO

➤ *To learn more about binding, see page 72.*

Remove network components

1. From the Control Panel, double-click on the **Network and Dial-up Connections** icon. The Network and Dial-up Connections dialog appears.

2. Select the **Local Area Connection** icon; then, select the **File** menu and click on **Properties**. The Local Area Connection Properties dialog appears, as shown in Figure 3.24.

FIGURE 3.24
Any installed protocol, client, or service can be uninstalled from the Local Area Connection Properties dialog.

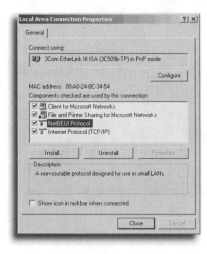

3. Select the desired client, service, or protocol, and click
   Uninstall.

4. A prompt similar to the one shown in Figure 3.25 appears. Click
   Yes to confirm the Uninstall.

FIGURE 3.25
Windows 2000 Pro
requires confirmation
before it will proceed
with the uninstall.

5. If prompted to restart the computer, click **Yes**.

part

II

NETWORK CONFIGURATION

chapter

4

Configuring the Network

Overview of Network Configuration

Installing network hardware and software as described in previous chapters provides all the components necessary to establish a peer network. This chapter reviews various procedures administrators can use to enhance the performance of network computers. These procedures are optional and when performed should increase overall network efficiency.

Part of designing the network involves deciding how to identify network resources and logically group them. Computers are identified by their computer names; they are displayed in Windows as lists or groups of computer names. A name can be used to provide important information to network users, such as the owner or location of a computer or the services it provides to the network.

A workgroup is a logical grouping of computers based on a logical organizational structure. For example, administrators can group computers by department or location. Using a department workgroup structure, an employee could browse the network looking for resources department by department.

Another component of network administration involves the configuration of individual computers to assign them roles on the network and improve their performance. Clients and servers are the two basic types of services on any network. On a peer network, most network computers perform some combination of both of these roles. The Client for Microsoft Networks Client provides client functionality, and server functionality is provided in the form of Network File and Print services. Normally, network computers will run both of these options. If a network computer has no resources to share, the Network File and Print services are not required and can be uninstalled. If a network computer is designated to serve as a dedicated file and print server that will not support local user access, the Client for Microsoft Network can be uninstalled. This allows the operating system to re-allocate resources that would have otherwise been assigned to the client.

Individual computer performance can also be enhanced by configuration of the amount of resources that Windows allocates to application programs. This allows an administrator to configure the amount of resources that Windows will assign to support the local user. The more responsive the computer is to the local user, the less responsive the computer will be to network users. Virtual memory is another important consideration in the management of computer performance. Virtual memory allows a computer to simulate physical memory by mapping out a special area of storage on local disk drives. When multiple hard drives and drive controllers are present, virtual memory can be spread across drives to provide increased performance.

One feature first introduced with Internet Information Server 4, and now a standard part of Windows 2000, is the Microsoft Management Console, or MMC. The MMC is a framework for gathering and administering various management utilities. The MMC provides the capability to perform remote administrative access on other Windows 2000 and NT computers. Microsoft provides a small collection of default consoles. In addition, administrators can create custom consoles designed to support individual working preferences.

In addition to everything previously mentioned, administrators need to be able to install new network applications and network components. Network components include additional protocols and services not provided during a default Windows 2000 installation.

Although the exercises presented in this chapter are not required for the network to operate, they can make it operate more efficiently and effectively. They represent another set of tools that network administrators use to keep things up and running as smoothly as possible.

Working with Workgroups

The primary organizational structure of a peer network is the *workgroup*. Every computer running a Windows operating system starting with Windows for Workgroups supports two organizational structures: the workgroup and the domain.

A domain is an organization construct applicable to Windows NT Server networks. The workgroup model is applicable to both the server and peer networking models. It is the only administrative model available on peer networks.

Network computers are identified by computer names. Computer names can be up to 15 characters long and must be unique on the network. Computer names should provide some type of information such as the computer's owner or location. A network computer's name is established during the installation of Windows 2000 Pro and can be changed from the System utility located on the Windows Control Panel.

Network computers are grouped into an organizational structure consisting of workgroups. Workgroup membership is established from the System utility on the Windows Control Panel. An administrator can join a network computer by simply specifying an existing workgroup name. For a small network of 2 to 10 computers, usually one or two workgroups exist, as shown in Figure 4.1.

SEE ALSO

➤ *For information about domains, see page 495.*

FIGURE 4.1
A network supporting
two workgroups.

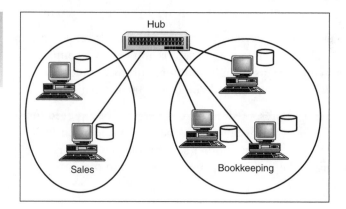

Workgroup membership is simply an organization tool that facilitates easier navigation of network resources. The assumption is that the network can be organized much in the same manner as people organize their companies. For example, a small company might have a sales and a marketing department. It might make sense then to organize their computers into workgroups that match their departments.

Workgroup membership is established by running the Network Identification Wizard from the System Properties dialog. Entering a completely new workgroup name on the network establishes the workgroup with the computer as its only member. Entering the name of a workgroup currently in use by other computers adds the computer to the specified workgroup.

Configuring a computer to join or create a workgroup

1. From the Windows 2000 Pro desktop, select **Start**, **Settings**, and then **Control Panel**.

2. Double-click on the **System** icon. The System Properties dialog appears.

3. Click on the **Network Identification** tab, shown in Figure 4.2.

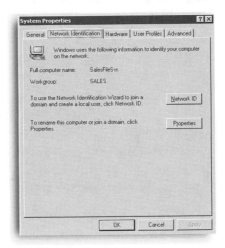

FIGURE 4.2
The Network Identification tab on the System Properties dialog manages computer name and workgroup membership.

4. Click the **Network ID** button. The Network Identification Wizard appears, as shown in Figure 4.3.

5. Click **Next** to Continue.

6. Two options are available on this dialog. The second option applies to standalone computers that will not join a network. Selecting this option allows for configuration of the computer logon process by either requiring or eliminating the mandate of entering a username and password. Select **This Computer Is Part of a Business Network, and I Use It to Connect to Other Computers at Work** (see Figure 4.4) and click on **Next**.

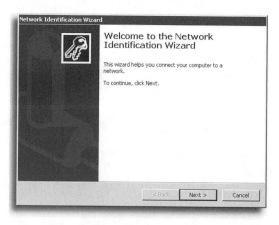

FIGURE 4.3
The Network Identification Wizard steps through the process of setting workgroup membership or controlling the logon process.

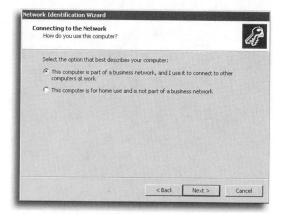

FIGURE 4.4
Establishing workgroup membership on the network.

7. The first option applies to a Microsoft client-server domain network and does not apply here. Select **My Company Uses a Network Without a Domain** to inform Windows 2000 that this computer will participate on a Windows peer network (see Figure 4.5), and then click **Next** to continue.

8. Type the name of a workgroup in the **Workgroup Name** field (see Figure 4.6). This name can be up to 15 characters in length. Entering an existing workgroup name adds the computer to that workgroup. Entering a new workgroup name creates the workgroup on the network with the computer as its only member. Click **Next** to continue.

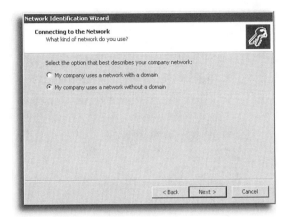

FIGURE 4.5
Specifying a peer
network.

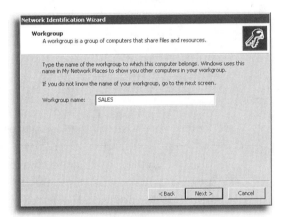

FIGURE 4.6
Identifying workgroup
membership.

9. The Network Identification Wizard completes the configuration
   process. Click **Finish**.

10. A prompt appears, stating that a reboot of the computer is
    required for the changes to take effect. Click **OK**.

11. A second prompt appears, asking for permission to restart the
    computer. Click **Yes**.

Another option presented on the Network Identification tab on the
System Properties dialog is the Advanced button. It allows the
administrator to configure the name of the computer. It also permits
changing workgroup membership without having to step through the
Network Identification Wizard.

Changing a computer's name and workgroup membership

1. Double-click on the **System** icon. The System Properties dialog appears.

2. Select the **Network Identification** tab.

3. Click the **Advanced** button (see Figure 4.7).

FIGURE 4.7
The Advanced option provides direct editing of a computer's name and workgroup membership.

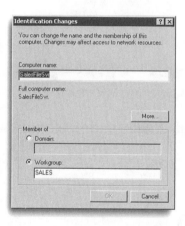

4. Enter a new name in the **Computer Name** field. This name can be up to 15 characters in length but cannot contain spaces. It must be unique on the network, meaning that no other computer or workgroup can use this name. Select the **Workgroup** option if it is not already selected, and enter the name of the workgroup that this computer will establish or join. This name can be up to 15 characters in length and does not have to be unique on the network. Click **OK**.

5. A prompt appears, welcoming the computer to the workgroup, as shown in Figure 4.8. Click **OK**.

FIGURE 4.8
An informational prompt indicates that the computer has successfully joined or created the workgroup.

6. A prompt appears, stating that a reboot of the computer is required for the changes to take effect. Click **OK**.

7. Click **OK** when returned to the System Properties dialog.

8. Another prompt appears, asking for permission to restart the computer. Click **Yes**.

Configuring Network File and Print Management

Windows 2000 Pro computers can act as both clients and servers. Adding the Client for Microsoft Services as described in Chapter 3, "Architecting a Network: Software," installs the software required to allow Windows 2000 Pro to access and use resources provided by servers on the network. In addition to this client role, a Windows 2000 Pro computer can share its local resources with other clients on the network, thus acting as a server. It is this combined client and server capability that defines peer networking.

This is one area of Windows 2000 Pro where Microsoft has made the user interface and configuration of processes resemble Windows 98 more than Windows NT 4.0. The Client for Microsoft Networks and Network File and Print Sharing are installed and uninstalled using a process that is very familiar to Windows 98 administrators. Microsoft allows the Network File and Print Sharing service to be installed independently of the Client for Microsoft Networks. Running this service alone still provides the capability to create and manage shared resources on the computer. It allows other network computers to map to its local shared drives and connect and submit print jobs to any shared printers. However, without the Client for Microsoft Network, other computers on the network will not be able to browse the computer's resources.

SEE ALSO

➤ *For information about configuring individual files, folders, or disks as shared network resources, see page 121.*

SEE ALSO

➤ *For information about applying security to shared resources, see page 189.*

SEE ALSO

➤ *For information about setting up a printer share on the network, see page 145.*

The Skinny on the Client for Microsoft Networks

On Windows 98 computers, the Client for Microsoft Networks is a prerequisite for file and print sharing. If the Client for Microsoft Networks is not already installed, Windows 95 and Windows 98 automatically install it as part of the process of installing file and print sharing. Windows 95 and Windows 98 file and print sharing cannot run without the Client for Microsoft Networks. Windows 2000 Pro, on the other hand, allows either of these two components to function independently of one another.

Another difference between Windows 2000 and Windows 95 and Windows 98 is that in Windows 2000 Pro, Network File and Print Sharing is self-configured on installation. On Windows 95 and Windows 98, both the file and the print sharing must be enabled after installation before any local resources can be shared over the network.

Configuring the Computer for Better Network Performance

For the network to operate efficiently, it is important that individual computers be configured according to the role they are assigned to perform. Windows 2000 Pro performance can be improved by the tweaking of either *application response* or *virtual memory*. These settings are configured on the Performance Options dialog in the System utility.

Application response controls the amount of resources Windows 2000 allocates to applications being run by a user logged in at the computer. Reducing the application response parameter frees up system resources, which can then be applied to supporting other system functions, including network services. Increasing application response improves the system response for the local user at the expense of network users.

Virtual memory allows the operating system to use a portion of reserved space on local hard drives to supplement physical memory. This allows the computer to support applications whose memory requirements exceed the amount of memory physically installed in the computer. In addition, configuring virtual memory can result in faster system response to local and network users.

Fine-tuning system performance

1. From the Windows 2000 Pro desktop, select **Start**, then **Settings**, and then **Control Panel**.

2. Double-click on the **System** icon. The System Properties dialog appears.

3. Click on the **Advanced** tab (see Figure 4.9).

4. Click on the **Performance Options** button. The Performance Options dialog appears, as shown in Figure 4.10.

5. There are two basic computer parameters for optimizing application performance on a Windows 2000 Pro computer. These are the support for applications and the support for background services. select the appropriate option and click **OK**. Click **OK** to close the System Properties dialog.

Configure as Either a Workstation or Server

A Windows 95 or Windows 98 computer can be configured as either a desktop computer or a network server. Any computer with at least 16MB of memory that shares resources over the network should be configured as a network server. To do this, click on the **File System** button on the Performance tab of the System Properties dialog.

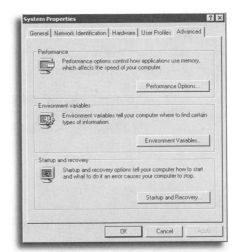

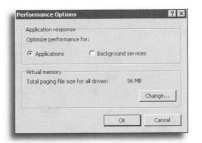

Application Response

Selecting the appropriate setting for application response is important because it adjusts the manner in which Windows 2000 Pro allocates computer resources.

Application response controls the amount of resources Windows 2000 Pro will provide to foreground and background services.

- *Foreground applications* are programs that users run as part of their normal operation on the computer. Examples include Microsoft Office and computer games.

- *Background services* are programs that Windows 2000 runs behind the scenes in support of computer operations. Examples of background services include the File and Print services, Simple TCP/IP services, and the Spooler service.

Configuring a computer to favor applications results in faster performance for the user who sits in front of the computer (locally). It provides more resources to running foreground applications and provides faster response time.

This option provides additional resources for providing File and Print services, enhancing its capability to perform as a network server. This results in slower user response time but provides faster support to network users.

Generally, most users will prefer that their computers be optimized for application performance. However, if any computers on the network are assigned to perform dedicated peer server roles, such as a print server, configuring support background services will provide better network performance.

Virtual Memory

Another configuration setting that can improve system performance is virtual memory. Virtual memory is an operating-system technique using a preset portion of a local hard drive to augment conventional memory. When a computer begins to run low on conventional memory (RAM), the operating system will begin to transfer pages of data stored in memory to a special file known as the paging file located on a local hard disk. This frees up memory, which is then made available to hold other data.

If the operating system or an application requires data that has been moved onto the paging file, the operating system will move other data from memory to the paging file to make room and will then retrieve that required data from the paging file and place it back into memory. The more conventional memory a computer has, the less virtual memory will be required and the faster a computer will operate.

Windows 2000 Pro assumes control of virtual memory by default. However, the following actions can potentially improve performance (see Figure 4.11):

- Creating multiple paging files
- Increasing the paging file size

Both of these options are described in the sections that follow.

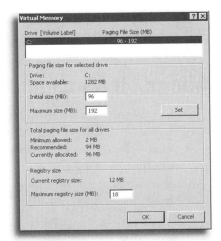

FIGURE 4.11
Virtual memory is provided by one or more paging files maintained on hard drives.

Creating Multiple Paging Files

If there is more than one hard drive and there are multiple disk controllers on the computer, performance can be improved by the creation of a paging file on each disk that is managed by a separate controller. This allows the disk controller to spread the processing load over multiple drives, enabling the controller to perform reads and writes to the drives at the same time, providing faster performance. Moving the paging file from the hard drive that contains the Windows 2000 Pro system files (typically, this directory is named \Winnt) to another drive speeds up performance. Because both the paging file and the systems files are highly used resources, moving them to separate drives spreads out the processing load and speeds up processing.

Increasing the Paging File Size

Even if a computer has only one hard drive, performance can be improved by an increase in the initial size of the paging file to match its maximum size. Windows automatically claims the amount of space on startup that has been specified for its initial paging file size. This space is then unavailable for data storage.

At system startup, Windows 2000 Pro creates a paging file of the size specified by the initial size setting. If, as the computer continues to operate, additional virtual memory is required, the operating system will have to increase the size of its paging file and expend resources in the process. This process will repeat every time Windows has to increase its paging file, until the maximum size limit is reached.

Microsoft Management Consoles

MMC Makes Its Debut

The MMC made its first appearance with Service Pack 3 for Windows NT 4.0, in which it was used as the primary management tool for Internet Information Server 4.0 (IIS 4.0).

One of the most difficult things in working with any new operating system is learning which administrative and configuration tools are available and how to use them. Often, each tool has its own unique interface, making the administrator's job more difficult. A new tool known as the *Microsoft Management Console (MMC)* has been added to Windows 2000 to address this issue.

The MMC helps standardize administrative utility program interfaces and consolidate them into manageable collections. The MMC itself is only an organizational tool and provides no administrative capabilities. Microsoft provides an initial set of default consoles that may provide all the administrative controls needed by network administrators. These consoles are outlined in greater detail in Chapter 10, "Administrative Tools."

An MMC contains one or more utilities known as snap-ins. A snap-in provides a unique administrative tool for managing a particular aspect of Windows 2000. For example, there are snap-ins for managing user accounts, services, and system logs. The MMC is an extensible architecture that allows third-party software developers to develop new add-on utilities or snap-ins.

Remote Administrations Snap-Ins

Many Microsoft Management Console snap-ins support both local and remote administration of Windows 2000 and Windows NT computers. Remote administration of Windows 9X computers is more limited.

Windows 95 and Windows 98 remote administration is enabled from the Remote Administration tab on the Passwords Properties utility located in the Windows Control Panel. After it's enabled, an administrator can run the Windows 95 or Windows 98 Net Watcher utility to administer shares for those operating systems.

Typically, MMC consoles are set up so that snap-ins are grouped to perform common or complementary sets of tasks. These consoles can then be saved as files with a .MSC extension and reused later or distributed to other administrators.

Two modes are used with MMC consoles: author and user. The author mode provides complete control over a console. After completing the construction of an MMC, the administrator can save it and change it to one of the user modes.

These are the three user modes:

- *Full access*: Allows users to traverse the entire console tree.
- *Delegated access with a single window*: Allows users to open multiple windows in the console and to view a limited subset of the console tree.

- *Delegated access with multiple windows*: Prevents users from opening multiple windows and can limit their access to a subset of the console tree.

Opening an MMC

1. Log on as an administrator.

2. From the Windows 2000 Pro desktop, select **Start**, **Settings**, and then **Control Panel**.

3. Double-click on the **Administrative Tools** icon. The Administrative Tools folder appears, containing a list of default consoles.

4. Double-click on one of the consoles to open it. Figure 4.12 shows the Computer Management console that is provided with Windows 2000 Pro.

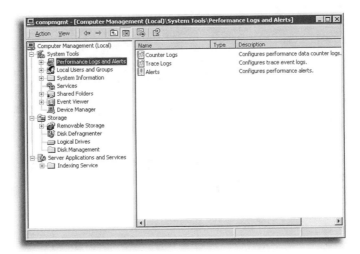

FIGURE 4.12
The Computer Management console is an MMC provided with Windows 2000 Pro.

An MMC is divided into two parts. The console tree is displayed in the left pane, and the right pane lists and provides access to the utilities provided by the snap-ins. Some MMC consoles contain utilities that allow remote administration of other network computers. Windows 2000 prompts the administrator for the name of a computer to administer when creating a console using a snap-in that provides this capability.

Creating a custom MMC

1. Log on as an administrator.

2. From the Windows 2000 Pro desktop, select **Start** and then **Run**. The Run dialog appears.

3. Type **MMC** and press Enter (see Figure 4.13). A blank console appears.

FIGURE 4.13
Creating a new Microsoft Management Console.

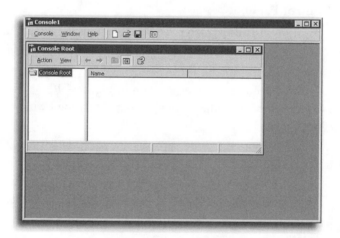

4. Select **Add/Remove Snap-in** from the **Console** menu. The Add/Remove Snap-in dialog appears, as shown in Figure 4.14.

FIGURE 4.14
By default, all snap-ins will be added to the console root.

5. Click the **Add** button. The Add Standalone Snap-in dialog appears, as shown in Figure 4.15. For example, to create an MMC that allows its user to administer user and group account management, select **Local Users and Groups**.

FIGURE 4.15
A large number of snap-ins are provided with Windows 2000 Pro.

6. After selecting a snap-in from the available list, click **Add**. To limit this console to the local computer, select **Local Computer** and click **Finish**. To allow the console to administer accounts on another computer, select **Another Computer** and either specify the name of the other computer or click on the **Browse** button to locate it (see Figure 4.16).

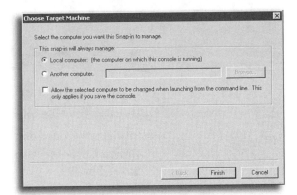

FIGURE 4.16
Snap-ins can support remote administration of other network computers.

115

7. If you clicked on Browse, a new dialog appears with a list of computers, as shown in Figure 4.17.

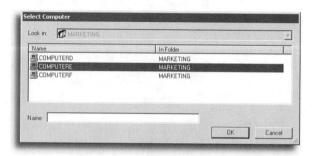

8. Select the target computer and click **OK**, then **Finish**, then **Close**, and finally **OK**. The new console reflects the newly added snap-in, as shown in Figure 4.18.

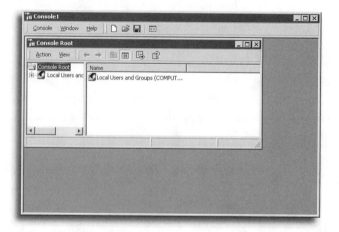

9. Repeat the preceding process as many times as necessary. When done, click **Options** on the **Console** menu.

10. Type the name of the new console in the field provided, and select the appropriate Console mode (see Figure 4.19). Then Click **Apply**, followed by **OK**.

11. Click **Save** on the **Console** menu and save the console.

12. Close the MMC utility.

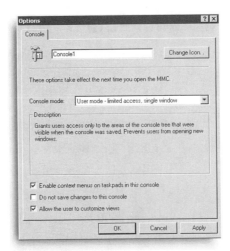

FIGURE 4.19
Naming the MMC and selecting a user mode.

The new console is now ready for use. Locate the console and double-click to open it (see Figure 4.20). The console can also be distributed to other administrators. You can share the console with other administrators by providing them with a copy of the .MSC files that contain the console's definitions.

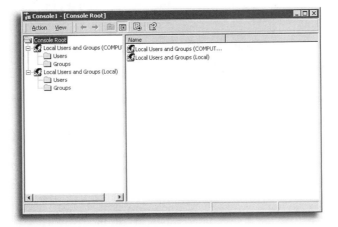

FIGURE 4.20
An example of an MMC console that has been set up to allow an administrator to administer user and group accounts on multiple computers.

SEE ALSO

➤ *For more information on Windows 2000 Pro security, see page 190.*

Installing Other Network Components

During the installation of Windows 2000 Pro, many different software components are installed by default. If a NIC is auto-detected during installation, Windows 2000 Pro configures the computer for networking. By default, Windows 2000 Pro installs the following networking components:

- Client for Microsoft Networks
- File and Print Sharing for Microsoft Networks
- TCP/IP

Windows 2000 Pro's network installation also allows for the selection of custom settings. This means that the administrator can deselect any of the options, as well as choose to install additional clients, services, and protocols.

Regardless of which software components are used to install Windows 2000 Pro on a computer, other components can always be added or removed later. To view all the components available for a Windows 2000 Pro computer, use the Windows Setup tab on the Add/Remove programs applet located in the Windows Control Panel.

Starting Add/Remove Programs

1. Log on as an administrator.
2. From the Windows 2000 Pro desktop, select **Start**, **Settings**, and then **Control Panel**.
3. From the Windows Control Panel, double-click the **Add/Remove Programs** icon to launch the Add/Remove Programs dialog, shown in Figure 4.21.

On the left side of the dialog are three options:

- Change or Remove Programs
- Add New Programs
- Add/Remove Windows Components

FIGURE 4.21
The Change or Remove Programs option provides a means for removing or reconfiguring installed programs.

The Change or Remove Programs option is selected by default. Both this and the Add New Programs option assist administrators in installing, modifying, and removing network applications and other supporting tools, such as the Windows 2000 Resource Kit.

The Add/Remove Windows Components option assists administrators in installing and removing network components that are included with Windows 2000 but that might not have been set up during its initial installation. For example, IIS, FTP, Simple TCP/IP services, and the SNMP protocol are all installed from this option.

Administrative Access

Any network users or administrators who receive a copy of an MMC must have the appropriate access privileges required to perform whatever task the console has been created to do. For example, only a person with Administrative accounts on both computers can make use of the MMC custom console demonstrated in this chapter.

chapter

5

Disk Sharing

Managing Data and Applications with Network Shares

Often, many users require access to the same file or sets of files. Windows 2000 Pro allows for remote access of hard disk drives, floppy drives, CD-ROMs, printers, and folders. Sharing a device or folder over a network establishes a *share*. The share can then be accessed from other computers on the network, provided that the network user has the appropriate permissions.

Establishing shares on peer computers allows them to provide file-serving capabilities similar to those provided by file servers on traditional client-server networks. Windows 2000 permits the sharing of drives and folders. For a file or group of files to be shared, they must reside in a shared drive or folder. Network administrators can establish shares to enable application sharing among network users, as well as sharing of data files. However, there are performance trade-offs here that must be carefully examined.

In addition to supporting file and application sharing, a special type of share known as a hidden share is used by Windows to facilitate communication and management over the network. Windows 2000 Pro automatically creates these shares. Network administrators use hidden shares to remotely manage shared resources over the network.

Understanding File Servers and Peer-Sharing

A file server is a network computer that stores files and provides shared access to multiple network computers. On a client-server network, a file server is a dedicated server that provides shared storage on one or more local hard drives. Client computers can communicate with the file server but not with each other. If a file needs to be shared among three computers, it is placed on a file server. On a peer network files are stored on individual computers that can be accessed by the other computers on the network. Figure 5.1 compares the two types of file servers.

On a peer network, selected computers can be assigned the task of providing shared access to files. This establishes dedicated peer computers that provide services similar to those provided by client-server file servers.

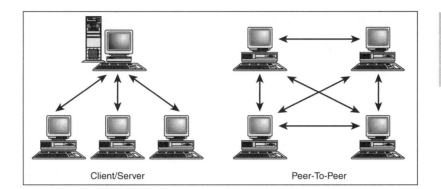

Client/Server   Peer-To-Peer

FIGURE 5.1
Client-server file servers
versus peer file sharing.

Likewise, users' computers can be set up to share local resources. On Windows 2000 Pro, sharing can be configured for an entire drive, a part of the directory tree, or individual folders. Before a networked computer can share a file resource, file sharing must be installed.

Important files can be grouped and stored in folders to be made available to users that require shared access to them. This type of file sharing offers many advantages. It makes finding and accessing important files easier for users and simplifies network administration. Centrally storing files makes backup simpler because administrators have to back up only the data stored on specified shares.

Windows 2000 Pro can support up to 10 simultaneous network connections. If greater access is required, Windows 2000 Server can be installed on computers as a standalone installation to provide unlimited access. On a small peer network, the 10-user access limit is usually not a concern. In addition, Windows 2000 can limit the number of users allowed to access a shared file to any number from 1 to 10. So, if there is a file that the network administrator wants only one person to access at a time, access can be restricted to allow only a single user at a time.

When administrators create network shares, they assign the shares a name and a description. They also can limit the number of users that

Sharing Folders and Drives Using Other Microsoft Operating Systems

Windows 95, Windows 98, and Windows for Workgroups all provide for the establishment of shared drives and folders. The drawback to sharing resources with these operating systems is their inherent lack of security. Windows NT 4.0, however, does support user-level security.

may simultaneously access the share and establish security over it. In addition, Windows allows multiple shares to be established for the same folder.

Shares for Applications

In addition to storing data on shared network folders, administrators might also want to store commonly used applications in network shares. This can be used as a tool for reducing the hard-drive storage requirements on users' computers because not all applications will need to be installed on every computer. It also makes upgrading from one version to the next easier because the administrator needs only to upgrade the centrally stored copy of the application rather than having to visit every computer on the network where the application could have been installed.

Of course, the capability to deploy applications in this manner depends on the application. Not all applications support this capability, and very large programs might load very slowly when not installed locally. Depending on the size of the application, additional burdens are also placed on the network bandwidth. Administrators can use Windows 2000 Pro's built-in security to provide read-only access to network users so that they can access and run application programs.

Understanding Hidden Shares

By default, Windows 2000 Pro automatically creates multiple hidden shares, as shown in Figure 5.2. A hidden share is the same as any other share except that a $ is appended to the end of its name. This prevents the share from appearing when network users browse the network. Only individuals who know about the existence of a hidden share and have appropriate permissions can access it.

A hidden share is automatically created for every hard disk on a Windows 2000 Pro computer. The name of the share is the drive letter assigned to the drive with a $ appended to the drive letter. In addition, Windows 2000 Pro creates other hidden shares:

- ADMIN$

  This share points to the *system root folder*, which is c:\WINNT by default during installation, and which is shared as ADMIN$.

During the installation of Windows 2000 Pro, the administrator has the option of changing the name and location of the system root folder. Regardless of what the folder is named or where it is located, the ADMIN$ share always refers to it. This provides other administrators with remote access to the share without knowing its name and location.

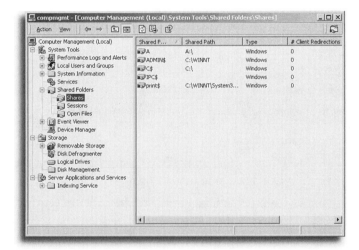

FIGURE 5.2
Windows automatically creates a number of hidden shares on installation.

- IPC$

  This share is an interprocess communication share used by Windows to support remote administration of computers.

- PRINT$

  This share is present if the administrator has established a shared printer on the computer.

Establishing Shared Network Folders and Drives

The same procedure is used to create shares for floppy drives, hard drives, CD-ROM drives, printers, or folders—all can be set up as a share. All resources on a Windows 2000 Pro computer have iconic representation. When a resource is shared, its iconic representation changes to show a hand under the original icon, as demonstrated by the floppy drive in Figure 5.3. When a local resource is shared, any user on the network can access it, provided that he has the proper permissions.

FIGURE 5.3
The My Computer window shows one nonhidden shared floppy drive on the local computer.

Sharing a local drive

1. Double-click on the **My Computer** icon on the main desktop. The My Computer dialog appears.

2. Right-click on a local hard drive and select the **Sharing** option from the menu that appears, as shown in Figure 5.4. The Properties dialog for the selected resource appears. If you want to share one folder on the drive, use the My Computer window to navigate to that folder and right-click on it instead of the hard-drive icon.

Sharing Tab Not Visible

If the Sharing tab is not visible, the file sharing services are not installed or enabled.

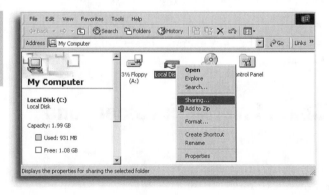

FIGURE 5.4
Creating a share for the local C: drive.

3. Windows displays the Local Disk (C:) Properties dialog (see Figure 5.5). The <u>S</u>hare This Folder option is automatically selected because Windows 2000 Pro has set up a default hidden share called C$ for the drive. The user limit is preset to allow the maximum number of users to connect to the drive. If the selected drive was not already shared, the Do Not Share This Folder option would have been selected. Select the **Share This Folder** option to enable sharing of the resource, and skip to step 5.

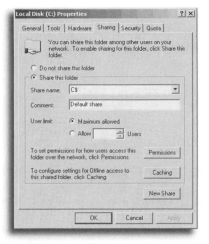

FIGURE 5.5
The Sharing property sheet in the Properties dialog.

Be Wary of Sharing an Entire Drive

Sharing an entire drive means that the entire contents of that drive are shared, including all folders. If only the data in a given folder needs to be shared, it is better to share only the individual folder. An unlimited number of shares can be created on a local drive.

4. Click on **N<u>e</u>w Share** to create another share for the drive. The New Share dialog appears, as shown in Figure 5.6.

FIGURE 5.6
Creating a new share for a local hard drive.

5. Enter a name and a description of the new share in the **<u>S</u>hare Name** and **<u>C</u>omment** fields. If required, establish a user connection limit and click **OK**. The Local Disk (C:) Properties dialog reappears, displaying the new share's information, as shown in Figure 5.7.

FIGURE 5.7
Configuration information for a new share.

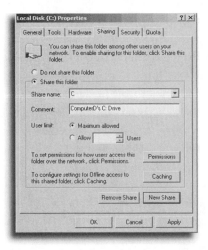

6. The iconic representation of the drive changes to show it as a shared resource, as demonstrated in Figure 5.8.

FIGURE 5.8
The My Computer dialog showing a shared hard drive.

① Shared icon

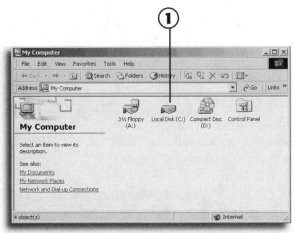

Establishing Tight Control over Network Resources

Windows 2000 Pro can apply two types of security to protect computer resources. These are share-level and user-level security. Share-level security is always available on Windows peer networks. User-level security is available on Windows 2000 and Windows NT 4.0 operating systems only if NTFS is installed as the computer's file system. However, if a computer has more than one hard drive or has a hard drive that has been partitioned into multiple volumes, user-level security can be applied only to volumes that have been formatted with NTFS.

By default, Windows 2000 Pro sets share-level security to provide every network user with complete control over the share. Clicking on the Permissions button on the Local Disk (C:) Properties dialog reveals this fact, as shown in Figure 5.9. Changing share-level permissions requires deselecting any of the available permissions or adding other users or groups of users and specifying a unique set of permissions for them. Specific levels of denied access can also be selected for each assigned user or group of users.

The available share permissions are Read, Change, and Full Control. Read access permits the viewing of files and subdirectories and the execution of applications. The Change permission allows everything that the Read permission allows, as well as the ability to add and delete files and subdirectories and to change file contents. Full Control allows everything that Change allows plus the ability to change NTFS permissions on the files and subdirectories and take ownership of them.

Feeling a Bit Insecure?

On Windows for Workgroups, Windows 95, and Windows 98 computers running as standalone computers on peer networks, only share-level security is supported, making these operating systems inherently less secure. A detailed overview of both types of security models is presented in Chapter 7, "Network Administration and Security."

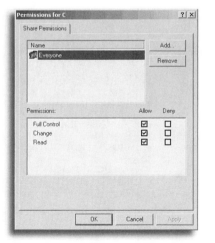

FIGURE 5.9
Default share permission gives every network user complete control over network shares.

Share-level security affects only network users. For example, a user with the Read permission on a share cannot change its contents from over the network. However, if the user logs on at the computer where the share resides, share-level security is not applied and therefore does not prevent the user from changing the contents of the share.

If the volume containing the shared drive or folders is formatted with NTFS, user-level security also affects user access. User security is effective for both local and network users, so a network user cannot bypass it by logging in at the computer where the shared resource resides.

The level of access granted to network users when both share- and user-level security are in place is determined by the most restrictive combination of the two security permissions. For example, if a user has the share access permission of Read and an NTFS permission of Change on a shared folder, the resulting access permission is Read.

SEE ALSO

➤ *For more information on applying share- and user-level security to network drives and folders,*
see page 223.

Accessing Shared Drives and Folders Across the Network

Network users can use several means to view and access shared resources on a peer network. These include using the following tools:

- My Network Places
- Windows Explorer
- Internet Explorer
- Windows dialog boxes
- Map Network Drive Wizard
- Run command1

Locating network resources involves one of two methods. The network user either supplies the name and location of a network resource or browses for them.

Using the Universal Naming Convention of Resources

When users know the name and location of network resources, they can provide them to Windows using the Universal Naming

Convention, or UNC, method. The UNC, a standard way of addressing network resources, uses the following syntax:

`\\Computer_name\Path\Resource_name`

For example, a folder named June_sales located just off the root directory on a network computer named SalesFileSvr would be located at `\\SalesFileSvr\June_sales`.

If the network user does not know the exact location of a network resource, it must be browsed for. Browsing is the process of navigating a computer or network looking for a resource by using utilities such as My Network Places, Internet Explorer, or Windows Explorer.

My Network Places

My Network Places is new in Windows 2000 Pro. It is a very powerful tool that has replaced the Network Neighborhood utility found in Windows NT 4.0, Windows 95, and Windows 98. My Network Places is located on the Windows 2000 desktop (see Figure 5.10). It contains three icons: Add Network Place, Computers Near Me, and Entire Network.

The Add Network Place icon launches a wizard designed to step the user through creating links to places on the network or Internet where documents are located that the user needs to access. The Computers Near Me icon instructs Windows to display a list of all computers on the network that belong to the current computer's workgroup. The Entire Network icon tells Windows to present a high-level view of the network so that the user can navigate to other workgroups or search for files, folders, or computers.

Entire Network

Clicking on the Entire Network icon presents a dialog resembling the one shown in Figure 5.11.

From here, three options are available:

- Search for Computers
- Search for Files or Folders
- Entire Contents

131

FIGURE 5.10
My Network Places pro-
vides tools for locating
network resources.

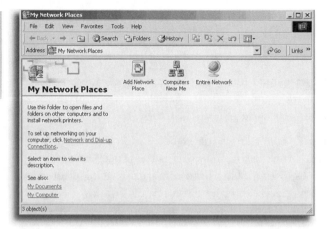

FIGURE 5.11
Selecting the entire net-
work provides access to
tools for searching and
browsing the network.

Search for Computers

Selecting Search for Computers allows the user to type the name of a
network computer in the Computer Name field on the left pane and
click Search Now. If found, the computer appears in the bottom portion of the right pane, as demonstrated in Figure 5.12. It can then be
selected and accessed via a double-click on its icon.

Search for Files or Folders

Selecting Search for Files or Folders allows the user to type the
name of a file or folder he needs to look for in the Search for Files
and Folders Named field. This utility can be used to search for files
and folders on the local computer or in shared network folders and
drives. If the file or folder belongs to a computer on the network, the
user can use the UNC naming convention to type the location of a

shared network resource that contains the folder or file and can then click Search Now.

FIGURE 5.12
The user can locate computers without knowing their workgroup membership.

In case the user does not know the exact location of the files, the Look In drop-down list provides a browsing option. If any matching folders or files are found, the results are displayed in the bottom portion of the right pane, as demonstrated in Figure 5.13. From here, they can be selected and accessed via a double-click on their icon.

FIGURE 5.13
Shared network files or folders can be searched for over the network.

Entire Contents

Clicking on Entire Contents presents the dialog shown in Figure 5.14, in which a list of networks appears. On a small Windows peer network, the Microsoft Windows Network appears. If other networks were installed, such as a Novell NetWare server, they would be represented here.

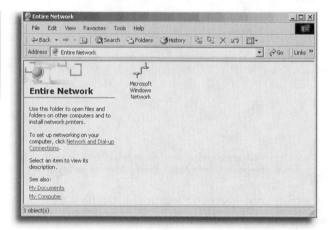

FIGURE 5.14
The Microsoft Windows Network represents the entire peer network.

Double-clicking on Microsoft Windows Network produces a list of all workgroups on the network (see Figure 5.15). On a Windows peer network that might be composed of several workgroups, users can select any workgroup and view its membership.

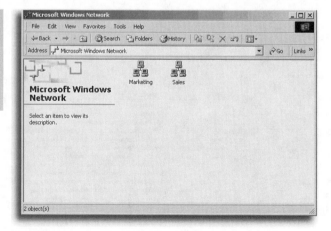

FIGURE 5.15
Double-clicking on the Microsoft Windows Network icon displays all network workgroups.

For example, double-clicking on the Sales icon produces a list of all the computers in the Sales workgroup, as shown in Figure 5.16. Any shared resources on any computer can be viewed and accessed, assuming that the network user has the appropriate permissions.

FIGURE 5.16
Double-clicking on a workgroup displays all its current members.

For example, double-clicking on SalesFileSvr produces a list of every shared resource on the computer (see Figure 5.17). To access any resource and view its contents, the user simply double-clicks on it.

FIGURE 5.17
Double-clicking on a computer displays all its shared resources.

Be Sure All Computers in the Workgroup Are Running

Other computers might be members of the workgroup, but if those computers are not up and running, they will not appear on the network. Therefore, actual workgroup memberships might be misleading if some computers on the network are not running.

Computers Near Me

Selecting Computers Near Me produces a dialog that displays a list of all computers in a local computer's workgroup. Because workgroups usually consist of computers owned by users that belong to

It Takes Time...
It takes a little time for computers that have disconnected from the network to stop appearing on other network computers' dialogs. Attempting to access these computers results in a brief delay, followed by an error message.

the same department or team, this arrangement offers an excellent means for organizing computers on the network. The Computers Near Me icon is designed to give users quick access to other computers in their workgroup.

Add Network Place

Selecting Add Network Place produces the Add Network Place Wizard. This wizard steps the user through the process of creating links to network locations where the user views, stores, or retrieves files. This wizard also supports the establishment of connections to the Web folders on the Internet and FTP sites.

Creating a link to a network drive or folder

1. Using the UNC naming convention, type the location of the resource in the **Type the Location of the Network Place** field in the Add Network Place Wizard dialog (see Figure 5.18), or click on the **Browse** button to locate the resource if its exact name or location is not known.

2. Type **Next** to continue.

FIGURE 5.18
The Add a Network Place Wizard allows a user to create links to network resources.

3. Windows displays a list of shared folders on the target computer (see Figure 5.19). Select one and then click **Next**.

4. Click **Finish** to instruct Windows 2000 to create the link (see Figure 5.20).

5. The link appears on the My Computer dialog as a folder with a network cable attached to it, as demonstrated in Figure 5.21.

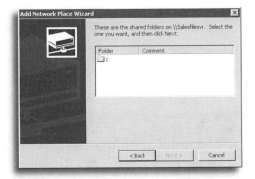

FIGURE 5.19
Select the resource that
is to be linked.

FIGURE 5.20
Windows completes the
link.

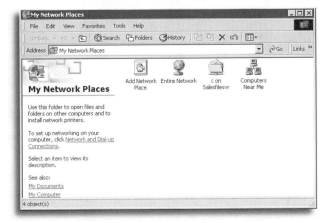

FIGURE 5.21
Linked network
resources appear in the
form of network folder
icons.

Windows Explorer

Windows Explorer is a tool that has been available in every Windows
operating system since Windows 95 first appeared. Most users are
familiar with this utility because they are accustomed to using it as a
tool for navigating local drives.

However, because Windows Explorer also contains a link to My Network Places, it provides complete access to the network as well. Figure 5.22 provides an example of navigating with Windows Explorer to view shared resources on a computer named SalesFileSvr.

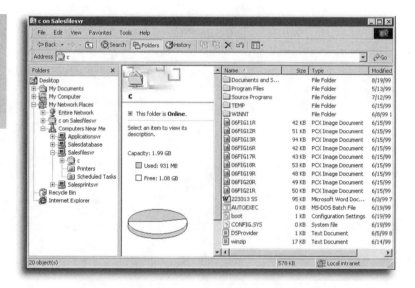

FIGURE 5.22
Windows Explorer incorporates My Network Places for providing access to network resources.

Internet Explorer

Most users are also familiar with using Internet Explorer as a tool for accessing the Internet. However, this utility can be used to access local network resources as well. By typing a UNC address in the Address field on the browser, a user can specify a network resource. For example, typing \\applicationsvr and pressing Enter produces a dialog similar to the one shown in Figure 5.23.

Windows Dialogs

Network-aware applications can use Windows 2000 Pro dialogs, such as the Open and Save dialogs, to access resources over the network. For example, Figure 5.24 shows the Windows 2000 Pro Open dialog.

Clicking on the My Network Places option allows the user to navigate to and open files stored on computer shares all over a network to which the user has the proper permissions. For older network applications that are not network-aware, the network drive can be mapped, thus providing access to legacy applications.

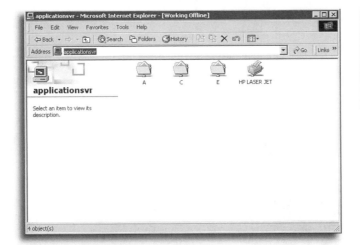

FIGURE 5.23
The Internet Explorer Address field provides a means for locating network resources.

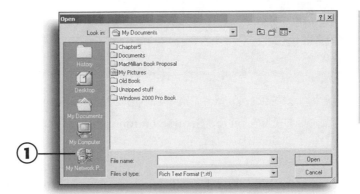

FIGURE 5.24
All Windows 2000 dialogs are network-aware.

① My Network Places

Map Network Drive Wizard

Mapping a network drive is a technique for assigning a local drive letter to a remote network drive or folder. This allows older programs that are not network-aware to connect to remote network shares because they appear as local drives.

This technique is especially helpful for older legacy software, such as Windows 3.1 programs like Microsoft Word 6. Another reason for establishing drive mappings is for convenience. After a network share has been mapped, the mapping can be moved or copied to the

Mapping Drives in Windows NT and Windows 9X

On Windows NT Workstation 4.0, Windows 95, and Windows 98, establishing network drive mappings requires right-clicking on the My Computer icon on the Windows desktop and selecting Map Network Drive.

Windows 2000 desktop, and from there it can provide quick access to the share.

Mapping a share to a local drive letter

1. Right-click on **My Network Places** on the Windows 2000 Pro desktop. A pop-up menu appears.

2. Select **Map Network Drive**. The Map Network Drive dialog appears (see Figure 5.25).

FIGURE 5.25
Mapping network drives provides fast and convenient access to the network drive and file shares.

Mapping Drives in Windows for Workgroups

Network drive mappings are established in Windows for Workgroups by the selection of Connect Network Drive from the Disk menu.

3. Select an available local drive letter from the **Drive** list.

4. Click on the **Browse** button to display the Browse For Folder dialog (see Figure 5.26).

or

Enter the full UNC location of the network share.

FIGURE 5.26
Browsing for network resources.

5. After locating the desired share, click **OK**.

6. Selecting **Reconnect at Logon** tells Windows 2000 to save the drive mapping for further use. Leaving this option cleared tells

Windows 2000 that the drive mapping should be made available only for the current session and should not be reestablished the next time the user logs on.

7. Click **Finish** when returned to the Map Network Drive dialog.

The mapped drive appears in the My Computer dialog as a drive icon with a network cable attached, as shown in Figure 5.27.

FIGURE 5.27
Viewing mapped network drives from the My Computer dialog.

Run Command

The Run command provides another way to quickly access computer resources. The Run dialog is accessed when Start and then Run are selected from the Windows 2000 desktop. The user can then type the UNC location of a network share or select Browse to locate a network share (see Figure 5.28). Clicking OK after the share has been found instructs Windows 2000 to open an Explorer dialog and display the contents of the share. If the entire path to a file inside a shared folder is provided, Windows 2000 attempts to open it if it is a file or execute it if it is a program or script.

Disconnecting Drive Mappings in Windows 2000, Windows NT 4.0, and Windows 9X

To disconnect mapped drives in Windows 2000 Pro, Windows NT Workstation 4.0, Windows 95, and Windows 98, right-click on the My Computer icon, select Disconnect Network Drive, and click OK after selecting a drive mapping.

FIGURE 5.28
The Run dialog provides quick access to network shares.

Removing Shared Network Access to Drives and Folders

Disconnecting Windows for Workgroups Drive Mappings

A mapped drive in Windows for Workgroups is disconnected using the Disconnect Network Drive option under the Disk menu in the File Manager.

Removing a share is a straightforward process. When a resource is unshared, it is unavailable to network users. The only way to access the resource is to log on to the local computer where the resource resides. Use the following steps to remove a share on a computer.

1. Locate the resource by using either the Windows Explorer or the My Computer dialog, and right-click on the resource. A pop-up menu appears.

2. Select the **Sharing** option. The Properties dialog for the selected devices appears, and the Sharing tab is automatically displayed.

3. If more than one share is established for this device, a Remove Share button appears at the bottom of the dialog. Click on the **Remove Share** button. The remaining shares are still intact.

   or

   If this is the only share for the resource, there is no Remove Share button. Select the **Do Not Share This Folder** option and click **Apply**.

4. Click **OK**.

The resource is no longer a share. Network users will not be able to view or access the resource remotely over the network.

Monitoring Shared Resources

An administrator can monitor locally shared resources as they are being accessed by other network users. The administrator can do so by using the Shared Folders snap-in located in the Computer Management MMC in the Administrative Tools folder located on the Windows 2000 Pro Control Panel.

The Shared Folders snap-in provides three views:

- *View by Share:* Displays currently shared network resources.
- *View by Sessions:* Displays currently connected networks users.
- *View by Open Files:* Displays files that are currently open.

Using the Shared Folders snap-in, an administrator can perform the following functions:

- Add and remove shared resources
- Monitor current network connections
- Disconnect users who are accessing a specified network resource
- Determine which resources are currently being shared

This utility allows the administrator to monitor only local resources. However, a custom MMC can be set up to enable an administrator to monitor shared resources for every Windows 2000 computer on the network.

SEE ALSO

➤ *For more information on the Shared Folders snap-in, see page 312.*

➤ *For more information on creating custom MMC consoles, see page 112.*

chapter

6

Installing and Managing Network Printers

Overview of Windows 2000 Pro Printing

Microsoft has worked hard to make local and network printing and print management as painless as possible. Windows 2000 represents its best work so far.

Windows 2000 Pro uses a device-independent print architecture. After a print device, either local or network, has been set up and configured on a Windows 2000 Pro computer, all applications will be able to work with it. A *local printer* is one that is physically attached to the computer, whereas a *network printer* is one that is available to both local and network computers. If a user's computer has been configured to work with multiple print devices, Windows 2000 Pro will seamlessly manage the print process. The user needs only to select which print device to send the print job to, and the operating system will manage the rest.

SEE ALSO

➤ *For an overview of Windows 95 and Windows 98 printing, see page 416.*

SEE ALSO

➤ *For an overview of Windows for Workgroups printing, see page 370.*

SEE ALSO

➤ *For an overview of Windows NT Workstation 4.0 printing, see page 466.*

Alternatives to Network Printing

The alternatives to sharing a printer over a network include purchasing a printer for every computer, implementing sneakernet and hardware solutions such as A/B switches. A/B switches allow multiple computers to be attached via parallel cables to an external device, which manages attached printers. A/B switches typically allow only a few computers to share a single print device, as demonstrated in Figure 6.1.

In this example, the user attached to port A is ready to print. For the computer attached to port B to print, the switch must be physically changed to B. More expensive switches support auto-detection of print jobs from connected computers and attempt to automatically manage the switching process. However, this does not always work and might result in two or more print jobs getting intermingled with very unpleasant results.

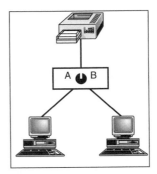

FIGURE 6.1
An A/B switch providing shared printer support.

Ways to Implement Network Printing

There are two ways in which to establish a shared network printer. One method is to attach a printer to a peer computer and share it. The other is to directly attach the printer to the network cable and manage it from a peer computer.

Peer Print Servers

On Windows 2000 Pro peer networks, most of the time a network printer is attached to a specific computer on the network, where it is shared with other networked computers as depicted in Figure 6.2. In this case the printer is locally attached and managed by an individual computer on the network. The owning computer then shares the printer with the rest of the network, making it a *peer print server*.

FIGURE 6.2
A network print server.

Network Printers

In some instances a printer might be directly attached to the network cable, as demonstrated in Figure 6.3.

This type of printer has its own built-in network interface card. This type of setup is more expensive and usually is found only on larger client-server networks. Common examples of this type of printer are HP printers with Jet Direct network interface cards.

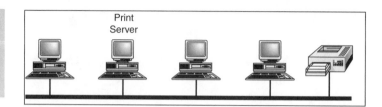

Print
Server

FIGURE 6.3
A network-attached
printer with a dedicated
print server.

Typically, a dedicated computer is assigned the role of providing print services. The DLC protocol is a common protocol used to facilitate communication with a network-attached print device. This protocol is installed on a single computer that will function as the print server for the network. No other computers on the network require this protocol. This protocol allows the print server to locate and communicate with the printer. The DLC protocol allows the computer to connect directly to the printer using the network rather than a physical port. After the DLC protocol is installed, the printer is added using the printer wizard. After the printer is installed, it can be shared by the print server with the rest of the network. Other network computers will then be able to use the print device without realizing that it is not physically installed on the printer server.

If a single computer is not designated as the print server for the network print device, the DLC protocol must be installed on any computer that needs to submit print jobs to the printer. However, this can present confusion and frustration for the network users because each network computer is unaware of when other computers are submitting print jobs to the print device. Figure 6.4 demonstrates this problem. In the left portion of the figure, three computers, each running the DLC protocol, are seen attempting to submit print jobs to the print device. However, only one of the three computers will be successful. The other two computers will fail, and error messages will appear on the other two computers, indicating that the print device is unavailable. By comparison, the model in the right portion of Figure 6.4 shows a dedicated print server.

Because the network-attached print device is installed on only one computer, network print management is greatly simplified. The print server provides spooling and print-queue management services. All computers on the network can submit print jobs to the print server.

The print server accepts the print jobs, adds them to the print queue, and submits them to the print device on a first-in-first-out, or FIFO, basis. The other printer can communicate with the print server using the common network protocol, TCP/IP.

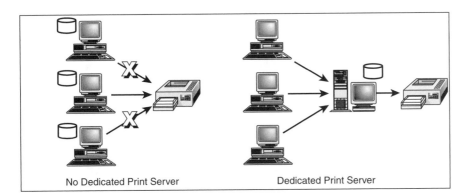

No Dedicated Print Server   Dedicated Print Server

FIGURE 6.4
Comparison of a nonded-icated versus a dedi-cated print server working with a network-attached print device.

Another available option is to purchase an *external print server*, as demonstrated in Figure 6.5. This device usually appears in the form of a small unit not much bigger than a small hub. It has its own processor and memory, is attached directly to an Ethernet RJ-45 connection on the network, and provides a port connection for a parallel printer.

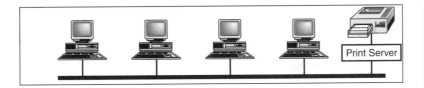

Print Server

FIGURE 6.5
An external print server allows any parallel printer to be attached anywhere on the net-work.

An Overview of the Windows Printing Process

Microsoft's printing terminology is a little different than you might expect and requires a quick overview before a review of the print process can be undertaken. The following list defines key terms.

Print device	The physical printer.
Printer	The software interface that is created using the Add Printer Wizard. Users interact and manage the print device from this interface.

continues...

...continued

Print device	**The physical printer.**
Software driver	Software that accompanies the printer that provides the operating system with control over the print device.
Spooling	The process of receiving a print job and copying it to a file on the hard drive, where it waits its turn before being submitted to the print device.
Print queue	The location on a hard drive where print jobs are spooled.

So What If I'm Using 9x or NT?

Windows 9X systems spool their print jobs to `C:\Windows\spool\printers`.

Note that Windows NT 4.0 spools its print jobs to `C:\Winnt\System32\spool\printers`.

Understanding Printer Driver Support

A Windows 2000 printer driver consists of instructions that inform the operating system how to manage and control the printer. Windows 2000 comes with hundreds of software drivers. In addition, printer vendors provide software drivers with their printers. This is especially important when the printer is new and Windows 2000 does not know about it. If the printer did not come with a Windows 2000 software driver, check the support area on the printer manufacturer's Web site.

The Windows print process is very straightforward and operates as outlined here:

1. A user's application submits a print job.

2. Windows 2000 Pro determines whether the print device that was selected is either a local or a network device. If the job is local, the print job is spooled to the local hard drive in the form of a temporary file, where it waits until the print device is ready to print it.

3. The Windows 2000 Pro print queue manages all spooled jobs. If there are other jobs ahead of this one, this job sits in the print queue until its turn comes.

4. Windows then submits the spooled print job to the printer.

5. After the print job has been printed, Windows deletes the print job from the print queue.

Windows print jobs are stored in the `\Winnt\System32\spool\printers` directory, as depicted in Figure 6.6.

When a print job is destined for a network printer, it is redirected across the network to the print server that manages the network printer, where, when received, it is spooled and managed by that computer's print queue manager, as depicted in Figure 6.7.

Another view of the Windows 2000 Pro print-management process is shown in Figure 6.8. Here, the print queue is depicted as containing two spooled print jobs. Print job 1 is submitted to the print device a page at a time. Print job 2 waits in the print queue for print job 1 to complete. All print processing is done in a FIFO fashion.

Print jobs 3 and 4 have been submitted on the wire from two different computers. Print job 3 will arrive just before print job 4.

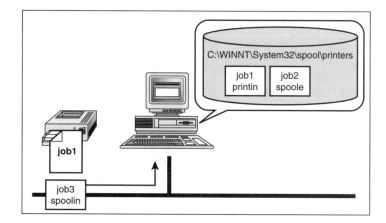

FIGURE 6.6
Windows 98 print-job management.

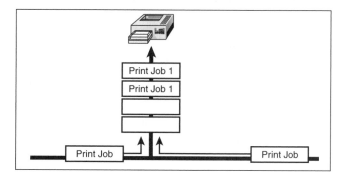

FIGURE 6.7
The local computer determines whether the requested resource is local and redirects the request over the wire if it is not.

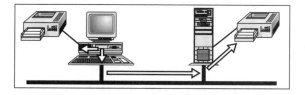

FIGURE 6.8
Windows 2000 FIFO print-queue management.

As each job is successfully printed, its temporary file on the hard drive is deleted. If something should disrupt the print device before the print jobs are completed, the jobs can either continue printing from the point of disruption or be reprinted from the beginning because the print file that contains the print job is still available in the print queue.

Figure 6.9 presents another view of the Windows 2000 Pro print queue. Here, two print jobs are being managed. The first job is currently printing while the second job is being spooled to the print queue, where it will await its turn.

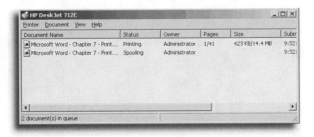

FIGURE 6.9
A Windows 2000 Pro print queue showing two print jobs.

The print queue provides a view of the status of the print jobs. It also provides management of the jobs in the queue. It allows an interface for such actions as pausing, deleting, and restarting prints jobs and changing their priorities.

Windows Print Management

All Windows 2000 Pro print management is controlled in the Printers dialog. The Printers dialog is accessed using one of the following methods:

- On the Windows 2000 Pro desktop, click **Start**, then **Settings**, and then **Printers**.
- On the Windows 2000 Pro desktop, click **Start**, then **Settings**, and then **Control Panel**. From the Control Panel select the **Printers** icon.
- From Windows Explorer, select **Control Panel** and then **Printers** (see Figure 6.10).

The Printers folder contains an icon for every installed print device. There is also an icon for launching the Print Wizard utility.

Viewing a Windows 2000 Print Queue

To view a print job after it has been submitted, the user must open the print queue that belongs to the targeted printer.

To view a printer's queue, select **Start**, then **Settings**, and then **Printers**. The Windows 2000 Print dialog appears. Double-click on a printer icon to view its print queue.

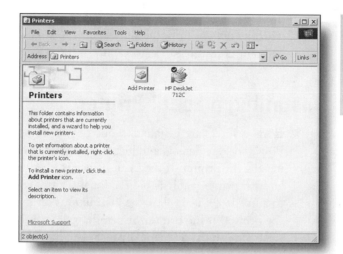

Examining Windows 2000 Pro Print Features

Windows 2000 Pro provides built-in support for hundreds of printers. It also features built-in support for adding other printers by allowing the user to supply vendor-provided software drivers.

Other features of Windows 2000 Pro include these:

- Support for user-friendly printer names up to 32 characters in length
- Plug and Play support for bidirectional printers
- Deferred offline printing for mobile computers
- Complete integration with the network printer process

Windows 2000's support for user-friendly names allows computer names to be up to 32 characters. Bidirectional communication support allows Windows 2000 to automatically detect a locally attached printer and use Plug and Play technology to install and configure it. Printers that support bidirectional communications can also provide Windows applications with status information, such as low-toner, out-of-paper, or paper-jam information. For portable computers that might not have access to a printer when on the road, Windows 2000 provides deferred printing that allows the user to create print jobs offline. When the user reconnects the printer to the network, the

Understanding Plug and Play Printer Configuration

As with other Windows 2000 Plug and Play devices, Plug and Play printers need only be connected to a computer with the appropriate hardware, and Windows will recognize and install the appropriate printer drivers and configure them.

To support Plug and Play printing under Windows 2000, the following requirements must be present:
- A bidirectional printer
- An IEEE 1284 printer cable
- A Windows 2000 software driver

print jobs are automatically submitted. Windows 2000's integration with the network printer allows users to submit print jobs to network printers as seamlessly as to local printers.

Installing a Local Printer

Local printers are installed in one of two ways. Either Windows 2000 Plug and Play detects and installs the printer, or the user manually installs the printer. If the print device is Plug and Play-compatible and the printer cable is bidirectional, Windows 2000 should be able to auto-detect it. Follow the instructions on the screen to configure the printer. If the printer or parallel printer cable is not bidirectional, the printer must be manually installed.

SEE ALSO

➤ *For information on how to install a printer in Windows 95 and Windows 98, see page 418.*

SEE ALSO

➤ *For information on how to install a printer in Windows NT Workstation 4.0, see page 466.*

SEE ALSO

➤ *For information on how to install a network printer in Windows for Workgroups, see page 372.*

Physical Installation of a Printer

Though not absolutely necessary, it is best to complete the physical installation of the print device before installing the printer driver and other software. This approach allows you to test the success of the printer installation by printing a test page.

Physically installing a parallel printer

1. Follow the directions provided with the printer device to assemble the printer. Plug it into a power outlet.

2. Attach a parallel printer cable to the port provided on the back of the printer.

3. Attach the other end of the cable to the parallel printer port on the back of the computer. Most modern computers come with one printer port known as LPT1.

The physical portion of the printer installation is complete.

Adding Printer Ports

Installing additional printer ports requires adding an I/O adapter card that supplies the additional ports. Another option is to acquire a printer that operates with the computer's serial port. A serial-port connection is not common, and unless there is a specific reason to use a serial connection, a parallel connection should always be used. Serial connections are much slower than parallel connections. This can cause delays when large graphically oriented print jobs are sent to the printer. Another option is to purchase a printer designed with the new universal serial bus, or USB, technology.

Plug and Play Installation of Parallel Printers

The software portion of a printer on a Windows 2000 computer is really just the process of installing the appropriate printer driver and supporting files on the computer. As such, the print device itself does not even have to be attached to perform this process. However, if the printer supports Plug and Play, it should be connected and then turned on; otherwise, Windows 2000 will be unable to auto-detect it, and it will have to be manually installed. In addition, the printer must be Plug and Play-compatible, and the parallel printer cable must be IEEE 1284-compliant. This type of parallel cable supports two-way communications between the print device and the computer.

PnP Not Available in NT 4.0

Windows NT 4.0 does not provide Plug and Play support. Printers must be manually installed on this operating system. Windows 9X systems provide Plug and Play support for printer hardware.

Plug and Play printer installation

1. From the Windows 2000 Control Panel, double-click on the **Printers** icon. The Printers dialog appears (see Figure 6.11).

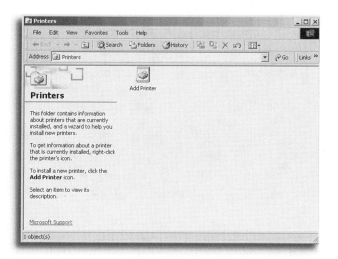

FIGURE 6.11
The Printers dialog displays all currently installed printers and provides access to the Add Printer Wizard.

2. The Add Printer Wizard is displayed. If there are any installed printers, they appear here as well. The Add Printer icon is used to launch the Add Printer Wizard. This wizard guides the user through the printer installation process. Double-click on the **Add Printer** icon. The Add Printer Wizard appears (see Figure 6.12).

FIGURE 6.12
The Add Printer Wizard steps the user through the printer installation process.

3. By default, both the **Local Printer** and the **Automatically Detect My Printer** options are selected (see Figure 6.13). To begin the printer installation process, click on the **Next** button.

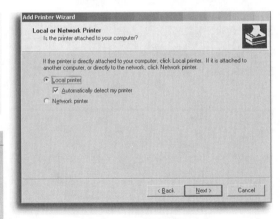

FIGURE 6.13
The wizard can set up both locally attached and remote network printers.

PnP Required to Autodetect

If Windows 2000 is unable to auto-detect the printer, make sure that the printer is Plug and Play-compatible. Verify that it is powered on and that the parallel cable is correctly attached to both the printer and the computer's parallel port. Make sure that the printer cable is an IEEE 1284–compliant parallel cable. If all these things check out, a manual install of the printer must be performed.

4. The prompt shown in Figure 6.14 appears. Click **Yes** to allow the Add Printer Wizard to attempt to auto-detect the print device (see Figure 6.14).

5. If the print device is detected, a message similar to the one shown in Figure 6.15 briefly appears.

6. After a few moments, the dialog shown in Figure 6.16 appears. Click **Next** to Continue.

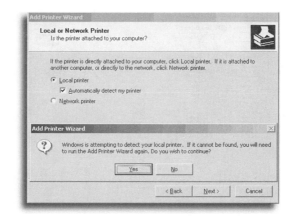

FIGURE 6.14
The Add Printer Wizard requests permission to begin the auto-detection process.

FIGURE 6.15
The wizard detects a local print device.

FIGURE 6.16
Windows reports that it has auto-detected the print device.

7. The wizard inquires as to the location of software drivers for the print device (see Figure 6.17). Select **Search for a Suitable Driver for My Device** and click **Next**.

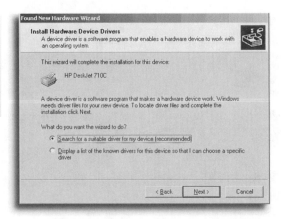

FIGURE 6.17
Windows needs to know the location of a software driver for the print device.

8. Insert the floppy disk or CD-ROM that contains the printer driver for the print device. Select the appropriate location for the driver from the **Optional Search Locations** check boxes (see Figure 6.18), and click **Next**.

FIGURE 6.18
Select the location to search for the Windows 2000 printer driver.

9. Windows searches for the appropriate software drivers. If successful, Windows displays a dialog similar to the one shown in Figure 6.19. The manufacturer and model of the printer appear, as does information about the name and location of the file that was found. Click **Next** to continue.

10. Windows completes the installation of the printer. Click **Finish**.

11. After the printer installation is complete, the Printer dialog displays an icon for the new printer (see Figure 6.20). If this is the only printer installed on the computer, it is made the default

printer, and a small check mark indicating this appears in the upper-left corner of the printer icon.

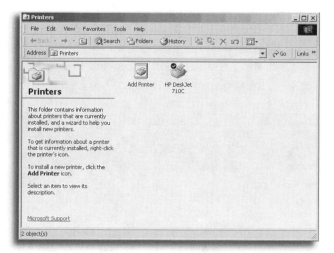

12. To verify that your printer has been installed correctly and is completely operational, you should print a test page. This will instruct Windows 2000 to print a one-page information sheet on the new printer. From the Windows 2000 Printer dialog, right-click on the printer's icon and select **Properties**. The Properties dialog for the printer appears.

13. The General tab is automatically selected by default, as shown in Figure 6.21. Click on the **Print Test Page** button.

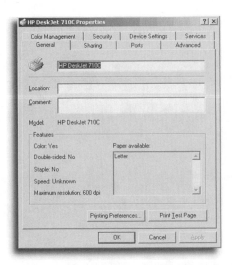

FIGURE 6.21
Clicking on the Print Test Page button creates a test which verifies that the print device is now operational.

14. Windows 2000 Pro submits the test page to the printer, and the prompt shown in Figure 6.22 appears. Wait for the test page to finish printing. If everything looks correct, click **OK**. If the test page does not print or looks scrambled or unreadable, click on the **Troubleshoot** button and follow the instructions presented by the Troubleshooting Wizard.

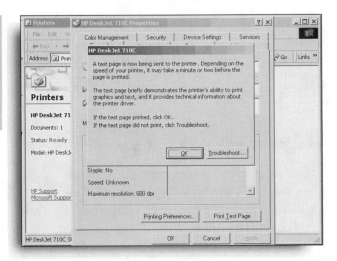

FIGURE 6.22
Windows automatically launches a trouble-shooter if informed that the test page did not print properly.

Manually Installing a Local Printer

Whenever possible, it is recommended that Plug and Play be used to install any new device. However, sometimes this is not possible. For printers this means a manual install. For example, if a new printer has been ordered and is scheduled to arrive at the end of the week on a day when the network administrator will not be at work, the administrator can manually install the printer and configure it as a shared device and then leave instructions for somebody to unpack the new printer and physically attach it. After this has been done, the printer will be immediately ready for use, and network users will not have to wait on the return of the administrator before using the new printer.

Manual printer installation

1. From the Windows 2000 **Control Panel**, double-click on the **Printers** icon. The Printers dialog appears.

2. Double-click on the **Add Printer** icon. The Add Printer Wizard appears. Click **Next** to continue.

3. By default, both the **Local printer** and the **Automatically Detect My Printer** options are selected. To manually install the print device, clear the **Automatically Detect My Printer** option. To begin the printer installation process, click on the **Next** button.

4. Select the parallel port where the printer is attached (see Figure 6.23). Most computers today have only a single parallel port known as LPT1. Select **LPT1**. Click **Next** to continue.

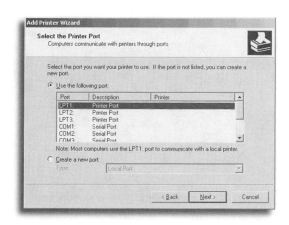

FIGURE 6.23
The Add Printer Wizard requires the user to identify the port where the printer is attached.

5. The printer wizard next inquires about the manufacturer and model type of the print device that is being installed (see Figure 6.24). Select the manufacturer of the printer from the Manufacturers list. A list of print devices made by that manufacturer appears in the Printers area. After selecting the manufacturer and printer type, click **Next** to continue.

FIGURE 6.24
The Add Printer Wizard provides a list of printer manufacturers and print devices.

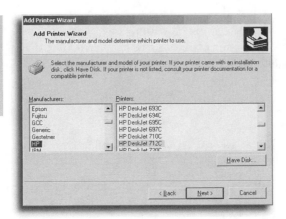

6. Windows 2000 prompts you to assign a name to this printer (see Figure 6.25). This is the name that will be displayed across the network if this printer is set up to be shared over the network. Limit the printer name to 31 or fewer characters. The printer name can be used to provide the user with helpful information such as the type or location of the printer. Click **Next** to continue.

FIGURE 6.25
The Add Printer Wizard allows the user to provide a customized name for the print device.

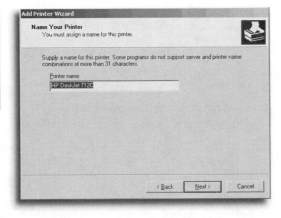

7. The Add Printer Wizard offers to configure the printer as a shared network device (see Figure 6.26). This means that other network users who have accounts with proper permission on this computer will be able to send print jobs to it. To set up the printer for local use only, select **Do Not Share This Printer**. Otherwise, select **Share As** and type a name for the share in the field provided. Windows 2000 suggests a default printer name that is the manufacturer's name and printer's model type combined. Click **Next** to continue.

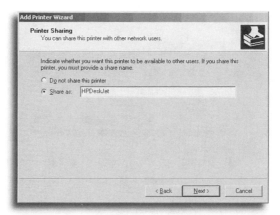

FIGURE 6.26
The Add Printer Wizard offers to automatically set up the printer as a shared device.

8. Type **Location** information and a **Comment** for the print device in the provided fields, and click **Next** to continue (see Figure 6.27).

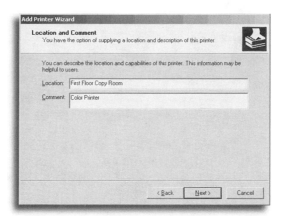

FIGURE 6.27
Windows allows for location and comment information to make it easier for network users to locate the print device.

9. Windows asks whether it should print a test page on the printer (see Figure 6.28). A test page should always be printed. It provides verification that the printer is correctly configured. Select the **Yes** option and click on **Next** to complete the printer installation.

FIGURE 6.28
The Add Printer Wizard offers to print a test page that provides immediate verification of the status of the printer install process.

10. A dialog similar to the one in Figure 6.29 appears, showing a summary of settings for the new printer. Click **Finish**.

FIGURE 6.29
The Add Printer Wizard displays settings information for the new printer.

11. Windows 2000 begins to load drivers for the specified printer. After completing the printer driver installation, Windows 2000 submits the test job to the printer. After the print device has finished printing the print job, make sure that it looks okay. If it does, the installation was successful. Click **OK**. If the test page does not print or prints incorrectly, something went wrong with the print driver installation. Click **Troubleshoot** and Windows

starts the Printer Troubleshooting Wizard. Follow the steps presented by the troubleshooting wizard to determine and correct the problem. The Windows 2000 Printers dialog now includes an icon representing the newly installed printer.

Setting Up a Printer to Share with Others

Sharing a printer makes it available to other users on the network. The computer where the printer is shared becomes a print server and will spool print jobs and manage the print process on behalf of other network computers.

SEE ALSO

➤ *For information on how to establish a shared printer in Windows 95 and Windows 98, see page 418.*

SEE ALSO

➤ *For information on how to establish a shared printer in Windows NT Workstation 4.0, see page 467.*

SEE ALSO

➤ *For information on how to establish a shared printer in Windows for Workgroups, see page 370.*

Sharing a printer with other network users

1. Select the **Sharing** tab on the printer's Properties dialog (see Figure 6.30). Select the **Shared As** option and type a name for the share. This is the name network users will see when they look for the printer.

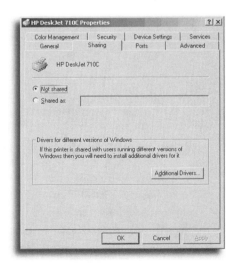

FIGURE 6.30
The Sharing tab of the printer's Properties dialog controls the sharing of the print device.

What About NT 4.0?

Windows NT 4.0 also supports the installation of drivers for other operating systems.

2. If any Windows 95, Windows 98, or Windows NT computers are on the network, click on **Additional Drivers**.

3. Select the computer operating systems you want to provide with software drivers from the Additional Drivers dialog. The software drivers for the selected operating system will be stored on the local computer and automatically downloaded to any computer that installs the print device as a network printer (see Figure 6.31). For example, to install software printer drivers for Windows NT 4.0 computer on the network, select **Intel Windows NT 4.0 or 2000** and click **OK**.

FIGURE 6.31
Windows 2000 can install and later download software drivers for other operating systems on the network.

4. Windows 2000 displays one or more prompts requesting the location of the driver and other related files for the specified operating system. Supply the appropriate floppy disks or CD-ROMs as requested, and continue to click **OK** until Windows 2000 has gathered all the information it requires.

5. The Additional Drivers dialog now shows that the drivers have been installed. Click **OK** to close the Additional Drivers dialog.

6. When returned to the Sharing tab, click **Apply** and then **OK**.

Security Settings Vary with the OS

The same set of security restrictions apply to Windows NT 4.0 as well. However, other operating systems, such as Windows for Workgroups, Windows 95, and Windows 98, do not place any restrictions on printers except for the application of share passwords.

Connecting to Network Printers

The process of connecting to a network printer is very similar to that of setting up a local computer. To connect to another Windows 2000 computer's shared printer, the user must have an account located on the other computer with sufficient rights. This is true even if the person is using the local administrator account. Unless the administrator user-accounts on both computers have the same password, access will be denied. For this exercise it is assumed that the administrator account is being used and that the passwords on both computers are the same.

Installing a network printer

1. Double-click on the **Add Printer** icon in the Printers dialog to open the Add Printer Wizard (see Figure 6.32).

2. To begin the process of connecting to a network process, click **N**ext.

FIGURE 6.32
The Add Printer Wizard guides the user through the process of installing a printer.

3. Select **N**etwork **Printer** and click **N**ext (see Figure 6.33).

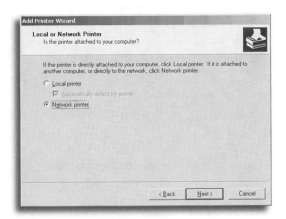

FIGURE 6.33
The Add Printer Wizard provides support for installing local and network printers.

The Add Printer Wizard asks for the location of the network printer (see Figure 6.34). Enter the location using the Universal Naming Convention, or UNC, method. If the computer where the printer resides is named ComputerA and the printer name is Marketing_Printer, the UNC path would be \\ComputerA\Marketing_Printer. If the location of the network computer is not known, click on the **Next** button. Windows then produces a dialog that allows you to navigate the network and select the printer.

FIGURE 6.34
The Add Printer Wizard requests a path to the network printer.

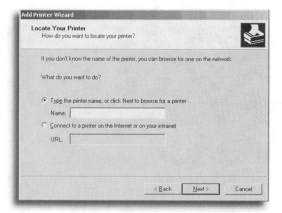

4. To locate the printer, drill down to the computer where the printer is attached by double-clicking on its workgroup and then on the computer (see Figure 6.35). Next, select the printer and click **Next**.

FIGURE 6.35
Browsing to locate a shared network printer.

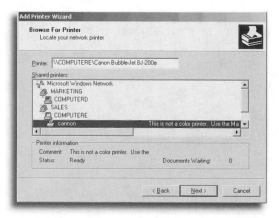

5. If this is not the first printer installed on the computer, Windows asks whether it should be set up as the computer's default printer (see Figure 6.36). Select the appropriate choice and click **Next**.

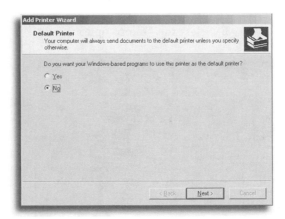

FIGURE 6.36
Windows 2000 can automatically set up the network printer as the default printer.

6. Windows announces the successful installation of the network printer and displays the printer's share name, its default status, and, if provided by the owning computer, location and comment information (see Figure 6.37). Click **Finish**.

FIGURE 6.37
Windows 2000 completes the network printer installation.

Uninstalling a Printer

Deleting a printer is a simple process. The process is the same whether it is a physically attached local printer or a connection to a shared network printer. Deleting a printer removes all references to the computer and deletes its icon.

Deleting a printer

1. From the Windows 2000 Control Panel, double-click on the **Printers** icon. The Printers dialog appears.

2. Right-click on the printer to be deleted. A menu appears (see Figure 6.38).

3. Select the **Delete** option.

FIGURE 6.38
Deleting an installed printer.

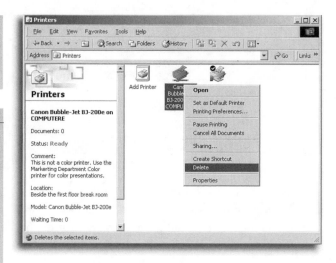

Think Twice Before Deleting Shared Printers

Deleting a printer that has been shared might create havoc among network users. Make sure that everyone is aware of the printer deletion before it occurs so that users who have installed it as their default printer have a chance to select a new default printer.

4. Windows 2000 displays a prompt asking for confirmation before deleting the printer (see Figure 6.39). Click **Yes** to proceed with the deletion.

FIGURE 6.39
Windows 2000 requires confirmation before deleting the selected printer.

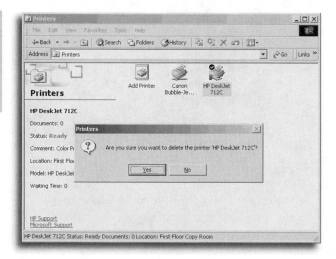

5. Windows 2000 deletes the printer. If the deleted printer was the current default printer and if another printer was installed, a prompt is displayed, stating that Windows has selected a new default printer. Click **OK** to acknowledge the prompt. If a new default printer was selected and it is not the desired default printer, the user might want to select a different printer to serve as the default.

Managing a Printer and Its Queue

Windows provides for the management of print jobs from the printer's print queue. Management tasks include such things as pausing print jobs before changing a printers ink or toner supply and resuming printing when done. Other activities might include canceling print jobs that were accidentally submitted to the wrong printer or adjusting print priorities of jobs to ensure that they print faster than other print jobs.

Printer management involves several other activities such as changing a printer's name, establishing a default printer, and managing the status of individual jobs in the print queue.

Changing a Printer's Name

Part of the process of installing a local printer is assigning a name to the printer. If the printer is a network printer, the computer where a printer is attached can make the printer available to network users as a shared device. As part of setting up the share, the device is named in the Share Name field on the Properties dialog for the printer. This is the name users browsing the network will use to identify the computer. This name should be indicative of the printer's type, capabilities, and location.

Regardless of whether the printer is a local or network shared printer, the name by which it is referred to on any computer where it has been installed can be changed.

Renaming a printer

1. From the Windows 2000 **Control Panel**, double-click on the **Printers** icon. The Printers dialog appears.

2. Right-click on the printer to be deleted. A menu appears (see Figure 6.40).

3. Select the **Rena̲me** option.

FIGURE 6.40
Renaming an installed printer.

4. Type a new name for the printer and press Enter.

Establishing the Default Printer

Watching Out for Printing Using Legacy Applications

Not all applications, especially legacy applications, recognize when the default printer has been changed, and as a result, the applications might not behave correctly. These applications will have to be individually reconfigured when the default printer is changed.

The default printer is the device where Windows 2000 submits all print jobs unless specifically instructed to do otherwise. If only one printer is installed on a computer (either locally or networked), Windows 2000 automatically makes it the default printer. If more than one printer is installed, the first printer installed is the default printer. Recognizing the default printer is easy. The default printer icon displays a small black circle with a check mark in the upper-left corner of its icon. Any printer installed after the first printer will not become the default printer unless the person installing the print device instructs Windows 2000 to make the new printer the default printer.

Changing the default printer

1. From the Windows 2000 **Control Panel**, double-click on the **Printers** icon. The Printers dialog appears.

2. Right-click on the printer that will become the new default printer. A menu appears (see Figure 6.41).

3. Select the **Set as Default Printer** option. Windows 2000 places a check mark to the left of the option to show that it has been selected.

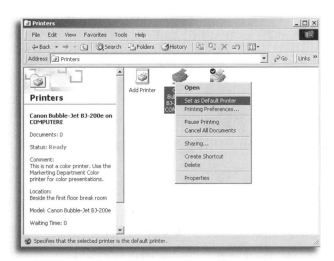

From this point on, Windows 2000 will submit all print jobs to this print device unless instructed to do otherwise from within an application. For example, Figure 6.42 presents the Microsoft WordPad Print dialog. The default printer is displayed in the Select Printer area at the top of the dialog. The Select Printer area shows that the default printer has been automatically highlighted. To send the print jobs to another printer, simply select the printer from the available list. This change affects only the current working session. If the user terminates the current session with Microsoft WordPad, opens it again, and submits a new print job, the default printer will be used unless overridden.

Managing a Printer's Queue

By default, users can manage only their own print jobs. This means that after a print job has been submitted to a print device, users can access the printer's print queue by clicking on the printer's icon in the Printer dialog, and they can pause and purge their own print jobs. In addition, Windows 2000 provides administrators full control, including the ability to manage the print device on a global scale with pause-all and purge-all capabilities. Figure 6.43 displays the print queue for a printer called the Marketing Color Printer. As the dialog shows, no print jobs are being processed on this printer.

FIGURE 6.42
Selecting the target printer from a Windows application allows the user to select a printer other than the default printer.

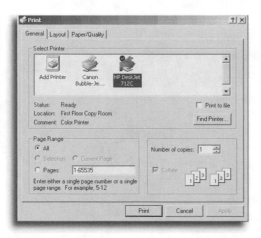

FIGURE 6.43
The Windows 2000 print queue displays a view of the status of the current state of print jobs.

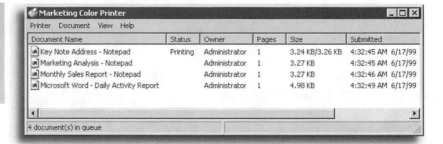

Understanding Global Controls

Figure 6.44 shows the global controls provided by Windows 2000 for managing the printer's print queue. These controls include the following:

Se<u>t</u> as Default Printer	Sets the printer as the new default printer.
P<u>a</u>use Printing	Pauses all print activity on this printer. Selecting this option a second time unpauses the print activity in this print queue.
Cance<u>l</u> All Documents	Deletes all print jobs from the print queue without printing them.

Sharing   Provides a means of creating and termi-
                           nating print shares.

Properties   Presents the print device's Properties dia-
                           log.

FIGURE 6.44
Windows 2000 provides menu commands for managing the print queue.

Figure 6.45 shows two print jobs in the printer's print queue. The information provided in this dialog includes the name of the print job, its status, the owner, the total number of pages, the size, and the time when the job originated.

The status of the first print job is Printing, which means that the print device is currently printing the print job. The status of the second print job is Spooling, which means that the computer is currently spooling or passing the print job into the printer queue. After the first job has been printed, Windows 2000 will delete it and begin to print the second print job.

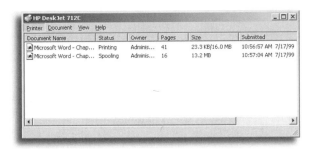

FIGURE 6.45
A Windows 2000 print queue showing the status of two print jobs.

Controlling Individual Print Jobs

Figure 6.46 demonstrates how to control individual print jobs by selecting a specific job and then clicking on the Document menu. Several options are available, including Pause, Resume, Restart and Cancel. Selecting Pause halts the printing of the selected print job.

Selecting Resume unpauses a previously paused print job. Print jobs can be deleted from the print queue with the Cancel option. Selecting a Restart on a paused job tells Windows 2000 to begin printing the print job from the beginning.

FIGURE 6.46
Windows 2000 provides menu commands for managing the status of individual print jobs.

Figure 6.47 shows the results of pausing a print job. The status for the print job now is displayed as Paused. The job remains in the print queue until either it is canceled out of the queue or it is unpaused. If new print jobs enter the queue while this job is still paused, the new jobs will print normally.

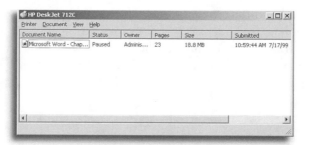

FIGURE 6.47
The print queue displays a single print job that has been paused.

Why Pause a Print Job?

One reason for pausing a print job might be that the print device is out of ink but still attempting to print and thus producing only blank pages. An administrator could pause any print jobs in progress, replace the printer's ink supply, and then unpause the print jobs to allow normal processing to continue.

Changing the Order of Print Jobs

By default, all print jobs are printed on a FIFO (first in, first out) basis. This order of jobs currently in the print queue can be changed, however.

Changing the order of documents in a print queue

1. From the Windows 2000 Pro desktop, click on **Start**, then **Settings**, and then **Printers**.

2. Click on the icon for the selected print device.

3. Right-click on a document and select **Properties**.

4. Use the cursor to move the bar in the **Priority** area to the right. Windows always prints higher priority jobs first.

Pausing All Printer Activity

Windows 2000 provides control of the entire print queue at a global level, meaning that the entire queue can be controlled with a single command. Two commands are available: Pause and Cancel. Pausing the print device causes all print activity to stop. Print jobs that are currently printing halt printing; spooled print jobs remain spooled. Print jobs currently spooling complete spooling but do not print, and new print jobs are accepted and spooled but do not print. No activity occurs on the print device until it is unpaused.

Pausing the entire print queue is an effective means of allowing maintenance to be performed on the device without severely impacting network users. For example, if a laser printer is running low on toner, an administrator can pause the printer on the controlling print server, allowing other users to continue to submit print jobs. Then, after waiting for the print device to finish printing any print jobs that might have already been loaded into its memory, the user can add additional toner, and when ready, the printer can be unpaused. The print server will continue printing where it left off.

Pausing all print activity

1. From the Windows 2000 **Control Panel**, double-click on the **Printers** icon. The Printers dialog appears.

2. Right-click on the printer that will become the new default printer. A menu appears.

3. Select the **Pause Printing** option (see Figure 6.48).

FIGURE 6.48
Windows 2000 provides the capability to pause all activity on a selected printer.

Purging All Print Jobs

Purging all print jobs on a print device's print queue deletes all printing, spooled, and spooling print jobs. Print jobs that arrive after the purge command has been completed will process normally.

Deleting all print jobs

1. From the Windows 2000 **Control Panel**, double-click on the **Printers** icon. The Printers dialog appears.

2. Right-click on the printer that will become the new default printer. A menu appears (see Figure 6.49).

3. Select the **Cancel All Documents** option. Windows 2000 deletes all print jobs currently printing, spooled, or spooling.

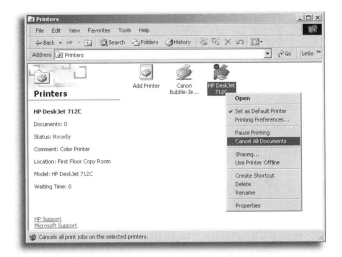

FIGURE 6.49
Windows 2000 provides the capability to purge all activity on a selected printer.

Configuring a Printer's Performance and Functionality

Like other hardware devices, Windows 2000 provides a host of configuration settings for controlling print-device performance and functionality. These settings are maintained individually for each printer on its Properties page. Because printers have different features, the Printer Properties dialog might look different for each printer. For example, settings offered by laser printers might not exist on ink-jet printers. Printer settings are grouped into a series of tabbed sheets on each printer's Properties dialog. Although some printers have more tabbed sheets with different options than other printers, there are some settings that most printers have in common. These common settings include the following:

- General
- Sharing
- Ports
- Advanced
- Security
- Device settings

Accessing a printer's Properties dialog

1. Right-clicking on a printer's icon accesses the Properties dialog. A menu appears.

2. Select the **Properties** option.

By default, the General property sheet is displayed. The number and type of property sheets displayed depends on the type of printer and its printer driver. In the following example, an HP DeskJet 712C printer that contains eight property sheets is displayed.

General Property Sheet

The General property sheet controls the name of the print devices and provides for location and description information that is shared with the rest of the network if this is a shared device (see Figure 6.50). Network users using a detail view setting in Network Neighborhood or Windows Explorer can view the description information when browsing the network.

The model type for the print device and various features are listed. The **Printing Preferences** button provides control over settings such as paper orientation, the order in which pages print, and the number of pages to print on one sheet. The **Print Test Page** button instructs Windows 2000 to submit a test page to the printer to validate that the printer is correctly configured.

FIGURE 6.50
The General property sheet on the printer's Properties dialog provides the capability to specify general printer settings and print a test page.

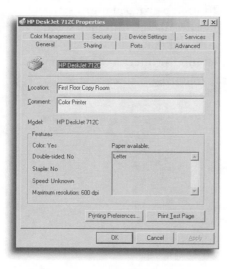

Sharing Property Sheet

The Sharing property sheet is used to enable or disable printer sharing and configure security (see Figure 6.51). To share a printer over the network, select the Shared As option. Unlike with disk or folder sharing, Windows 2000 does not offer share-level security over print devices. Therefore, there are no corresponding share security fields on this property sheet. Provide a name for the printer in the Shared As field. The **Additional Drivers** button allows software drivers for other operating systems to be installed on the local computer. When other operating systems install the printer as a network printer, the software drivers appropriate for their system can then automatically be downloaded.

Share Level Security Not Available with NTFS Filesystem

Windows NT 4.0 systems running NTFS do not provide share-level security over print devices. Only user-level security is provided.

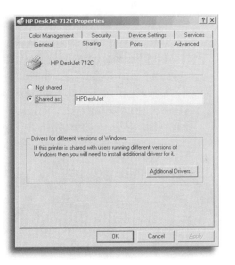

FIGURE 6.51
The Sharing property sheet on the printer's Properties dialog provides a means for sharing a printer on the network and dispersing software drivers to other operating systems.

The Ports Property Sheet on the Printer Properties Dialog

The Print to the Following Port(s) area shows the port used by a locally connected printer or the path used to establish a network printer. Clicking on the **Add Port** button produces a dialog that allows the addition of either a local port or a TCP/IP port. The addition of a local port would be appropriate if an I/O card with another parallel port was added to the computer. Clicking on the **Delete Port** button allows a port to be removed from the system.

Password Access Provided in 9x

Windows 9X systems provide share-level security over print devices by assigning a password to each locally installed printer. Anyone who knows the password can submit print jobs to the printer.

Clicking the **Configure Port** button displays a dialog that allows specification of Transmission retry. The default value of this setting is 300 seconds. Transmission retry specifies how many seconds Windows 2000 will wait for the printer to be ready to print before reporting an error.

The last two options are **Enable Bidirectional Support** and **Enable Printer Pooling**. Bidirectional devices can provide Windows with detailed information about the status of the print device, such as out-of-paper conditions or low toner. This option is available only if the printer supports it.

Printer pooling is a technique by which two or more printers that use the same printer driver can be set up to operate as one logical printer. For example, if two printers of the same model were installed on a Windows 2000 computer, a pool containing the two printers could be established. Whenever a print job was submitted, it would be routed to the first available printer in the pool. There is no way to know which of the two printers will actually print the print job, so it is advisable that the two print devices be kept close to one another. To establish a printer pool of two print devices, select the **Enable Printer Pooling** option (see Figure 6.52) and then select the check boxes for the two ports where the printers are attached.

FIGURE 6.52
The Ports page on the printer's Properties dialog provides a means for configuring printer ports.

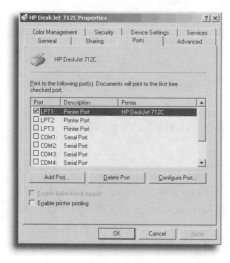

The Advanced Property Sheet on the Printer Properties Dialog

This property sheet provides a range of administrative options that include the capability to specify hours of availability for the printer, configure its priority assignment, specify how it should manage the spooling of print jobs, configure printing defaults, and provide for the addition of separator pages between print jobs. In addition, this property sheet includes an option for installing a new print driver.

Controlling Printer Availability

The top portion of the Advanced property sheet provides control over the availability of the print device. For example, an administrator might install a printer, instruct users to submit only large print jobs to it, and then configure it to be available between 5:00 p.m. and 6:00 a.m., thus preventing large print jobs from printing during the day. This allows users to submit their large jobs and then collect them from the printer in the morning. The administrator could then install a second printer for the same print device and instruct users to send all regular print jobs to it. This way, users can immediately print normal print jobs without having to wait on large print jobs that otherwise might have consumed much of a print device's time. The key here is to remember that although there might be only one print device, multiple printers can be defined for each, and each can be configured differently.

Managing printers using availability times

1. Install a printer normally using either Plug and Play or a manual install.

2. Install the printer a second time using a manual install.

3. Access the printer properties for the first printer.

4. Select the **Advanced** property sheet.

5. Note that by default the printer is always available.

6. Access the printer properties for the second printer.

7. Select the **Advanced** property sheet.

8. Restrict the available hours of printer operations.

Administrators can also manage the printers by installing multiple logical printers and assigning different priorities to the different

Multiple Printers Supported

Windows NT 4.0 also provides support for installing multiple printers for a single print device and then managing the printers using availability times. This feature is not supported by Windows for Workgroups or Windows 9X operating systems.

Managing Printers Under NT 4.0

Windows NT 4.0 also provides support for managing printers using print priorities. This feature is not supported by Windows for Workgroups or Windows 9X operating systems.

Drag and Drop Supported

Windows 9X operating systems support the use of drag and drop within the print queue as a means of changing the printer order of batch jobs. On these systems, jobs print in a FIFO order. To instruct one of these operating systems to submit a print job that is on the bottom of the print queue before any other jobs, simply select the print job by right-clicking on it and, while still holding the mouse button down, drag and release it at the top of the print queue. This will be the next print job submitted.

Be Careful When Replacing Drivers

Replacing a driver with a newer one might result in additional property sheets or changes in the settings on existing property sheets. These changes reflect new capabilities that have been provided by the new driver software.

instances. For example, if the sales and marketing departments share a laser printer but the sales department requires that its jobs finish first, an administrator can install two logical instances of the printer, assigning one a low priority and the other a high priority. Users in the marketing department could then be instructed to send their print jobs to the printer with the low priority, and sales staff could be told to send their print jobs to the printer assigned the higher priority.

Managing printers using print priorities

1. Install a printer normally using either Plug and Play or a manual install.
2. Install the printer a second time using a manual install.
3. Access the printer properties for the first printer.
4. Select the **Advanced** property sheet.
5. Notice that the priority is set to 1.
6. Access the printer properties for the second printer.
7. Select the **Advanced** property sheet.
8. Set the priority to 99.

The software driver for the printer can be changed via the New Driver button. This launches the Add Printer Driver Wizard, which steps through the process of installing the new driver. Currently installed printer drivers can be replaced with newer ones provided by the printer manufacturer. Replacing the old driver with a new one requires clicking on the New Driver button.

Controlling Spooling Options

The middle portion of the Advanced property sheet controls how print jobs are spooled. The default setting is **Spool Print Documents So Program Finishes Printing Faster**. Under this option are two choices. If enough disk space is available to store the entire print job, selecting the **Start Printing After Last Page Is Spooled** option can speed up printing.

Selecting **Print Directly to the Printer** provides a means for troubleshooting spooling problems by bypassing spooling and feeding the print job directly to the printer. The drawback to this option is that it will take more time for the program submitting the print job to free up.

Additional Options

Other options managed on this property sheet include these:

_Hold Mismatched Documents__:_ Instructs Windows 2000's spooler not to print any print job whose document setup does not match printer setup. Mismatched documents are held in the print queue until manually deleted by either their owner or an administrator.

_Print Spooled Documents First__:_ Instructs the Windows 2000 spooler when deciding which document to print next to give preference to print jobs that finished spooling.

_Keep Printed Documents__:_ Instructs the Windows 2000 spooler not to delete any print jobs after they have been printed. For example, this feature would be useful if payroll checks were being printed. After the checks are printed they could be proofed to make sure that the checks had been properly aligned and printed correctly. If the alignment was off, the alignment could be fixed, and then the print job could be restarted.

_Enable Advanced Printing Features__:_ This setting instructs Windows 2000 to enable advanced capabilities (see Figure 6.53). If it's not enabled, certain printing options might not be available. These options depend on the type of printer and can include such things as determining the page order and providing support for booklet printing.

FIGURE 6.53
The Advanced property sheet's settings allow the establishment of printer priorities and pooling.

The **Printing Defaults** button allows global control over default document properties for every user of this printer.

The **Print Processor** button allows selection of data type. This option should not be selected unless a program specifically requires a particular print processor and data type in order to work correctly.

The **Separator Page** button allows a specific separator page to be inserted in between every print job. This feature assists users in locating their print jobs when multiple users share the same print device. You can use any Windows metafile (.wmf) for a separator page.

The Security Property Sheet on the Printer Properties Dialog

The Security property sheet allows an administrator to provide or deny different levels of access to users and groups. Printer security is explained in detail in Chapter 7, "Network Administration and Security."

The Device Settings Property Sheet on the Printer Properties Dialog

The Device Settings property sheet provides control over printer features such as the type of paper loaded in the print device's paper trays.

Troubleshooting Printing Problems

From time to time, every network experiences problems. Networking printing is no exception. Unlike computers, printers need constant care and maintenance. Papers trays run empty; printer ribbon, ink, or toners become depleted. Many things can cause a lapse in the availability of a print device. This is especially true when print devices are attached to peer computers and the owner of a computer powers off the printer or the computer which manages that printer without realizing the effect it might have on network users. For help, look to the Windows 2000 Print Troubleshooting Wizard, as shown in Figure 6.54.

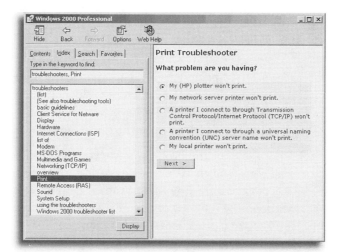

FIGURE 6.54
The Windows 2000 Print
Troubleshooting Wizard
provides assistance in
solving most common
printer problems.

Using Drag and Drop to Print Documents

An alternative to opening a program and then using it to access and
print a file is drag and drop. For example, a user can quickly print a
file on a local drive by simply dragging it on top of the icon representing the destination print device and dropping it, as demonstrated
in Figure 6.55.

FIGURE 6.55
Drag and drop provides
a means for printing a
document without open-
ing the application that
created it.

Using drag and drop to print files

1. Using either the **My Computer** or the **Windows Explorer** utilities, locate the file to be printed.

2. Open the Printers dialog to display available print devices.

3. Click on the desired file and continue to hold down the left mouse button while dragging the mouse over the top of the selected print device. Then, release the mouse button. The application associated with the document might open for a moment during the print process before closing again. Windows 2000 proceeds to print the document.

To make drag and drop easier to work with, shortcuts can be created and placed on the Windows desktop for the destination printer. Users need only drag files to the desktop instead of having to go through the motions of opening and locating the printer's dialog every time a print operation is required.

Validating Printer Operability

The Windows 2000 Printer Test Page button located on the General property sheet of a printer's Properties dialog provides a means for immediately testing any printer. If the test page prints correctly, the printer is operating correctly. As the first sentence of the printed test page states, if you can read this information, you have correctly installed your printer. In addition to providing a visual proof of a successful printer installation, the process provides a wealth of information, including the following data:

- The printer name
- The printer model
- The printer driver name
- The version of the printer driver
- A listing of installed driver and DLL Files and their location on the local computer

---

Adding a Printer Shortcut to the Desktop

To place a shortcut on the desktop, simply open the Printers dialog and locate the desired printer. Then, right-click on the printer's icon and, while still holding down the right mouse button, drag the icon onto an open area on the Windows desktop; then, release the right mouse button. Windows responds by displaying a menu. Click on the **Create Shortcut(s) Here** option. An icon for the print device appears on the Windows desktop. In the lower-left portion of the icon, a small arrow is present, signifying that this is a shortcut to the original printer.

chapter

7

Network Administration and Security

Examining Windows 2000 Security

Windows 2000 Professional is substantially more secure than Windows 95 or 98. It inherits the rich set of security features found in Windows NT 4.0. These include User and Group account management, share and NTFS security, security policies, and auditing. Windows 2000 Pro was designed from the ground up with security in mind.

Logon Accounts

Unlike with Windows 95 or 98, one cannot simply gain access to a Windows 2000 Pro computer by clicking Cancel at the logon prompt. Nor can one create a new user account by simply typing a new account name at the login prompt. Windows NT 2000 Pro requires that every user have a user account before logging in to the computer. User accounts have to be created by a user with administrative privileges.

On a peer network, user accounts are stored in the local security database on each Windows 2000 Pro computer. This means that if there are five computers on the network to which a user needs access, a user account must be created on each computer, as depicted in Figure 7.1.

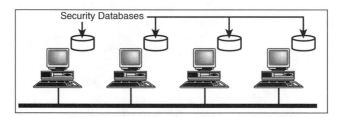

FIGURE 7.1
Every computer on a Windows 2000 Professional peer network maintains its own local security database.

After a user's account has been established, the user can log on to that computer. Windows 2000 Pro presents a logon prompt that requires the user to press the Ctrl+Alt+Delete keystroke combination. This presents the user with a logon dialog. The user enters the username and password as assigned by an administrator.

The username is a unique name to identify the user to the computer. A password is assigned to every user account. The computer requires the password as proof that the person trying to log on is really the owner of the user account. For this reason, passwords are considered highly confidential and are not shared with anyone. As the password is typed, asterisks (*) appear in place of typed characters. This helps prevent others from stealing passwords by looking over someone's shoulder.

User Groups and Account Management

Windows 2000 Professional provides two means for managing user and group accounts. The first is the Users and Passwords utility located on the Windows 2000 Control Panel. The second is the Local Users and Groups snap-in. The Users and Passwords utility provides a link to the Local Users and Groups snap-in.

If the only requirement is to manage local user and group accounts, the Users and Passwords utility will suffice. However, if the requirement is to be able to manage all user and group accounts on all computers on the network from a single location, the Local Users and Groups snap-in is the proper solution. This snap-in can provide remote administration over other Windows 2000 Pro and Windows NT 4.0 workstations. Without this snap-in, an administrator would have to physically visit each network computer to perform account management.

Remote Administration

On a small network of only a few computers, configuring shared resources at each computer might not pose a significant inconvenience. However, when the network grows to 9 or 10 computers dispersed over an entire suite of offices, the level of inconvenience increases. Windows 2000 offers remote administration as a means of allowing an administrator to manage security over users, groups, and shared resources from a single computer on the network.

Windows 2000 Pro provides many utilities that support remote computer administration over the network. Many of these utilities automatically connect the administrator to the remote computer as long as the network administrator's user accounts and passwords are the same on both computers. If the user accounts are out of sync, many of these utilities will prompt the administrator for a user account name and password on the remote computer that should be used to establish the connection. However, not all these utilities provide this prompt, and instead, the administrator receives a message saying that the connection cannot be established.

Enabling Remote Administration

On Windows 9X operating systems, remote adminis-tration is enabled from the Password utility on the Windows Control Panel. A password is assigned to protect remote access. Any user who knows the pass-word specified can access and administer shares on the computer. A special share is created for every hard disk on the computer. This allows for complete remote access and control of the file system on the remote computer.

If this occurs, close the utility and use the My Network Places to browse and locate the network computer. Attempt to access a resource on the target computer. When prompted, supply a user-name and password. Close the My Network Places dialog and subor-dinate dialogs, and attempt to open the original utility and remotely access the network resource.

Share and NTFS Security

In addition to establishing user and group accounts, administrators need to administer share and NTFS security. Share security controls network access to locally shared resources. Share security is available on any Windows 2000 computer that has the Windows File and Print Sharing service installed. NTFS security provides a very high level of security that protects computer resources by assigning spe-cific permissions to users and groups and prevents local and network users from doing anything without permission.

To implement NTFS security, Windows 2000 Pro requires that *New Technology File System*, or *NTFS*, be installed as the computer's file system. NTFS is the most secure of Windows 2000's available file systems. The NTFS file system is installed as part of the Windows NT Workstation installation process.

As a part of his responsibility for securing the network, the adminis-trator must set up a security policy that governs user accounts. Another facet of protecting both the network and each network computer is monitoring for possible attempts to breach security. This is achieved by implementation of auditing.

Logon and Logoff

Windows 2000 Professional employs user accounts and passwords to identify and authenticate users. Every person who logs on to the computer is assigned a unique username. The Windows 2000 Pro logon process provides the means for the user to give the computer this information.

The Access Token

After the user enters a valid username and password, Windows 2000 attempts to authenticate the account information. It does this by searching the local security database to find a matching user account and password. If it is unsuccessful, the logon is rejected, and the user is denied access. If the search finds a match, Windows creates an access token for the user and completes the logon.

An access token contains the System ID assigned to the user's account and any Group IDs assigned to groups of which the user is a member (see Figure 7.2). The system uses this token to determine when a user can access a given resource.

The Windows logon process then starts the Windows Explorer process and attaches the access token to it. From there every application the user starts is assigned the same access token. Every time a user attempts to access an object and perform an action on it, Windows 2000 references the user's access token to determine whether the user's account or group membership provides sufficient permissions.

Security-ID
Sales_Group
Managers_Group
Administrators

FIGURE 7.2
An access token contains the user's SID and all group account IDs to which the user belongs.

Security on an Object Model

On Windows 2000 Pro, security is applied to individual objects. Everything on Windows NT is an object. For example, files, directories, drives, and printers are all objects. On Windows 2000, every object consists of three parts: type, functions, and attributes, as shown in Table 7.1. Every object has a type such as file or folder and a series of functions that can be applied to it such as open and close. In addition, the object consists of a filename, a data portion, and an *Access Control List*, or *ACL*.

Table 7.1 A Sample ACL for a File

Type	Functions	Attributes
File	Open	Filename
	Close	Data
	Read	ACL
	Write	
	Delete	
	Change	

Windows 2000 uses the ACL to decide whether a user may access the object. The ACL is composed of a series *of Access Control Entries*, or *ACEs*. For example, a file with a filename of DOCUMENT1 might have an ACL that grants Read access to an SID belonging to a user named Bob, Read access to a user named Sue, Read access to a Group ID belonging to the Sales group, and No Access for a Group ID belonging to the Marketing group, as depicted in Table 7.2.

Table 7.2 A Sample of ACE Entries in an ACL

User/Group	Permission
Bob	Read
Sue	Read
Sales	Read
Marketing	No Access

If Bob is a member of the Marketing group, he will be unable to access the file. Windows NT first examines all the access permissions assigned to a user (including group memberships) looking for an explicit No Access permission. If No Access is specified, the user cannot access the file. If Windows 2000 does not find a No Access permission, it checks again to see whether the user should be given access. Using the preceding example, Sue and all members of the Sales group have Read access to the file, and Bob and all members of the Marketing group are denied access. The actual application of security is performed by comparing the SID and Group IDs stored in a user's assigned token to the ACE entries in the ACL of the object.

The Local Account Scheme

On the peer network, all user accounts are local accounts. This means that each computer maintains its own database of user accounts. If a user is to log on to more than one computer or use the network to access other computers, a user account must be established on each computer.

For a network administrator, this means that an account must be created on every computer on the network the administrator is responsible for managing. To make network administration easier, administrators should try to keep all user account names and passwords synchronized across the network. Otherwise, the administrator must remember what his account name and password are on every computer. If the network consists of 9 or 10 computers, this can become a difficult task. The disadvantage of this strategy is that if someone discovers your user account and password on one computer, every computer on the network can be compromised.

Logging Off

After a user has logged on and completed working, it is appropriate for the user to log off. This does not require the user to perform a system shutdown. If the computer is shared by multiple users or is accessed often during the day, it might be preferable to simply log off and leave the system running. If the computer is providing a shared resource, it must be left running to provide support to network users.

Users can log off of Windows 2000 using one of two means. The most common option is to use the Log Off option located on the Shut Down Windows dialog.

Using the Shut Down Windows dialog to log off

1. Select **Start** and then **Sh<u>u</u>t Down**. The Shut Down Windows dialog appears.

2. Select Log Off from the drop-down list in the **What Do You Want the Computer to Do?** area.

3. Click **OK**. Windows should display a prompt stating that the Ctrl+Alt+Delete keys must be pressed to initiate a new login.

The second means for logging off is through the Windows 2000 Security dialog, as described in the next section.

The Security Dialog

One particularly useful security feature in Windows 2000 Pro is the Security dialog box. After logging on to a Windows 2000 computer, the user can access this dialog by pressing Ctrl+Alt+Delete (see Figure 7.3). The name of the computer and the currently logged-on user are displayed. Six options are available, as outlined in Table 7.3.

FIGURE 7.3
The user accesses the Windows 2000 Security dialog by pressing Ctrl+Alt+Delete.

Using Ctrl+Alt+Delete

On Windows 9X computers, pressing the Ctrl+Alt+Delete keystroke combination produces the Close Program dialog. From here, programs that are not responding to the operating system can be terminated, and a shutdown of the computer can be initiated. Windows 9X provides the Passwords utility located in the Windows 9X Control Panel for changing the password of the currently logged-on user.

Table 7.3 Windows 2000 Security Dialog Options

Option	Description
Lock Computer	Provides a fast way for a user to secure the computer without logging off completely. This option is typically used when the user needs to step away from the computer for a few minutes.
Log off	Provides a fast way for the user to log off the computer and shut down all running applications. Windows 2000 Pro continues to operate and waits for the next user to log on.
Shut Down	Instructs Windows 2000 Pro to display a dialog that allows the user to shut down the computer.
Change Password	Presents a dialog allowing the user to change his current password.
Task Manager	Launches the Task Manager utility. This utility displays real-time information about the performance of the computer and allows the user to terminate a program that has stopped responding.
Cancel	Instructs Windows 2000 to close the Windows Security dialog.

Examining the Differences Between NTFS and FAT

Windows 2000 supports several types of file systems, including FAT, FAT32, and NTFS. Windows 2000 Pro security depends on which type of file system is installed. The following sections discuss the different systems and how they relate to Windows security.

Understanding the FAT16 File System

The *File Allocation Table*, or *FAT*, file system was created back in the early 1980s. Created in an age when computers were viewed only as separate standalone systems, it is an insecure file system.

The FAT file system is an excellent choice to use when the drive must be accessed by different local operating systems, as is the case when a computer is running in a dual-boot mode in which an operating system such as Windows 95 might also reside on the computer. Other features of FAT include the following:

- FAT filenames are limited to a length of eight characters with a period and a three-character extension.
- Each file entry also contains a date and time stamp and attribute information such as read-only and hidden.
- FAT file systems are limited to partitions less than 2GB.
- FAT works better than NTFS on drives smaller than 200MB.

If either FAT or FAT32 is installed, Windows 2000 Pro is limited to share security.

Understanding the FAT32 File System

The *FAT32* file system expands the original FAT file system by adding support for filenames up to 255 characters in length, including spaces and multiple periods. FAT32 automatically creates eight-by-three file aliases for each long filename. This provides support for older software that cannot work with long filenames.

Understanding the NTFS File System

The *New Technology File System*, or *NTFS*, is the most secure of the available file systems. The NTFS file system is installed as part of

Converting File Systems

Windows drives that are running with the FAT file system can be changed to NTFS using the Convert command.

the Windows NT Workstation installation process. Windows 2000 supports NTFS Version 5, and Windows NT 4.0 supports NTFS Version 4. Other operating systems such as Windows for Workgroups, Windows 95, and Windows 98 cannot read an NTFS drive. NTFS provides several features that make it more dependable and secure than the other file systems.

In addition to being more secure than FAT, NTFS-formatted partitions offer many advantages, including these:

- NTFS provides for partitions as large as 16 exabytes.
- Windows 2000 provides file compression for NTFS partitions.
- NTFS includes fault tolerance that ensures the integrity of the file system.
- NTFS has the capability to back out or finish any incomplete transactions when the system is restarted.
- NTFS provides significantly better security than the share security to which FAT files systems are limited.

One drawback to NTFS is that it incurs a higher overhead than FAT and is not recommended for drives smaller than 50MB.

Establishing a Password Policy

Working with Policies

On Windows NT 4.0, system policies are established using the User Manager utility. On Windows 9X operating systems, policies are established using the System Policy Editor.

Before creating user and group accounts, you need to think about several considerations. For instance, what are your password policy requirements? Will an account lockout policy be enforced? Will you follow a user-naming convention when creating account names?

Password Policies and the Group Policy Snap-In

A password policy is a set of rules that Windows 2000 enforces on the creation of user accounts. On a Windows 2000 peer network, password policy is established locally on each Windows 2000 computer using the Group Policy snap-in.

Locating the password policy

1. Create an MMC console containing the Group Policy snap-in for the local computer, as demonstrated in Figure 7.4. There are two different security types in Group Policy. User Configuration provides the capability to restrict such things as the user's ability

to change desktop settings or view and access certain Windows components such as the My Network Places. Computer Configuration affects every user who logs on to the computer; it includes such items as the Password, Account, and Audit policies.

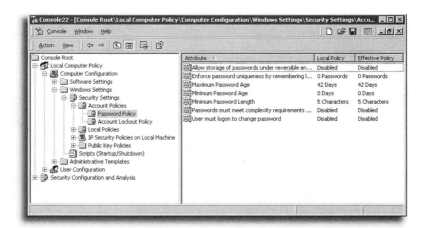

FIGURE 7.4
An MMC containing the Group Policy snap-in.

SEE ALSO

➤ *For information on adding snap-ins to custom MMC consoles, see page 112.*

   2. Expand the view in the left pane by using the following path: **Local Computer Policy**, **Computer Configuration**, **Windows Settings**, **Security Settings**, **Account Policies**, and then **Password Policy**.

The available Password Policy entries and their default entries are listed in Table 7.4.

Table 7.4   Available Password Policy Entries on Windows 2000 Professional

Description	Local Policy	Effective Policy
Allow Storage of Passwords Under Reversible Encryption	Disabled	Disabled
Enforce Password Uniqueness by Remembering Last...	0 Passwords	0 Passwords
Maximum Password Age	42 Days	42 Days
Minimum Password Age	0 Days	0 Days

continues...

Table 7.4 Continued

Description	Local Policy	Effective Policy
Minimum Password Length	5 Characters	5 Characters
Passwords Must Meet Complexity Requirements of Installed Password Filter	Disabled	Disabled
User Must Logon to Change Password	Disabled	Disabled

Understanding Policy Settings

The Minimum Password Age setting instructs Windows 2000 not to allow a user to change his password until a specified number of days has passed since the last time the password was changed. The maximum password age setting instructs Windows 2000 to force users to change their passwords after the specified number of days has passed. Windows 2000 prompts the user to change the password before it expires as part of the logon process.

The User Must Logon to Change Password setting specifies that a user must be able to log on before changing his password. If users allow their accounts to expire, they will be unable to change their passwords and will have to notify the administrator. The Enforce Password Uniqueness By Remembering Last setting instructs Windows to store a history of previously used passwords for every user account and to not allow a user to try to reuse an old account until this setting's value has been passed.

For example, suppose that the policy setting for a computer was set as outlined in Table 7.5.

Table 7.5 Sample Windows 2000 Professional Password Security Settings

Description	Policy
Enforce Password Uniqueness by Remembering Last	6 Passwords
Maximum Password Age	30 Days
Minimum Password Age	20 Days
Minimum Password Length	8 Characters

A Windows 2000 computer with the settings specified in Table 7.5 would force users to change their passwords every 30 days. The more often users change their passwords, the greater the security. If someone manages to find out what a user's password is, the longest he could possibly use it would be 30 days, after which time the user would be forced to change it or else have the account locked out. Setting a minimum password age of 20 days along with a uniqueness requirement of six passwords eliminates the possibility that a user might try to outsmart the security policy. Some users might be particularly fond of using a certain password. If forced by Windows 2000 to change the password to something different every 30 days, this user might attempt to change it again right away to what it used to be. By requiring a minimum 30-day password age and keeping a history of six passwords, this user must wait 180 days before being able to recycle the password. The longer a password, the stronger it is generally regarded to be because it is harder to guess a longer password.

Changing a Policy Setting

The Local Policy column displays any changes made to a policy that are not yet in effect. The Effective Policy column displays currently enforced policy settings. To change a policy setting, double-click on it. For example, use the following steps to change the Minimum Password Age.

Changing a policy setting

1. Double-click on the policy setting to be changed. A dialog for that setting appears, as shown in Figure 7.5.

FIGURE 7.5
The Minimum Password Age dialog allows the administrator to enforce a minimum password length requirement on all passwords.

Allow Time for Policies to Take Effect

Policies might take some time to become completely enforced. For example, changing the minimum password length from zero to six and restarting the computer will cause the new policy to be immediately enforced for any new user accounts. However, existing accounts that already have shorter passwords will continue to function. When their password finally expires, the new policy setting will force the user to create a password that complies with the new policy.

Be Consistent with Policies

It is a good idea to make all policies the same on every computer on the network. If policies get out of sync, network users might become confused. For example, if the Minimum Password Length setting was set to zero on some Windows 2000 computers and to eight on others, users might become confused then they find that a six-character password is allowed on one computer and not another.

Make Everyone Aware of Policies

Make sure that all network users are aware of policies. This enables them to comply with policies without the headache of having to figure them out on a trial-and-error basis.

2. Modify the value of the policy setting by altering its value or configuration in the **Local Policy Setting** area.

3. Click **OK**.

4. The Local Policy column now reflects any changes that have been made. Close the MMC console and reboot the computer. When the computer restarts, the new policy setting will be in effect.

Managing Accounts

Network administrators need to create a formal policy for naming user accounts so that they are easy to identify and manage. Another issue that should be addressed is the establishment of an account lockout policy that limits the number of login attempts that can be made before an account is locked out. This policy prevents unauthorized users from trying to break into the computer by trying to repeatedly guess an account's password.

User-Naming Policy

A user-naming policy is a set of guidelines for creating new user and group accounts. A naming convention makes usernames easy to remember and locate. There are multiple approaches for developing a naming convention.

On a peer network, where administrators and users need to be able to access resources on multiple computers, a logon account must be created on every computer that each user needs to access. Therefore, you might want to consider creating accounts of the same name on every computer for each user. This way, a user needs to remember only one account name when logging on to any computer. An example of a simple naming convention often used on small networks is to take the user's last name or a portion of it and to append it with a portion of the user's first name. For example, a naming convention might state that a user's account name will consist of the first four characters of the user's last name and the first two characters of the user's first name, followed by a two-digit number. The two-digit number is added so that if there are two users whose combinations of first- and last-name characters end up producing the same logon name, they can still be distinguished.

Table 7.6 demonstrates how this naming convention can be applied when new user accounts are being created.

Table 7.6 Example of a User-Naming Policy

User's Name	Account Name
Jerry Vale	valeje01
Jerry Valentine	valeje02
Elvis Presley	presel01
Tom Jones	joneto01

Account Lockout Policy

An *account lockout* policy governs what happens if a user attempts to log on but misspells his password too many times. This policy can also be managed using the Group Policy snap-in. Table 7.7 provides a description of the options available in the account lockout policy.

Table 7.7 Options Available in the Account Lockout Policy

Description	Local Policy	Effective Policy
Account Lockout Count	0 Invalid Logon Attempts	0 Invalid Logon Attempts
Lockout Account For	Not Defined	Not Defined
Reset Account Lockout After	Not Defined	Not Defined

Specifying a number such as 3 for Account Lockout Count tells Windows 2000 to lock a user account after a user has tried unsuccessfully three times to log on. The lockout account allows the administrator to specify how long a user account that has been locked out by Windows 2000 should remain locked out. For example, the policy setting might specify that after 15 minutes the account should become unlocked. If this option is not defined, only an administrator can unlock the account. The Reset Account Lockout After option instructs Windows 2000 to reset the lockout to 0 after the specified amount of time has passed.

Guidelines for Secure Passwords

Although there is no one set formula or standard for creating a secure password, there are some general guidelines. Never use the same password twice. Never share your personal password with anyone. If you believe that your password might be compromised, change it immediately. Make passwords a minimum of six characters in length. Do not use common words such as your name or the names of family members. Mix upper- and lowercase letters and include at least one numeric character.

203

Understanding User Profiles

User profiles support individual configuration of system settings on a user-by-user basis. When multiple users share the same computer, they can log on to that computer with a unique username and password, and Windows 2000 establishes a profile for that user where any customizations will be stored. For example, users can select their own preferred screen savers, desktop background, setup shortcuts on the desktop, and a host of other changes. Because the private configurations are stored in users' individual profiles, they do not affect other users. Each time a user logs on to the computer, Windows loads any user-defined customizations stored in that user's profile.

The types of things stored in user profiles include these items:

- Windows desktop settings
- Network settings including mapped drives and defined printers
- Windows application settings for applications that support per-user customization
- Shortcuts
- Changes made to the Start menu and Programs folder

After user profiles are activated, every time a new user logs on, the computer prompts for a username and password. After receiving the user ID and password, Windows 2000 looks to see whether the user has logged on to this computer before. If that is the case, the user's previously saved profile is loaded. If this is the first time the user has logged on to the computer, a new profile is created for that user. If the administrator has created an account for a user but that user has not yet logged on to the computer, that user profile has not yet been established. The user profile is established the first time the user successfully logs on to the computer.

The default user profiles are stored in the Documents and Settings folder off the root directory where Windows 2000 was installed. For most computers this is C:\Documents and Settings. Under the Documents and Settings folder is a folder for every user who has logged on to the computer. For example, the profile for a user whose username is Roberta would be C:\Documents and Settings\Roberta.

Managing User Accounts

When Windows 2000 Pro is installed on the computer, two accounts are automatically created. These are the Administrator account and the Guest account. In addition, if the installation of Windows 2000 was an upgrade from another operating system such as Windows NT Workstation 4.0, other user accounts might have been migrated.

Windows 2000 provides a utility in the Windows Control Panel for local account management and a snap-in for remote account administration. Windows also provides a means for controlling account logon for all users of a computer.

The Administrator and Guest Accounts

The Administrator account and password are established during Windows 2000 installation. This account is used to manage the computer and to create other user accounts on the computer. This account can be renamed but cannot be locked out or deleted.

The Guest account is created during installation but is automatically placed in a disabled state. This account can be enabled and used to provide temporary computer and network access to individuals who do not have an account on the computer. By default, this account can operate the computer and save files but cannot make configuration changes or perform other changes. This account can be renamed and disabled but cannot be deleted.

Guidelines for Creating New Accounts

Before creating additional Windows 2000 user accounts, keep the following points in mind:

- Passwords can be from 0 to 128 characters long. Eight is generally considered to be a good length.
- Passwords can consist of any combination of numbers, letters, and special characters, except for these characters: "[ ]/\p;:|+=,.><?*.
- It is best to always require a user to change his password the first time he logs on to the computer so that no one, even an administrator, knows a user's password after he has logged on.

Performing Group and Remote Account Management

The Users and Passwords utility does not permit the creation of new groups or the addition of user accounts to multiple groups. If these capabilities are required, the Local Users and Groups snap-in must be used. For network administrators the Users and Passwords utility will prove too limiting. For local users who are allowed to perform account management on their own PC, this tool should be just fine. The Users and Passwords dialog consists of two tabs. The Users tab is displayed by default and provides user account-management capabilities. The Advanced tab provides control over how secure the local computer's boot is and provides a link to the Local User Manager MMC.

Using the Local Users and Groups snap-in to manage accounts has the added benefit of allowing the snap-in to be added multiple times to accommodate the remote administration of user and group accounts on other network computers, thus allowing centralized account management.

- Initial passwords should be a random set of numbers, letters, and special characters to make them more secure.

- All user account names must be unique on the computer.

- User account names are limited to 20 characters in length.

- User account names are not case-sensitive.

The Users and Passwords Utility

The Users and Passwords utility provides a means for users who have access to the Administrator account or are a member of the Administrators groups to manage user accounts on their local computer. It also allows the assignment of a user account to a single group account.

SEE ALSO

➤ For information about adding snap-ins to custom MMC consoles, see page 112.

Accessing the User and Passwords utility

1. Select **Start**, then **Settings**, then **Control Panel**.

2. Double-click on the **Users and Passwords** icon. The Users and Passwords dialog appears (see Figure 7.6).

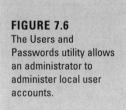

FIGURE 7.6
The Users and Passwords utility allows an administrator to administer local user accounts.

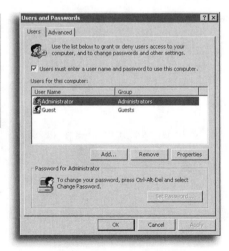

Automatic Logon

One Windows 2000 Pro logon option controlled from the Users and Passwords dialog is **Users Must Enter a User Name and**

Password to Use This Computer. When this option is selected, each user who sits down in front of the computer to log on must supply a unique username and password before access is permitted. When this option is not selected, the computer can be set up so that all users who access it are automatically logged on using a single, preconfigured account. For example, a company might set aside one computer for use by visitors and preconfigure it to allow anyone to log on using the Guest user account. This would allow anyone to power on the computer and gain access without logging on yet limit access to the permission granted to the Guest account.

Configuring automatic logon

1. Remove the selection of the **Users Must Enter a User Name and Password to Use This Computer** option on the Users and Passwords dialog. The Automatically Log On dialog appears (see Figure 7.7).

2. Click **Apply**.

FIGURE 7.7
Configuring a Windows 2000 computer to automatically establish a user logon when the computer is started.

3. Enter the username of the account that will be used to establish the automatic log in the **User Name** field, and press the **Tab** key.

4. Enter the password associated with this account into the **Password** field, and press the **Tab** key.

5. Enter the password associated with this account into the **Confirm Password** field.

6. Click **OK**.

Creating, Modifying, or Deleting Accounts

A list of all currently established user accounts is displayed in the **Users for This Computer** area on the dialog. Accounts are displayed by username. Group membership is also visible. The Add,

Remove, and Properties buttons provide the capability to create, delete, and configure user accounts on the computer.

Creating a New Account

Creating new accounts from the Users and Passwords utility adds the new account to the local computer. It does not provide the capability to perform remote account management on other network computers. It allows for the definition of an account name, a description, an initial password, and other basic account settings including a single group membership.

SEE ALSO
➤ *To learn more about remote account management, see page 215.*

Creating a new user account

1. Click the **Add** button on the Users and Passwords dialog. The Add New User dialog appears (see Figure 7.8).

2. Enter a name for the new user account in the **User Name** field, and press the **Tab** key.

3. Enter the name of the person who will be assigned this account in the **Full Name** field, and press the **Tab** key.

4. Enter an optional description for the account in the **Description** field.

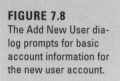

FIGURE 7.8
The Add New User dialog prompts for basic account information for the new user account.

5. Click **Next** to continue.

6. Enter an initial password for the new account in the **Password** field, and press the **Tab** key.

7. Enter the password a second time in the **Confirm password** field (see Figure 7.9).

8. Click on **Next** to continue.

9. Select an appropriate group of which the user account should be a member (see Figure 7.10). Standard User is the default. Selecting Standard User provides a common set of access privileges that will be required by most users. Selecting Restricted User limits the user's ability to make any changes that might affect the computer but allows the user to perform actions such as creating, saving, and printing files. Selecting Other allows for the selection among any existing groups on the computer. These groups include the built-in Windows groups, as well as any groups that an administrator has created. Selecting one of these groups provides the capability to specify a more specific set of access privileges.

10. Click **Finish**. The new account appears in the Users for This Computer area on the Users and Passwords dialog.

Modifying an Existing Account

Modifying user accounts allows administrators to change account-name and description information to reflect changes in user status, such as when an employee's last name changes due to a marriage. In addition, group membership can be modified.

Configuring an account

1. Select an account and click on the **Properties** button on the Users and Passwords dialog. A dialog for the selected account appears, as shown in Figure 7.11.

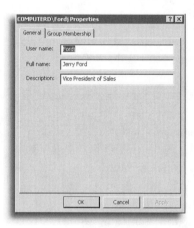

FIGURE 7.11
Basic account information can be modified for existing user accounts.

2. If appropriate, modify **User Name**, **Full Name**, or **Description**.
3. Select the **Group Membership** tab.
4. Modify the group membership as required (see Figure 7.12).
5. Click **OK**.

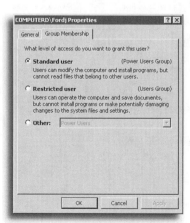

FIGURE 7.12
Group membership can also be modified.

The changes will not take effect until the next time the user logs on to the computer and a new access token reflecting the changes is created.

Deleting a User Account

When a user no longer requires access to a computer or network resource, steps should be taken to terminate the user's account access. For example, if a user leaves the company, his account should be deleted. Accounts are deleted from the local security database using the Remove option.

Removing a user account

1. Select an account and click on the **Remove** button on the Users and Passwords dialog. The Users and Passwords prompt appears, as shown in Figure 7.13.

FIGURE 7.13
Windows requires confirmation before deleting a user account from the local security database.

2. Click **Yes** to delete the account. The account no longer appears in the **Users for This Computer Area** on the Users and Passwords dialog.

Changing a User Account Password

From time to time, every user forgets a password. When this occurs, an administrator can log on and give the user a new password. This works for every computer account stored in the local computer account database with the exception of the Administrator account. The only way to change the password for this account is by pressing the Ctrl+Alt+Delete keys and selecting the Change Password option.

Changing account passwords

1. Select an account and click on the **Set Password** button on the Users and Passwords dialog. The Set Password dialog appears, as shown in Figure 7.14.

2. Enter a new password for the account in the **New Password** field and press the **Tab** key.

3. Enter the new password a second time in the **Confirm New Password** field.

4. Click **OK**.

Advanced User Management and Security Boot Settings

The Advanced tab on the Users and Passwords dialog shown in Figure 7.15 provides access to several advanced security features. Among these are Advanced User Management and Secure Boot Settings. The Advanced User Management section provides a link to an MMC that contains the Local Users and Groups snap-in. This snap-in provides an advanced interface for managing user and group accounts. The Secure Boot Settings section contains just one option, which controls whether the Ctrl+Alt+Delete key sequence is required before allowing users to log on to the computer.

Securing the Windows Logon

By default, the **Require Users to Press Ctrl-Alt-Delete Before Logging On** option is selected when Windows 2000 is installed. This option forces users to simultaneously press the Ctrl+Alt+Delete key combination to start the Windows logon process. This ensures that the logon dialog where users will type their username and password is what it appears to be because this key sequence instructs Windows 2000 to stop all foreground applications during the logon process.

Leaving the option on prevents someone from running a program to spoof the Windows logon process by preventing the spoofing program from executing during logon. Disabling this option opens a security hole. For example, someone wanting to acquire an administrator's password might load a program that displays a dialog that appears to be the Windows logon dialog. If an administrator later attempts to log on to the computer and enters her account name and password, the utility could save this information to a file, display a false error message, and terminate while also logging off the original user. The unsuspecting administrator would then see the real Windows logon dialog and proceed to log on to the computer unaware of what had just occurred. Later, the owner of the impersonating program could come back and collect the file where the trapped username and password had been stored. If the administrator has accounts and passwords on other network computers that are in sync with her local account, the perpetrator can attack the entire network.

> **Windows May Automatically Turn On the Ctrl+Alt+Delete Key Sequence Requirement**
>
> The Require Users to Press Ctrl-Alt-Delete Before Logging On option is automatically cleared if the Users Must Enter a User Name and Password to Use This Computer option is cleared on the Users tab of the Users and Passwords dialog.

If **Require Users to Press Ctrl-Alt-Delete Before Logging On** option is not selected, Windows 2000 automatically presents a logon dialog when booted or when a user logs off. This provides the advantage of saving users one step during login. However, the time savings provided by eliminating this option are usually more than offset by the danger it presents. This option is not appropriate for business settings.

Advanced User Management

The Advanced button in the Advanced User Management area provides a link to the Local User Manager MMC, as shown in

Figure 7.16. From this MMC the administrator can manage both local user and group accounts, as well as make user accounts members of multiple user accounts.

This MMC contains the Local Users and Groups snap-in, which means that it is limited to managing user and group accounts for the local computer. The Local Users and Groups snap-in is also contained in the Computer Management MMC.

SEE ALSO

➤ *For information on adding snap-ins to custom MMC consoles, see page 112.*

Accessing the Local Users and Groups snap-in in the computer management MMC

1. Select **Start**, then **Settings**, then **Control Panel**, and click on the **Administrative Tools** icon.

2. Double-click on the **Computer Management** icon.

3. Double-click on **System Tools** in the left pane.

4. Select **Local Users and Groups**. The Users and Groups folders appear in the right pane (see Figure 7.17).

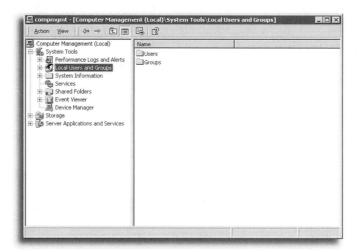

FIGURE 7.17
The Computer
Management MMC pro-
vides local user and
group account manage-
ment using the Local
Users and Groups snap-
in.

Local Users and Groups Snap-In

So far, all the options that have been examined provide account management only for the local computer. However, by creating a custom MMC, an administrator with account privileges on other Windows 2000 computers can create a console from which account management can be performed on any Windows 2000 computer on the network. Figure 7.18, shown a bit later, demonstrates a custom MMC console that has been configured to allow the administrator to manage three network computers using the Local Users and Groups snap-in. Note that the Local Users and Groups snap-in is also available by default on the Computer Management MMC, where it can provide local and group account management only on the local computer.

Remotely Managing Network Users and Group Accounts

Although the Users and Passwords utility provides limited control over local user account and group membership, it lacks several features required by network administrators. The Local Users and Groups snap-in provides these missing capabilities and, when added to a custom MMC, can provide them for every Windows 2000 and Windows NT 4.0 computer on the network.

These features include the capability to do the following:

- Force users to change their password at next logon
- Prevent users from changing their password
- Prevent password expiration
- Lock and unlock accounts
- Disable an unused account without deleting it
- Add a user to more than one group
- Administer user and group accounts remotely
- Control user-profile information and establish home directories

Creating New User Accounts

Creating a user account with the Local Users and Groups snap-in allows a more granular specification of account options than is provided with the Users and Passwords utility. The snap-in allows specification of the following additional features:

- Forcing users to change their password the next time they log in
- Preventing users from changing their passwords
- Preventing passwords from expiring (this overrides the account expiration rule in an existing account policy if one has been established)
- Disabling selected user accounts

Creating a Local Account

1. Open an MMC that contains the Local Users and Groups snap-in (see Figure 7.18).
2. Expand the tree view in the left pane for a selected computer.
3. Select **Users**. A list of all user accounts appears in the right pane.
4. Select **New User** from the **Action** menu option. The New User dialog appears, as shown in Figure 7.19.
5. Type the username, the full name, and a description for the new user account.
6. Type a password for the new account and type it a second time in the Confirm Password field.

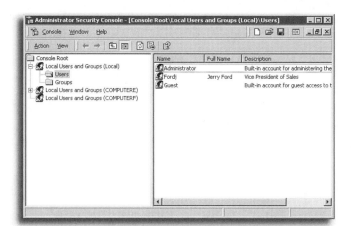

FIGURE 7.18
An example of an MMC containing three instances of the Local Users and Groups snap-in.

FIGURE 7.19
The New User dialog collects basic account information and provides several controlling options.

7. The default of User Must Change Password at Next Logon is automatically selected. Leave this option in place for most user accounts.

8. If this account is a special-purpose account, such as the Guest account, you might want to deselect the User Must Change Password at Next Logon option. This automatically enables the next two options, which are otherwise unavailable.

9. User Cannot Change Password can be chosen for shared accounts that have been set up with very restricted user access.

10. Selecting Password Never Expires overrides the Maximum Password Age policy setting.

11. Selecting Account Disabled allows the user account to be created but prevents it from being used until the administrator later clears it.

12. Click **Create** and then click **Close**. The new account appears in the left pane of the MMC console window.

Now that you have created a new account, you need to establish group membership. Optionally, you can configure the user's profile and create a home directory.

To establish a group membership

1. Select the new account and then select **Properties** from the **Action** menu. The Properties dialog for the account appears, containing three tabs with additional configuration options.

2. Select the **General** tab to modify any of the account settings that were just established.

3. Select the **Member Of** tab and click the **Add** button to add the user account to one or more groups (see Figure 7.20). Select a group to which the user account should be added, and click the **Add** button. The group then appears in a list at the bottom of the dialog. Continue to add additional user accounts as required. When done, click **OK**.

FIGURE 7.20
The Member Of tab on the account's Properties dialog provides the means for adding user accounts to multiple groups.

4. Select the **Profile** tab to configure the user profile or home directory, as shown in Figure 7.21. These features are automatically established by Windows 2000. If the user of this account will be working from multiple Windows 2000 computers on the network and wants to have his profile follow him from computer to computer, set the **Profile Path** to a shared folder on a

network computer set aside to hold user profiles. This way, when the user logs on to any Windows 2000 computer, his profile will be downloaded from the computer where it is stored to the computer that is being logged on to. If this option is not set in this manner, a unique user profile will be created on every computer that the user logs on to. The syntax for this field follows the UNC and is `\\computer_name\path\folder`, where *folder* is the name of the folder where the user profile is stored.

FIGURE 7.21
The Profile tab on the account's Properties dialog allows the administrator to establish a network profile and home directory for user accounts.

6. Select **Local Path** if a share has been set aside on a network computer that is designated as the user's personal storage location. For example, it might be desirable to create a home directory for every network user on one computer and instruct all users to store their data on that computer. This would make the backing up of user data easier because all user data would be stored in a single location. The UNC for the home directory can be provided in the Local Path field, or a mapping can be established by selecting a free drive letter from the Connect drop-down list and then typing a UNC to the shared folder. When done, click **Apply** and then **OK**.

SEE ALSO
➤ *For information on establishing disk quotas, see page 237.*

Unlocking a User Account

From time to time, users forget their password and attempt to guess it when logging on to their computer. If an account policy has been established that sets a limit on the number of attempts that can be made, Windows 2000 automatically locks out the account if this limit is exceeded. When the user next attempts to log on to the computer, the following prompt appears: Unable to log you on because your account has been locked out, please contact your administrator.

Unlocking User Accounts

1. Open an MMC that contains the Local Users and Groups snap-in.

2. Expand the tree view in the left pane for a selected computer.

3. Select **Users**. A list of all user accounts on that computer appears in the right pane.

4. Double-click on the user's account. The Properties dialog for that account appears (see Figure 7.22). Clear the **Account Locked Out** option.

FIGURE 7.22
The Properties dialog for the selected user account indicates that the account has been locked out.

5. Click **Apply** and then **OK**.

Creating a Group Account

Except when there are only a few user accounts, managing users with group accounts is much easier than managing them individually. For example, adding 20 users to two group accounts means that instead of managing all 20 accounts one at a time, an administrator can make changes to just the two group accounts, and the changes will automatically govern their user account members.

Creating group accounts

1. Open an MMC that contains the Local Users and Groups snap-in.

2. Expand the tree view in the left pane for a selected computer.

3. Copy and modify this portion from the Users section.

4. Select **Groups** on a selected computer in the left pane, and then select **New Group** from the **Action** menu (see Figure 7.23).

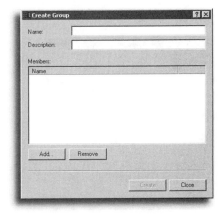

FIGURE 7.23
The Local Users and Groups snap-in provides the capability to create and manage group accounts.

5. Type a name and comment for the new group in the **Name** and **Description** fields.

6. Click on the **Add** button. The Select Users or Groups dialog appears, as shown in Figure 7.24.

7. To add users to the new group, select one from the list at the top of the dialog and click on the **Add** button. The account appears in the display area at the bottom of the dialog. Continue to add as many accounts as necessary. Click **OK** when done.

8. The Create Group dialog reappears (see Figure 7.25). The accounts that were added to the group now appear in the Members area. Click **Create** and then **Close**.

The new group now appears on the right pane of the MMC console, as shown in Figure 7.26.

FIGURE 7.24
Adding members to the group.

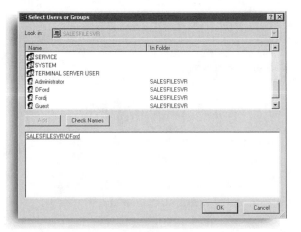

FIGURE 7.25
The Create Group dialog displays a list of all user and group accounts that have been added to the new group.

FIGURE 7.26
The new group account is now visible in the right pane when the Groups folder in the Local Users and Groups snap-in is selected.

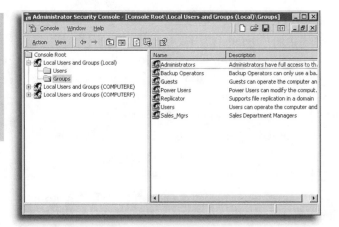

Implementing Share Security

Sharing resources over Microsoft peer networks requires establishing shared resources, or *shares*. This approach enables other network users to access these shared resources remotely. You can share an entire drive or a folder (which can contain subfolders). The default permission for a shared resource permits everyone on the network to have complete control over what has been shared. This might be acceptable for some types of files, but many pieces of network data, though they must be shared, should not be made available to all users. For example, a company might have confidential records to which only a few individuals or perhaps a department should have any access. Perhaps different individuals and groups require different levels of access. When it comes to security, the rule of thumb is to provide users with only the minimum level of access they need to perform their jobs.

Understanding Share Security

There are several very important things to understand about share security:

- Shares cannot be applied to individual files. To share a file or files, you should create a share folder and move files into it.

- Share access is not as secure as NTFS security.

- Share security is in effect only when users try to access files from over the network. Any user who logs on locally is not governed by share security.

- The default permission for shared drives and folders is Full Control.

- If the file systems on a local drive are FAT, then NTFS security is not available, but share security is.

There are three levels of share security to select. Windows 2000 allows any combination of them to be selected. Each permission can be implemented in two ways, either by allowing the permission or by denying it. Table 7.8 outlines the share permissions.

Table 7.8 Share Permissions

Permission	Function
Read	Allows a user or group to display folders and files and to run programs.
Change	Permits users and groups to create, modify, and delete folders and files, and permits all the items that the Read permission allows.
Full Control	Allows users and groups to take ownership of files, modify permissions, and do all the items permitted by the Change permission.

Understanding Allow and Deny

By assigning a user or group a permission with the Allow setting, you are enabling them to perform any actions provided by that permission. By assigning a user or group a permission with the Deny setting, you are denying them those same capabilities. One important rule to remember is that a denied permission overrules any allowed permission. Also, permissions are cumulative, meaning that if a user has a certain set of permissions assigned to a resource and is also the member of one or more groups that also have assigned permission over the resources, the resulting permission granted to the user is the accumulation of all assigned permissions.

For example, assume that a user account named Bob has the following permission assigned to it for a folder named Data_Folder.

Permission	Type of Access
Read	Allow

Also assume that Bob is a member of a group that has the following permission assigned to the folder named Data_Folder.

Permission	Type of Access
Change	Allow

The result of combining these two permissions is that the user has the Change permission over the shared resource. Again, remember that if the user logs on to the computer where the resources are shared, share security does not apply and the resource can be secured only if the file system active on the computer is NTFS.

Another example demonstrates the effect of applying Deny to a permission. Assume that a user account named Bob has the following permission assigned to it for a folder named Data_Folder.

Permission	Type of Access
Read	Allow

Also assume that Bob is a member of a group that has the following permission assigned to the folder named Data_Folder.

Permission	Type of Access
Read	Deny

The result of combining these two permissions is that the user has no access to the shared resource. This is because the Deny setting always takes precedence over the Allow permission.

Securing a Resource

Securing a resource with share security means selecting a resource and assigning specific permissions to user or group accounts. The default permission for each new share is to allow every user complete access to it. However, this setting does not provide any security over the resource and should therefore be changed.

Securing a shared drive or folder

1. Right-click on a shared folder or drive, and select the **Sharing** option from the menu that appears. The Properties dialog for the shared resource appears, and the Sharing tab is automatically selected.

2. Click on **Permissions**. The Permissions dialog for the shared resource appears, as shown in Figure 7.27.

3. By default, only the Everyone group is assigned all permissions over the shared resource. To remove the Everyone group, select it and click **Remove**. To modify the permissions assigned to the group, select or deselect any of the three permissions in the **Permissions** area and assign **Allow** and **Deny** as required.

4. To add another user or group and manage its permissions, click **Add** and select the user or group from the available list on the Select Users, Computers, or Groups dialog. Then, click **Add** followed by **OK**. Configure the new user or group as required,

Watch Out

Be very careful when copying or moving shared folders. When a shared folder is moved, it is no longer shared. When a shared folder is copied, the original folder remains shared, but the new folder is not shared.

225

and continue adding groups as necessary. When done, click
Apply and then **OK**.

FIGURE 7.27
An example of the
default permissions
assigned to a new share.

5. When returned to the Properties dialog for the shared resources,
   click **Apply** and then **OK**.

6. Figures 7.28 and 7.29 demonstrate the results of modifying the
   shared resource. In this case the permissions assigned to the
   Everyone group have been limited to allow Read access, and the
   user account for Bob has been added and granted Full Control.

FIGURE 7.28
The Everyone group has
been granted only Read
access.

FIGURE 7.29
The user account Bob has been granted Full Control over the shared resource.

SEE ALSO

➤ *For information on establishing a share, see page 125.*

Getting a Handle on NTFS Security

In addition to share security, Windows 2000 supports NTFS security, or *resource-level security*. NTFS security works by assigning access permissions to users or groups for each object. To implement resource-level security, the NTFS file system must be used on the local hard drive. Windows 2000 security depends on an identification of a user during logon using the user ID and password. As part of the logon process, Windows creates an access token for the user that contains the System ID assigned to the user's account and any Group IDs assigned to groups of which the user is a member. The system uses the token to determine when a user can access a given resource.

On Windows 2000, security is applied to individual objects. Everything on Windows 2000 is an object. For example, files, directories, drives, and printers are all objects. Every object maintains an Access Control List, or ACL, that Windows 2000 uses to decide whether a user may access the object. The ACL is composed of a series of Access Control Entries, or ACEs.

Like share security, NTFS security governs what a network user can and cannot access. In addition, it protects resources when users are logged on at the computer where the resource resides.

Keep It to Yourself

Of course, the ultimate security is to stop sharing the resource. If it is not essential that network users have access to a folder or drive, do not share it.

Managing Shared Resources

When planning how to make shared resources available, consider gathering them in a few places rather than allowing them to be scattered all over the network. Also, try to group them in such a way that all files on the same folder require the same level of permissions.

227

Understanding NTFS Permissions

There are more NTFS permissions than share permissions. In addition, the permissions applied to folders are different than those for files, as shown in Tables 7.9 and 7.10.

Table 7.9 NTFS Folder Permissions

Permission	Description
Full Control	Allows users and groups to take ownership of files, modify permissions, and do all the operations provided by every other NTFS permission.
Modify	Allows users and groups to delete folders and do all the operations allowed by the Read & Execute permission.
Read & Execute	Allows users and groups to navigate folders and drives and do all the functions permitted by the List Folder Contents and Read permissions.
List Folder Contents	Allows users and groups to view the contents of subfolders and see their contents.
Read	Allows users to view folders and files and to view their properties.
Write	Allows users and groups to create new folders and files and to view their properties.

Who Can Apply NTFS Security?

Three groups of users can apply NTFS security permissions. These are the members of the Administrators group, users with the Full Control permission on a folder or file, and the owner of the folder or file.

Table 7.10 NTFS File Permissions

Permission	Description
Full Control	Allows users and groups to take ownership, modify file permissions, and do all the operations provided by every other NTFS file permission.
Modify	Allows users and groups to change or delete the file and do all the functions allowed by the Read & Execute permission.
Read & Execute	Allows users and groups to run programs and do all the functions permitted by the Read permissions.
Read	Allows users to view a file and its properties.
Write	Allows users and groups to write over or change files and view their properties.

How Permissions Work

Like share permissions, NTFS permissions accumulate such that the system examines the permissions assigned to the user's account and any group account to determine whether the user has enough accumulative permission to perform a required action on an object, such as read or write. If there is a conflict between folder and file permissions, file permissions take precedence. For example, if a user has permissions on a file in a folder to which he does not have permission, the user can access the file using UNC syntax even though he is unable to navigate and view the contents of the folder using browsing. One other important point to remember about NTFS security is that, as with share security, the Deny setting overrides any instance where the permission is granted.

By default, NTFS permissions on folders are passed down to or inherited by any subfolders they contain. However, this setting can be overridden during the assignment of permissions.

For example, a file with a filename of DOCUMENT1 might have an ACL that grants Read access to an SID belonging to a user named Bob, Read access to a user named Sue, Read access to a Group ID belonging to the Sales group, and No Access for a Group ID belonging to the Marketing group, as depicted in Table 7.11.

Table 7.11   A Sample of ACE Entries in an ACL

User/Group	Permission
Bob	Read
Sue	Read
Sales	Read
Marketing	No Access

If Bob is a member of the Marketing group, he cannot access the file. Windows 2000 first examines all the access permissions assigned to a user (including group memberships) looking for an explicit No Access permission. If No Access is specified, the user cannot access the file. If Windows 2000 does not find a No Access permission, it checks again to see whether the user should be given access. Using the preceding example, Sue and all members of the Sales group have Read access to the file, and Bob and all members of the Marketing

229

group are denied access. The actual application of security is performed by comparing the SID and Group IDs stored in a user's assigned token to the ACE entries in the ACL of the object.

Applying NTFS Security

NTFS permissions are applied from the Security property sheet on each resource's Properties dialog. Windows 2000 establishes a set of default permissions for every resource on the computer. Unlike share security, which establishes permissions only at the drive and folder level, NTFS security can also set permissions at the file level.

Applying NTFS security

1. Right-click on a shared folder or drive, and select the **Properties** option from the menu that appears. The Properties dialog for the shared resource appears.

2. Select the **Security** tab (see Figure 7.30).

FIGURE 7.30
The Security tab on the Properties dialog for a Windows 2000 folder.

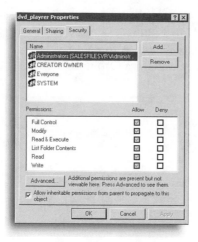

3. The top portion of the Security tab displays a list of accounts that have NTFS security permissions set for the object.

4. To view or change the specific permission for any account, select it. The permissions assigned to that account are displayed in the Permissions area on the dialog. Making changes requires selecting or clearing the appropriate entries in the Permissions area.

5. To add an account and assign it permission, click on **Add**. Select an account from the dialog that appears, and click **Add** and then

OK. When returned to the Security tab, assign NTFS permission as required, and click **Apply** and then **OK**.

6. To remove an account, select it and click **Remove**.

7. To prevent inheritance of permissions to files and subfolders of this folder, clear the **Allow Inheritable Permissions from Parent to Propagate to This Object** option.

8. If there are any advanced settings modifications, click **Advanced**. Otherwise, click **Apply** and then **Close**.

Copying and Moving Files

Like share security, NTFS permissions can be changed when files and folders are moved or copied from one location to another on a computer. Windows applies the following rules when performing copy and move operations:

- If a file is copied from one folder to another or from one volume to another, Windows creates a new file in the destination folder, and the permissions of the destination folder are inherited by that file.

- If a file or folder is moved to another folder on the same NTFS volume, the file or folder retains its current permissions.

- If a file or folder is copied from one NTFS volume to another NTFS volume, the permissions of the destination folder are inherited.

- If a file or folder is copied from an NTFS volume to a non-NTFS volume, all permissions are lost because only NTFS supports NTFS permission.

More Control

The Advanced security settings allow for more granular control over permission, the establishment of auditing (as discussed in the next section), and changing the ownership of files and folders.

Changes Take Effect at Next Login

Any changes made to user accounts will not take effect until the next time the user logs on and a new access token is created for that user reflecting the changes in permissions.

Resolving Share and NTFS Permissions

When both share and NTFS permissions are applied to computer resources, both types of security must be added together to determine the level of security granted to a network user. If resources are accessed locally, only NTFS permissions are applied. If accessed from over the network, both share and NTFS permissions are applied by taking the most restrictive level of access provided by each type of security.

For example, assume that a user named Bob has been granted the Read permission to a file using share security and Read & Execute permission to the same file using NTFS security. The resulting level of access provided to the user would be Read.

Keeping an Eye on Security with Auditing

Windows 2000 provides auditing as a means of tracking user activity and logging problem information. Windows 2000 can monitor any system event as long as NTFS is being used as the file system. Windows 2000 defines an event as any significant occurrence on a computer. For example, when a user logs on, logs off, opens, modifies, deletes, or saves a file, an event occurs. Events are recorded in one of three event logs, where they are archived and available for later viewing. These are the logs:

- System
- Security
- Application

Windows 2000 logs messages relating to the core operating system, as well as from software drivers, to the system log. The application log contains messages generated by applications that have been written to use the log. For example, an old 16-bit version of Microsoft Office will not write messages to the application log, whereas the Office 2000 version will. The security log contains audit information as specified by the audit policy. A snap-in called the Event Viewer is used to view and manage the event logs.

Understanding Audit Policies

An audit policy is established by the enabling of any of the audit events listed in Table 7.12. There are four types of auditing statuses. No Auditing means that the selected policy event is not being audited. Success means that any successful events of the selected type will be recorded. Failure means that any failed events of the selected type will be recorded. In addition, both Success and Failure events can be captured simultaneously for any selected audit event.

Audit policies are established individually on each computer using the audit policy located in the Local Computer Policy snap-in.

Table 7.12 Audit Policy Events

Event Type	Description
Audit Account Logon Events	When a domain controller receives a logon request. Not valid on peer networks.
Audit Account Management	When an attempt is made to create, delete, or modify user or group accounts.
Audit Directory	When a user accesses an Service Access Active Directory object. Not valid on peer networks.
Audit Logon Events	When a user logs on or off or connects via the network to a shared resource.
Audit Object Access	When a user accesses files, folders, or printers.
Audit Policy Change	When a change is made to audit policies or user rights.
Audit Privilege Use	When a user performs a right as defined in the User Rights Assignments Policy.
Audit Process Tracking	When an application performs an action.
Audit System Events	When the computer is started or stopped or any significant event occurs that affects security.

Establishing and Modifying an Audit Policy

On Windows 2000 Pro auditing is enabled in two steps. First, an audit policy needs to be established and turned on. Establishing an audit policy informs Windows of which categories of information you want to audit. Next, auditing needs to be configured on individual resources such as files, folders, and printers.

Establishing an audit policy

1. Create an MMC console containing the Local Computer Policy snap-in for the local computer, as demonstrated in Figure 7.31. There are two security types in Group Policy. User Configuration provides the capability to restrict such things as

the user's ability to change desktop settings or view and access certain Windows components such as My Network Places. Computer Configuration affects every user who logs on to the computer and includes such items as the password, account, and audit policies.

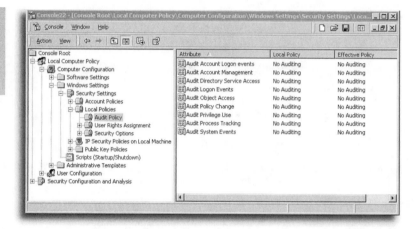

2. Expand the view in the left pane using the following path: **Local Computer Policy**, **Computer Configuration**, **Windows Settings**, **Security Setting**, **Local Policies**, and then **Audit Policy**.

3. In the right pane, double-click on the audit setting to be changed. A dialog for that setting appears, as demonstrated in Figure 7.32.

4. Modify the value of the policy setting by altering its value or configuration in the **Local Policy Setting** area.

5. Click **OK**.

6. The Local Policy column now reflects any changes that have been made. Close the MMC console and reboot the computer. Until the computer is restarted, the changes to the audit policy will not take effect.

Auditing Specific Resources

After the audit policy has been set, the next step is to establish auditing on specific computer resources. The process of establishing auditing over files, folders, and printers is essentially the same as previously discussed and is outlined in the following sections.

File and Folder Auditing

After auditing has been configured and enabled, the establishment of auditing of specific resources can be set up. Auditing is established on a resource-by-resource basis.

Enabling file and folder auditing

1. Select the **Security** tab on the Properties dialog for a file or folder on the computer.

2. Click **Advanced**. The Access Control Settings dialog for the resource appears, as shown in Figure 7.33.

FIGURE 7.33
Auditing is enabled on an object-by-object basis for specified users and groups.

3. Select the **Auditing** tab and click **Add**. The Select User, Computer, or Group dialog appears.

4. Select a user or group to be audited and click **OK**. The Auditing Entry dialog appears.

5. Select the manner in which the auditing should be applied from the **Apply Onto** drop-down list. The available choices allow you to specify how auditing is inherited by subfolders and files.

6. Choose the **Successful** or **Failed** options for as many of the available Access options as required, and click **OK**.

7. The Access Control Settings dialog reappears, displaying the auditing options selected for the user or group. Continue to add and configure as many users and groups as necessary. When done, click **Apply** and then **OK**.

Printer Auditing

Like file and folder auditing, printer auditing is established on a printer-by-printer basis and involves selecting the users or groups to be audited and the types of access to monitor.

Enabling printer auditing

1. Select the **Security** tab on the Properties dialog for a printer on the computer.

2. Click **Advanced**. The Access Control Settings dialog for the resource appears.

3. Select the **Auditing** tab and click **Add**. The Select User, Computer, or Group dialog appears.

4. Select a user or group to be audited and click **OK**. The Auditing Entry dialog appears.

5. Select the manner in which the auditing should be applied from the **Apply Onto** drop-down list. The available choices allow you to specify whether auditing is applied to the printer, documents, or both.

6. Choose the **Successful** or **Failed** options for as many of the available Access options as required, and click **OK**.

7. The Access Control Settings dialog reappears, displaying the auditing options selected for the user or group. Continue to add and configure as many users and groups as necessary. When done, click **Apply** and then **OK**.

Activating Audit Policies

If a Security prompt appears, stating that the current audit policy is not turned on, go back and make sure that steps 1 through 4 in the "Establishing and Modifying an Audit Policy" section were successfully completed.

The Event Viewer snap-in is used to view and manage system logs and can be accessed using the Computer Management MMC or as an add-in on a custom MMC.

SEE ALSO

➤ *For information on working with the Event Viewer, see page 304.*

Establishing Disk Quotas

One interesting feature that is new in Windows 2000 Pro is the capability to set *disk quotas*. A disk quota is a preset limit on the amount of space a user may use on a computer. For example, an administrator might limit each user to 100MB of storage on a network computer. Individual users who require greater storage requirements can be individually configured to a greater threshold.

Windows 2000 applies disk quotas on a per-user basis on every volume. This means that if a hard disk is partitioned into multiple logical drives, each logical drive's quota setting is separate from those for the other logical drives.

Any time a user creates a new file or folder or copies a file, the amount of space occupied by the file or folder is debited against the user's quotas. If new software needs to be installed, the Administrator account can be used. Using this account allows the application to be installed without the space it occupies being credited against any user account. For disk quotas to be turned on, the volume must be running NTFS.

Enabling Disk Quotas

Disk quotas are enabled only at the drive level. Space cannot be restricted within a specific folder. The establishment of disk quotas affects all users. However, it can be overridden on a user- or group-account basis to accommodate individuals or groups with different storage requirements.

Enabling disk quotas

1. Select the **Quota** tab on the Properties dialog for a disk drive on the computer.

2. By default, quotas are not enabled. Select the **Enable Quota Management** option (see Figure 7.34).

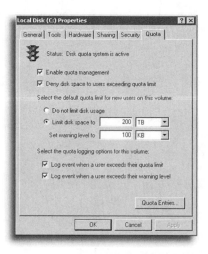

FIGURE 7.34
Enabling disk quotas is
performed on a disk-by-
disk basis from the
Quota tab on the drive's
Properties dialog.

3. Select the **Limit Disk Space To** option and select a unit of measurement from the drop-down list. Type a space limit in the field provided.

4. Type a space limit in the **Set Warning Level** field.

5. To instruct Windows 2000 to write log messages when disk-space limits or warning levels are reached, select both options in the **Select the Quota Logging Options for This Volume** section.

6. Click **Apply**. Windows displays a disk Quota prompt stating that it will take several minutes to scan the computer to create usage statistics. Click **OK**.

7. Click **OK**.

Overriding Disk Quotas

After disk quotas have been set for all users of the computer, the administrator can establish higher or lower quotas for users who have differing storage requirements.

Overriding disk quotas

1. Click the **Quota Entries** button on the **Quota** tab of the driver's Properties dialog. The Quota Entries dialog for the drive appears (see Figure 7.35).

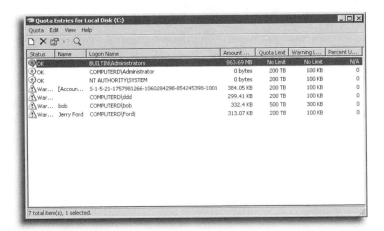

FIGURE 7.35
The Quota Entries dialog displays detailed quota information about every user account on the system.

2. Select a user account and click on **Properties** from the **Quota** menu. The quota setting for the selected user appears.

3. Type quota limits in the **Limit Disk Space To** and **Set Warning Level To** fields.

4. Click **Apply** and then **OK**.

chapter

8

The Internet

Understanding the Internet

The origins of the Internet can be traced back to the late 1960s. It began as result of funding efforts by the U.S. Department of Defense's Advanced Research Projects Agency, or ARPA, in a network technology known as packet switching. *Packet switching* was designed to allow data communications between computers in different locations by breaking data into small numbered packets that were then routed over the network to their destination. Because each packet contained its own addressing information, the packets could travel down different routes as they moved toward their destination. On receipt of the packets, the destination computer reassembled the packets using their sequence numbers.

One of the basic goals of the DoD was to create a network that could support a nuclear war and continue to operate even if parts of the network were destroyed. Packet switching provided this solution because packets could travel different routes to their destination, thus eliminating any single point of failure.

The network that was developed as a result of this research was known as the Advanced Research Projects Agency Network, or Arpanet. It originally ran a protocol known as the Network Core Protocol, or NCP, and connected only a small handful of universities. TCP/IP later grew out of NCP and made its appearance in 1983.

Because the DoD was also providing funding to the University of California at Berkeley for its implementation of UNIX, it imposed the requirement that it also support TCP/IP. This led to the rapid spread of TCP/IP and the network because most of the universities in the United States ran this version of UNIX.

For most of its existence the Internet was the exclusive property of universities, research institutions, and the military. However, by the mid-1990s all this changed as more of the Internet came to be managed and run over commercial lines and government funding was replaced by commercial investment. Today, the Internet is in the process of expanding by leaps and bounds as millions of users continue to get online every year.

Internet Resources

The Internet offers a range of communication services unprecedented in human history. Information on every subject is available. Internet-based companies are being created every day. It is possible to buy just about anything over the Web. New technologies are being developed that support radio, television, and telephone over the Internet. Internet email is changing the face of communications around the world.

Software and hardware manufacturers use the Internet as a means of communicating with their customers. Software drivers, fixes, documentation, and help are published at their Web sites and made readily available. Microsoft has integrated the Internet into the Windows 2000 operating system by integrating the Web browser into the graphical user interface. Microsoft has established a Windows 2000 Update Web site that works with a Windows 2000 Update utility to provide an automatic means for keeping Windows 2000 computers up-to-date.

Shareware and freeware software are flourishing on the Internet. Entire Web sites are devoted to making this software available free. Freeware is just that—free. Shareware is software that can be downloaded and used for a period of time. The user has the opportunity to kick the tires for a while before deciding to either uninstall the software or contact the software vendor and buy it.

The Internet offers untold opportunities for businesses. On the Internet the smallest company can compete with the largest international corporation on an equal footing. For the home user it provides unparalleled access to information, shopping, and electronic communications. Microsoft provides access to the Internet via its Dial-Up Networking and Internet Explorer 5 software. It also provides Outlook Express as a client email application that allows network users to send and receive email to and from other networks all around the world. *Dial-Up Networking* is the client component of Windows 2000 *Remote Access Service*, or *RAS*.

The Best of Both Worlds

Like many of Windows 2000's features, the Windows Update feature is borrowed from Windows 98. The Windows 98 version provides the same service for that operating system. Microsoft maintains separate update sites for both operating systems.

Internet Tools: Internet Explorer and Outlook Express

Microsoft provides two applications that enable network users to engage in meaningful interactions with the Internet. These are Internet Explorer 5.0 and Outlook Express. With these two tools users can surf the Internet and communicate with other users, companies, and networks.

Internet Explorer is Microsoft's Web browser. A Web browser is an application that is used to surf the World Wide Web or WWW pages on the Internet.

Outlook Express provides a complete set of tools for creating and managing email. It also functions as a news viewer, allowing users to search news servers for information on virtually any subject. Following is a partial list of the features Outlook Express offers users:

- An address book for managing email addresses.
- The capability to view a message list and read email simultaneously.
- The capability to manage email using folders and to create rules for automatically sending incoming email to those folders.
- On Internet Service Providers (ISPs) that provide IMAP mail servers, the ability to read and store email messages on the mail server without downloading them. This enables the user to view the same email later on another computer.
- The capability to search for newsgroups using keywords.
- The capability to subscribe to newsgroups.
- Support for offline reading of newsgroup messages by downloading either messages or entire newsgroups.
- The capability to manage multiple mail and news accounts.

Windows and the Internet: Point-to-Point Protocol (PPP)

Communication with another computer over a communication medium such as a telephone line is achieved using a point-to-point connection that usually involves a serial, parallel, or modem connection. *Modem* stands for modulation/demodulation. A modem is a device that can convert a computer's digital signal into a format that can be sent over the communications line to another computer. The modem on the receiving computer receives the analog signal and converts it back into a digital signal.

By default, Windows 2000 uses the Point-to-Point Protocol, or PPP, to support TCP/IP communications to the Internet. PPP supports dynamic IP assignment. PPP performs the same essential function as Ethernet does over a hardware LAN connection. PPP encapsulates the transport protocol, which in the case of the Internet is TCP/IP, and transports it across the phone line, as depicted in Figure 8.1.

SEE ALSO

➤ *For more information on the Point-to-Point Protocol, see page 536.*

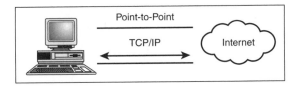

FIGURE 8.1
Windows uses the Point-to-Point protocol to encapsulate transport protocols providing a wide area network connection.

PPP also supports the transport of other network protocols besides TCP/IP. These include NetBEUI and IPX/SPX. Windows 2000 supports PPP dial-up connections as both a client and a server. This allows Windows 2000 computers to use PPP to accept or initiate dial-up using any combination of the three transport protocols. For example, Figure 8.2 shows a situation in which a Windows 2000 computer is set up as a dial-up client. When connecting to the Internet, PPP encapsulates TCP/IP packets. However, when PPP is used to dial into a Windows computer or network, PPP can encapsulate any of the transport protocols, thus allowing the dial-up computer to connect using a protocol supported by the network.

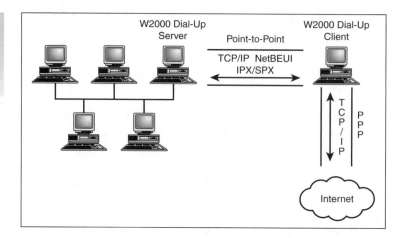

FIGURE 8.2
Using a Windows 2000
Workstation as a dial-up
client.

Remote Access Using Modems

A *modem* is a device that converts digital signals used by the computer into analog signals so that they can be transported over communication lines to their destination. At the destination, another modem receives the analog signals and converts them back into their digital equivalent. The current standard for conventional modems is the V9.0 standard, which supports a data transfer rate up to 56K. Data transfer rates of 56K are never really achieved because of such circumstances as noise on the wire.

Modems are connected to standard telephone jacks. Most modems provide a second jack that allows a phone to be plugged into the back of the modem. When the modem is not in use, the second jack provides a pass-through connection for making normal phone calls.

By subscribing to an Internet Service Provider, users can establish accounts that provide a connection to the Internet. A monthly subscription fee is charged for the service. Often, companies or home users install a second line to be used for accessing the Internet. Otherwise, the existing line ties up the phone line and denies normal phone service until the connection to the Internet is disconnected.

Installing a Modem

Windows 2000 should be able to use Plug and Play to install most modems made within the past few years. When you're purchasing a modem, it is best to make sure that it is Windows 2000 plug-and-play–compatible. If it is, Windows 2000 should be able to auto-detect it during startup and complete its installation. However, if the modem was built before 1995 or is not plug-and-play–compatible, a manual install must be performed. Even with Windows 2000 plug-and-play technology, at times it will fail to auto-detect new hardware.

There are several ways to install a modem. One is using the Add/Remove utility in the Windows 2000 Control Panel. Another option is to call the Hardware Wizard from the Hardware tab on the Systems utility located in the Windows 2000 Control Panel. The most straightforward and intuitive way is to use the Phone & Modem Options utility.

Manually installing a modem

1. Double-click on the **Phone & Modem Options** icon in the Windows 2000 Control Panel. If no modems are currently installed on the computer and this is the first time this utility has been run, a Location Information dialog appears. Windows requests information regarding the location of the computer, including the country and area code in which the computer will be used (see Figure 8.3). Windows also needs to know whether the phone system over which the computer will be operating requires a number, such as 9, to gain access to an outside line. By default, Windows assumes that tone dialing is used. However, some older systems might use pulse dialing. After providing the requested information, click **OK**.

2. The Phone & Modem Options dialog appears, and the location information just collected is displayed (see Figure 8.4). Select the **Modems** tab. A list of any currently installed modems appears. Click on **Add**.

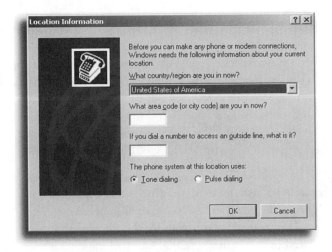

FIGURE 8.3
Windows 2000 needs to collect information about where the computer is located and how an outside line is reached.

FIGURE 8.4
The Phone & Modem Options dialog displays a list of currently installed modems.

3. Windows 2000 offers to try to auto-detect your modem (see Figure 8.5). If you know that the search will be unsuccessful, you can select the **Don't Detect My Modem; I Will Select It from a List** option, click **Next**, and skip to step 5. Otherwise, leave this option clear and click **Next**.

FIGURE 8.5
Windows 2000 offers two options when manually installing a modem: auto-detect and manual.

4. If the auto-detect option selected, Windows attempts to locate the modem by checking each installed communication port and displays status information as it examines each port. If Windows 2000 is unable to auto-detect the modem, the dialog shown in Figure 8.6 appears. Click **Next** to continue.

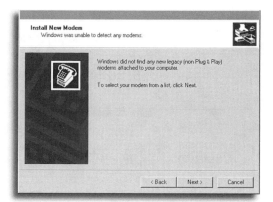

FIGURE 8.6
Windows 2000 reports that it has been unable to locate a new modem attached to the computer.

5. Windows presents a list of modem manufacturers. Select the name of the modem manufacturer from the Manufacturers list (see Figure 8.7). A list of all modems made by the selected manufacturer appears in the Models section. Select the entry that matches the modem, or click on the **Have Disk** button and supply the software driver that was shipped with the modem.

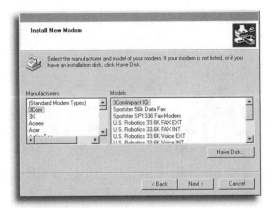

FIGURE 8.7
The Install New Modem Wizard requests specification of the modem manufacturer and model.

6. If the modem cannot be located from the available choices, another option is to attempt to install a generic modem driver from the Standard Modem Types selection. The software driver supplied by the modem's manufacturer is written specifically to take advantage of the unique features of the modem. Installing a generic software driver might result in some lost functionality. Whenever possible, always install the manufacturer's driver.

7. The Install New Modem Wizard displays the name of the modem and some feature information (see Figure 8.8). Verify that the information is correct and click **Next** to continue.

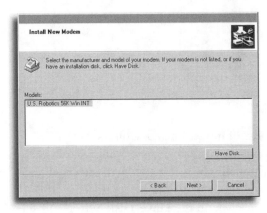

FIGURE 8.8
The Install New Modem Wizard requests confirmation of the modem name and attributes.

8. Windows next asks for port information. If this is an external modem, choose **Selected Ports** and then click on the port where the modem is attached. Click **Next** to continue.

If this is an internal modem, choose **Selected Ports**, click on an available port that you want to assign to the modem, and click **Next** to continue (see Figure 8.9).

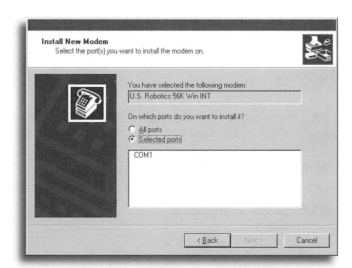

FIGURE 8.9
Windows provides a list of available ports, requesting information about which one will be used to support the modem.

9. Windows 2000 completes the modem installation. A dialog informs the user that the settings for this modem can be changed by double-clicking on the Phone and Modems icon in the Control Panel. Click **Finish**. The modem now appears as an entry on the Phone & Modem Options dialog.

Modem Configuration

After a modem is installed, it can be configured and tested from its properties dialog. To access a modem's properties, double-click the **Phone & Modem Options** icon on the Windows 2000 Control Panel and select the **Modems** tab. A list of all modems installed on the computer appears (see Figure 8.10).

Changing modem properties

1. From the Phone & Modems Option dialog, select a modem and click on **Properties**. The Properties dialog for the selected modem appears (see Figure 8.11).

No Digital Signature

Windows might display a dialog stating that it does not have a digital signature for the specified modem. This might appear if you are installing an older modem. The absence of this signature means that Microsoft has not tested this device with Windows 2000. You can still click on **Yes** on this prompt to instruct Windows to continue installing the device.

It is always best to use hardware that has been certified by Microsoft as Windows 2000-ready. Microsoft makes a Windows 2000 Hardware Compatibility List, or HCL, at its Web site that contains the most current list of Microsoft-tested hardware.

FIGURE 8.10
The Phone & Modems Options dialog displays a list of installed modems.

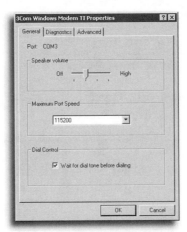

FIGURE 8.11
The Modem Properties dialog provides access to modem configuration and diagnostics.

2. Select the **General** property sheet. This property sheet provides control over the volume of the modem's internal speaker and the maximum port speed the modem supports. The Maximum Port Speed setting specifies the computer-to-modem speed and not the speed at which the modem will be able to communicate with other modems. The General property sheet also provides dial control. By default, **Wait for Dial Tone Before Dialing** is selected. This option should be cleared only if the modem is having trouble recognizing the dial tone.

3. Select the **Diagnostics** property sheet. This property sheet displays modem information. Clicking the **Query Modem** button provides a test of the modem. After this button is pressed, Windows takes a few moments to test the modem. The results are displayed under the Command and Response columns in the Modem Information section. The Command column identifies common AT commands that were sent to the modem, and the Response column displays the modem's response. Problems with the modem can appear in the form of error messages in the response column. The Logging option controls whether Windows 2000 Pro clears the modem log file at the start of each session. Selecting this option instructs Windows 2000 Pro to append each session's log messages to the bottom of the current log file. The View Log button displays the contents of the log.

4. Select the **Advanced** property sheet. This property sheet allows customized commands to be added to the modem initialization string. Modify this setting only if you have an application that specifically requires it.

   The Port Settings button allows for configuration of the receive and transmit buffers. The Advanced button provides access to advanced options. The Advanced Port Setting provides tuning control of the Transmit and Receive buttons and can be used to compensate for poor connection problems. The Change Default Preferences button controls basic connection preferences and hardware settings. Unless instructed otherwise, it is best to leave the options on the Advanced tab with their default settings.

Removing a Modem

Removing a modem from a Windows 2000 computer is a two-step process. The first step is to uninstall the modem driver, and the second step is to physically uninstall the device.

Uninstalling a modem

1. Double-click on the **Phone & Modems Options** icon in the Windows 2000 Control Panel.

2. Select the **Modems** tab.

3. Select the modem from the list of installed modems.

4. Click on **Remove**. Windows 2000 displays a prompt that asks for confirmation. Click **Yes**.

5. Click **OK**.

6. Physically disconnect the modem from the computer.

Driver Versus Physical Uninstallation

Removing a modem from the Modem Properties dialog removes only the modem software driver. After the driver is removed, the modem should be physically uninstalled. Otherwise, Windows might plug-and-play the device the next time the computer is restarted.

Dial-Up Connections

A dial-up connection provides a computer with the capability to connect to another computer, a network, or the Internet using a modem and a conventional phone line. In the context of this discussion, a dial-up session is a communication link to an *Internet Service Provider*. Dial-up connections use PPP by default. PPP supports the encapsulation and transport of multiple protocols. A PPP connection is by definition a wide area network connection. It allows Windows 2000 dial-up computers to establish WAN connections to a wide range of computers and networks. The most common use of dial-up connections is for communicating with the Internet.

Establishing a Dial-Up Connection

To make this process as easy as possible, Microsoft has provided the Network Connection Wizard. This wizard can be used to perform any of the following activities:

- Dial up to a private network
- Dial up to the Internet
- Create a Virtual Private Network, or VPN, by connecting through the Internet to another computer or network
- Set up a computer to accept incoming connections
- Connect directly to another computer

Creating a dial-up connection to your ISP

1. Right-click on the **My Network Places** icon on the Windows 2000 Pro desktop, and select **Properties** from the menu that appears (see Figure 8.12).

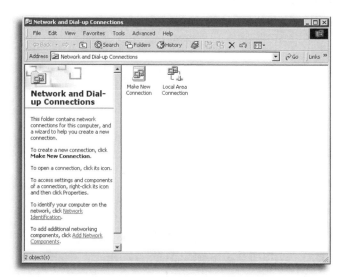

FIGURE 8.12
The Network and Dial-up
Connection dialog dis-
plays dial-up connec-
tions and contains the
Make New Connection
icon.

2. Double-click on the **Make New Connection** icon (see
   Figure 8.13).

3. The Network Connection Wizard appears Click **Next**.

FIGURE 8.13
The Network Connection
Wizard simplifies the
creation of new dial-up
connections.

4. Select **Dial-up to the Internet** and click **Next** (see
   Figure 8.14).

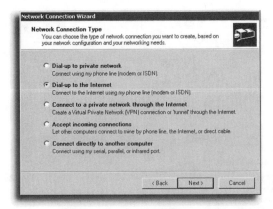

5. The wizard supports the establishment of connections over
modems of the area network if a proxy server has been set up.
To manually configure an existing account, select **I want to Set
Up My Internet Connection Through a Local Area
Network (LAN)** and click **Next** (see Figure 8.15).

6. Select **I connect Through a Phone Line and a Modem** and
click **Next**.

7. Type the required information about your ISP in the **Area Code**
and **Telephone Number** fields and click **Next** (see Figure 8.16).

8. Type the username and password assigned by your ISP in the
User Name and **Password** fields and click **Next** (see
Figure 8.17).

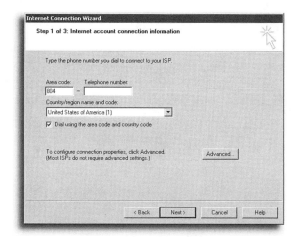

FIGURE 8.16
Provide the phone number of your ISP.

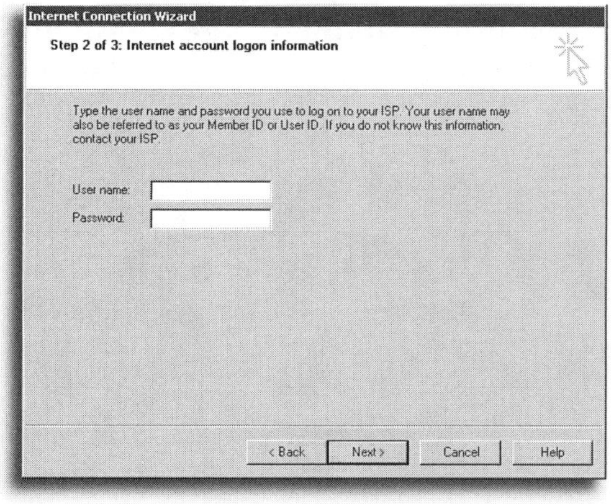

FIGURE 8.17
Provide the username and password assigned by the ISP.

9. Type a name describing the dial-up connection in the **Connection Name** field and click **Next** (see Figure 8.18).

10. The Internet Connection Wizard announces that it has completed collecting all the information it needs to create a dial-up connection. Click **Finish**.

An icon for the dial-up connection appears in the Network and Dial-Up Connections dialog. Repeat the preceding steps to create additional dial-up connections.

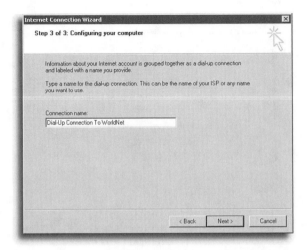

FIGURE 8.18
Provide a name for the dial-up connection.

Connecting Using a Dial-Up Connection

After a dial-up connection has been established, it can be used to connect to the Internet.

Connecting to the Internet

1. From the Network and Dial-up Connections dialog, double-click on the dial-up connection you created to connect to your ISP. Windows displays a dialog similar to the one shown in Figure 8.19.

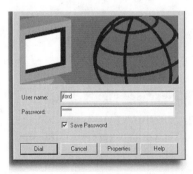

FIGURE 8.19
The Connect Dial-Up Connection for Your ISP dialog appears.

2. Verify that all the information presented is correct, and click on the **Dial** button. You might hear the modem activate and dial the ISP's telephone number, followed by a brief series of screeching sounds. After the ISP's computer answers the call, the two

computers will exchange information. The username and password are passed to the remote computer for authentication. Finally, the Connection Complete dialog appears.

3. You might want to select the **Do Not Display This Message Again** option to instruct Windows 2000 not to display this dialog in the future. Click **OK**.

4. Windows 2000 places a small icon representing the dial-up connection in the system tray on the right side of the taskbar (see Figure 8.20). Double-click on this icon to view connection statistics. Connection information is provided on two tabs. Click **Close** to minimize this dialog back to the system tray, or click **Disconnect** to terminate the dial-up connection. Selecting the **Properties** button produces the Dial-Up Connection Properties dialog, from which connection settings can be modified. This includes the capability to select which protocols and services can use this connection, change the phone number being dialed and the modem selected to support the connection, and configure Internet connection sharing (see Figure 8.21).

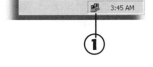

FIGURE 8.20
An icon representing your dial-up connection appears in the system tray on the taskbar.

① Dial-Up Connection icon

FIGURE 8.21
Windows maintains detailed statistics about the active dial-up connection.

After a dial-up connection has been established, you can start Internet Explorer and begin surfing the Internet if you already have an established Internet account.

Proxy Servers

On a small network, individual computers typically connect to a network through a locally installed modem. Before Windows 2000, network administrators had to turn to third-party *proxy server* products to allow computers on the network to access the Internet by sharing the modem installed on a single computer. The advantage of proxy software is that it can result in significant cost savings by reducing the number of modems, phone lines, and Internet connections.

The Windows Proxy Server

The Windows proxy server receives requests from network clients and forwards them onto the remote network through its connection. Proxy servers provide an effective means for providing shared access to the Internet, as demonstrated in Figure 8.22. The proxy server translates between local network addresses and the account used to communicate with the ISP. It then records the local network address of the computer making the requests and issues the request itself on behalf of the network computer. When the results are returned to the Windows 2000 proxy server, it passes them back to the requesting network computer.

FIGURE 8.22
A proxy server permits multiple computers on the network to access the Internet by sharing a connection established on a single computer, which is known as the proxy server.

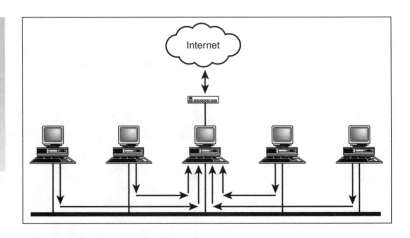

Other Solutions

An alternative to proxy servers is to attach a modem directly to every computer that requires Internet access, as depicted in Figure 8.23. This option is more expensive. It requires a modem and phone line for each computer, as well as multiple Internet accounts.

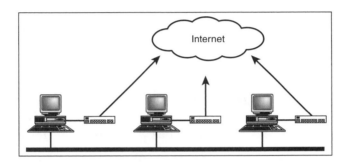

FIGURE 8.23
Windows 2000 provides the capability to connect individual computers to the Internet using a modem and a standard phone line.

Another means of delivering proxy services on a network is to purchase dedicated proxy server hardware. In this case, the proxy server is actually a specialized piece of hardware with its own built-in processor and one or more modems. The device is typically placed directly on the network wire. Typical features include on-demand dialing, one or more modems, firewall, and routing services.

Windows Proxy Server Prerequisites

For a computer to operate as a proxy server on the network, it must have both a modem and a NIC. By default, Microsoft auto-configures Windows 2000 computers to join the 169.254.0.0 network. However, Microsoft changes this configuration when modem sharing is enabled.

Microsoft automatically turns the Windows 2000 Pro computer designated as the proxy server into a DHCP allocator. A DHCP allocator automatically assigns an IP address, a subnet mask, and a default gateway to every computer on the network that has the Obtain an IP Address Automatically option enabled.

This means that the proxy server will act as a simple DHCP server on the network. The network address assigned to the proxy server is automatically changed to 192.168.0.0 with a subnet mask of

255.255.255.0. The IP address of the proxy server is changed to 192.168.0.1. All IP address assignments made by this server will be for this network. This means that except for computers with statically defined address information, every machine on the network will be automatically reconfigured on the 192.186.0.0 network. For computers with static address assignments to access the proxy server, they must have their IP addresses changed to join this network as well.

According to Windows 2000 online help, the "Internet connection sharing feature is intended for use in a small office or home office where network configuration and the Internet connection are managed by the computer running Windows 2000 where the shared connection resides. It is assumed that on its network, this computer is the only Internet connection, the only gateway to the Internet, and that it sets all internal network addresses." You cannot modify the network address or the proxy server's IP address without disabling this modem sharing. If this solution is not acceptable, the only way to provide proxy services on the network is by acquiring another proxy server product. This network-address configuration is demonstrated in Figure 8.24. In this example, the computer in the middle is the proxy server, and the remaining computers reflect their new IP address assignments.

FIGURE 8.24
Windows 2000 Pro's modem sharing service requires a new network address of 192.168.0.0.

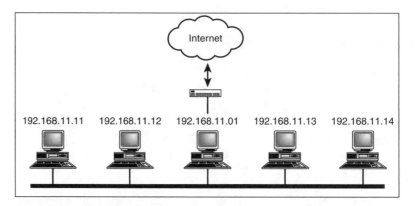

Windows 2000 automatically enables the on-demand dialing feature to allow other network computers to instruct the proxy server to initiate a dial-up connection when one is not already active. When a connection is already established, client requests should be immediately serviced.

Client Prerequisites

For a peer network to take advantage of the Windows 2000 Pro proxy server, the following criteria must be met:

- Every computer that requires proxy services must have TCP/IP loaded.

- Computers should be set to obtain IP address information automatically.

- Any computers with statically defined IP addresses must be set up as a member to the 192.168.0.0 network with a subnet mask of 255.255.255.0 and a default gateway of 192.168.0.1.

Establishing a Proxy Server

A proxy server is configured on the properties dialog on an existing dial-up connection. Only an administrator can configure this service.

Enabling modem sharing

1. Open the Network and Dial-Up Connections dialog.

2. Select the dial-up connection that will provide proxy service for the network (see Figure 8.25).

3. Right-click on the dial-up connection that will provide proxy service for the network, and click on the **Properties** option.

4. Select the Sharing tab (see Figure 8.25).

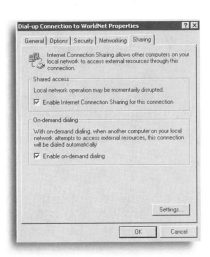

FIGURE 8.25
Each dial-up connection has its own configuration options.

5. By default, all options on this tab are disabled. Select the **Enable Internet Connection Sharing for This Connection** option, and the rest of the options will become enabled. Select the **Enable On-Demand Dialing** option to allow other network computers to instruct this computer to automatically dial up and connect to the Internet when requested. Click **OK**.

6. Windows 2000 Pro responds with a prompt which states that the computer must be configured with a static IP address of 192.168.0.1. This will cause all network connections to this computer to be lost because the computer must change IP addresses. Other network computers will temporarily be unable to contact this computer. Click **Yes** to continue.

Connecting to a Proxy Server

Proxy clients are established on other Windows 2000 computers on the network. After these clients are configured, they will be able to connect to the Internet using the proxy services provided by the proxy server. If the proxy server already has an active dial-up connection to the Internet, the user should get immediate access to the Internet. If the proxy server does not have an active dial-up connection, a brief delay will ensue as the proxy server establishes the connection.

Configuring a proxy client

1. Open the Network and Dial-Up Connections dialog.

2. Double-click on the **Make New Connection** icon.

3. The Network Connection Wizard starts. Click **Next** to continue (see Figure 8.26).

4. Select **Dial-Up to the Internet** and click **Next**.

5. Select **I want to Set Up my Internet Connection Manually** or **I want to Connect Through a Local Area Network (LAN)** and click **Next**.

6. Select **I Connect Through a Local Area Network (LAN)** and click **Next**.

7. The default option is set to **Automatic Discover of Proxy Server.** Click **Next**. Alternatively, an administrator can manually configure the address information of the proxy server by selecting **Manual Proxy Server**. This option is useful if a third-party proxy service is being used.

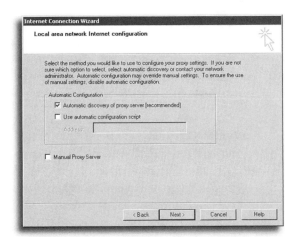

8. Select **No** when prompted to set up an email account to instruct Windows to complete the connection. Otherwise, click **Yes** and follow the provided instructions.

9. The Internet Connection Wizard displays a dialog announcing that it has completed its configuration. Click **Finish**.

The client computer is now ready to access the Internet via the proxy server. Open Internet Explorer and the client computer will automatically contact the proxy server and begin accessing the Internet.

Creating a Virtual Private Network

A *virtual private network* is a secure network that runs on top of a public or private network. VPNs are best known as a means for allowing companies to establish a WAN using the Internet as its transmission medium. A VPN can be as simple as two connected computers or as complex as two interconnected networks. VPNs deliver secure, on-demand establishment of WAN connections using dial-up connections. Figure 8.27 demonstrates a VPN in which one computer connects to a remote network using the Internet.

Verifying the Right IP Settings

If the client computer fails to locate or establish communications with the proxy server, make sure that the Obtain an IP Address Automatically option is selected on the TCP/IP Properties dialog. You can also statically define the client computer IP information. Make sure that you assign an IP on the 192.168.0.0 network with a 255.255.255.0 subnet mask and that the default gateway is set to 196.168.0.1.

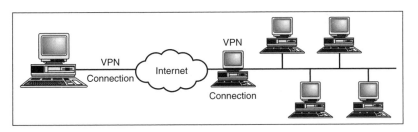

FIGURE 8.27
An example of a VPN connecting a user to a remote network using the Internet.

A VPN is established between two computers, and if the computers are connected to networks, they can be configured to provide a gateway into their respective networks. Before any data can be sent, both machines must agree on session parameters such as encryption and compression. After the logical tunnel is negotiated, data transmission begins.

Windows 2000 Pro supports the well-known *Point-to-Point Tunneling Protocol*, or *PPTP*, as well as the newer *Layer-2 Tunneling Protocol*, or *L2TP*, and *IP Security Protocol*, or *IPSec*. Secure VPN transmissions depend on key management. A key is a unique mathematical code that both computers know and use to encrypt and decrypt data. For PPTP and L2TP, a key is created during user authentication.

These protocols provide various forms of data encryption, user authentication, and multiple protocol support:

- Data is encrypted before it is transported over the VPN connection to make sure that if someone other than the intended destination intercepts the data, it will be unreadable.

- User authentication is required before the destination computer or network will permit the remote computer to connect.

- Multiple protocol support means that VPNs will encapsulate (tunnel) whatever protocols the computers and networks are running (NetBEUI, IPX/SPX, or TCP/IP) inside of IP and transmit them over the Internet.

Alternative to VPN

An alternative to a VPN is to lease a dedicated communications line from a telecommunications company, as depicted in Figure 8.28. This option is significantly more costly because leased lines have to be set up at specific locations. This method is by far the most expensive, requires dedicated equipment and expertise, and does not support roaming mobile users.

FIGURE 8.28
An example of a WAN connecting a computer to a remote network using a dedicated communications line.

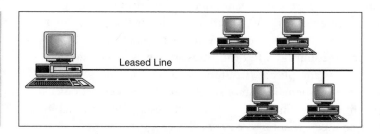

Leased Line

A VPN can be established over both public networks and private networks. For small companies and home users, establishing a VPN typically means using the Internet. Windows 2000 Pro provides the Network Connection Wizard to make the establishment of a VPN connection an easy chore.

Using Microsoft 2000 Pro, one computer is configured to accept incoming connection requests while connected to the Internet, and the other computer is configured to initiate a VPN connection.

One prerequisite for establishing a VPN is that the computer set up to accept the incoming connection request must have a permanent IP address assignment with an optional fully qualified hostname. Contact your ISP for information about leasing a dedicated IP address and registering a domain name.

The process of configuring computers to initiate and accept a VPN connection over the Internet is outlined in the following two sections.

Setting Up a Computer to Accept a Connection

Configuring a computer to accept a VPN connection over the Internet

1. Right-click on the **My Network Places** icon on the Windows 2000 Pro desktop, and select **Properties**. The Network and Dial-Up Connections dialog appears.

2. Double-click on the **Make New Connection** icon. The Network Connection Wizard appears.

3. Click **Next**.

4. Select **Accept Incoming Connections** and click **Next** (see Figure 8.29).

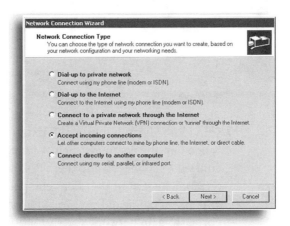

FIGURE 8.29
Select the type of network connection that is to be set up.

5. Select the communications device that will be used to provide support for the VPN connection, and click **Next** (see Figure 8.30).

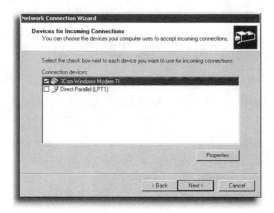

FIGURE 8.30
Select the communications device to be used to support this connection.

6. Select **Allow Virtual Private Connections** and click **Next** (see Figure 8.31).

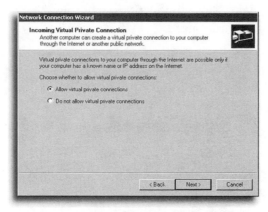

FIGURE 8.31
Configuring the connection to support a VPN connection.

7. Windows displays a list of all the user accounts that have been added on the computer. Select which user accounts will be permitted to connect using the VPN, and click **Next** (see Figure 8.32). The user at the client computer will be required to supply the logon name and password for one of the selected accounts in order to gain network access. Optionally, the administrator can add or remove user accounts on the computer from this dialog.

FIGURE 8.32
Specific accounts must
be selected in order to
grant access permission
over a VPN connection.

8. Select the networking components that will be supported over this connection. It is important to remember that a common protocol must be supported on both computers for the VPN connection to be successful. Click **Next**.

9. Provide a name for the VPN connection, and click **Finish**.

An icon for the new VPN connection appears in the Network and Dial-Up Connections dialog. To have this computer start monitoring for incoming VPN connection requests, use an existing dial-up connection to connect to your ISP. When a client connection request is received, Windows 2000 will automatically answer and attempt to authenticate the user.

Testing VPN Functionality

VPN functionality can be tested without having a registered Internet domain name or IP address. Log on to your ISP, open a command prompt, and type `IPCONFIG`. The IP address that has been temporarily leased to the computer for the current dial-up session will be displayed. When setting up your VPN dial-up connection on a VPN client computer, provide the Network Connection Wizard with this IP address. Of course, this test will be valid only until the computer set up to accept the VPN connection disconnects from the Internet. The next time the VPN server connects, the ISP will dynamically assign a different IP address, and testing would require the creation of a new VPN client connection.

Setting Up a Computer to Initiate a Connection

Configuring a computer to initiate a VPN connection using the Internet

1. Right-click on the **My Network Places** icon on the Windows 2000 Pro desktop, and select **Properties**. The Network and Dial-Up Connections dialog appears.

2. Double-click on the **Make New Connection** icon. The Network Connection Wizard appears.

3. Click **Next**.

4. Select **Connect to a Private Network Through the Internet**, and click **Next** (see Figure 8.33).

FIGURE 8.33
Select the type of network connection that is to be set up.

5. Select **Automatically Dial This Initial Connection**, and select the dial-up account that has been established for your ISP from the drop-down list (see Figure 8.34). Click **Next**.

6. Type either the Internet name or the IP address of the VPN server, and click **Next** (see Figure 8.35).

7. If this connection is going to be shared with other users of this computer, select **For All Users**. Otherwise, select **Only for Myself** and click **Next** (see Figure 8.36).

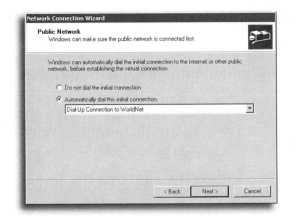

FIGURE 8.34
Windows can automatically establish a dial-up connection to your ISP.

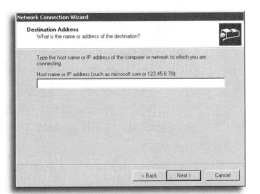

FIGURE 8.35
Identify the name or IP address of the VPN server.

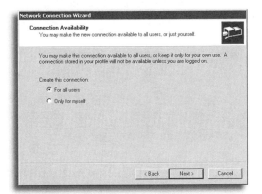

FIGURE 8.36
The VPN connection can be shared with other users of the computer.

8. Provide a name for the VPN connection, and click **Finish**.

An icon for the new VPN connection appears in the Network and Dial-up Connections dialog.

Establishing a VPN Connection

After the host and client have been configured, you are ready to establish the VPN connection. The host will monitor for incoming VPN connection requests as soon as it connects to the Internet and will respond when it receives a client request, as demonstrated next.

Establishing a VPN connection

1. On the VPN server computer, right-click on the **My Network Places** icon on the Windows 2000 Pro desktop, and select **Properties**. The Network and Dial-Up Connections dialog appears.

2. Double-click on the icon representing the dial-up connection to the ISP. The computer establishes a dial-up connection.

3. On the VPN client computer, right-click on the **My Network Places** icon on the Windows 2000 Pro desktop, and select **Properties**. The Network and Dial-Up Connections dialog appears.

4. Double-click on the icon representing the VPN dial-up connection.

5. Windows 2000 Pro displays a prompt requesting confirmation before initiating a dial-up connection (see Figure 8.37). Click **Yes**.

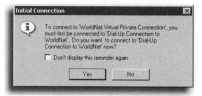

FIGURE 8.37
Click Yes to start a dial-up connection to your ISP.

6. The next dialog presents information that will be used to connect to your ISP. Verify that the connection information presented is correct, and click **Dial**. Windows 2000 Pro dials your ISP and establishes a connection.

7. After a connection with your ISP has been established, Windows presents another connection dialog. The information presented will be used to connect to the VPN server. Make sure that the username and password information provided is correct, and click **Connect** (see Figure 8.38).

FIGURE 8.38
Verify connection settings for the VPN server before connecting.

8. A series of messages will be displayed on the client computer as the VPN connection is established:

- `Connecting to xxx.xxx.xxx.xxx`

- `Verifying user name and password`

- `Registering your computer on the network`

- `Authenticated`

9. Click **OK** when the Connection Complete prompt appears.

At this point, multiple icons will be seen on both the VPN client and the VPN server representing their respective dial-up and VPN connections. Selecting the icon representing the VPN connection on one of the computers produces the Virtual Private Connection Status dialog. Two tabs are displayed: the General tab and the Details tab.

The General tab displays information about session status and activity and provides the Disconnect button for terminating the session (see Figure 8.39).

The Details tab provides information about the connection, as demonstrated in Figure 8.40.

Using the Current Connection

If a dial-up connection to the Internet is already established, Windows does not prompt the user or attempt to initiate a second dial-up connection. Instead it uses the current connection.

No Logon Domain for Windows Peer Networks

The Logon Domain field in the Connect Dial-Up Connection dialog is not a valid option on Windows peer networks. This field can be ignored. You can remove it from the dialog by clicking on **Properties** and then clearing the **Prompt for and Include Windows Logon Domain** option on the Options tab.

FIGURE 8.39
The General tab provides VPN connection statistics and the capability to terminate the session.

FIGURE 8.39
The General tab provides VPN connection statistics and the capability to terminate the session.

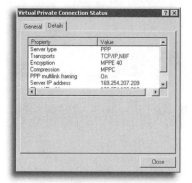

FIGURE 8.40
The Details tab provides VPN information about the current connection.

At this point, the computers on both sides of the VPN connection can communicate with one another. For example, on the VPN client computer, open Internet Explorer and type the internal network IP address of one of the computers on the VPN server's side of the connection in the URL field; press Enter. The shared resources for the VPN server appear (see Figure 8.41). The user will be able to access any resource for which his account has been given access permissions. Windows 2000 treats a VPN connection just as it would any other network connection.

Dealing with Dynamic IPs

Typing an IP address to access the network resources of a VPN works only if static addressing is used. If your network is using dynamic IP assignments, typing IP addresses is not an option because they are constantly changing and you will not know what they are.

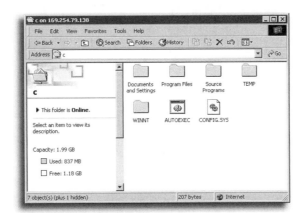

FIGURE 8.41
Viewing information over the VPN connection.

A simple solution to this problem is to install NetBEUI on every computer that will participate over the VPN and make sure that NetBEUI is configured as a transport protocol on the dial-up VPN client computer. This will allow the use of NetBIOS names. For example, a user at the VPN client could type \\computerf\c in place of the dynamic IP address belonging to the computer, and NetBEUI would take care of the rest.

part

III

NETWORK UTILITIES

chapter

9

Remote Access

Overview of Remote Access

Remote access permits users to use a modem and a regular phone line to dial into a computer or computer network and access shared resources. According to Microsoft, a dial-up connection between two computers is a network connection. Therefore, dial-up networking provides some of the same set of network services as are made available by a network connection with a NIC, except that network data is routed through a modem instead of the NIC.

Another form of remote access is *remote control*. A third-party software application such as PCAnywhere can be installed on two computers, giving each the capability to dial into the other and take complete control of the remote computer's mouse and keyboard and to view all output displayed on the remote computer monitor. The drawback to this type of remote connection is that it is usually very slow and requires the purchase of the remote-control software. Windows 2000 dial-up networking itself does not provide remote control over the target computer. Instead, it permits each computer to access resources that have been shared on its counterpart. A dial-up server can also serve as a gateway and provide access to the network if the appropriate protocols are installed on both computers (see Figure 9.1).

FIGURE 9.1
A remote access server on a Windows 2000 peer network provides access to its shared resources and can serve as a gateway to the rest of the network.

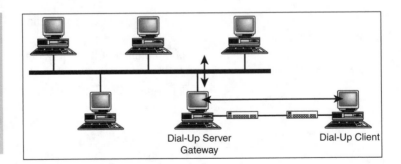

Dial-Up Server
Gateway

Dial-Up Client

Uses for Remote Access

Remote access is a particularly useful tool for businesses that have employees who spend a lot of time traveling but still need access to the company's LAN to perform activities such as these:

- Accessing email
- Synchronizing copies of documents on the network

- Releasing print jobs that have been deferred on a network printer

- Accessing the Internet through a network proxy server

- Copying files to and from the network

- Accessing a database server

The computer selected as a remote access server will incur a small performance hit when being used by dial-up client. The impact on the owner of the computer depends on the activities of the remote user. If the remote user requires only occasional access and copies and moves small files, the impact will be minimal. However, if the remote user remains logged on for extended periods and moves large amounts of data through the connection, the local user might see a noticeable performance loss. Adding more memory to the dial-up server might alleviate the situation. Another option is to set aside a dedicated computer to provide remote access.

When a computer dials into the dial-up server, a network connection is made. To communicate with the dial-up server or the rest of the network, a common protocol must be installed. These are the available options:

- NetBEUI

- IPX/SPX

- TCP/IP

Prerequisites for Remote Access

Setting remote access on a Windows 2000 peer network involves several components, including these:

- Installation of a modem on both the server and the client computers

- Installation and configuration of a dial-up server

- Installation and configuration of a dial-up client

- RJ-11 cables for both computers

- A 9- or 25-pin serial cable for external modems

- Access to phone lines

- An account on the dial-up server for each remote user

Adding TCP/IP to Windows for Workgroups

Windows for Workgroups does not support TCP/IP out of the box. Instead, an update must be downloaded and installed from Microsoft's Web site to provide TCP/IP support.

Gateways Provide Access to the Network

A *gateway* is a device or computer that provides access to the rest of the network. After the remote computer has connected to the gateway, it performs just as if it were physically attached via a NIC with the exception that performance is significantly slower. Peer networks usually operate in the 10Mbps or 100Mbps ranges, whereas a typical modem operates at just 56Kbps. Although an ISDN line offers improved capacity, it still performs substantially slower than a network connection.

Only One Connection Per Computer

Windows 2000 Pro supports three types of dial-up access—modem, ISDN, and x.25—per incoming dial-in connection. Only one incoming connection can be defined per computer. Any attempt to create a second incoming connection using the Network Connection Wizard only changes the original incoming connection. Windows 2000 can connect to as many as one of each type of dial-up for a total of three connections. If your network requires support for more than one dial-up connection of each type at a time, consider setting up a Windows 2000 Server to support remote access. Windows 2000 Server's dial-up support is limited only by its installed hardware. However, multiple Windows 2000 Pro computers can be set up as dial-up servers to provide additional connections. Remote users need to be aware of the multiple phones associated with each inbound line.

Providing Dial-Up Access (by Version)

Windows 95, Windows 98, and Windows NT Workstation 4.0 can also provide dial-up access to the network for a single connection. Windows NT Server 4.0 can support up to 256 in-bound connections.

X.25 is an older WAN technology designed to provide 64Kbps transmission rates over unreliable communication networks and is not commonly used today.

To access a Windows 2000 Pro dial-up connection, the user must have a valid account on the dial-up server. Otherwise, authentication will fail and access will be denied. If access is granted, the user will have whatever access permission has been granted just as if the user were logged onto the network from a locally attached computer.

Windows 2000 Pro provides gateway functionality for TCP/IP, IPX/SPX, and NetBEUI protocols.

Windows 2000 dial-up clients can connect many different types of dial-up servers, including these:

- Windows for Workgroups 3.11
- Windows 95 with Microsoft Plus
- Windows 98
- Windows NT 4 Workstation
- Windows NT 4 Server
- Windows 2000 Server
- Windows 2000 Professional

Reviewing the Point-to-Point Protocol

The *Point-to-Point Protocol*, or *PPP*, is a wide area network, or WAN, protocol. It supports the transmission of multiple protocols including TCP/IP, IPX/SPX, and NetBEUI. Additional PPP features include password encryption and compression. Windows 2000 uses PPP as its default dial-up protocol based on the assumption that the Internet is the most common connection (see Figure 9.2).

Windows 2000 uses PPP to manage the communications session between the dial-up client and the dial-up server. Windows 2000 dial-up clients can also use *Serial Line Internet Protocol*, or *SLIP*, to connect with *UNIX* servers. SLIP is an outdated protocol seldom found anymore.

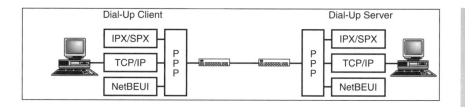

FIGURE 9.2
Windows 2000's dial-up architecture consists of standard network protocols combined with the Point-to-Point protocol.

SEE ALSO

➤ *For more information on the Point-to-Point protocol, see page 245.*

Configuring a Dial-Up Server

The Windows 2000 Pro Network Connection Wizard manages the setup of a dial-up server as well as a dial-up client.

Setting up a dial-up server

1. Right-click on the **My Network Places** icon on the Windows 2000 Pro desktop, and select **Properties** from the menu that appears.

2. Double-click on the **Make New Connection** icon.

3. The Network Connection Wizard appears. Click **Next**.

4. Select **Accept Incoming Connections** and click **Next**.

5. Select the modem that will be used to support the dial-up connection, and click **Next** (see Figure 9.3).

Gateway Support (By Version)

Windows 95 and Windows 98 computers can provide gateway support only for the IPX/SPX or NetBEUI protocols. Windows 98 Second Edition, however, includes gateway support over TCP/IP.

Windows NT Workstation can provide gateway functionality for TCP/IP, as well as the NetBEUI and IPX/SPX protocols.

FIGURE 9.3
Select the modem that will support the dial-up connection.

6. Because you don't want to offer a VPN, but want to offer only a dial-in connection, select **Do Not Allow Virtual Private Connections** and click **Next** (see Figure 9.4).

FIGURE 9.4
Select Do Not Allow Virtual Private Connections.

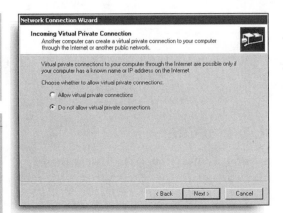

Refining User Account Settings Added from the Network Connection Wizard

The option to add a new user from the Network Connection Wizard permits the definition of only the User Name, Full Name, and Password for each new account. Use the Local Users and Groups snap-in to further refine user account settings, such as establishing group memberships or user profiles.

7. A list of all user accounts defined on the dial-up server appears. Adding and removing user accounts from the Network Connection Wizard is the same as adding them using the Users and Groups snap-in in an MMC. After these accounts have been created, they are managed like any other user account on the computer. Select the users that will be permitted to connect to this computer, and click **Next** (see Figure 9.5).

FIGURE 9.5
Specify which users are to be granted remote access.

8. Select the network components to be supported by this connection (see Figure 9.6). Be sure to select every protocol that dial-up clients are likely to require. Click **Next**.

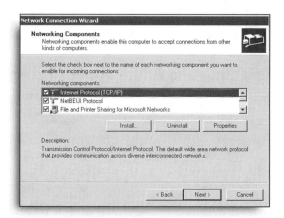

9. Type a name that describes this dial-up connection, and click **Finish** (see Figure 9.7).

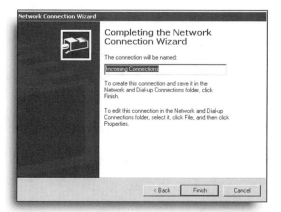

An icon for the dial-up connection now appears in the Network and Dial-Up Connections dialog. Windows 2000 Pro begins monitoring the connection's assigned modem for incoming connection requests and automatically monitors for incoming connection requests every time the computer is started.

Effects of Deleting Access

The option to delete a user from the Network Connection Wizard affects more than just dial-up access. Deleting a user account using this wizard instructs Windows 2000 to remove the account from its security database.

Callback Options Found Under Properties

The Properties button allows for configuration of the callback options for each individual user account as outlined later in this chapter.

Managing a Dial-Up Server

A dial-up connection is managed from its Properties dialog. Reaching the Properties dialog requires right-clicking on the **Incoming Connections** icon and selecting **Properties**.

Configuration options include adding or removing remote access for user accounts and the selection or removal of network components.

Selecting and Adding User Access

Although the Network Connection Wizard presents an opportunity to establish user account access for dial-up connections during the configuration of the dial-up server, additional account access might be required. New users might be added to the computer that require dial-up access, or users with existing access might need their callback options changed. This section explains how to configure existing accounts and add and remove new user accounts.

Adding or removing remote user access for existing user accounts

1. Right-click on the **My Network Places** icon on the Windows 2000 Pro desktop, and select **Properties** from the menu that appears.

2. Double-click on the icon representing the dial-up connection. The Incoming Connections Properties dialog appears.

3. Select the **Users** tab. To allow remote access to an existing account, select it from the Users Allowed to Connect section (see Figure 9.8). To remove an account's remote access, clear its selection. Click **OK** when done.

Dial-Up Security (By Version)

Windows 2000 and Windows NT 4 are significantly more secure dial-up services than the other Windows operating systems, which support only share-level security. The other operating systems can protect a dial-up connection only by assigning it a password. Anyone who learns the password can dial in. Windows 2000 and Windows NT 4 computers running NTFS security will still protect their resources, but computers not running NTFS will be open to possible intrusion.

FIGURE 9.8
Managing account access for a dial-up connection.

The process of adding and deleting user accounts from the connection's Properties dialog is very similar to the process presented by the Network Connection Wizard.

Adding and deleting user accounts

1. Right-click on the **My Network Places** icon on the Windows 2000 Pro desktop, and select **Properties** from the menu that appears.

2. Double-click on the dial-up connection icon. The Incoming Connections Properties dialog appears.

3. Select the **Users** tab. To add a new user account on the computer, click on **New**. Type new account information into the User Name, Full Name, and Password and Confirm Password fields, and click **OK**. To remove an account, select **Delete** and click **Yes** when asked for confirmation. Click **OK** when done.

Callback Options

To further enhance remote access security, Windows 2000 also provides callback options, which can be configured user by user (see Figure 9.9). Establishing a callback for a user account instructs Windows 2000 Pro to hang up immediately after connecting to a dial-up client and call the dial-up client. These are the available callback options:

- Do Not Allow Callback
- Allow the Caller to Set the Callback Number
- Always Use the Following Callback Number

Selecting Do Not Allow Callback instructs Windows 2000 to allow any properly authenticated dial-up connection to continue. Selecting Allow the Caller to Set the Callback Number tells Windows 2000 to collect the phone number being used by the dial-up client and to disconnect and then dial the remote computer and reestablish the connection. This has the advantage that not only will Windows 2000 Pro have a record of the user account that accessed the computer but it also will have a record of the phone number from which the communications session occurred. The most secure option is Always Use the Following Callback Number. This option disconnects the dial-up client and calls it back at a predetermined number. This option

---

Installing Dial-Up Access

Dial-up networking is automatically installed as part of the Windows 98 setup. However, the dial-up server must be manually installed.

Setting up a Windows 95 Remote Access Server requires purchasing Windows 95 Plus. Microsoft chose to sell it as an add-on feature in its Windows 95 Plus product offering.

Increasing Dial-Up Server Performance

Dial-Up Server performance can be increased by removal of any unnecessary protocols from the incoming connection. This keeps Windows 2000 from attempting to establish a connection with a protocol not supported by dial-in clients. Protocol configuration is performed from the Networking properties sheet on the Incoming Connection tab.

increases security by ensuring that users can connect to the network only from known locations.

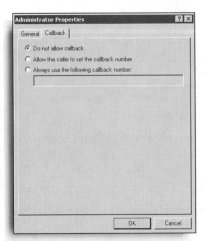

Configuring an Incoming Connection

The Properties button allows for configuration of the callback options for each user account as outlined earlier in this chapter. It also allows an administrator to reset account passwords.

Use the User and Groups Snap-In to Create New Accounts

Although user accounts can be established from the Properties dialog for the dial-up connection, it is usually better to create them with the User and Groups snap-in. Only user accounts can be created from within the dial-up connection's Properties dialog. Detailed account configuration and group assignment are not supported.

Establishing callback options

1. Right-click on the **My Network Places** icon on the Windows 2000 Pro desktop, and select **Properties** from the menu that appears.

2. Double-click on the dial-up connection icon. The Incoming Connections Properties dialog appears.

3. Select the **Users** tab.

4. Select a user account and click on **Properties.**

5. Select the **Callback** property sheet.

6. Select the appropriate option. If **Always Use the Following Callback Number** is selected, type the phone number for the callback connection in the field that is provided, and click **OK**.

Securing a Connection

Any external connection to a network opens it to the possibility of attack. To help combat this threat, the dial-up connection is protected by requiring user accounts and passwords. Requiring that user account and password information be transmitted in an encrypted format further protects the connection.

Securing the dial-up connection with encryption

1. Right-click on the **My Network Places** icon on the Windows 2000 Pro desktop, and select **Properties** from the menu that appears.

2. Double-click on the dial-up connection icon. The Incoming Connections Properties dialog appears.

3. Select the **Users** tab.

4. Select **Require All Users to Secure Their Passwords and Data**, and click **OK.**

Client and Server Encryption Settings Must Match

For dial-up clients to connect to the dial-up server when the encryption requirement is established, the clients must have this same requirement selected on the Security tab on the Dial-Up Connection Properties dialog.

Creating a Client Dial-Up Connection

A dial-up connection provides access to a remote computer or network. Windows 2000 supports dial-up connections over regular telephone lines and ISDN lines. Most users will have only one or two dial-up connections. The first will be to the Internet, and the second will be to a company network.

Creating a new dial-up connection

1. Right-click on the **My Network Places** icon on the Windows 2000 Pro desktop, and select **Properties** from the menu that appears.

2. Double-click on the **Make New Connection** icon.

3. The Network Connection Wizard appears. Click **Next.**

4. Select **Dial-Up to Private Network** and click **Next** (see Figure 9.10).

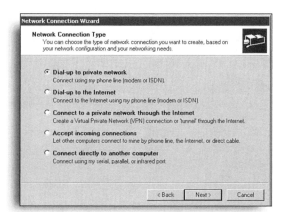

FIGURE 9.10
Select the Dial-Up to Private Network option.

5. Type the phone number of the dial-up server in the Phone Number field, and click **Next** (see Figure 9.11).

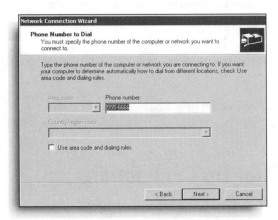

FIGURE 9.11
Provide the phone number for the dial-up server.

6. If this connection is going to be shared with other users of this computer, select **For All Users**. Otherwise, select **Only for Myself** and click **Next** (see Figure 9.12).

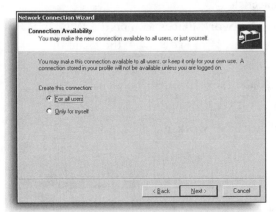

FIGURE 9.12
Determine who will access this connection.

7. The Network Connection Wizard announces that it is ready to complete the connection. Type a name describing the connection and click **Finish**.

Windows 2000 displays the Connect dialog to allow for the initiation of a session with the dial-up server as described in the next section.

Connecting to a Dial-Up Server

After both a dial-up server and a dial-up client have been configured, you are ready to test the connection. The following example assumes that no callback requirements have been established on the dial-up server.

Connecting to a dial-up server

1. Make sure that the dial-up server is powered on and that its modem is connected to a phone line.

2. At the dial-up client, double-click on the dial-up connection. The Connect Dial-Up Connection dialog appears.

3. Type the username and password to be used for the connection, and click on **Dial** (see Figure 9.13).

FIGURE 9.13
Provide dial-up connection logon information.

4. The modem on the client computer dials the dial-up server and begins synchronization. A series of prompts appear on the client computer, announcing that the computer is dialing and then authenticating itself to the dial-up server. If the Connection Complete prompt appears, click **OK**.

5. An icon representing the dial-up connection appears on the system tray on the taskbars of both computers. Double-clicking on one of these icons brings up the Dial-Up Connection Status dialog. From here, session statistics can be viewed. The dial-up connection can be terminated from either computer by the **Disconnect** button.

Use Caution When Disconnecting Users

Be careful when using the Disconnect User button to kick a remote user off the dial-up server computer. If the remote user is in the process of working with a file of the dial-up server, any unsaved user work will be lost.

291

After a connection between a dial-up client and server is established, the shared resources on both machines are available to each computer. For example, if the dial-up client is connected to a dial-up server named SalesPrintSvr, the user can view SalesPrintSvr's shared resources from the dial-up client computers using Windows Explorer by typing \\Computere in the Address field. On the dial-up server, client resources are also available (see Figure 9.14). For example, open the Network Neighborhood and navigate to the dial-up client computer. Remember that communications between dial-up computers will be substantially slower than normal network access.

Other actions that can be performed over a dial-in connection include the following:

- Installing a network printer using the network printer option on the Add Printer Wizard
- Submitting print jobs to a network printer on the other side of the dial-up connection
- Accessing drive and folder shares on the dial-up server and its attached network using the My Network Places dialog and the UNC address of network resources
- Copying and moving files
- Running Microsoft Management Consoles and performing remote administration

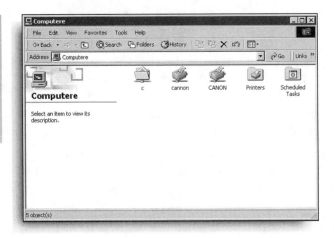

FIGURE 9.14
Any dialog that provides the capability to browse the network or enter network addresses can be used by the client and server computers.

Removing a Dial-Up Connection

Dial-up connections are deleted in the Network and Dial-Up Connections dialog. After a connection is deleted, it can be reestablished only if it is created again.

Removing a dial-up connection

1. Right-click on the **My Network Places** icon on the Windows 2000 Pro desktop, and select **Properties** from the menu that appears.

2. Select the icon representing the dial-up connection.

3. Select **Delete** from the **File** menu.

4. When prompted for confirmation, click **Yes**.

Dealing with Lost Dial-Up Connections

Sometimes, the connection between a dial-up client and a server is terminated accidentally. This can be caused by excess noise or static on the phone line or if someone accidentally picks up another phone while the two computers are in session. Windows 2000 computers do not display a prompt or message to indicate that the connection has been dropped. However, the icon representing the connection disappears from the system tray on the taskbar, and access to the remote connection is lost. To reestablish the communications session, have the dial-up client start the connection over again.

chapter
10

Administrative Tools

Overview of Microsoft Management Consoles

The Administrative Tools folder provides a collection of *Microsoft Management Consoles*, or *MMCs*, that are automatically created when Windows 2000 Professional is installed. These consoles provide convenient groupings of snap-ins. *Snap-ins* are management utilities that allow administrators to manage computers. By default, Windows 2000 Pro creates the following groups of MMCs:

- Component Services
- Computer Management
- Data Sources (ODBC)
- Event Viewer
- Local Security Policy
- Performance
- Services

These consoles are located in the Administrative Tools folder on the Windows 2000 Pro Control Panel as shown in Figure 10.1.

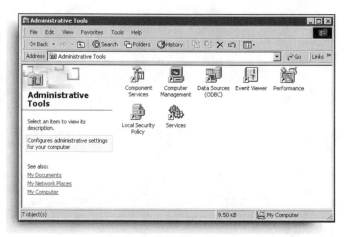

FIGURE 10.1
The Administrative Tools folder contains a default set of Microsoft Management Consoles.

Windows 2000 Pro also allows administrators to create their own custom consoles to which they can add any snap-in. It is important to understand that it is the snap-in and not the MMC that provides management functionality. The MMC only provides a means for organizing and working with snap-ins.

Whether you are working with one of the default consoles or your own custom set of consoles, you will want to use certain snap-ins when managing local and network computers:

- Services
- Event Viewer
- System Information
- Shared Folders
- Device Manager
- Local Users and Groups
- Group Policy
- Performance Monitor

Many snap-ins support both local and network computer management. The remainder of this chapter is devoted to covering these snap-ins.

SEE ALSO

➤ *For detailed information on creating custom Microsoft Management Consoles, see page 112.*

Managing Services

Windows 2000 Pro is a modular operating system. One of the key components of the operating system is services. A service is a part of the operating system that performs a given function. For example, the services listed in Table 10.1 are just a few of the many services that are active on a typical Windows 2000 Pro computer.

Table 10.1 A Sampling of Windows 2000 Pro Services

Service	Description
DHCP Client	Manages computer configuration on IP networks
Event Log	Logs system, security, and applications information that is viewed by the Event Viewer snap-in
Plug and Play	Manages the installation and configuration of hardware
Print Spooler	Manages the print queue for locally installed printers
Server	Manages file and printer services for remotely connected computers
Workstation	Manages network connections with network computers

By controlling the status of services, administrators can limit or provide functionality on the computer. For example, if the Print Spooler service was paused or stopped, the computer would not be able to accept or process print jobs.

Using the Services Snap-In

Services are viewed and managed from the Services snap-in as demonstrated in Figure 10.2. Service management includes such activities as stopping, pausing, and starting services; configuring service recovery; and accessing accounts. By default, this snap-in is available in the Component Services MMC, in the Computer Management MMC, and as its own MMC named services.

Managing Services in Windows NT Workstation 4.0

The Services applet located in the Windows NT Workstation 4 Control Panel provides that operating system with similar control over services.

FIGURE 10.2
The Services snap-in as viewed from the Computer Management MMC.

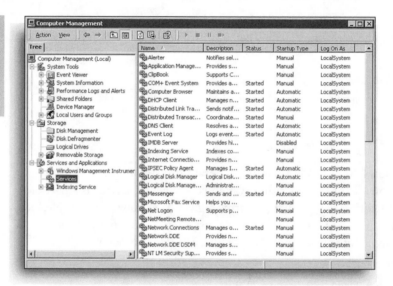

The Services snap-in displays the name and description of every installed service on the computer. Other information provided includes the status of the service and its startup type. A service can have several different statuses, including these:

- Started
- Stopped
- Paused

Changing the status of a service

1. Open an MMC that contains the Services snap-in.

2. Select **Services**.

3. Select a service.

4. Select one of the options **Start**, **Stop**, **Pause**, **Resume**, or **Restart** from the **Action** menu. Note that not every one of these actions is supported by every service.

Selecting a Service's Startup Type

Not every service on a Windows 2000 computer is active all the time. Some services, such as the Microsoft Fax Service, might be useful only on certain occasions, and others might not be required at all. Still other services, such as the Workstation and Server services, must be active at all times to ensure that basic system functionality is in place.

The Startup Type column displays the action Windows 2000 takes on the service when the computer is started. A startup type of Automatic means that the service is automatically started when the computer is started. A startup type of Manual means that the service is not automatically started but can be started from the Services snap-in or when called on by a system process. A startup type of Disabled prevents the services from being started other than through manual intervention by the administrator.

Modifying service startup type

1. Open an MMC that contains the Services snap-in.

2. Select **Services**.

3. Select a service.

4. Select **Properties** from the **Action** menu. The Properties dialog for the selected service appears. By default, the General tab is selected as shown in Figure 10.3.

5. Select **Automatic**, **Manual**, or **Disabled** from the **Startup Type** drop-down list, and click **OK**.

SEE ALSO

➤ *For more information on configuring services to work with accounts, see page 303.*

Service Property Sheets

In addition to the General property sheet, each service includes the Log On and a Recover property sheet. The Log On sheet allows the administrator to provide account access to services. The Recovery sheet provides a means of telling the operating system which actions to take if a service fails.

FIGURE 10.3
Modifying a service's startup type.

Changing a Service's Recovery Options

In the event that a problem occurs that causes a service to stop, the administrator can configure recovery options that instruct Windows 2000 how to handle service recovery. Recovery is configured on a service-by-service basis. Recovery options include the following:

- *Take No Action*

  The Take No Action recovery option instructs Windows 2000 not to take any action on the failed service. Windows 2000 will display an error message and log an event message in the system event log. This option is the default for most services. It notifies the administrator of the problem so that it can be researched and corrected before the administrator manually restarts the service.

- *Restart the Service*

  The Restart the Service option instructs Windows 2000 to automatically restart a failed service. Services can fail for various reasons, including failed or stopped prerequisite services, damaged or deleted files that the services depend on, and unexpected system malfunctions. Often, recovery from service failures is simply a matter of restarting the service. For example, during system startup, a service might fail if it attempts to start before a prerequisite resource is available. Allowing a restart of the service might solve this problem.

- *Run a File*

  The Run a File option allows the administrator to specify a program or custom script to be run if a service fails. A custom script can be written to perform a series of recovery actions, including the restart of the service.

- *Reboot the Computer*

  The Reboot the Computer option is used when the administrator has determined that the only means of recovering from the service failure is a complete reboot of the system. Unlike the other options, this option causes a disruption of other services provided by the computer and should be used only when specified by the vendor documentation.

Configuring service recovery options

1. Open an MMC that contains the Services snap-in.

2. Select **Services**.

3. Select a service.

4. Select **Properties** from the **Action** menu. The Properties dialog for the selected service appears.

5. Select the **Recovery** tab as shown in Figure 10.4.

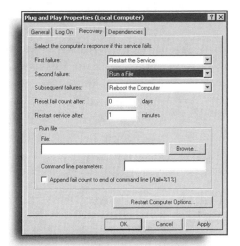

FIGURE 10.4
Modifying service recovery options.

6. Select the appropriate recovery options for the first, second, and subsequent failures. This allows administrators to configure an escalating series of recovery options. For example, on initial

failure Windows 2000 can be instructed to restart the service. If the service fails again, Windows 2000 could then either run a custom recover script or restart the computer.

7. Modify the **Reset Fail Count After** field to control how much time must pass before the failure count is returned to zero. Windows 2000 allows the administrator to decide when enough time has passed to consider the problem resolved and resets the failure count to zero for a service that successfully restarts and runs for a predetermined number of days. When the failure count is returned to zero, any subsequent failure will be handled by the First Failure recovery option. For example, the administrator might decide that if the Print Spooler service is successfully restarted and continues to provide print services for seven days without failing, any new failures should be treated as a new problem and therefore should be handled by the First Failure recovery action.

8. If Restart the Service was selected as one of the recovery options, type a number for the number of minutes the system should wait before attempting a restart of the service in the **Restart Service After** field.

9. If the Run a File recovery option was selected, the Run File section of the dialog will become enabled. Provide the name and location of the script or executable you want to run.

10. If the Reboot the Computer option was selected as a recovery option, click the **Restart Computer Options** button. The Restart Computer Options dialog appears. Type the number of minutes the computer should wait before restarting, and optionally type a warning message that should be broadcast to all network computers. Click **OK**.

11. Click **Apply** and then **OK**.

Checking Service Dependencies

Some services are dependent on other services. Stopping one service might impact other services. Care should be taken to make sure that the ramifications of stopping a service are known before any actions are taken.

Checking service dependencies

1. Open an MMC that contains the Services snap-in.

2. Select **Services**.

3. Select a service.

4. Select **Properties** from the **Action** menu. The Properties dialog for the selected service appears.

5. Select the **Dependencies** property sheet as shown in Figure 10.5. The top portion of the Dependencies property sheet shows a list of all services on which this service depends. The bottom portion lists all the services that are dependent on the selected service.

6. Click **OK**.

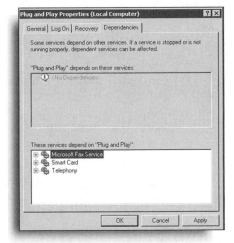

FIGURE 10.5
Viewing service dependencies.

Configuring Account Access for Services

Other third-party software might add new services to the computer as part of its installation. Sometimes, these add-on services require the assignment of a special user or system account in order to run. This account might have access to files and folders that would otherwise not be accessible.

Establishing service account access

1. Open an MMC that contains the Services snap-in.

2. Select **Services**.

3. Select a service.

4. Select **Properties** from the **Action** menu. The Properties dialog for the selected service appears.

5. Select the **Log On** tab as shown in Figure 10.6.

FIGURE 10.6
Establishing account associations for selected services.

6. Select the **This Account** option and provide the name of the account with which the service will be associated.

7. Type the account's password in the **Password** and the **Confirm Password** fields, and click **Apply** and then **OK**.

Using Event Viewer

Looking for the Event Viewer in Other Microsoft Operating Systems

The Event Viewer applet located in the Windows NT Workstation 4.0 Administrative Tools menu provides that operating system with similar control over event logs. Windows for Workgroups also supports an Event Viewer utility, though it provides substantially less functionality. There is no similar tool in Windows 9X operating systems.

Like any other operating system, Windows 2000 Pro needs a means of communicating problems to the user. For critical problems, the operating system usually displays a message on the screen, such as when a service fails to start upon system initialization. Windows 2000 Pro logs most other events to event logs, where they are available for later viewing. Windows 2000 Pro logs event information in three different logs:

- System
- Security
- Application

Windows 2000 logs messages relating to the core operating system, as well as from software drivers, to the system log. The security log contains audit information as specified by the audit policy. The application log contains messages generated by applications that have been designed to use the log. For example, an old 16-bit version of Microsoft Office will not write messages to the application log, whereas the Office 2000 version might.

Working with the Event Viewer

The Event Viewer snap-in can be used to research hardware, software, and system problems and to monitor Windows 2000 Pro operation. When an audit policy is activated, the Event Viewer can be used to audit user activities. One of the first things an experienced administrator does when trying to troubleshoot a problem is check event logs for clues. For example, when a service fails, a message is written to the system log. An examination of the system log might reveal that another resource that the failed service depends on is missing.

In the steps that follow, we will look at how to use and manage system event logs from the Event Viewer. This will include viewing and configuring event logs and archiving and restoring them.

In addition to any custom MMCs, the Event Viewer snap-in is available in the Component Services MMC, in the Computer Management MMC, and as its own MMC named Event Viewer.

Viewing event logs

1. Open an MMC that contains the Event Viewer snap-in.

2. Select **Event Viewer** as shown in Figure 10.7.

3. Select one of the three available logs. The contents of the log appear in the right pane of the console as demonstrated in Figure 10.8.

4. Double-click on an event. The Event tab displays the date, time, type, source, and category of the event as demonstrated in Figure 10.9. The Description section provides detailed information on the event.

5. Click the **Up** or **Down** arrow to view other events. Click **OK** when done.

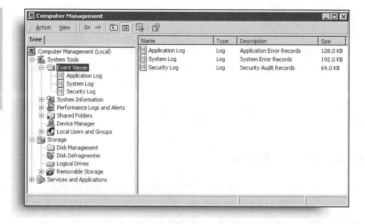

FIGURE 10.7
Use the Event Viewer to examine any of the three logs maintained by Windows 2000 Pro.

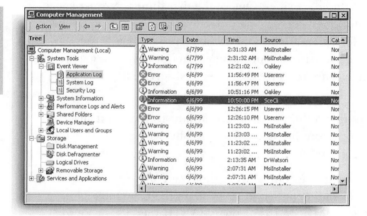

FIGURE 10.8
Event types are identified by icons in the Type column.

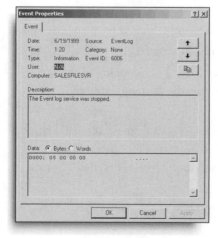

FIGURE 10.9
Detailed event information.

Configuring Event Logs

Log files provide critical information on the performance of a computer and its applications. Administrators need to configure log files so that they are always available. Log files are configured individually. Available configuration options include establishing the maximum log size in kilobytes and specifying how to handle full logs. Setting a maximum log size limits the amount of information that can be stored. On systems with large hard drives, the default size of 512KB can be expanded. The Event Log Wrapping options include the following:

- Overwrite Events As Needed
- Overwrite Events Older Than X Days
- Do Not Overwrite Events (Clear Log Manually)

Setting a log to overwrite as needed allows Windows to overwrite older events when the log becomes full. This ensures that information is always logged. However, unless saved, older event information will eventually be overwritten.

Setting a log to overwrite events greater than a specified number of days allows Windows to overwrite older events only a certain number of days. This ensures that log messages will be around for a given period. However, if the log file fills before this number of days passes, Windows 2000 will be unable to record events in that log. It might be necessary either to reduce the number of days that event messages are retained or to expand the size of the event log to accommodate logging requirements.

Setting the log file so that Windows cannot overwrite old events protects older events. However, if the log fills up, Windows will be unable to record the new event. This option makes the administrator responsible for managing the log.

Configuring event logs

1. Open an MMC that contains the Event Viewer snap-in.
2. Select **Event Viewer**.
3. Select an event log and click on **Properties** in the **Action** menu.
4. Make changes as required; then, click **Apply** and then **OK**.

Identifying the Types of Events Found in Event Logs

There are three event types. An icon appears under the Type column identifying the event type. Information events appear with a white *I*, warning events appear with a yellow *!*, and error events are reported with a red *X*.

Clearing a Log File

If a log file has been set not to overwrite events, the administrator must manually manage it. One option is to clear the log file. This option deletes the contents of the log file without saving them.

Clearing a log file

1. Open an MMC that contains the Event Viewer snap-in.

2. Select **Event Viewer**.

3. Select an event log and click on **Clear all Events** in the **Action** menu.

4. Click **No** when prompted to save the log.

Saving and Retrieving Log Files

As a general rule, it is better to save log files than to clear them. This way they can be retrieved for later viewing. An experienced administrator knows that many times users will not report a problem until days or even weeks after the problem occurs. By archiving log files, administrators can go back and retrieve the log file that contains events for the period during which the user's problem occurred and can research the problem.

Saving a log file

1. Open an MMC that contains the Event Viewer snap-in.

2. Select **Event Viewer**.

3. Select an event log and click on **Save Log File As** in the **Action** menu.

4. Supply a log name and folder where the log should be stored when prompted by the Save dialog, and click **Save**.

Retrieving archived event logs

1. Open an MMC that contains the Event Viewer snap-in.

2. Select **Event Viewer**.

3. Click on **Open Log File** in the **Action** menu. The Open dialog appears.

4. Select the appropriate log type from the **Log Type** drop-down list. Locate the desired log file and click **Open**.

Tips for Archiving Your Event Logs

When you're saving log files, it is generally best to save them in a common location using a naming scheme that includes both the type of the log and the dates of its starting and ending event records.

Gathering System Information

The System Information snap-in displays a computer's system configuration information. It includes a wide variety of information in the following categories:

- System Summary
- Hardware Resources
- Components
- Software Environment
- Applications

In addition to any custom MMCs, the System Information snap-in is available as a snap-in on the Component Services MMC.

System Summary

System Summary displays information about such resources as the operating system, its version and manufacturer, the computer name and processor type, BIOS information, and physical and virtual memory as shown in Figure 10.10.

Finding System Information in Other Windows Operating Systems

The Windows NT Diagnostics utility located in the Windows NT Workstation 4.0 Administrative Tools menu provides that operating system with similar information. Windows 98 provides similar information with the Microsoft System Information utility.

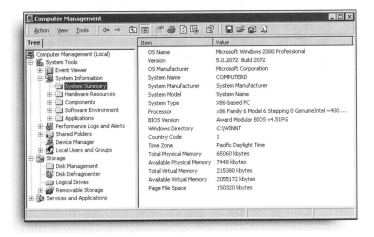

FIGURE 10.10
System Summary provides a high-level overview of basic system information.

Hardware Resources

Hardware Resources displays hardware information using the following categories:

- Conflicts/Sharing

- DMA
- Forced Hardware
- I/O
- IRQs
- Memory

For example, selecting IRQ displays a list of used and available IRQs. Similar information is presented by the DMA, I/O, and memory options. The Conflicts/Sharing option displays a list of devices with resource conflicts and identifies the conflicting resources as shown in Figure 10.11.

FIGURE 10.11
The Conflicts/Sharing option displays a list of conflicting resources.

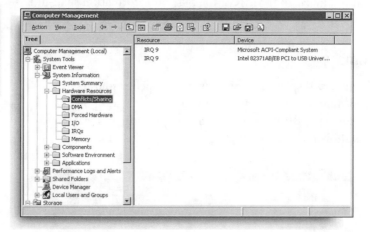

Components

The Components category provides information about major system components, including such things as multimedia, modem, network, ports, storage, printing, and problem devices. Obtaining detailed information requires drilling down into a component category, as demonstrated in Figure 10.12.

Software Environment

The Software Environment category displays information about such resources as installed software drivers, environmental variables, running jobs, active network connections, active tasks, and the status of system services. For example, Figure 10.13 shows the status of every software driver on the computer. An administrator can use this option to view the status of a NIC driver when troubleshooting network connectivity problems.

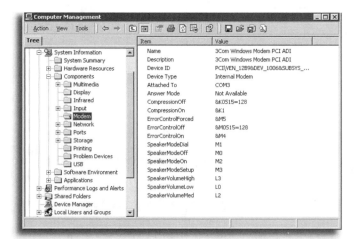

FIGURE 10.12
The Components category of System Information provides detailed information about major system components.

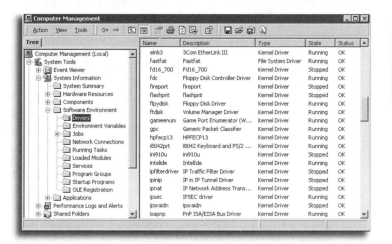

FIGURE 10.13
Viewing the status of every drivers installed on the computer.

Applications

The Applications category provides information on installed applications that have been written to work with Windows 2000, as shown in Figure 10.14. Available information can include the name of applications and their version and build numbers.

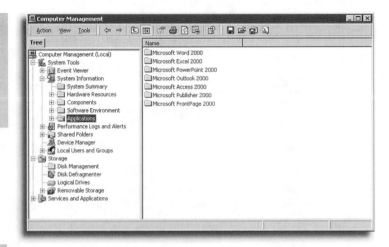

Monitoring Shared Folders

The Shared Folders snap-in provides a tool for administering shared folders on local and network computers. In addition to any custom MMCs, the Shared Folders snap-in is available as a snap-in on the Component Services MMC. Three views are available:

- Shares
- Sessions
- Open Files

Shares

The Shares option displays the name, path, type, and comment information for all shared resources on the selected computer as shown in Figure 10.15. A count of connected users is also presented in the # Client Redirections column.

Shares that end with a $ are hidden shares. This means that they will not appear when network users browse the computer. By default, Windows 2000 creates the following hidden shares:

- ADMIN$
- *DriveLetter*$
- IPC$
- Print$

ADMIN$ is used by the computer during remote administration. A hidden share is created for every drive on the computer. By default, only an administrator or backup operator can connect to these shares. IPC$ is used to support a programming technique referred to as named pipes that facilitates remote operations. Print$ allows remote administration over locally installed printers.

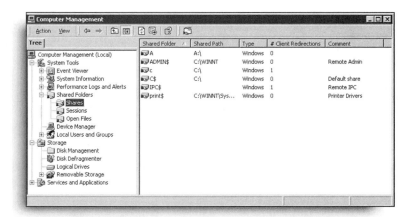

Managing shared resources

1. Open an MMC that contains the Shared Folders snap-in.

2. Select **Shared Folders**.

3. Select a shared resource and click on **Properties** in the **Action** menu. The Properties dialog for the selected resource appears as demonstrated in Figure 10.16.

   The Properties dialog for the shared resource appears. It contains three property sheets. The General sheet allows a comment to be added for the share and for a limit to be placed on the number of network users that can connect to the share at the same time.

   The Share Permissions sheet allows administrators to specify which user and group accounts can access the share and to specify which permissions are assigned to each account. This sheet manages share-level permission and not NTFS permission. Therefore, these permissions do not apply to users who log on locally at the computer.

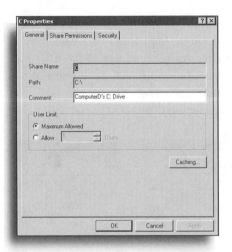

FIGURE 10.16
Administering a shared resource.

The Security sheet allows the administrator to configure NTFS permissions for the shared resource. NTFS permissions affect both local and network users and are more specific than share permissions.

4. Make any required changes and click **Apply** and then **OK**.

Stopping a Share of a Resource

You can also use the Shared Folders snap-in to stop the sharing of resources. There are many reasons for stopping the sharing of a drive or folder. It might be that a given resource no longer needs to be shared. For security reasons it is proper to limit sharing to only those resources that require access over the network. In addition, an administrator might need to reorganize the contents of a shared drive or folder and might want to ensure that no other users are accessing it while it is being worked on. In this case the administrator can stop sharing the resource and reshare it after the task has been completed.

Stopping the sharing of a resource

1. Open an MMC that contains the Shared Folders snap-in.

2. Select **Shared Folders**.

3. To stop sharing a resource, select the resource and click on **Stop Sharing** in the **Action** menu. Click **OK** when requested to confirm the action.

Creating a New Share

Shared folders can be created locally on each computer where the resource resides. However, using this snap-in, an administrator can remotely create new shares. This allows the administrator to create new shares without having to physically visit the remote computer. In addition, this tool allows the administrator to administer shares on the remote computer even if a user is currently working on the computer.

Creating a new shared folder

1. Open an MMC that contains the Shared Folders snap-in.

2. Select **Shared Folders** and then click **Shares**.

3. Click on **New File Share** in the **Action** menu. The Create Shared Folder Wizard appears as demonstrated in Figure 10.17. Identify the folder to be shared, provide a name and description, and then click **Next**.

FIGURE 10.17
Creating a new shared folder.

4. Select the appropriate security permission for the shared folder as demonstrated in Figure 10.18 and click **Finish**.

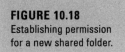

FIGURE 10.18
Establishing permission for a new shared folder.

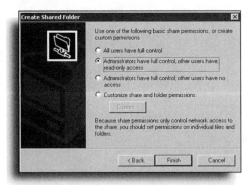

5. Click **No** when prompted by Windows to share another resource.

Sessions

The Sessions option displays information about all network users who are connected to the selected computer, including the user's name, the computer, the type of connection, the total number of connections established by the user, the amount of time the user has been connected, and how much time has passed since the user last performed an action as shown in Figure 10.19. Administrators can disconnect all sessions to the selected computer or close an individual session from the <u>A</u>ction menu.

FIGURE 10.19
The Sessions view of the Shared Folders snap-in.

Open Files

The Open Files option displays information about all open files, including filenames and the names of the users who are accessing the files as shown in Figure 10.20. Administrators can disconnect all open files on the selected computer or close an individual open file from the <u>A</u>ction menu.

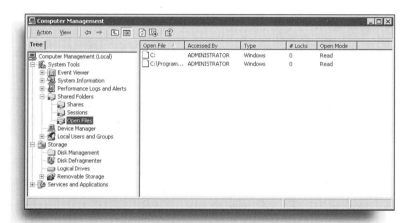

Using the Device Manager

The Device Manager snap-in provides a graphical overview of a computer's hardware as shown in Figure 10.21. It also allows you to view and configure hardware settings. The Device Manager is typically referenced after Plug and Play has installed a new piece of hardware to verify that no hardware conflicts have been introduced to the computer. In addition, this snap-in allows you to install and uninstall new (non–plug-and-play) hardware and to enable and disable installed hardware.

In addition to any custom MMCs, the Device Manager snap-in is available as a snap-in on the Component Services MMC.

Looking for the Device Manager in Other Windows Operating Systems

There is no tool similar to the Device Manager in Windows NT Workstation 4.

Windows 9X operating systems supply similar functionality with their own version of the Device Manager located in the Windows Control Panel.

Save Printed Reports

One useful feature of the Device Manager snap-in is its capability to produce a printed report of the computer hardware configuration. This allows the administrator to print a report before and after every hardware installation or hardware configuration change so that it can be referenced if a problem occurs.

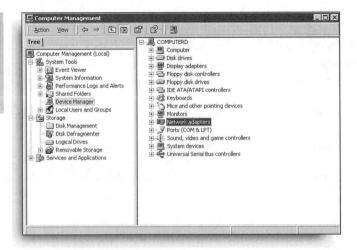

FIGURE 10.21
The Device Manager snap-in provides a graphical overview of a computer's hardware.

Printing hardware resources

1. Open an MMC that contains the Device Manager snap-in.

2. Select **Device Manager**.

3. Select the icon representing the computer.

4. Select **Print** from the **View** menu.

5. Click **Print** to send the report to the default printer.

SEE ALSO

➤ *For detailed information on working with the Device Manager snap-in, see page 54.*

Managing Local Users and Groups

Working with User and Group Accounts in Windows NT 4.0

The User Manager utility located in the Windows NT Workstation 4 Administrative Tools menu provides that operating system with a similar tool for managing user and group accounts.

In addition to any custom MMCs, the Local Users and Groups snap-in is available as a snap-in on the Component Services MMC. It can also be called from the Users and Passwords utility located in the Windows 2000 Pro Control Panel.

This snap-in provides an interface for performing user and group account management. Every user of a Windows 2000 Pro computer must have a user account. For convenience, administrators often group users' accounts into groups so that account management can be performed for multiple users from a single group account as demonstrated in Figure 10.22. Windows 2000 allows user and group members to perform actions based on their assigned rights and permissions.

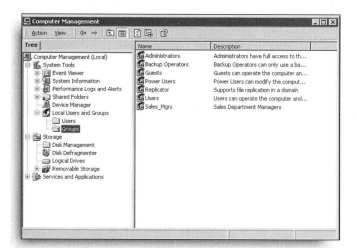

FIGURE 10.22
The Local Users and Groups snap-in allows for user and group account management.

SEE ALSO

➤ *For detailed information on working with the Local Users and Groups snap-in, see page 191.*

Establishing Policies

In addition to any custom MMCs, the Group Policy snap-in is available as a snap-in named Local Security Policy.

This snap-in provides an interface for the establishment and maintenance of system policies as shown in Figure 10.23. Policies are rules that govern behavior on the computer. Important policies include these:

- Password Policy
- Account Lockout Policy
- Audit Policy

A password policy is a set of rules that Windows 2000 enforces upon the creation of user passwords. On a Windows 2000 peer network, password policy is established locally on each Windows 2000 computer. This policy is used to enforce certain rules over passwords such as a minimum length, maximum age, and uniqueness requirements as shown in Figure 10.23.

Establishing Policies on Other Microsoft Operating Systems

Policies are set on Windows NT Workstation 4 computers from the Policy menu on the User Manager utility. Windows 9X operating systems provide support for policies using the System Policy utility.

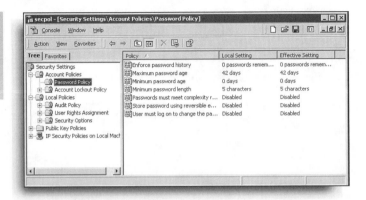

FIGURE 10.23
The Group Policy snap-in is available in the Local Security Policy MMC.

An account lockout policy governs what happens when users attempt to log on but misspell their passwords too many times. Available options include the capability to automatically unlock the account after a predetermined period to force users to contact an administrator when they lock out their accounts.

An audit policy is established when auditing is enabled on individual resources. Audit policies are established individually on each computer.

SEE ALSO

➤ For detailed information on establishing policies, see page 202.

Monitoring with Performance Monitor

Monitoring Windows NT and Windows 9X Operating Systems

The Performance Monitor utility located in the Windows NT Workstation 4 Administrative Tools menu provides that operating system with similar tools for monitoring local and remote computers. Windows 9X provides similar functionality with the System Monitor utility.

In addition to any custom MMCs, the Performance Monitor snap-in is available in its own MMC named Performance. When adding it to an MMC, look for it in ActiveX Control and select System Monitor Control when prompted.

Windows 2000 views a computer as a collection of objects. As it runs, it collects performance data about these objects. Multiple counters for each object represent specific measurements of its performance. For example, the Network Interface object represents the computer's NIC, and the Bytes Received/Sec counter measures the rate at which bytes are received on the card.

Performance Monitor can be used to view real-time statistical information on system performance as demonstrated in Figure 10.24.

Three views of collected data are available:

- Chart
- Histogram
- Report

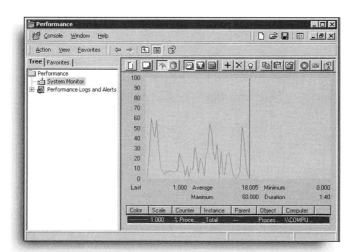

FIGURE 10.24
Performance Monitor provides access to historical and real-time data.

Monitoring system performance

1. Open an MMC that contains the Performance Monitor.

2. Select **Performance Monitor**. By default, System Monitor displays a graph view. Click on the **Add** button on the toolbar. The Add Counters dialog appears as shown in Figure 10.25.

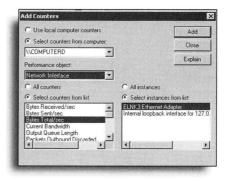

FIGURE 10.25
Adding the Bytes Total/Sec counter for the selected instances of the Network Interface object.

3. Select the type of object you want to monitor from the **Performance Object** drop-down list.

4. Select a counter from the available list for that object in the **Select Counters from List** area.

5. Select a specific instance for the selected counter in the **Select Instances from List** area.

6. Click **Add**. To add additional counters, repeat the preceding steps. When done, click **Close**.

Refer to Windows 2000 Pro online help for more information on working with Performance Monitor.

chapter

11

Troubleshooting

Overview of Troubleshooting

Even the best network will experience occasional problems. Network problems can range from a simple configuration error that inhibits a single computer to the crashing of the entire network. Troubleshooting is one of the most important skills a network administrator can develop. This chapter highlights some of the more common problems that occur on networks and helps identify how to isolate and solve them.

Troubleshooting network problems can be a laborious process and requires a methodical approach. Network administrators should resist the temptation to begin powering off and on network computers and devices in an effort to find a quick solution and to appease network users. Though occasionally successful, this approach usually results in lost time and can damage computer hardware and cause data loss.

However, many problems can be resolved without detailed troubleshooting. One of the first things you should do is ask whether any of the following considerations is applicable to your situation:

- Has anything recently changed? If new hardware or software was just added, uninstall it and return the network to its preceding configuration.

- Does the problem affect just one computer or the entire network? If every network computer is affected, the problem is likely to be hardware related. Perhaps a cable has been cut or disconnected or a terminator is loose. If only one computer is having problems, either it's a configuration problem or the computer's NIC or cable connection is the problem.

- During startup of the computer, do any error messages appear that indicate the problem? Did you check for errors in the system log using the Event Viewer snap-in? When there are error message, they can sometimes point directly to the problem or at least point you in the right direction.

Of course, the best way the solve problems is to plan for dealing with them. This means using antivirus protection software, maintaining an emergency repair disk for each network computer, and making regular backups.

Troubleshooting Hardware Problems

Hardware problems can disable an entire network or a single computer and can be difficult to diagnose. This section outlines a basic approach for resolving problems with cabling, hubs, and NICs.

Diagnosing Cable Problems

Although a simple faulty cable could be the culprit in any network problem, other cable problems vary depending on the type of cable that is being used to connect the network. The following sections break down problems by specific cable type.

Coax Cable Problems

Often network cable problems are intermittent. This can make them very tough to diagnose and resolve. If only one computer is experiencing problems, look for a faulty BNC-T connector or NIC at the computer experiencing the problem. If the entire network is experiencing a problem, look for one of the following causes:

- Faulty, missing, or improperly connected terminators

  Even if the terminators are present, try disconnecting and reconnecting them to make sure that one of them is not improperly connected. If the problem still persists, try replacing them with a new set of terminators.

- A portion of the network cable located too close to a device that is producing electromagnetic interference

  Certain devices, such as fluorescent lights and portable heaters, can generate electromagnetic interference that can wreak havoc on a network. Consider either moving the offending device or moving the cable away from it.

- A physical break somewhere in the network cable

  A break in the cable results in two network segments, neither of which is properly terminated at the point of the break. To fix the problem, you must locate and replace the damaged section of cable. Unfortunately, coax cable problems are not always visible to the naked eye. In this case, pick an arbitrary point somewhere in the middle of the network, disconnect the network into two segments, and then terminate both sections. One section should begin to operate properly. On the side of the segment of cable that does not work, repeat this "halving" process as many times as necessary to isolate the problem. When the faulty segment has been found, replace it and then reconnect the network in its original configuration.

Another thing to look for when working with coax cabling is to make sure that you stay within the official standards for 10BASE-2 cabling. For example, the total length of the network cannot exceed 185 meters, nor can more than 30 network nodes be placed on a network.

SEE ALSO

➤ *For more information about coax cable wiring standards, see page 540.*

➤ *For more information on working with coaxial cable, see page 30.*

➤ *To learn more about working with coax cable, BNC connectors, and BNC-T connectors, see page 39.*

Twisted-Pair Cable Problems

Solving cable problems on networks in which twisted pair is used is considerably easier than solving them on coax-cable networks because the hub isolates each network connection. If only one computer is experiencing problems, look for a fault in the cable connecting the computer to the hub, a problem with the port on the hub, or a bad NIC in the computer. If the entire network is experiencing a problem, look for the problem to be in the hub.

If you suspect a twisted-pair cable problem, first try disconnecting and reconnecting the cable between the NIC and the hub to see whether the problem goes away. If this does not work, try connecting another computer to the connection to see whether it also experiences problems. If it does not, the problem is in the NIC or the software configuration on the original computer. However, if the problem still persists, try replacing the cable.

SEE ALSO

➤ *For more information on working with twisted-pair cable, see page 34.*

➤ *To learn more about twisted-pair cable, see page 41.*

As with coaxial cable, the operation of a network based on twisted-pair cable has a set of governing standards that must be closely followed. For example, a run of twisted-pair cable from the hub to a computer is limited to 100 meters and can support only a single computer connection.

SEE ALSO

➤ *For more information about twisted-pair cable wiring standards, see page 541.*

Isolating Hub Problems

If the problem affects the entire network, the hub is where the problem lies. Use the following checklist to troubleshoot the problem:

- Are the power lights lit on the hub?
- Are the status lights on the hub reporting any errors?
- Try pressing the reset switch on the hub.
- Replace the hub with a different one.

If only one computer is experiencing the problem and you think that the problem does not lie in the connecting cable or the computer's NIC, look for a faulty port on the hub. If this is the case, moving the twisted-pair cable for the computer to another open port on the hub should fix the problem.

SEE ALSO

➤ *For more information on working with network hubs, see page 36.*

Examining the Software Configuration

When only one computer is experiencing a problem, the problem is either in the computer's software configuration or in its NIC or its cable connection. Because checking the software configuration in the fastest and easiest of these options to examine, it should be tried first. Configuration information is checked from the Local Area Connection Properties dialog. Make sure that the correct client, service, and protocols are installed and configured correctly and that the NIC has been properly installed.

SEE ALSO

➤ *For more information on installing client software, see page 89.*

➤ *For more information on installing services, see page 92.*

➤ *For more information on installing protocols, see page 87.*

➤ *For more information on installing a NIC's software driver, see page 82.*

Troubleshooting NICs

If the software configuration is correctly set, the decision as to whether to next troubleshoot the NIC or the cable connection usually depends on which is easier to do. The best and easiest way to check a faulty NIC is simply to replace it with another NIC of the same make and model that is known to function properly.

SEE ALSO

➤ *For more information on physically installing a NIC, see page 82.*

Troubleshooting TCP/IP Communications

TCP/IP communications between two computers can occur only if both machines are running the TCP/IP protocol and it is correctly configured. On a peer network, this means that all computers must have the same subnet mask and have IP addresses, which exist on the same logical network.

Identifying the Current Configuration

The easiest way to gather TCP/IP configuration information is by using the ipconfig command from a Windows command prompt. The output of an ipconfig command is shown here:

```
C:\WINDOWS>ipconfig
Windows 2000 IP Configuration
Ethernet adapter Local Area Connection:
        Connection-specific DNS Suffix  . :
        Autoconfiguration IP Address. . . : 169.254.101.163
        Subnet Mask . . . . . . . . . . . : 255.255.0.0
```

Examining Other Windows Operating System Configurations

To check software configuration on Windows NT 4.0, Windows 95, and Windows 98, you right-click on **Network Neighborhood** and select **Properties**. On Windows for Workgroups computers, it is checked on the Network Setup utility located in the Network group.

Save Time and Money by Replacing NICs

One thing seasoned administrators quickly learn is that it is far more cost-effective to simply replace a NIC than to try to troubleshoot it.

Standardize on a Single NIC

Whenever possible, standardize on a single NIC card. It is difficult enough to troubleshoot hardware problems, especially NICs, without having to support different NIC types and brands. This approach will allow you to purchase an extra NIC for emergencies that is compatible with all existing configurations.

```
          Default Gateway . . . . . . . . . : 169.254.0.1
PPP adapter MyInternetProvider:
          Connection-specific DNS Suffix  . :
          IP Address. . . . . . . . . . . . : 152.172.248.212
          Subnet Mask . . . . . . . . . . . : 255.248.0.0
          Default Gateway . . . . . . . . . : 152.172.248.212
```

In this example, the computer has one NIC and a dial-up adapter for an installed modem. The top portion of the command results displays IP information for the local network. The bottom portion shows IP settings assigned by the ISP that provided the Internet connection. Make sure that the IP address, subnet mask, and default gateway assigned to the computer are correct. If any of these settings is incorrect, the computer cannot communicate with other network computers.

SEE ALSO

➤ *For information on how to work with TCP/IP settings, see page 527.*

➤ *To learn more about the ipconfig command, see page 529.*

Testing Communications with Ping

After you have determined that every computer has the correct TCP/IP configuration and that there are no physical problems such as cable problems or a bad NIC, you can try the ping command. The ping command is an excellent means of verifying that there is a good physical connection between network computers. The results of the ping command tell you whether communications could be established with target computers. If communications were established, the results would include information about the amount of time it took to contact the target computer.

The following example shows a failed attempt to ping a computer with an IP address of 169.254.111.113. In this case, all four attempts to communicate resulted in a timeout.

```
C:\>ping 169.254.111.113

Pinging 169.254.111.113 with 32 bytes of data:

Request timed out.
```

Watch Out for an Empty Subnet Mask

If the subnet mask appears as 0.0.0.0, the computer has an IP address conflict with another computer on the network, and therefore TCP/IP could not initialize during system startup. In this case, the IP address assignment of one of the two computers must be changed.

Windows 9X Users Need to Use the *winipcfg* Command

Windows 9X systems do not support the ipconfig command. Instead, these operating systems provide the winipcfg command, which results in a graphical dialog that provides the same essential information as the ipconfig command.

```
Request timed out.
Request timed out.
Request timed out.

Ping statistics for 169.254.111.113:
    Packets: Sent = 4, Received = 0, Lost = 4 (100% loss),
Approximate round trip times in milli-seconds:
    Minimum = 0ms, Maximum =  0ms, Average =  0ms
```

If this occurs, check for all the following conditions:

- A typo in the IP address portion of the ping command
- A hardware problem on the local and target computers
- A hardware problem on the network (hub, cable, BNC connectors)
- Improper TCP/IP configurations at one of the two computers
- A NIC software driver problem

After you have determined the problem and fixed it, try the ping command again. The following example shows a successful attempt to ping a computer whose IP address is 169.254.111.113. The results show that TCP/IP connectivity exists between the two computers.

```
C:\WINDOWS>ping 169.254.111.113
Pinging 169.254.111.113 with 32 bytes of data:
Reply from 169.254.111.113: bytes=32 time=1ms TTL=32
Reply from 169.254.111.113: bytes=32 time=1ms TTL=32
Reply from 169.254.111.113: bytes=32 time=1ms TTL=32
Reply from 169.254.111.113: bytes=32 time=1ms TTL=32
Ping statistics for 169.254.111.113:
Packets: Sent = 4, Received = 4, Lost = 0 (0% loss),
Approximate round trip times in milli-seconds:
Minimum = 1ms, Maximum =  1ms, Average =  1ms
```

If the ping command is still failing to communicate with the target host, you should try to ping the local computer loopback address. The loopback address on all Microsoft computers is 127.0.0.1. This is a special IP address reserved for special purposes, one of which is verifying the success of a TCP/IP installation on a computer.

The following example demonstrates the result of a successful ping to the loopback IP address:

```
C:\>ping 127.0.0.1

Pinging 127.0.0.1 with 32 bytes of data:

Reply from 127.0.0.1: bytes=32 time<10ms TTL=128
Reply from 127.0.0.1: bytes=32 time<10ms TTL=128
Reply from 127.0.0.1: bytes=32 time<10ms TTL=128
Reply from 127.0.0.1: bytes=32 time<10ms TTL=128

Ping statistics for 127.0.0.1:
    Packets: Sent = 4, Received = 4, Lost = 0 (0% loss),
Approximate round trip times in milli-seconds:
    Minimum = 0ms, Maximum =  0ms, Average =  0ms
```

If pinging the loopback address fails, there is a problem with the installation of TCP/IP on the local computer. Uninstall TCP/IP, install and configure it again, and then try to ping the loopback address again.

After you've successfully pinged the loopback address, try pinging the local computer–assigned IP address. This verifies that the address has been correctly assigned on the network.

When the ping of the loopback and local IP address is successful, go back and try pinging the target network computer. Also, make sure that you can ping the computer from another computer on the network.

Other Useful Commands and Utilities

Several other TCP/IP commands besides the `ipconfig` and `ping` commands provide information that might be useful when troubleshooting TCP/IP problems. These commands are summarized here:

Netstat	Provides statistics about the TCP/IP protocol and shows current TCP/IP network connections.

| Tracert | Provides a listing of the path used to establish communications with the target computer. This command is useful on a network that employs routers to connect multiple network segments. It shows a list of all routers that were traversed during the communications process. |
| Nbtstat | Provides statistical information for TCP/IP connections that use NBT (NetBIOS over TCP/IP). |

More information on these commands can be obtained from Windows 2000 Help.

Microsoft Problem Recovery Tools and Help System

Microsoft provides additional tools that system administrators will find invaluable in resolving network problems. These aids include backup software, the capability to create recovery disks, and an extensive help system. The following sections examine each of these features.

Archiving Important Data

Windows 2000 is equipped with a backup utility that provides the capability to store and restore important system and data files. One of the administrator's most important jobs is to prevent common problems from turning into disasters. For example, establishing a shared folder to store all account and sales information for the entire company places a lot of important data in a single location. Network users need to know that the data they store on network shares is safe. This means that if a few files are accidentally deleted or an entire disk drive crashes, the administrator can recover the lost information.

Network data can be lost for various reasons, including these:

- A network user accidentally deletes a file or folder
- Users power down their computer without performing a complete shutdown while data is still in the process of being saved
- A computer crashes before saving any open files
- A computer locks up and forces the user to hard-boot the computer
- A hard disk crashes

The backup utility can be run by the selection of **Start**, **Programs**, **Accessories**, and then **System Tools**. The backup utility appears, as shown in Figure 11.1.

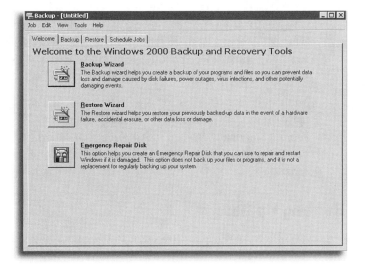

Backups can be written to any of the following types of storage devices (see Figure 11.2):

- Network drivers
- Tape backup units
- Writable compact disk drives
- Backup hard drives located on the computer
- Floppy disks

Establishing Permission to Run the Backup Utility

To use the backup utility you must have the appropriate permissions. All users have permission to back up and restore their own folders and files. Administrators, server operators, and backup operators have permissions to back up and restore all folders and files.

FIGURE 11.1
The Windows 2000 backup utility provides for the creation of backup jobs, the restoration of lost or damaged files, and the creation of an ERD.

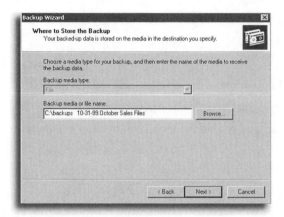

The main backup dialog has four tabs representing property sheets. The Welcome tab allows the user to create and restore from backups using built-in wizards and to create an *emergency repair disk*, or *ERD*. The Backup and Restore tabs allow for manually archiving and retrieving files. The Schedule Jobs tab provides the capability to schedule the automatic execution of backup jobs.

You can create backups in three ways: run the Backup Wizard, manually execute a backup from the Backup tab, or schedule a backup to run automatically from the Schedule Jobs tab. The following sections demonstrate how to create and restore files using wizards and the job scheduler.

Backing Up Data

The Backup Wizard allows you to back up all files, selected files, or just system state data. System state data are key system components that Windows 2000 requires for proper operation. They include such things as the Registry and boot files.

Five different types of backups are supported, as outlined in Table 11.1. Some of the backup operations use attributes that mark a file as having changed since the last backup. This way, the operating system can flag which files need to be backed up and then clear the attributes after the backup is completed.

Table 11.1   Windows 2000 Provides Multiple Backup Options

Type of Backup	Description
Normal	Backs up all selected files and folders and clears all attributes.
Copy	Backs up all selected files and folders but does not clear all attributes. This type of backup does not affect the data that is archived by other scheduled backups.
Incremental	Backs up files and folders that have backup attributes which indicate that they have been altered since the last backup and clears their attributes.
Differential	Backs up files and folders that have backup attributes which indicate that they have been changed since the last backup but does not clear their attributes.
Daily	Backs up files and folders that have been changed that day without examining or altering any backup attributes.

A good backup plan usually involves more than one of the available backup options. For example, you might want to perform a normal backup every Sunday night and then do incremental backups every evening for the rest of the week. Restoring from an incremental backup takes less time than from a full backup because it contains only files that have been changed since the last backup. In a restore situation you could use the most recent incremental backup that contains the damaged or lost files and folders. If the data in question is not on any of the incremental backups because no changes were made to them during the preceding week, you could restore from the last normal backup. For more information about the selecting the right type of backup scheme, refer to Windows 2000 Help.

Creating a backup

1. Click on the **Backup Wizard** button on the Welcome tab of the Backup utility.

2. The Back Up Wizard appears. Click **Next** to continue.

3. Select **Backup Everything on My Computer**; **Back Up Selected Files, Drives or Network Data**; or **Only Back Up the System State Data**. Then, click **Next**. If you choose to back up selected files, drives, and folders, you are presented with an Explorer-style dialog that allows you to browse and select what to back up for the local computer and any other computer on the network.

335

4. In the **Backup Media or File Name** field, provide the location where the backup should be stored and include a name for the backup, as demonstrated in Figure 11.2. The options available depend on what hardware you have installed. After selecting the proper location, click **Next**.

5. The Backup Wizard displays a dialog announcing that you have successfully completed the Backup Wizard. Click on the **Advanced** button to specify the backup type, or click **Finish** to accept the default backup type of Normal. The backup executes immediately. If you choose to specify a specific backup type, Windows presents a dialog that allows you to pick one of the five backups types from the Select the Type of Backup Operations to Perform list.

6. As the backup job executes, the dialog shown in Figure 11.3 appears. It provides detailed information on the status of the backup job.

FIGURE 11.3
Detailed information is provided as the backup job runs.

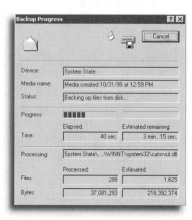

7. When the backup job completes, the dialog changes to reflect summary information. Click on **Close** to terminate the dialog, or click on **Report** to instruct Windows to open Notepad and create a summary report as demonstrated next. This report can then be printed or saved.

```
Backup Status
Operation: Backup
Active backup destination: File
Media name: "Media created 10/31/99 at 12:59 PM"
```

```
Backup of "System State"
Backup set #1 on media #1
Backup description: "Set created 10/31/99 at 1:20 PM"
Backup Type: Copy

Backup started on 10/31/99 at 1:20 PM.
Backup completed on 10/31/99 at 1:24 PM.
Directories: 59
Files: 1625
Bytes: 218,476,454
Time:  3 minutes and  53 seconds

. . . . . . . . . . . . . . . . . . . . .
```

Restoring Data

When network users accidentally delete critical data or system files, they can be retrieved or restored from backups. The following process outlines how to restore a backup job using the Restore Wizard.

Restoring from a backup

1. Click on the **Restore Wizard** button on the Welcome tab of the Backup utility.

2. The restore Wizard appears. Click **Next** to continue.

3. Windows displays a dialog that allows you to locate the backup, which you will use to perform the restore as demonstrated in Figure 11.4. Navigate the left pane to locate and select the backup file. Its contents are displayed in the right pane. Click **Next**.

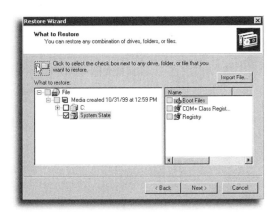

FIGURE 11.4
Locating the backup file with which you will perform the restore.

Performing a Partial Restore

When restoring system state data, you must restore the entire backup. But when restoring from other types of backup jobs, you have the option of restoring either from the entire backup job or from selected files contained in the backup job. You can choose to restore only specific files and folders by selecting them in the right pane instead of selecting the entire backup job in the left pane.

4. The Restore Wizard displays a dialog announcing that you have successfully completed the Restore Wizard. Click on the **Advanced** button to specify the location where the selected files and folders should be restored, or skip to step 8 to complete the restore. The available locations for restoring from the backup are Original Location, Alternate Location, and Single Folder. The default is Original Location. Selecting either of the other options allows you to examine the contents of the restored data before accepting and manually move them to their final destination.

5. If you selected Advanced and specified an option other than Original Location, Windows prompts you for the location where the restored files and folders should be placed, and you must click **Next** to continue.

6. Windows presents three options for determining what it should do when a file or folder of the same name already exists during a restore operation. The choices are Do Not Replace the File on My Disk, Replace the File on Disk Only If It Is Older Than the Backup Copy, and Always Replace the File on Disk. After making the appropriate selection, click **Next**.

7. The Advanced Restore Option dialog appears. Three options are available for selection. These are Restore Security, Restore Removable Storage Database, and Restore Junctions Points, Not the Folders and File Data They Reference. Restore Security works only for Windows 2000 NTFS volumes. It restores the security settings for each file and folder, including permissions, audit entries, and ownership. The Restore Removable Storage database works with systems that have tape backup drives. In this case Windows maintains a Removable Storage database located in *Systemroot*\System32\Ntmsdata for managing the drive and its data. A *junction point* is a physical location on a disk drive that points to another location on your hard disk where data is stored or to a different disk drive; this topic is beyond the scope of this book. Generally, it is best to leave all of these options blank and click **Next**.

8. Click **Finish** to execute the restore.

9. The Enter Backup File Name dialog appears, as shown in Figure 11.5. Verify that the correct backup job is selected, and click **OK**.

FIGURE 11.5
Verify the name and location of the backup job.

10. A dialog appears as the restore job executes, providing detailed information on the status of the restore operation. When the restore completes, the dialog changes to reflect summary information. Click **Close** to terminate the dialog, or click **Report** to instruct Windows to open Notepad and create a summary report. This report can then be printed or saved.

Scheduling Jobs

Manually executing backup jobs can quickly become a tedious and mundane task. This often means that backups are skipped or not performed regularly. This can result in disastrous consequences. Fortunately, Windows 2000 provides a solution in the form of a backup job scheduler. This allows administrators to set up automated backup schedules that manage the backup process.

To set up a scheduled backup job, select the Scheduled Jobs tab on the Backup utility, as demonstrated in Figure 11.6. The wizard steps you through the backup process, which is as described in the preceding backup example except that this time additional dialogs appear to allow you to choose between replacing and appending to the current backup media, to prompt you for a backup job name, and to assist you in creating a schedule for running the backup job.

Creating an Emergency Repair Disk

If a computer is not properly shut down or the user accidentally deletes important system files, the computer might not be able to restart the next time it is rebooted. To address this problem, Microsoft provides the capability to create an ERD that can be used to store damaged or missing system files.

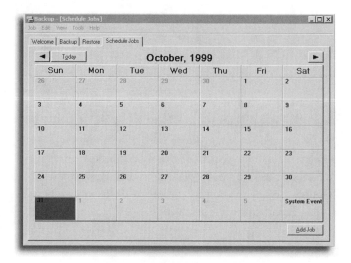

FIGURE 11.6
Select the date on which to schedule the backup job.

An ERD is created by the selection of the Emergency Repair Disk option on the backup utility's Welcome screen. When this option is selected, Windows 2000 Pro displays a prompt instructing the user to insert a blank disk in the A: drive. Windows 2000 Pro then proceeds to save critical system files and configuration information to the disk. The ERD can later be used to try to repair the Windows 2000 Pro computer in the event that it fails to start.

An ERD should be created for every computer and should be updated after every significant change to a computer, such as the installation of a new piece of hardware. When used, the ERD will restore system files and configuration information to the state they were in when the ERD disk was made. Any changes made to the system since that time might be lost. It is therefore critical to keep the ERD current.

The ERD is used to recover a Windows 2000 Pro computer that is failing to start. The following procedure outlines the basic steps required to use the ERD.

Using the emergency repair disk

1. Start the computer using the Windows 2000 setup disks.

2. When prompted, select the repair option.

3. Select either a fast or a manual repair.

4. Supply the ERD and the Windows 2000 Pro CD-ROM.

5. Restart the computer.

Using Windows Help

Windows 2000 introduces a new HTML-based help engine. It provides seamless integration of help topics located either on the computer or on the Internet. Windows 2000 Help is accessed on the Windows 2000 Pro desktop by the selection of **Start** and then **Help**. Windows 2000 Help presents a dialog with four tabs: **Contents**, **Index**, **Search**, and **Favorites**.

The Help dialog is divided into two panes. The left plane displays the appropriate selections for the selected tab, and the right pane displays actual help information based on the selection made in the left pane.

Contents

The Contents tab lists Windows 2000 help in the form of books in the left pane of the dialog, as shown in Figure 11.7. Books represent top-level topics. The right pane displays the currently selected topic.

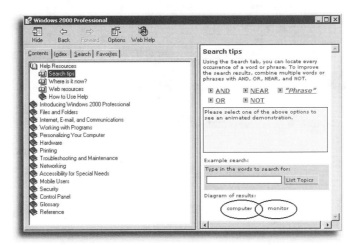

By drilling down into selected books, you can access specific topics. Among the information available are the Windows 2000 troubleshooters, as shown in Figure 11.8.

FIGURE 11.7
The Contents tab provides access to information located in the form of books.

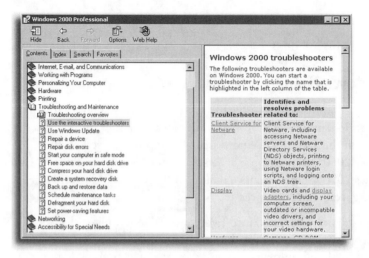

FIGURE 11.8
Windows 2000 troubleshooters provide extensive help information for solving many common problems.

Index

The Index tab provides a comprehensive index of Windows 2000 help topics. The Windows 2000 index can be searched quickly by letters or keywords. For example, typing the letter *T* instructs Windows 2000 to immediately display all help topics beginning with that letter, as demonstrated in Figure 11.9. Typing a whole word (or phrase) moves the selection to the applicable word or phrase in the index (or to the closest match if no exact match exists).

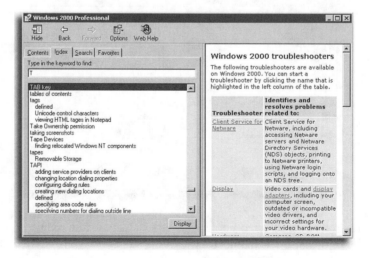

FIGURE 11.9
The Index tab provides an alphabetical list of help topics.

Search

The Search tab provides a search field that can be used to find help topics based on keywords or phrases supplied by the user. If Windows finds multiple hits based on the search criteria, it displays a list of entries that can be selected in the topics area. Individual topics, when they're selected, are displayed in the right pane, as shown in Figure 11.10.

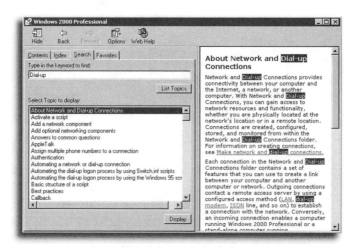

FIGURE 11.10
The Search tab provides a list of matching topics based on keyword searches.

Though similar to the Index option, which displays a listing of indexed help entries, the Search option locates every occurrence of a word or phrase and can be used to locate help information that is not necessarily indexed.

Favorites

The Favorites tab lists any help pages the user has added to it, as demonstrated in Figure 11.11. This feature allows the user to create a custom collection of help topics that are of personal interest. For example, after using the Search tab to find a useful help page, the user can select the Favorites tab and click on Add. A link to the help page is then added to the Topics area and will be available the next time the user visits this tab.

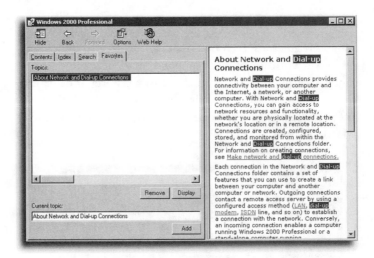

FIGURE 11.11
The Favorites tab allows users to create a collection of links to help topics.

Wizards

In addition to problem recovery tools and an extensive online help system, Microsoft provides troubleshooting wizards to assist you in working through your network problems. If you are unable to troubleshoot the problem yourself, try looking for answers here before pursuing some of the alternative options presented later in this chapter.

These wizards help to solve many common problems as shown in Figure 11.12. Several of these troubleshooters are directly related to Windows networking. Among the key troubleshooters are the following:

Hardware	Provides help for solving common problems with hardware such as NICs.
Internet Connections	Provides help for resolving problems with connecting to your ISP.
Modem	Provides help for solving most modem problems.
Networking (TCP IP)	Provides help for diagnosing TCP/IP-related problems.
Print	Provides help for solving most printing problems.
Remote Access (RAS)	Provides help for solving Dial-Up Networking problems.

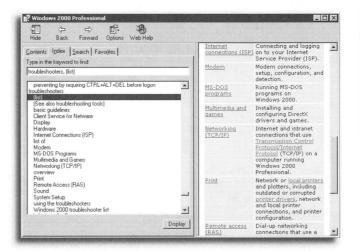

FIGURE 11.12
Windows 2000 comes equipped with a series of troubleshooters that guide the user through the steps required to solve various problems.

To execute a troubleshooter, simply double-click on it and follow the provided instructions. For example, Figure 11.13 shows the Networking (TCP/IP) Troubleshooter, which begins by asking the user what type of problem is being experienced. After the user selects from the available list of answers and clicks on Next, the wizard begins to provide troubleshooting instructions to the user.

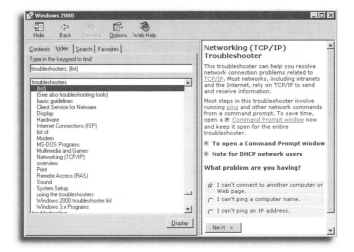

FIGURE 11.13
The Networking (TCP/TP) Troubleshooter asks what type of problem you are experiencing.

Web Help

For situations in which the Windows 2000 help system cannot provide the required information, there is the Web Help feature. It is selected via a click on **Web Help** on the toolbar, as shown in Figure 11.14.

FIGURE 11.14
Windows 2000 HTML-
based help provides
seamless integration
with Internet-based help.

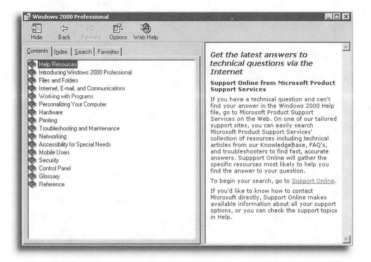

If an Internet connection is established, clicking on **Support Online** instructs Windows 2000 to launch its default Web browser and connect to the Microsoft On line Support Web page, as shown in Figure 11.15. To reach the page directly from the browser, type `http://support.microsoft.com/support` in the URL field of the Web browser.

FIGURE 11.15
Windows 2000 provides
links to help information
located on Microsoft's
Web site.

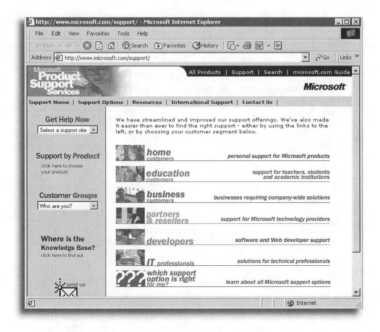

Additional Support Avenues

Microsoft provides a wide assortment of alternative support options for its products and operating systems. One of the best sources is found at Microsoft's Web site located at http://www.microsoft.com. In addition, many other avenues of support are available, including these:

- A subscription to Microsoft TechNet at www.microsoft.com/TechNet

- A subscription to Microsoft email newsletters

- The Microsoft Windows Update Web site

- Computer antivirus products

- Microsoft technical support

Help can also be found from sources other than Microsoft. Manufacturers of hardware and software also maintain their own Web sites, from which they make software drivers and fixes available as free downloads. If a peripheral device is not functioning properly on Windows 2000, the solution might be a new software driver. These manufacturers, as well as Microsoft, usually publish Frequently Asked Questions, or FAQs, at their Web sites. FAQs contain the answers and workarounds to common problems.

Researching Problems with TechNet

Microsoft has established a resource known as TechNet, which contains information on various topics including technical papers, software drivers, and resource kits and service packs. Microsoft's TechNet is sold as a subscription service with CD-ROMs mailed out every month. For more information about TechNet or on subscribing to TechNet, see http://support.microsoft.com/support.

Subscribing to the Microsoft Email Newsletter

The Microsoft Windows electronic newsletter is a free publication from Microsoft that provides tips and tricks on all Microsoft operating systems. It also includes news updates, as well as other relevant pieces of information. Microsoft makes this newsletter available to everyone at no charge. To subscribe, visit http://www.microsoft.com and perform a search on "newsletter."

347

Visiting the Windows Update Site

Microsoft and other vendors continuously improve their products. Microsoft creates software updates to fix bugs and make products enhancements. Other vendors' updates are typically software-driver updates. Microsoft added the Windows Update utility to Windows 2000. When activated, the utility connects to Microsoft's Web site and presents a list of software updates, fixes, and utilities available for download.

Using the Windows Update Wizard

1. Click on **Start** and then **Windows Update**. Internet Explorer starts and attempts to connect to Microsoft's Update Web site, as shown in Figure 11.16.

FIGURE 11.16
The Microsoft Windows Update Web site provides a list of available products updated for Windows 2000.

2. Select the **Products Updates** option. If this is the first time you have used the Windows Update feature, the dialog shown in Figure 11.17 appears. Select **Yes** to continue.

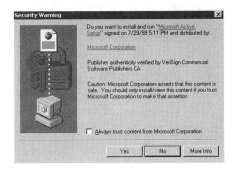

3. After a brief delay, a custom list of updates is presented, as shown in Figure 11.18.

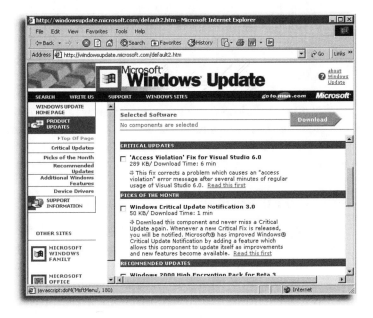

Several categories of software are available, including these:

- Critical Updates
- Picks of the Month
- Recommended Updates
- Additional Windows Features
- Device Drivers

4. To download an update, select a specific update and click on the **Download** button. A Web page appears, asking for confirmation and offering instructions on downloading the update.

5. Click **Start Download** to download and automatically install the update. A license agreement might be presented, depending on the update selected. Click **Yes** to continue.

6. The update is downloaded and then installed. Windows might require a restart of the computer.

Visiting Manufacturers' Web Sites

Peripheral manufacturers are always making improvements or providing fixes for their products that usually are provided in the form of software drivers. These software updates are usually available as free downloads from the manufacturer's Web site. It is not unusual to purchase a network card that includes a disk or CD-ROM that has software drivers only for Windows 95 or Windows 98. This does not mean that the manufacturer has not created drivers for Windows 2000 or Windows NT 4; they might be available in the download area on the manufacturer's Web site. In addition, many manufacturers make help information available. Sometimes diagnostic utilities or other helpful programs are also provided.

Checking for Viruses

Computer viruses can attack networks in various ways. They can hide in files downloaded from the Internet, in files attached to emails, or on floppy disks. Though it is rare today, viruses can even be introduced from software programs purchased from the local computer store.

There are several good rules for preventing computer viruses from harming network resources:

- Download files only from reputable locations on the Internet.
- Never load a floppy received in the mail from an unknown source.
- Purchase and regularly update an antivirus program.
- Never open an email attachment from an unknown sender.

Registering Products

The importance of taking a few minutes to register a new product or piece of software cannot be overestimated. By registering with vendors, you supply them with information they can use to contact you and keep you informed of problems and fixes. In addition, should a problem occur that requires a call to the vendor, things will proceed more smoothly if you have registered your product in advance.

Microsoft Technical Support

If all else fails, a problem can be submitted to Microsoft technical support. To find out how to get help from technical support, look for the Phone Numbers link on the Microsoft Support Web page `http://support.microsoft.com/support`.

part

IV

OPERATING SYSTEMS

chapter

12

Windows for Workgroups

Overview of Windows for Workgroups

Windows for Workgroups, or *WFW*, is an update of the Microsoft Windows 3.1 operating system. It is available through either the full version of *Windows 3.11* or the *Workgroup Add-On for Windows*, which is essentially an upgrade that converts a preexisting installation of Windows 3.1 to Windows for Workgroups.

Windows for Workgroups was Microsoft's first operating system specifically directed at providing network services. Surprisingly, Windows for Workgroups provides most of the core functionality and features provided by Windows 95 and Windows 98. It does have a few limitations that Windows 95 and Windows 98 do not have, such as a limit of four protocols supported per network interface card.

Also, Windows for Workgroups does not provide support for TCP/IP out of the box. A TCP/IP add-on for WFW can be obtained from *Microsoft's Developer Network*, or *MSDN*. As of the publishing of this book, that Web site address is

```
http://msdn.microsoft.com/developer/downloads/subscriber.htm
```

The TCP/IP add-on is a 32-bit protected-mode protocol stack that provides WFW with a full range of Microsoft TCP/IP functionality and features.

In addition to adding base networking support to the operating system, WFW brought with it many new network utilities and applications, including these:

- Chat
- Net Watcher
- Remote Access
- Schedule +
- WinMeter
- WinPopup
- Mail
- Fax

Since the release of Windows 95 in late 1995, the role of Windows for Workgroups has gradually declined in the business world. Nevertheless, it still has a large installation base and can be found running on older computers around the world. These computers are still providing a useful service and can continue to do so when added to a peer network.

Often, home users with more than one computer have one newer computer running either Windows 2000 Pro or Windows 98 and an older computer running either Windows for Workgroups or Windows 95. While falling prices have made it easier than ever to purchase a new computer, they have also driven down the resale value of older PCs to the point where they might not be worth selling. These machines often become the kids' computer or the family's backup computer.

Adding a Windows for Workgroup computer to a peer network extends both its longevity and its usefulness. It usually runs on older computers that lack the memory or the CPU power to run other Windows operating systems, and computers running Windows for Workgroups typically have a limited storage capacity. Membership on the network provides additional storage capacity in the form of network access to shared drivers and folders on other network computers. This allows companies and home users to extend their network and exploit their current investment in existing hardware and software.

SEE ALSO

➤ *To learn more about the hardware requirements for running Windows for Workgroups, see page 26.*

Working with User Accounts

When Windows for Workgroups is started, a logon dialog appears, querying the user for a logon name and the associated password (see Figure 12.1).

FIGURE 12.1
The Windows for Workgroups logon dialog.

It's Unlikely That WFW Will Have the NIC Driver You Need

With an operating system as old as WFW, it is highly likely that it will not have the installed network adapter in its list or will be unable to auto-detect it. In that case choosing the option to supply the vendor-supplied software driver is the required method of NIC installation. Most NICs come with a disk or CD-ROM that contains software drivers for most Windows operating systems. If Windows for Workgroups drivers are not supplied with your card, check the supplied documentation and search the vendor's Web site to see whether a Windows for Workgroups driver is available.

A user can establish a new user account by simply entering a new user ID and password in the dialog and clicking OK. The password can be up to 14 characters long. WFW recognizes the new information and creates a new account.

When creating a new account, WFW also asks the user whether a *password-list*, or *PWL*, file should be created. The password-list file is named *xxxxxxxx*.PWL where *xxxxxxxx* is the first few unique letters of the user ID of the new user. In this file, Windows stores passwords the user uses when accessing network resources such as share drives that are password-protected. After the user has initially accessed the network resource successfully, the system does not ask the user to supply a password the next time the resource is accessed. The only time the user will be prompted for a password in the future is if the associated device's password is changed. In this case Windows asks the user to supply a new password, which is then saved in the password-list file. Unlike other Windows operating systems, Windows for Workgroups does not support multiple user profiles. Windows for Workgroups uses the password-list file only to simplify accessing network resources and not for allowing the customization of individual desktops or settings.

If the user decides not to create a password-list file, the system always prompts the user when a password-protected network resource is accessed.

Adding, Removing, and Configuring NICs, Clients, Protocols, and Services

A network interface card, or NIC, must be installed before Windows for Workgroups networking can be configured. If the NIC is installed before Windows for Workgroups is installed, the operating system installation process will ask the user whether the computer will be connected to a network and will step the user through a network setup process similar to the manual one outlined next. If the NIC was added to the computer after WFW installation, the user will have to initiate the NIC installation process manually.

SEE ALSO

➤ *For information on installing a NIC, see page 51.*

Network configuration is performed from the Network Setup icon in the Network group.

Windows for Workgroups NIC setup

1. After the network card is installed, from the Windows Program Manager double-click on the **Network** group. The contents of the Network group appear (see Figure 12.2). All Windows for Workgroups networking functions are accessed from this location.

2. Double-click on the **Network Setup** icon to start the network configuration process.

FIGURE 12.2
The contents of the Windows for Workgroups network group.

3. The Network Setup dialog provides the interface for configuring all networking features (see Figure 12.3). These are the three primary configuration options provided by this interface:

   - *Networks:* Specifies the type of network the computer will be attached to.

   - *Sharing:* Specifies whether the computer will offer file or print sharing services.

   - *Drivers:* Installs software drivers for the installed NIC.

   Click on the **Networks** button to specify the network type that the computer will join.

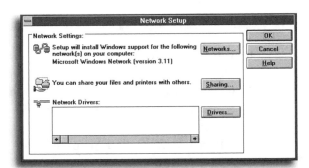

FIGURE 12.3
The Windows for Workgroups Network Setup dialog.

4. Select the **I̲nstall Microsoft Windows Network** option (see Figure 12.4). As the option indicates, this allows the computer to share both its local drives and its printer over the network, as well as interact with other types of networks. To add a WFW computer to a Windows 2000 Pro peer network, no other options need to be selected. Click **OK** to continue network setup.

FIGURE 12.4
Specifying the type of network.

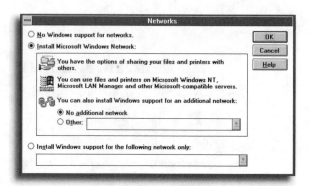

5. When returned to the main Network Setup dialog, click on the **S̲haring** button. The Sharing dialog appears as shown in Figure 12.5. From here, the type of services the computer will make available over the network can be selected. If the role of this computer is to provide resources over the network, click on one or both options and click **OK**.

FIGURE 12.5
Configuring device sharing.

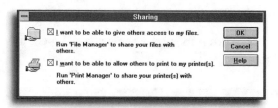

6. When returned to the main Network Setup dialog, click on the **D̲rivers** button. The Network Drivers dialog appears. This dialog provides support for adding and removing NICs and protocols (see Figure 12.6). Configuration of these two types of resources is controlled from this dialog as well. To add a new NIC, click on the **Add A̲dapter** button. The Add Network Adapter dialog appears.

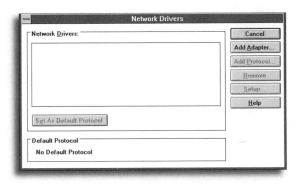

FIGURE 12.6
Adding a network
adapter card.

7. WFW displays a list of network adapters. If the installed NIC matches one of the entries in this list, select it and click **OK** (see Figure 12.7). If you want WFW to attempt to automatically locate the card and determine its type, click on the **Detect** button. If the card is not supplied in the list and if the detection process fails, select the **Unlisted or Updated Network Adapter** entry and click **OK**. This tells WFW that the user will provide the software required to configure the card. Usually, this comes in the form of a disk or CD-ROM supplied with the network adapter.

FIGURE 12.7
Selecting a network
interface card driver.

8. A prompt appears if WFW is instructed to try to auto-detect the network adapter card. Click **Yes**.

9. A prompt appears if WFW fails to auto-detect the network adapter card. Click **OK**.

10. Choosing to provide the software driver causes the Install Driver dialog box to appear. Insert the floppy disk or CD-ROM where the WFW software driver is located, and either type the location into the dialog or click on the **Browse** button to browse the system and find the proper location. Click **OK**.

11. WFW checks the location provided for the NIC drivers and displays a dialog asking for confirmation that the information found matches the card that was installed (see Figure 12.8). Verify that the information is correct and click **OK**.

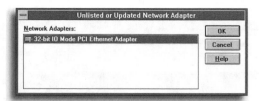

FIGURE 12.8
Confirmation of the software-driver selection.

12. WFW proceeds with the installation of the NIC and automatically installs the Microsoft NetBEUI protocol. If the computer has more than 6MB of RAM, the IPX/SPX protocol is also installed; otherwise, only NetBEUI is present. To view or change the network adapter card settings, select the card and click **Setup**.

13. From this dialog, the driver type can be changed and card settings can be altered (see Figure 12.13). To view advanced network adapter card settings, click on **Advanced** (see Figure 12.9).

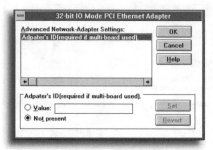

FIGURE 12.9
Viewing advanced network-adapter settings.

WFW Supports Only Four Protocols

WFW supports a maximum of four protocols per network adapter card.

14. Whenever possible, it is best to keep the default settings. Care should be taken when network-adapter card settings are being altered. Always record original settings so that they can be restored if the new settings do not perform as expected. Click **OK** to close this dialog. Click **OK** a second time to return to the Network Drivers dialog.

Windows for Workgroups protocol setup

1. To configure a protocol, select the protocol and click on the **Setup** button. A dialog appears for the selected protocol, displaying all configurable parameters (see Figure 12.10). Make any required parameter adjustments and click **OK**. In most cases no changes are required to the default parameter settings.

FIGURE 12.10
Viewing NetBEUI protocol settings; a similar dialog appears for any selected protocol.

2. When more than one protocol is selected, WFW sets one as the default protocol as designated in the Default Protocol display area of the Network Drivers dialog. To change the default protocol, select the desired protocol and click **Set As Default Protocol** (see Figure 12.11).

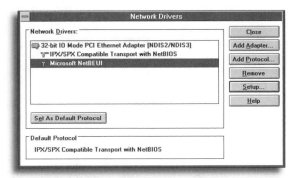

FIGURE 12.11
Changing the default protocol.

3. To remove a protocol, select the desired protocol and click on **Remove**.

4. WFW prompts for confirmation of the removal before proceeding. Click **Yes** to remove the protocol.

5. WFW returns to the Network Drivers dialog. The selected protocol has been removed.

6. Click **Close** when done. Window displays the main Network Setup dialog (see Figure 12.12). All NICs and associated protocols are displayed in the Network Drivers display list.

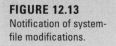

FIGURE 12.17
The main Network Setup dialog with the network adapter and protocols.

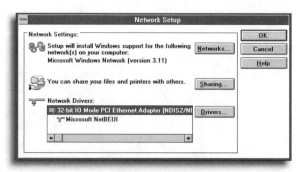

Finishing the network install

1. When you are finished, click **OK** on the Network Setup dialog.

2. Windows asks for the WFW installation disks so that it can complete the changes that have been made. Insert the appropriate WFW disks when prompted by the system.

3. When the installation process is complete, WFW displays the prompt shown in Figure 12.13 to notify that changes have been made to several Windows configuration files. Click **OK**.

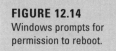

FIGURE 12.13
Notification of system-file modifications.

4. WFW requires a restart of the computer. Until the system is rebooted, the networking changes will not be effective. Click on the **Restart Computer** button (see Figure 12.14).

FIGURE 12.14
Windows prompts for permission to reboot.

Tuning Windows for Workgroups Performance

Like its Windows 95 and Windows 98 counterparts, WFW manages network functionality from the Network icon in the Windows Control Panel. The WFW Control Panel is located by default in the Main group, as shown in Figure 12.15. Double-clicking the Control Panel icon displays the dialog shown in Figure 12.16.

FIGURE 12.15
The Windows for Workgroups Main group.

FIGURE 12.16
The Windows for Workgroups Control Panel.

Microsoft Windows Network Control Panel

The Network icon provides access for controlling the following network features:

- Managing computer and workgroup names
- Logging off the network
- Managing workstation network startup settings
- Changing passwords
- Managing the Event Log

The Microsoft Windows Network dialog displays the **Computer Name**, **Workgroup**, and **Comment** boxes. These fields can be edited directly from this dialog (see Figure 12.17). The drop-down arrow beside the **Workgroup** field can be used to display a list of known active workgroups on the network.

The Logon Status area displays the user ID of the currently logged-on user. The **Log Off** button allows the user to log off the network while still remaining active on the local computer.

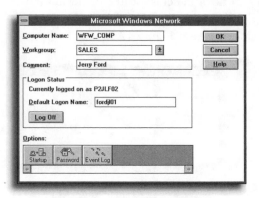

Selecting the **Log Off** button on the Microsoft Windows Network dialog logs the user off the network. If there are any active network connections such as a mapped drive, WFW displays a prompt asking the user to verify the decision to log off the network (see Figure 12.18).

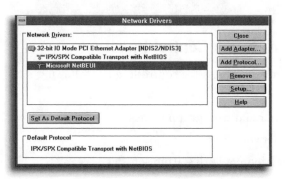

Selecting **Yes** disconnects the user's network session. The user can then continue using the computer but is restricted to the resources available only on the local computer. Selecting **No** cancels the operation and leaves the user connected to the network.

Additional Functions of the Control Panel

At the bottom of the Microsoft Windows Network dialog are three buttons that provide access to the following dialogs:

- Startup Settings
- Change Logon Password
- Event Log Settings

Startup Settings

Selecting the Startup button on the Microsoft Windows Network dialog produces the Startup Settings dialog. It offers three sets of options:

- Startup Options
- Options for Enterprise Networking
- Performance Priority

Startup Options   Windows for Workgroups provides four startup options that determine the network status when the computer is first started. These options are outlined here:

- *Log On at Startup:* When selected, this option instructs WFW to display the network login prompt at startup.

- *Enable Network DDE:* This option is required to support network applications such as chat.

- *Ghosted Connections:* Selecting this option instructs WFW not to restore all drive mappings at startup and instead to restore them the first time they are accessed. This speeds up system startup.

- *Enable WinPopup:* Selecting this option instructs WFW to automatically start the WinPopup broadcasting utility at system initialization (see Figure 12.19).

Options for Enterprise Networking   Log On to Windows NT or LAN Manager Domain is a feature that permits the WFW computer to try to join a Windows NT domain or an older LAN Manager domain. Neither is relevant on a peer network.

Get the Right Drivers

Manufacturers of computer peripherals, especially NIC manufacturers, usually build their cards to support multiple operating systems. For example, most NIC cards are supplied with software drivers for WFW, Windows 95, Windows 98, Windows NT 4, OS/2, and NetWare. It might be necessary to provide the entire path to the WFW driver directory, which must be supplied in order for the installation process to locate the correct driver. A software driver written for a different operating system will not work for a WFW installation.

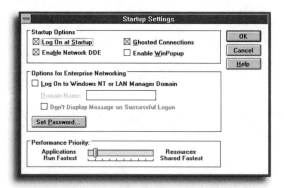

FIGURE 12.19
Configuring network startup options.

Performance Priority   Performance Priority provides a means for configuring the WFW computer to provide additional resources to network sharing. Sliding the bar toward the Resources Shared Fastest option instructs WFW to allocate additional resources to providing file and print servers for network clients. Moving the bar to the Applications Run Fastest option instructs WFW to allocate more resources to applications running on the local computer at the expense of network clients that might be attempting to access the computer's shared resources.

Change Logon Password

Clicking the **Set Password** button on the Microsoft Windows dialog (previously shown in Figure 12.19) produces the Change Logon Password dialog (see Figure 12.20). The **Change Password for User** field permits the selection of a user ID. The **Change Password On** field applies to Windows domains and is not used on peer networks. The **Old Password** field is used to type the current password for the selected user ID. The **New Password** and **Confirm New Password** fields are used to enter a new password for the selected account. The dialog permits a user ID belonging to someone who is not the currently logged-on user to be changed providing that the current user knows the current (old) password associated with the selected account.

Event Log Settings

The WFW Event Log serves the same basic function as does the Microsoft Windows 2000 Pro Event Log snap-in (see Figure 12.21). It provides a location to which WFW can write system messages.

To instruct WFW to begin maintaining log data, click the **Event Log** button. The rest of the options on the dialog then become enabled.

FIGURE 12.20
Changing a user password.

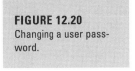

FIGURE 12.21
The WFW Event Log records system messages.

The **Record These Events** list displays the categories of data that WFW is logging during normal operations (see Figure 12.22). The **Do Not Record These Events** list displays categories of data that WFW is capable of logging but is not currently recording. The **Add** and **Remove** buttons are used to move logging categories from one list to another. The **Add All** button allows selection of all available data.

At the bottom of the dialog is the **Limit Event Log Size** field. It defines the maximum size that the event log can grow to before old events begin to be overwritten by new events. It is measured in kilobytes. The default size is 4KB.

Event Viewer Not Available in Windows 9X

The Event viewer did not make its way into Windows 95 or Windows 98. It is available in Windows NT 4. It also available as a snap-in in Windows 2000.

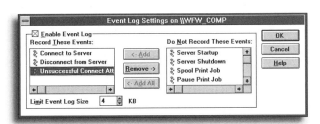

FIGURE 12.22
Selecting events to monitor.

Sharing Local Resources

After a Windows for Workgroups computer has been configured, it is ready to access network resources and share its own resources. WFW supports both print and file sharing. Before either of these types of resources can be shared, sharing must be enabled as described earlier in this chapter in step 5 of "Adding, Removing, and Configuring NICs, Clients, Protocols, and Services."

File Sharing

File sharing is established in the File Manager application. An entire drive or individual folder can be shared. WFW can assign passwords to its shared folders for security. The available types of share security are listed here:

- Read-only
- Full
- Depends on password

Sharing a local folder

1. Start the **File Manager** application located in the **Main** group.

2. Select a drive or folder to be shared and select **Share As** from the **Disk** menu. This brings up the Share Directory dialog (see Figure 12.23).

3. Type a name for the share and a comment in the **Share Name** and **Comment** fields.

4. Select **Re-share at Startup** to make this share permanent.

5. Select the appropriate type of security and supply a password.

6. Click **OK**.

FIGURE 12.23
Establishing a shared network folder.

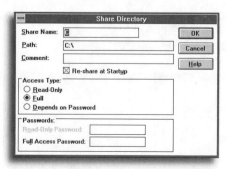

7. WFW displays a prompt requesting confirmation of the password. If this share is being established for the first time, leave the **Re-enter Old Password** field blank and type the password in the **Confirm New Password** field. Click **OK**.

8. WFW displays a message warning about the effects of changing share passwords. Click **OK**.

Print Sharing

Print sharing is established in the Print Manager application. A password can be assigned for security. Any network user who knows this password can submit print jobs to the printer.

Sharing a local print device

1. Start the **Print Manager** application located in the **Main** group.

2. Select a locally installed printer, and click on **Share Printer As** from the **Printer** menu. This selection brings up the Share Printer dialog (see Figure 12.24).

FIGURE 12.24
Establishing a shared network printer.

3. Type a name, comment, and password in the **Share As, Comment**, and **Password** fields.

4. Leave the **Re-share at Startup** option selected to make this a permanent share.

5. Click **OK**.

6. WFW displays a message warning about the effects of changing share passwords. Click **OK**.

Do not attempt to close the Print Manager after establishing a shared printer. This causes WFW to terminate the sharing of the printer. WFW will automatically start the Print Manager the next time WFW is started if the shared printer was set to be permanently shared.

Connecting to Network Resources

Access to network folders is established in the File Manager application by the assignment of local drive letters to network folders. When the mapping is to a shared folder on a Windows 2000 or Windows NT 4 computer, the username and password of the user at the WFW computer must be synchronized with the user's account on the Windows 2000 or Windows NT 4 computer; otherwise, access will be denied. Accounts do not have to be synchronized when mapping to Windows 95 and Windows 98 computers. If a share password is established on these computers, a security dialog appears on the WFW computer, allowing the user to provide the share password for the selected resource.

Connecting to a network folder

1. Start the **File Manager** application located in the **Main** group.

2. Select **Connect Network Drive** from the **Disk** menu, and Windows displays the Connect Network Drive dialog (see Figure 12.25).

FIGURE 12.25
Mapping a network folder.

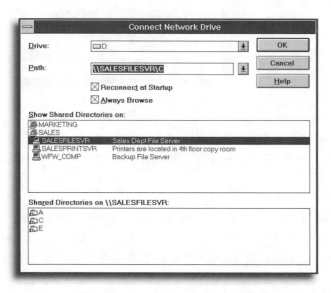

3. Select an available drive letter from the **Drive** drop-down list.

4. Select **Reconnect at Startup** to restore this mapping when the computer is restarted.

5. Navigate to the computer where the shared folder resides in the **S**how Shared Directories On area.

6. A list of all shared folders on the selected network computer appears. Select the desired folder and click **OK**.

Connecting to a network printer

1. Start the **Print Manager** application located in the **Main** group.

2. Select **C**onnect **Network Printer** from the **P**rinter menu. The Connect Network Printer dialog appears (see Figure 12.26).

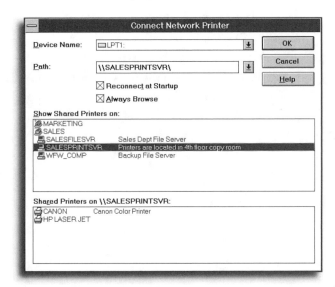

FIGURE 12.26
Setting up a connection to a network folder.

3. Select an available port from the **D**evice **Name** drop-down list to assign to the network printer.

4. Navigate to the computer where the shared printer resides in the **S**how Shared Printers On area.

5. A list of all shared printers on the selected network computer appears. Select the desired printer and click **OK**.

6. Click **Y**es when prompted to install the network printer on the selected port.

7. The Printers dialog appears. Select **A**dd.

8. The Printers dialog expands to display a list of printers for which WFW has device drivers. It is unlikely that WFW will have a matching entry for your printer. If it does, select it from the list and click **Install**. Otherwise, select **Install Unlisted or Updated Printer** and click **Install**.

9. When prompted, supply WFW with the location of the disk or CD-ROM containing a WFW printer driver for the network printer, and click **OK**.

10. The Add Unlisted or Updated Printer dialog appears and displays the model type of the network printer. Click **OK**.

11. WFW might require some files from the WFW installation disks. Supply them as requested.

12. WFW completes the network printer installation and the printer appears in the Installed Printers section on the Printers dialog. Click **Close**.

chapter

13

Installing and Configuring Windows 9X Networking

Overview of Windows 95 and Windows 98

Windows for Workgroups was Microsoft's first operating system to include integrated network support. Windows 95 built on this initial offering by adding TCP/IP protocol support, an improved graphical user interface, and easier network administration. Like Windows for Workgroups, Windows 95 features integrated 32-bit networking. Windows 95 further refined the network components and added Plug and Play support for easier configuration and an improved graphical user interface complete with software wizards to make network setup, configuration, and management considerably easier than in Windows for Workgroups.

Windows 98 represents the most recent evolution in this line of operating systems. It features improvements in performance, an integrated Internet shell, support for universal serial bus hardware, faster program execution, more efficient use of disk space, and support for MMX and virtual private networking. With all these improvements, Windows 98 is a more capable and user-friendly network operating system.

SEE ALSO

➤ *For more information on Internet Explorer or Outlook Express, see page 244.*

SEE ALSO

➤ *To learn more about sharing an Internet connection, see page 260.*

Windows 98 is designed to provide robust network services, and it does this very well. However, the operating system provides many of these new features at the expense of security. Windows 98 lacks a sophisticated security model on the level provided by Windows 2000 or Windows NT 4.0. The result is that although it makes building networks easy, it also makes them more open to outside attack, which makes the job of the network administrator more difficult.

Microsoft markets Windows 98 to the home user. As such, its focus is not on security but on delivering functionality and ease of use. For customers in businesses in which security is a major concern, Microsoft offers Windows 2000.

Windows 98 Second Edition

In June of 1999, Microsoft released Windows 98 Second Edition. This version of Windows 98 fixes many bugs found in the original version, adds improved support for universal serial bus hardware, and provides better support for networking. Among its new features are Internet Explorer 5 and Outlook Express 5. This version of Windows also provides support for Internet connection sharing, which allows multiple network computers to share access to the Internet using a single modem and an ISP account.

Overview of Features

Microsoft targets Windows 9X operating systems at home users and low-end corporate desktops. Microsoft targets Windows NT Workstation 4 and Windows 2000 Pro at corporate users and high-end desktops. Windows 9X operating systems provide a full suite of networking tools that enable them to perform both as a client on a client-server network and as an effective participant on a peer network. Both provide file and print sharing services and can access network resources.

In addition to these common features, Windows 98 provides network support for the following:

- Automatic IP addressing for networks based on the TCP/IP protocol
- Built-in support for Virtual Private Networking
- Improvements in the Microsoft Logon
- A built-in dial-up server
- Complete integration with Internet Explorer
- Automatic operating-system update through Internet access
- Software wizards to make Internet connection easier
- Support for the universal serial bus
- Fixes to thousands of bugs found in Windows 95

Security Options

Windows 9X is primarily designed to serve as a network client and not a server, although it does maintain some qualities of both. In Windows networking there are two primary types of security, NTFS and share security. Windows 2000 and Windows NT 4 provide for both types of security, but the Windows 9X operating systems provide only share security. On these operating systems, share security essentially provides protection for a given resource such as a network drive or printer by assigning a password and permitting access only to users who provide the password. Share security becomes cumbersome as the number of shared devices requiring security increases. Maintaining and remembering the password for a few shared devices is decidedly easier than doing so for dozens of them.

Works in Both Windows 95 and Windows 98

Looking at Windows 98, it is very difficult to distinguish its networking features from those of Windows 95. As a result, just about everything covered in this and the next chapter can be applied to both operating systems with little or no adjustment. When referring to common aspects of both operating systems, these two chapters refer to both operating systems collectively as Windows 9X and refer to each operating system by name when making specific references or when pointing out unique differences. Although Windows 98 offers many improvements over Windows 95, most have been made in the base operating system rather than in the networking components. For illustrative purposes, these two chapters use Windows 98 screen shots.

Transport Protocols

Windows 9X operating systems support the following transport protocols:

- NetBEUI
- IPX/SPX
- TCP/IP

System Network Defaults

Each Windows operating system has its own unique set of system defaults that are automatically installed when a network adapter is detected on a computer.

Windows 95 Installation Defaults:

- Client for Microsoft Network
- Network adapter card driver
- NetBEUI

Windows 98 Installation Defaults:

- Client for Microsoft Network
- Microsoft Family Client
- Network adapter card driver
- TCP/IP—network card

Working with Network Components

Windows 9X networking components include NICs, protocols, clients, and services. These components provide the same capabilities and features as their Windows 2000 counterparts.

Installing a Network Interface Card Driver

Windows 9X operating systems supply a hardware installation wizard that assists in the installation and configuration of a NIC. The wizard can be instructed to attempt to auto-detect the NIC or can present a dialog that permits a NIC card to be manually specified. It is usually easiest to allow Windows to auto-detect the card and configure it. If Windows cannot perform this operation, the NIC can still be added manually.

SEE ALSO

➤ *For information on installing a NIC, see page 82.*

Installing a NIC on a Windows 98 computer

1. Select **Start**, **Settings**, and then **Control Panel**. The Control Panel dialog appears.

2. Double-click on the **Add New Hardware** icon to initiate the Add New Hardware Wizard (see Figure 13.1).

3. Click on the **Next** button to start the hardware setup process.

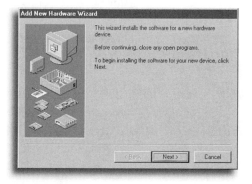

FIGURE 13.1
The Add New Hardware Wizard installation dialog box.

4. Windows displays a dialog stating that it will search for Plug and Play devices on the computer. Click **Next**.

5. Next, Windows displays a dialog asking you to wait while it begins the search process. After a few moments, a new dialog appears (see Figure 13.2). Windows 98 can automatically attempt to detect new hardware. Windows also gives you the option to specify the new hardware either from a list of known vendors or by supplying Windows with a disk or CD-ROM with a vendor-supplied software driver. If you know that the Plug and Play process will not detect your NIC, select **No** and then click on the **Next** button. Otherwise, leave the default option of **Yes** and click on the **Next** button.

6. If you selected the default option to have Windows 98 auto-detect your NIC, a confirmation dialog appears. Select **Next** to continue.

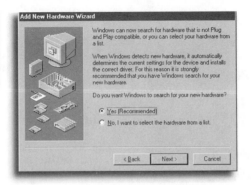

FIGURE 13.2
The hardware detection option.

7. Windows begins the hardware detection process (see Figure 13.3). As the dialog states, this process will take several minutes.

FIGURE 13.3
Hardware detection in progress.

8. If the wizard fails to detect the network adapter, a dialog stating such appears. Click on **Next** to specify the network adapter card. If Windows successfully finds the network adapter, the dialog offers its findings. Click the **Next** button and skip to step 11.

9. Windows produces a dialog and prompts for the selection of the type of card to be installed (see Figure 13.4). Click **Network Adapters** and then click **Next**. The Select Device dialog appears.

10. Locate the manufacturer of the network adapter from the Manufacturers list and then select your specific card from the Models list (see Figure 13.5). Click **OK**. If the network adapter cannot be located, click the **Have Disk** button, and when prompted, supply either the disk or the CD-ROM that came with the NIC card to provide Windows with the software driver required for the operating system to manage the NIC.

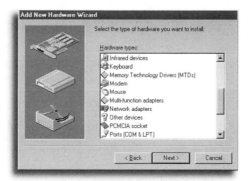

FIGURE 13.4
Selecting the type of hardware to install.

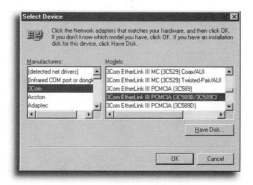

FIGURE 13.5
Selecting the card manufacturer and type.

11. Windows displays a confirmation dialog. Click the **Next** button to continue.

12. If the Windows 98 CD-ROM is not in the CD-ROM drive, you might be prompted to insert it and then click on **OK**.

13. Specify the location of the Windows source files on the CD-ROM. The files should be located in the \WIN98 directory. Click **OK**.

14. Windows copies the required files from the CD-ROM to the hard drive. After Windows completes the process of copying files, it prompts you to reboot the computer so that it can initialize and manage the newly installed network adapter. Click on **Yes**.

Installing a Network Protocol

At least one default protocol is installed as part of the network adapter installation. Windows supports several major LAN protocols. For example, the NetBEUI protocol is installed as shown next.

Installing the NetBEUI protocol

1. From the Control Panel, double-click on the **Network** icon. The Network dialog appears (see Figure 13.6).

FIGURE 13.6
The main Network dialog.

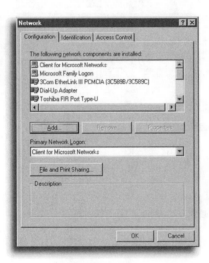

2. Click on the **Add** button to display the Select Network Component Type dialog (see Figure 13.7). Four categories are displayed.

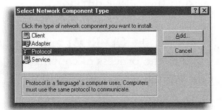

FIGURE 13.7
Selection of the network component type.

3. Select **Protocol** and click on **Add** to display the Select Network Protocol dialog.

4. Under Manufacturers, select **Microsoft**.

5. Under Network Protocols, select **NetBEUI**, and click **OK** (see Figure 13.8).

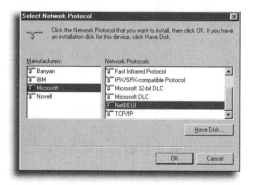

FIGURE 13.8
Selection of the network protocol.

6. The Network dialog appears. Click **OK**.

7. Windows begins the protocol installation process. You might be prompted to insert the Windows CD-ROM.

8. After the protocol installation process is complete, you are prompted to restart the computer. Until the computer is restarted, the new protocol will not be available to the system. Click **Yes** to restart the system.

Installing a Network Client

At least one default client is installed as part of the NIC installation. Windows supports the execution of multiple concurrent networking clients. For example, if the network supports a NetWare server, the Client for NetWare Network is required on any computer that will communicate with that server. The process of installing a new client is outlined next.

Installing a client

1. From the Control Panel, double-click on the **Network** icon. The Network dialog appears.

2. Click on the **Add** button to display the Select Network Component Type dialog. Four categories are displayed.

3. Select **Client** and click on the **Add** button to display the Select Network Client dialog.

4. Under Manufacturers, select **Microsoft**.

5. Under Network Protocols, select one of the available network clients, and click **OK**.

6. The main Network dialog appears. Click **OK**.

Connecting to Other Networks

Microsoft knows that its customers might not always be connecting to Microsoft networks. Therefore, it provides clients for connecting to different networks, including Banyan and Novell, which can be selected during client installation. However, for a computer attached to a Windows peer network, the Client for Microsoft Networks is all you need.

---

7. Windows begins the client installation process. You might be prompted to insert the Windows CD-ROM.

8. After the client installation process is complete, you are prompted to restart the computer. Until the computer is restarted, the new client will not be available to the system. Click **Yes** to restart the system.

Installing a Network Service

At least one default service is installed as part of the NIC installation. Windows can provide multiple concurrent services. For example, the File and Printer Sharing for Microsoft Networks Service is installed by the process shown next.

Installing file and print services

1. From the Control Panel double-click on the **Network** icon. The Network dialog appears.

2. Click on the **Add** button to display the Select Network Component Type dialog.

3. Select **Service** and click on the **Add** button to display the Select Network Service dialog.

4. Under Manufacturers, select **Microsoft**.

5. Under Network Services, select **File and Printer Sharing for Microsoft Networks**, and click **OK**.

6. The main Network dialog appears. Click **OK**.

7. Windows begins the service installation process. You might be prompted to insert the Windows CD-ROM.

8. After the service installation process is complete, you are prompted to restart the computer. Until the computer is restarted, the new service will not be available to the system. Click **Yes** to restart the system.

Removing Network Adapters, Protocols, Clients, and Services

The same process outlined previously is used to remove network adapters, protocols, clients, and services.

Uninstalling a network component

1. From the Control Panel, double-click on the **Network** icon. The Network dialog appears.

2. Select the **Configuration** tab.

3. Select the item that is to be removed, and click on the **Remove** button.

4. Windows removes the selected item. Click on the **OK** button. Windows prompts you to restart the system. Click **Yes**.

Managing Workgroup Membership

Establishing workgroup membership requires entering a workgroup name in the Workgroup field on the Identification tab of the Network dialog. Entering a completely new workgroup name establishes the workgroup on the network with the computer as its only member. Entering the name of a workgroup currently in use by other network computers adds the computer to the workgroup. Figure 13.9 shows a computer named SalesPrintSvr that is a member of a workgroup called Sales.

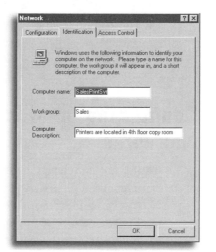

Be Careful What You Remove

Removing a top-level resource such as a NIC results in the unbinding of all lower-level resources that have been bound to it. These lower-level resource include clients and services. If a lower-level resource was bound only to the removed top-level resource, it will be completely uninstalled. If you decide to later reinstall the top-level resource, you might have to reinstall some or all of the lower-level resources.

FIGURE 13.9
The Identification tab in the Network dialog manages the computer name and workgroup membership.

Changing computer name, workgroup assignment, or description

1. From the Windows 9X desktop, right-click on the **Network Neighborhood** icon and then click on **Properties**. The Network dialog appears.

2. Click on the **Identification** tab.

3. Type a new computer name in the **Computer Name** field. This name can be up to 15 characters long but cannot contain spaces. It must be unique on the network, meaning that no other computer or workgroup can use this name. In the **Workgroup** field, type the name of the workgroup that this computer will establish or join. This name can be up to 15 characters long and must be unique on the network. In the **Computer Description** field, type an optional description for the computer. This description can be up to 48 characters long.

4. Click **OK**. Windows asks for permission to restart the computer so that the changes can take effect. Click **Yes**. When the computer finishes rebooting, the new settings are in effect.

Workgroup membership is simply an organizational tool that facilitates easier navigation of network resources. The assumption is that the network can be organized in the same manner as people organize their companies. When users browse the network on a Windows 9X computer using the Network Neighborhood or Windows Explorer utilities, they are initially presented with a view of three items:

- An icon representing their computer
- An icon representing every computer in their assigned workgroup
- An icon representing the entire network

Configuring the Client for Microsoft Networks

Configuration of the Client for Microsoft Networks involves making two choices. The first is whether the computer will join a Windows NT domain. The second choice is between the two network logon methods. The Quick Logon option logs a user on to the network without checking the status of any mapped network drives. The Logon and Restore Network Connections option logs the user on to the network and immediately checks the status of mapped network drives and notifies the user of any failed connections.

You can access configuration options for the Client for Microsoft Networks on the main Network dialog by selecting **Client for Microsoft Networks** from the **Configuration** tab and clicking on the **Properties** button (see Figure 13.10).

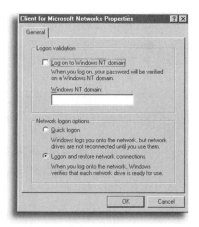

FIGURE 13.10
Configure the validation and logon options here.

The Log on to Windows NT Domain option in the Logon Validation section is used only for Windows 9X computers that will connect to a Windows NT domain. Therefore, this field is not used on peer networks.

Network Logon Options section has two options that control how Windows handles mapped drives. Quick Logon logs the user into the network but does not attempt to reestablish connections with any existing network connections. Any mapped drives that are unavailable are not reported because there is no attempt to reconnect them. Logon and Restore Network Connections logs the user on to the network and attempts to restore all network connections. Any mapped drivers that are unavailable are reported as errors with an option to delete the mapping or keep it available for future use.

Installing and Configuring File and Print Sharing

Windows 9X computers can act as both clients and servers. Adding the Client for Microsoft Services allows Windows 9X computers to access and use resources provided by other computers on the network. In addition to this client role, a Windows 9X computer can

387

Windows 98 Autoconfigures to Work with All Installed Protocols

By default, Windows 98 configures file and print sharing to work with all currently configured protocols. This means that if TCP/IP is currently installed when file and print sharing is installed, it will be configured to work over TCP/IP-based connections. Any computer that fits the preceding description opens a security hole if it also connects to the Internet. Anyone on the Internet then is able to access the computer's shared resources. This is especially dangerous if the shared resource does not have an associated password. In this case, it leaves the system open to attack.

For example, an Internet user using Windows 98 might open his Network Neighborhood utility and

continues...

share its local resources with other clients on the network, thus acting as a server.

The Client for Microsoft Networks is a prerequisite for file and print sharing. If the Client for Microsoft Networks is not already installed, Windows 9X automatically installs it as part of the installation process of installing file and print sharing. A Windows 9X computer can share local folders and printers. The File and Printer Sharing Service only enables Windows 9X computers to make local resources available over the network. It does not actually share specific local resources. Resources are shared on a resource-by-resource basis.

Enabling file and print sharing does not make local resources available to the network. It only enables the capability to share local resources. After selecting file or print sharing or both, the user must select a specific file or printer and individually step through the sharing process before the resource is available on the network.

Managing file and print sharing

1. From the Network Configuration dialog, click on the **File and Print Sharing** button. The File and Print Sharing dialog appears (see Figure 13.11). If file and print sharing for Microsoft network clients is not installed, Windows 9X installs it as part of this process.

2. To enable file sharing, select **I Want to Be Able to Give Others Access to My Files**.

3. To enable print sharing, select **I want to Be Able to Allow Others to Print to My Printer(s)**.

4. Click **OK**.

FIGURE 13.11
Managing file and print sharing.

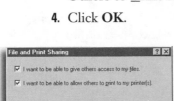

5. To complete the configuration of the selected services, Windows 9X prompts the user for the Windows 9X CD-ROM. Insert the CD-ROM into the CD-ROM drive and click **OK**.

6. Windows 9X requests a restart of the computer before file or printer sharing will be enabled. Click **Yes**.

Configuration of file and print sharing is performed on each individual shared resource. Configuration involves such selections as the types of access allowed on a resource, its hours of availability, and the application of password security.

SEE ALSO

➤ For instructions on how to configure file sharing, see page 412.

Configuring a Workstation for Network Performance

For the network to operate efficiently, it is important that individual computers be configured according to the role they are assigned to perform. A Windows 9X computer can be optimized for three basic computer configurations:

- Desktop computer
- Mobile or docking system
- Network server

Computers that will not share any locally attached resources over the network should be set up as desktop computers. Computers that share local resources with the rest of the network should have the Network Server option selected. Laptop computers should be configured with the Portable option.

Selecting the appropriate option is important because it adjusts the manner is which Windows 9X allocates memory cache. *Cache* is a portion of the local memory Windows 9X uses to store information retrieved from the hard drive. Windows 9X sets aside a portion of available memory to retrieve more data stored on a disk than is required in an effort to anticipate what might be asked for next. When Windows 9X correctly anticipates the next disk read request, system performance improves because the data needed is already in cache ready for retrieval. This saves Windows 9X from having to go through the much slower process of locating and retrieving the data from the drive.

Selecting the Desktop Computer setting tells Windows 9X to set aside a smaller area of cache, thus making more memory available to programs. Selecting the mobile or docking system setting tells

---

...continued

enter random IP addresses using the command syntax *XXX.XXX.XXX.XXX* *C*, where *XXX.XXX.XXX.XXX* represents the IP address and *C* represents the default name for a share of the local hard drive. If this IP address belongs to one of the company's computers, that computer is now subject to attack. If Full Control has been set for the shared resource and no share password is in place, the Internet user can copy or delete selected files or plant a virus. If a printer is shared on the computer, the Internet user can submit a flood of print jobs to try to exhaust the printer's supply of paper or ink.

In an effort to warn the user about this danger, Windows 98 might produce a message prompt warning of the dangers and offer to turn off file and print sharing over TCP/IP. Windows 95 does not display any warnings, though the same security hole exists in that operating system.

If You Have More than 16MB of RAM...

If a computer has more than 16MB of RAM, it is generally advisable to choose the Network Server option even if the computer is to be used only as a standalone system.

Windows 9X to allocate a larger cache pool. This might reduce the power required to access the hard drive by reducing the number of times that Windows 9X needs to request data retrieval. Selecting the Network Server setting allocates the largest amount of cache. This provides less memory for local programs but provides more cache, which improves network performance.

Other configuration settings include parameters for controlling virtual memory and CD-ROM. Windows 9X assumes control of virtual memory by default, and it is best not to change this setting unless there is a specific need to do so. CD-ROM configuration is also automatic and consists mainly of identifying the speed of the drive and allocating the amount of cache memory to associate with it. As with virtual memory, it is best to leave these settings with their default values unless there is an application that specifically requires the adjustments.

Assigning a network role to a computer

1. From the Windows 9X Control Panel, double-click on the **System** icon. The System Properties dialog appears. The General tab is displayed by default.

2. The **General** tab presents basic information about the system, such as the operating system version, the processor type, and the amount of memory installed on the computer, as shown in Figure 13.12. Select the **Performance** tab.

FIGURE 13.12
The General tab on the System Properties dialog.

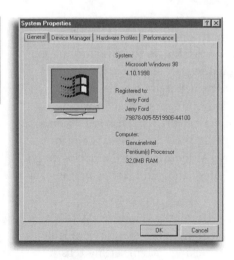

3. In the Advanced Settings section, click on the **File System** button, shown in Figure 13.13. The File System Properties dialog appears.

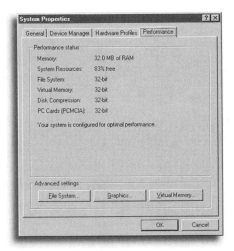

FIGURE 13.13
The System Properties dialog.

4. The assigned role for the computer is configured in the Settings section on the Hard Disk tab (see Figure 13.14). There are three roles to select. They are located in the **Typical Role of This Computer** drop-down list. For peer computers the correct setting is usually the **Network Server** option, because by definition most peer computers spend at least part of their time and resources providing locally shared resources with other computers on the network. Unless you have an application that specifies a need to change the **Read-Ahead Optimization** settings, it is best to leave the default setting in place. Moving the Read-Ahead Optimization setting toward **Full** instructs Windows 2000 to allocate additional memory to the process of trying to anticipate what will be retrieved next when reading data from a hard disk. When it guesses correctly, system performance is improved.

5. Click **OK** to complete the configuration process.

FIGURE 13.14
Windows 98 file-system properties.

Working with Modems

Although Windows 9X operating systems support both Plug and Play and manual installation of modems, Windows 95 and the original version of Windows 98 do not provide built-in support for modem sharing. However, Windows 98 Second Edition does provide this support.

Installing a Modem

Whether the modem is an internal or external modem, the installation process is essentially the same. After inserting an internal modem into an open expansion slot or plugging an external modem into an open serial port, power on the computer and Windows 9X should be able to auto-detect it. If Windows 9X fails to auto-detect the new modem, it must be added manually. The following example demonstrates the installation of a modem on a Windows 98 computer.

Installing a modem on a Windows 98 computer

1. The Plug and Play installation process displays a dialog similar to the one shown in Figure 13.15 when it detects the modem. Information about the device is displayed. Click **Next** to continue.

2. The Add New Hardware Wizard requests instructions on how to find the software driver for the modem (see Figure 13.16). Windows 98 recommends selecting **Search for the Best Driver for Your Device** option. This provides a means for specifying the location of the driver that was supplied on a disk or

CD-ROM by the modem manufacturer. Click **Next** to continue with the installation.

FIGURE 13.15
The Add New Hardware Wizard displays information about the modem that was detected by Plug and Play.

FIGURE 13.16
Select the location where the modem's software driver is located.

3. Windows presents a dialog displaying a list of locations it can search for an appropriate software driver (see Figure 13.17). Windows 98 allows you to specify multiple locations in case you are unsure of the specific location of the driver. Select the appropriate locations and click **Next**. If the driver is supplied on a disk or CD-ROM, remember to insert it into the computer before proceeding.

4. Windows begins its search for a software driver. Windows reports the success of its driver search by displaying the name and location where it was found (see Figure 13.18). Click **Next** to install the driver.

FIGURE 13.17
A list of locations in which to search for a software driver.

FIGURE 13.18
Windows reports the results of its search.

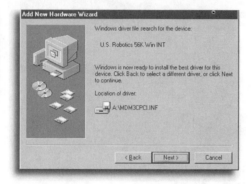

5. Windows completes the driver installation. Click **Finish** (see Figure 13.19).

6. Windows displays a dialog that shows the newly installed modem. Select **Yes, I Am Finished Installing Devices** and click **Next** (see Figure 13.19).

FIGURE 13.19
Windows asks for confirmation that all devices have been installed.

7. Click **Finish**.

Modem Configuration

After a modem is installed, it can be configured and tested from its Properties dialog. To access a modem's properties, double-click the **Modems** icon on the Windows 9X Control Panel. A list of all modems installed on the computer appears. The General tab provides access for adding and removing modems, as well as viewing and configuring their properties. Dialing preferences are managed here as well. The Diagnostics tab provides information about each modem's software driver and provides a means of testing modems. The first time you access the Modems utility, the Location Information dialog appears, requiring area-code and other dialing information.

Viewing and changing modem properties

1. From the Modems Properties dialog, select a modem and click the **Properties** button. The Properties dialog for the selected modem appears (see Figure 13.20).

FIGURE 13.20
The Modems Properties dialog displays entries for all installed modems.

2. There will be at least two tabs, General and Connection. Other tabs might be present, depending on the features offered by the modem. The General tab provides access to viewing and changing the communications port where the modem is attached, controlling the volume of the modem's internal speaker, and setting the maximum speed the modem supports (see Figure 13.21). The Maximum Speed setting specifies the computer-to-modem speed and not the speed at which the modem will be able to communicate with other modems. Specify the maximum speed

your modem supports. If you do not see an exact match, select the next-highest setting.

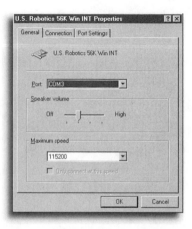

3. The Connection tab provides access to multiple settings (see Figure 13.22). Unless there is a specific reason to change these settings, it is best to leave the default settings in place. The Port Settings button allows for configuration of receive and transmit buffers. The Advanced button provides access to advanced options such as whether to require data compression. It also allows configuration and access to a log containing information about modem activity.

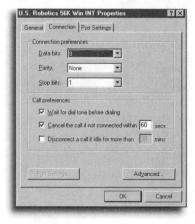

Changing modem dialing properties

1. From the Modems Properties dialog click on **Dialing Properties**. The Dialing Properties dialog for the selected modem appears (see Figure 13.23).

2. Computers such as laptop computers are often used in multiple locations. If the country/region or area-code information changes from location to location, Windows can be configured to store information about each individual location. This allows for quick retrieval of dialing information about each area. Dialing locations can be added or removed via the **New** or **Remove** buttons. When a new location is being created, the information from the previous location is used as a template. The drop-down list provides a list of all existing locations. The rest of the fields on the dialog configure the currently displayed dialing location.

3. After making any required changes to a dialing location, click **OK** to complete the process.

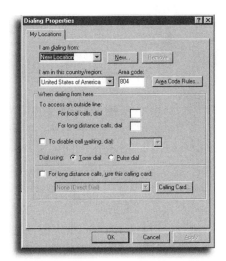

FIGURE 13.23
The Windows 98 Dialing Properties dialog allows new dialing locations to be established and existing locations to be edited or removed.

Viewing driver information

1. Double-click on the **Modems** icon in the Windows 9X Control Panel. The Modems Properties dialog appears.

2. Select the **Diagnostics** tab. A list of installed modems appears (see Figure 13.24).

FIGURE 13.24
The Modems Properties
Diagnostics tab provides
access to driver informa-
tion and modem diag-
nostics.

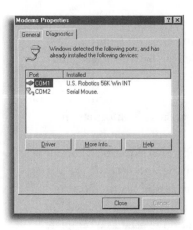

3. To get information on the software driver used to manage a modem, select the device from the list of installed modems, and click on **Driver**. Windows displays a prompt that contains information about the software driver, including its name and size (see Figure 13.25).

FIGURE 13.25
The Current
Communications Driver
prompt displays informa-
tion about the selected
modem's software driver.

Performing diagnostics on a modem

1. Double-click on the **Modems** icon in the Windows 9X Control Panel. The Modems Properties dialog appears.

2. Select the **Diagnostics** tab. A list of installed modems appears.

3. Select a modem and click on **More Info**. Windows responds by displaying a message that Windows is gathering information. After a few moments, the message disappears, and a dialog similar to the one shown in Figure 13.26 appears.

Among the information provided is the assigned communications port and the highest speed at which the modem can operate. The bottom portion of the screen displays a series of information gathered by Windows when it's communicating with the modem.

FIGURE 13.26
The More Info dialog displays the results of Windows 9X's attempt to communicate with the modem.

Managing Dial-Up Communications

Windows 9X operating systems provide limited support as a dial-up server, as well as complete dial-up client support. Dial-up communications can be protected by share passwords and can provide gateway access to the network. However, dial-in access is limited to one connection at a time per Windows 9X computer.

Configuring a Dial-Up Server

A dial-up server is a computer with a modem that is set up to access incoming connection requests from other computers. Windows 98 provides dial-up client and dial-up server services. However, out of the box Windows 95 supports only dial-up client capability. Microsoft provides Windows 95 with this capability in the form of an add-on product called Microsoft Plus for Windows 95.

When Dial-Up Networking is installed, Windows 98 automatically installs the dial-up adapter, TCP/IP, and the Microsoft Family Logon Client. These default characteristics are sufficient for dialing into the Internet. However, depending on the protocols in use on a small network, they might not suffice. Many small peer networks do not support TCP/IP as the primary protocol. NetBEUI might be the protocol of choice. If this is the case, the NetBEUI protocol must be added on the workstation, along with the dial-up adapter.

By default, Windows 98 uses PPP as its default protocol based on the assumption that the Internet is the most common PPP connection. However, Windows automatically binds any already-installed

Only One Dial-Up User Supported in Windows 98

Windows 98 supports only a single dial-in user at a time. If your network requires support for more than one dial-up connection at a time, consider setting up Windows 2000 Professional to support remote access. Windows 2000 Professional supports up to 10 users, assuming that the appropriate hardware is present. Windows 2000 Server supports up to 256 simultaneous dial-up connections. However, another option would be to set up multiple Windows 98 computers as dial-up servers to provide additional connections.

protocols to Dial-Up Networking when it is installed. Windows 98 uses PPP to manage the communications session between the dial-up client and the dial-up server.

Dial-up networking is automatically installed when Windows 98 is set up. However, the dial-up server must be manually installed.

Installing a dial-up server

1. Double-click on the **Add/Remove Programs** icon in the Windows Control Panel.

2. Select the **Windows Setup** tab.

3. After a few moments, Windows presents a list of component categories. Select **Communications** and click on the **Details** button. A window appears with a list of communication utility options.

4. Select **Dial-Up Server** and click **OK**. The Add/Remove Programs Properties dialog reappears. Click **Apply**. Windows might request that the Windows 98 CD-ROM be placed in the CD-ROM drive. Windows then proceeds to copy files and install the dial-up server.

5. Click **OK**.

Managing a Dial-Up Server

After the dial-up server application has been installed, it must be configured. The dial-up server is accessed from the Dial-Up Networking folder.

Configuring a dial-up server

1. Select **Start**, **Programs**, **Accessories**, **Communications**, and **Dial-Up Networking**.

2. The dial-up server is located on the **Connections** menu. It is visible on this menu only if it has been installed. Select **Connections** and then **Dial-Up Server**.

3. The Dial-Up Server dialog appears (see Figure 13.27). A tab is displayed for each modem attached to the computer. To enable the dial-up server to accept incoming connections on a given modem, select the modem's tab and select **Allow Caller Access**.

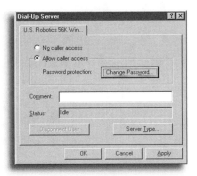

FIGURE 13.27
The Dial-Up Server dialog provides the means for configuring dial-up server access.

4. If security is required, click on the **Change Password** button. The Dial-Up Networking Password dialog appears (see Figure 13.28). Because this is a new installation of a dial-up server, there is no old password. Leave the Old Password field blank. Enter a new password in both the **New Password** and the **Confirm New Password** fields, and then click **OK**. The dial-up server is now ready for use. Either click **Apply** to instruct the dial-up server to start monitoring and then **OK** to close the dialog, or click **Server Type** to configure advanced dial-up server options. When the dial-up server is activated, an icon representing the dial-up server appears on the Windows taskbar. Double-click the icon to display the Dial-Up Server dialog.

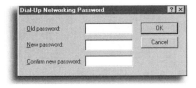

FIGURE 13.28
The Dial-Up Networking Password dialog provides a means for establishing password protection on the dial-up server.

Additional Options

Additional configuration options include entering an optional comment in the **Comment** field to describe the purpose of the dial-up server. The **Status** field provides the current status of the connection. Idle indicates that there is currently no active connection. If a connection is currently active, the dial-up server offers the option of forcibly disconnecting the user with the **Disconnect User** button.

Windows 2000 Provides a More Secure Dial-Up Server

For a more secure dial-up server, consider using Windows 2000 Professional. Windows 2000 Pro supports the NTFS file system, which is more secure than the FAT file system supported by Windows 98. Windows 2000 also supports NTFS security, which is more secure than the share-level security supported by Windows 98.

Server Type, Compression, and Encryption

Selecting the **Server Type** button produces the Server Types dialog (see Figure 13.29). From here, additional configurations can be performed:

- The type of dial-up server can be set
- Software compression can be enabled
- The requirement of an encrypted password can be set

The type of dial-up server can be set to one of three options:

- Default
- PPP: Internet, Windows NT Server, Windows 98
- Windows for Workgroups and Windows NT 3.1

By default, software compression and encryption are enabled. Software compression increases the speed of the connection. It will be used only if both the dial-up server and the client are using a compatible compression type. Encrypting the password increases security. However, as with compression, the client must also support this feature.

FIGURE 13.29
The Server Types dialog provides advanced configuration options.

Be Careful When Kicking a Remote Server

Be careful when using the **Disconnect User** button to kick a remote server off the dial-up server computer. If the remote user was in the process of working with a file, any unsaved work will be lost.

Monitoring and Establishing a Connection

After the dial-up server is configured and started, the Status field displays the value of Monitoring to indicate that it is waiting for a dial-up client to initiate a session (see Figure 13.30).

When a communication session is established with a dial-up client, the Status field displays a message stating the logged-on user's name and initial connection time, and the **Disconnect User** button becomes enabled. When either the user disconnects the session or is forcibly disconnected, the status returns to Monitoring.

FIGURE 13.30
A status of Monitoring indicates that the dial-up server is actively monitoring for incoming dial-up client login requests.

Disabling the Dial-Up Server

To disable the dial-up server, open the Dial-Up Server dialog and select the **No Caller Access** option; then, click **Apply** followed by **OK**.

Using Multiple Modems

A Windows 98 dial-up server can manage only one dial-up connection at a time. However, it can see and monitor any modem connection to the dial-up server. Figure 13.31 shows a dial-up server with two installed modems. Each modem is represented by a tab to permit individual configuration.

FIGURE 13.31
Every modem on a dial-up server is available to the dial-up server for monitoring.

Creating a Dial-Up Connection

Dial-Up Networking provides a computer with the capability to connect to another computer or network using a modem and a conventional phone line. Microsoft treats a computer that dials into a network using Dial-Up Networking as just another network node. The dialed-in computer has all the same access to the network as a computer connected directly to the network with the exception that the speed of the connection is much slower.

Before a Dial-Up Networking connection can be set up, it must first be installed. To see whether Dial-Up Networking is installed, double-click on the **My Computer** icon and look for a Dial-Up Networking icon. If the icon is not there, the application is not installed. If Dial-Up Networking is not installed, use the Add/Remove Programs utility located in the Windows Control Panel to install it.

The following example demonstrates how to create a dial-up connection on a Windows 98 computer.

Creating a dial-up connection

1. Double-click on the **Dial-Up Networking** icon in the My Computer dialog. If this is the first dial-up connection, the dialog shown in Figure 13.32 is displayed. Click **Next** to continue.

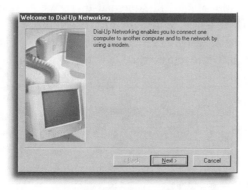

FIGURE 13.32
Windows is ready to install Dial-Up Networking.

2. Otherwise, the Dial-Up Networking dialog appears (see Figure 13.33).

3. Double-click on the **Make New Connection** icon. The Make New Connection Wizard appears (see Figure 13.34).

4. Type a name identifying the connection in the **Type a Name for the Computer You Are Dialing** field. The **Select a Device** option provides a drop-down list of all the modems installed on the computer. Select the modem that will be used to make the connection, and click **Next**.

5. Enter the area code and telephone number of the dial-up server (see Figure 13.35). Make sure that the correct country code is selected, and then click **Next**.

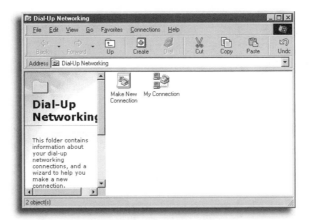

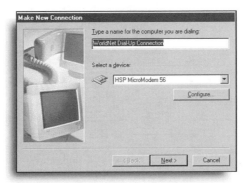

FIGURE 13.34
The Make New Connection Wizard requests a name for the new connection and the selection of a modem.

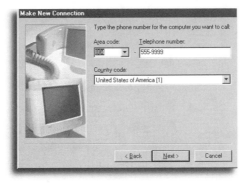

FIGURE 13.35
Windows requires speci-fication of the area code and phone number of the new connection.

6. Windows 98 is ready to complete the new dial-up connection (see Figure 13.36). Click **Finish**.

FIGURE 13.36
The Make New Connection Wizard completes the creation of the new connection definition.

The new connection appears in the Dial-Up Networking dialog. By default, Windows 2000 sets up a point-to-point connection and binds all installed protocols. To configure the connection, right-click on it and select **Properties**. Available configuration options include changing the phone number and area code assigned to the connection, changing its assigned modem, and selecting the protocols that are to be supported over the connection.

SEE ALSO

➤ *For more information on the Point-to-Point Protocol, see page 245.*

➤ *To learn more about the Point-to-Point Protocol, see page 536.*

To create additional dial-up connections, double-click on the **Make New Connection** icon.

Connecting to a Dial-Up Server

After a dial-up connection has been created, it can be used to connect to the remote computer or network.

Establishing a dial-up connection

1. Double-click on the icon representing the connection in the Dial-Up Network dialog. The Connect To dialog for the defined connection appears (see Figure 13.37).

2. Verify that all the information presented is correct, and click on **Connect**. Windows begins the logon process by dialing the dial-up server. The dial-up server must be active and monitoring.

FIGURE 13.37
The Connect To dialog allows connection to a dial-up server.

3. After the dial-up server answers the connection request, the two computers begin to negotiate the login process. If the dial-up server has been configured with a password, a dialog appears on the dial-up client computer requesting the password. If an incorrect password is provided, the connection is terminated. When the correct password is provided, the logon is established, as shown in Figure 13.38. If the dial-up server does not require a password, the two computers proceed to complete the login.

FIGURE 13.38
The Connected To prompt displays information about the connection and provides a means for terminating it.

4. The connection is established. On the client, the Connected To prompt shows the speed at which the connection was established, the length of time it has been active, and the number of bytes sent and received between the two computers. On the dial-up server, the name of the logged-on user is displayed, along with the time when the connection occurred.

5. Clicking on the **Details** button provides additional information about the connection (see Figure 13.39), including the following:

- The name of the modem used to establish the connection
- The type of dial-up server that the client is currently connected to
- The protocol used to establish the network connection

FIGURE 13.39
The Details button provides more details about the current connection between the dial-up client and server.

If this is the first time the dial-up client has established a connection, the dialog shown in Figure 13.40 appears when the connection is established. To prevent the screen from appearing in the future, select the **Do Not Show This Dialog Box in the Future** option and then click **Close**.

FIGURE 13.40
The Connection Established dialog provides instructions for terminating the connection or gathering more information.

After a connection between a dial-up client and server is established, the shared resources on both machines are available to each computer. For example, if a dial-up client is connected to a dial-up server named SalesFileSvr, the user can view and access all SalesFileSvr's shared resources using Windows Explorer by typing \\SalesFileSvr in the Address field.

Sometimes, the connection between a dial-up client and server is terminated accidentally. This can be caused by excess noise or static on the phone line, or if someone accidentally picks up a phone while the two computers are in session. This prompt also appears on the dial-up client if the Disconnect User button is clicked on the dial-up server computer (see Figure 13.41). To reestablish the session, click **Reconnect**.

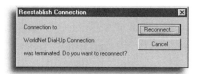

FIGURE 13.41
Reestablish Connection prompt appears on the dial-up client computer if something causes the connection between the dial-up client and server to disconnect.

chapter
14

Managing and Administering Windows 9X Networking

Managing Shared Drives and Folders

This is the second of two chapters on networking with the Windows 95 and Windows 98 operating systems (collectively known as Windows 9X). Because of their similarities, both operating systems are covered in parallel, with differences pointed out where appropriate. Windows 98 is used to present examples of administrative procedures throughout the chapter.

On Windows 9X operating systems, sharing can be configured for an entire drive or folder in much the same manner as it is configured in Windows 2000 Professional. There are, however, a few key points to keep in mind when networking a Windows 9X machine:

- Before a networked computer can share a drive or folder, file sharing must be installed and configured.
- Windows 9X operating systems do not support NTFS security. This means that they do not provide security on a user or group basis.
- Windows 9X does provide share security. Share security applies only when the computer is accessed over the network. If the computer is accessed locally, all resources are available to the user. Windows 9X share security works by assigning passwords for read-only access and full access to shared resources and then distributing the passwords to authorized users. Anyone who knows a password can use it to access the resource to which it belongs.

SEE ALSO

➤ *To learn how to enable and configure file sharing, see page 387.*

Creating a Share

A share is a local drive or folder that is made available to other computers on the network. Any resource that can be accessed from the network is referred to as a share. The same procedure is used to create shares for floppy drives, hard drives, CD-ROM drives, and folders. All resources on Windows 9X computers have iconic representation. When a resource is shared, its iconic representation changes to show a hand under the icon. When a Windows 9X resource is shared, any user on the network can access it, provided that he knows the password. Three share security options are available for shared drives and folders, as shown in Table 14.1.

Table 14.1 Share Security Options

Security Option	Description
Read-Only	Allows users to access the drive, view its contents, and read stored files. A password is optional.
Full	Allows users to access the drive; view its resources; and read, change, or delete its contents. A password is optional.
Depends on Password	Allows passwords to be assigned to the resource. Forces network users to provide the password before access to the resource is granted.

Sharing a drive or folder

1. Double-click on the **My Computer** icon on the main desktop. The My Computer dialog appears.

2. Right-click on a local drive or folder, and select the **Sharing** option from the menu that appears. The Properties dialog for the selected resource appears. If the Sharing option is not present, the file-sharing service is either not installed or not enabled.

SEE ALSO

➤ *For instruction on how to install file and print sharing, see page 384.*

SEE ALSO

➤ *For information on how to configure file and print sharing, see page 387.*

3. By default, the Not Shared option is selected. To share the local drive, select the **Share As** option. This selection activates several fields on the dialog.

4. A default name is provided for the share. It is often advisable to replace the default name with a more descriptive name. Enter a name in the **Share Name** field and an optional comment in the **Comment** field.

5. Select the access type to be assigned to the resource.

   ■ If **Read-Only** access is selected, an optional password can be supplied in the **Read-Only Password** field.

> **Sneaky Sharing**
>
> If you place a $ at the end of the share name, it becomes a hidden share, and that shared resource will not appear in network browse lists. This allows users and administrators to share local resources without allowing those resources to appear when network users browse the network. The share is still available to network users who are aware of its existence; they can access it by using the UNC command syntax of `\\computername\resourcename$` from any Windows utility that accepts it.

- If **Full** access is selected, an optional password can be supplied in the **Full Access Password** field.

- If **Depends on Password** access is selected, optional passwords can be supplied in either of the password fields, as shown in Figure 14.1.

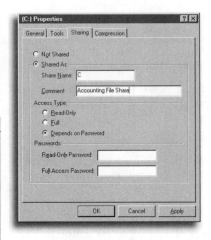

FIGURE 14.1
Establishing secured access on a shared resource.

Less Is Better

If most users require only read-only access to a shared device, it is strongly recommended that only read-only access be granted. If a few of the users need full control, apply both types of access using different passwords for each type of access, and provide only trusted users with the password that provides full access.

6. Click **Apply** and then **OK**.

Removing a Share

After a resource is no longer shared, it is unavailable to network users. The only way to access the resource is to log on at the local computer where the resource resides. This works the same way for printers when sharing has been terminated.

Terminating shared access on a drive or folder

1. Open either **Windows Explorer** or **My Computer**, and right-click on the drive or folder.

2. On the menu that appears, click on the **Sharing** option. The Properties dialog for the selected device appears, and the Sharing tab is automatically displayed.

3. Click on the **Not Shared** option. The fields under the Shared As section then become disabled.

4. Click **Apply** and then **OK**.

Working with Shared Drives and Folders

Several means can be used to view and work with shared resources on a peer network. These include the Windows Explorer, Internet Explorer, Network Neighborhood, and various Windows dialogs. In addition, Windows 9X supports the establishment of drive mappings that, after they've been established, allow direct access to network resources.

Accessing a Share Across the Network

The processes of viewing resources with the My Computer dialog and Windows Explorer are very similar. Windows dialogs, such as File Open or File Save, are provided by Windows applications. As long as the applications are network-aware, these dialogs will allow the user to access shares on remote computers.

Accessing network resources with Network Neighborhood

1. Double-click on the **Network Neighborhood** icon on the Windows 9X desktop.

2. Navigate the dialog as necessary to locate a computer, as shown in Figure 14.2.

FIGURE 14.2
Using Network Neighborhood to locate shared resources.

3. To see whether a computer has any shared resources, double-click on it.

4. The dialog changes to display a list of all shares available on the selected computer. To view the contents of a given share, double-click on it. If the share is password-protected, supply the appropriate password when prompted.

Mapping Shared Drives

Now You See It, Now You Don't

Although you'll be able to access networked drives and folders through network-aware applications, such as Microsoft Office 97, Office 2000, or Lotus SmartSuite, some older software programs or software that is not network-aware might not be able to view or access drives or folders over the network. If sharing files via a network is essential to your work, your best bet is to upgrade applications.

For convenience, remote shares located on other computers on the network can be mapped to local drive letters. Mapping a drive in this manner makes it appear as if the drive is local to the computer. An iconic representation of the mapped drive appears in the My Computer and Windows Explorer dialogs, resembling a regular drive icon with the addition of a cable connection under it.

With a remote resource mapped to a local driver letter, these application programs are able to view the share as a local resource. Figure 14.3 presents an example of two mapped drives, one of which is broken. A broken mapping is a situation in which either the local computer has lost connectivity with the remote computer that provides the share, or the remote computer has stopped sharing the resource, thus making it unavailable. A broken mapping is represented by an icon that looks like a mapped drive with a red × at the bottom, as shown in Figure 14.3.

FIGURE 14.3
Viewing a mapped resource from the My Computer dialog.

① Broken links are marked with an ×.

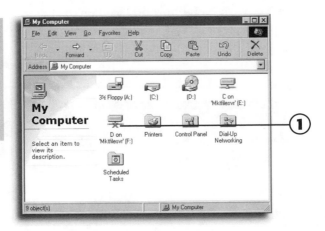

Overview of Windows 9X Printing

Like Windows 2000 Professional, Windows 9X uses a device-independent print architecture. After a print device has been set up and configured, all applications will be able to work with it. The user only needs to select the desired print device, and the operating system manages the rest of the process.

The Windows 9X print queue manages all spooled jobs. After the print job has been printed, Windows removes it from the print queue. Print jobs are stored in the `\Windows\spool\printers` directory. If the print job is destined for a network printer, it is redirected across the network to the print server that manages the network printer, where it is spooled and managed by that computer's print queue manager. By default, all print jobs are printed on a FIFO (first in, first out) basis. However, the order of jobs currently in the print queue can be changed.

Changing the print order in the print queue

1. From the Windows 98 desktop, select **Start**, **Settings**, and then **Printers**.

2. Double-click on the icon for the selected print device.

3. Press and hold the left mouse button on a document and drag it to a new position in the queue; release the button.

All Windows 9X print management is controlled in the Printers dialog. The Printers folder contains an icon for every installed print device, as well as an icon for launching the Print Wizard utility, as shown in Figure 14.4.

FIGURE 14.4
The Printers folder displays the Add Printer icon and a list of installed printers.

Windows 9X provides built-in support for hundreds of printers and provides support for other printers by allowing the user to supply vendor-provided software drivers.

Other features of Windows 9X operating systems include these:

- Support for user-friendly printer names up to 32 characters in length

- Plug and Play support
- Complete integration with the network print process
- Support for spooling MS-DOS print jobs

Installing and Configuring Printers

The process of installing a printer is essentially the same for Windows 95 and Windows 98, with only minor differences. The following sections demonstrate how to set up a local and a network printer using Windows 98.

Installing a Local Printer

Local printers are installed in one of two ways. Either Windows 9X Plug and Play detects and installs the printer, or the user manually installs the printer. If the printer is a parallel printer and the print device is plug-and-play–compatible and the printer cable is bidirectional, Plug and Play should be able to detect it. In this case, follow the instructions on the screen to configure the printer. If the printer or parallel printer cable is not bidirectional, the printer must be manually installed. If the printer is a USB printer, Windows 9X should be able to auto-detect and install it after it has been connected.

Printer installation involves two steps. The first step is the physical installation of the print device. The second step is the installation of the printer driver.

Installing the printer driver

1. From the Windows 98 Control Panel, double-click on the **Printers** icon. The Printers dialog appears.

2. All defined printers are displayed. In addition, the Add Printer icon is displayed. Double-click on the **Add Printer** icon, and the Add Printer Wizard appears. Click **Next**.

3. Windows asks for the location of the printer. Select the **Local Printer** option and then click **Next**.

4. The printer wizard next inquires about the manufacturer and model type of the print device. Select the manufacturer and printer type and click **Next**.

Unsupported Print Features

Two printing features available in Windows 2000 Pro and Windows NT Workstation 4.0, but not supported by Windows 9X, are printer pools and print priorities. Windows 9X does allow you to change the order of print jobs in the print queue by dragging and dropping a print job to a new location in a queue.

5. If either the manufacturer or the type of printer is not displayed, click the **Have disk** button; when prompted, supply the disk or CD-ROM that contains the printer driver supplied by the vendor, and click **OK**. Otherwise, skip this step and click **Next**.

6. Next, Windows prompts for selection of the port where the printer is attached. Most computers have only a single parallel port, known as LPT1. Select **LPT1**. If MS-DOS applications that require print service will run on this computer, click **Configure Port**. Otherwise, click **Next** and skip to step 8.

7. If support for MS-DOS print jobs is required, select the **Spool MS-DOS Print Jobs** option and click **OK**. The printer port selection options reappear. Click **Next** to continue.

8. Windows 98 prompts you to assign a name to this printer. This is the name that will be displayed across the network if this printer is set up to be shared over the network. The default printer name is the manufacturer's name and model type combined.

9. Windows asks whether it should print a test page on the printer. A test page provides a visual verification that the printer was correctly configured. Select the **Yes** option and click on **Finish** to complete the printer installation.

10. Windows 98 immediately begins to load drivers for the specified printer. If you have not already done so, Windows 98 prompts you to insert the Windows 98 CD-ROM and then click **OK** to continue.

11. After completing the printer-driver installation, Windows 98 submits the test job to the printer. After the print device has finished the print job, make sure that it looks okay. If it does, the installation was successful. Click **Yes**. If the test page did not print or printed incorrectly, something went wrong with the printer installation. Click **No** and Windows starts the Printer Troubleshooting Wizard. Answer the questions and follow the steps presented by the troubleshooting wizard to determine and correct the problem.

The Windows Printers panel now includes an icon representing the newly installed printer.

What's in a Name?

A printer name should be used to provide some idea of the purpose of the printer. The printer name can be used to provide the user with helpful information such as the type or location of the printer. Click **Next**.

Connecting to a Network Printer

The process of connecting to a network printer is very similar to that of setting up a local computer.

Installing a network printer

1. Double-click on the **Add Printer** icon to open the Add Printer Wizard. Click **Next**.

2. Select **Network Printer** and click **Next**.

3. The Add Printer Wizard asks for the location of the network printer. Enter the location using the Universal Naming Convention, or UNC, method. If the computer where the printer resides is named SalesPrintSvr and the printer name is Color_Printer, the UNC path would be this:

   ```
   \\SalesPrintSvr\Color_Printer
   ```

4. If the location of the network computer is not known, click on **Browse**. Windows then produces a dialog that allows you to navigate the network and select the printer. After finding the computer where the printer resides and selecting the printer, click **OK**. If this printer will be used to print MS-DOS print jobs, select **Yes.** Otherwise, select **No**. Click **Next**.

5. The printer wizard next inquires about the manufacturer and model type of the print device that is being installed. Select the manufacturer of the printer from the **Manufacturers** list. A list of print devices made by that manufacturer appears in the printers area. Select the manufacturer and printer type and click **Next**.

6. If either the manufacturer or the type of printer is not displayed, click the **Have disk** button; when prompted, supply the disk or CD-ROM that contains the printer driver supplied by the vendor, and click **OK**. Otherwise, skip this step and click **Next**.

7. Supply a name your computer will use to refer to the network printer. If you want this printer to become the default computer, click **Yes**. Otherwise, click **No**. Click **Next**.

8. If the network printer is protected by a password, you are prompted to provide it. Type the password and click **OK**.

9. Windows asks whether it should print a test page on the printer. A test page provides a visual verification that the printer was

correctly configured. Select the **Yes** option and click on **Finish** to complete the printer installation.

10. Windows 98 immediately begins to load drivers for the specified printer. If you have not already done so, Windows 98 prompts you to insert the Windows 98 CD-ROM and then click **OK** to continue.

11. After completing the printer driver installation, Windows 98 submits the test job to the printer. After the print device has finished printing the print job, make sure that it looks okay. If it does, the installation was successful. Click **Yes**. If the test page did not print or printed incorrectly, something went wrong with the printer installation. Click **No** and Windows starts the Printer Troubleshooting Wizard. Answer the questions and follows the steps presented by the troubleshooting wizard to determine and correct the problem.

Deleting a Printer

Deleting a printer is a simple process. The process is the same whether it's a physically attached local printer or a connection to a shared network printer. Deleting a printer removes all references to the computer and deletes its icon.

Removing a printer

1. From the Windows 98 Control Panel, double-click on the **Printers** icon. The Printers dialog appears.

2. Right-click on the printer to be deleted.

3. Select the **Delete** option.

4. Windows 98 displays a prompt asking for confirmation before deleting the printer. Click **Yes**.

5. Windows 98 might display another prompt. If this printer or another printer that uses the same software driver will be installed later on this machine, you might want to select the **Yes** option. This tells Windows 98 to keep the software driver and related files for the printer, thus making a future installation easier. Select **No**. This instructs Windows 98 to delete the Printer and remove all related files for the printer.

6. Windows 98 deletes the printer. If the deleted printer was the current default printer and if another printer is installed, a prompt is displayed, informing the user that Windows has selected a new default printer. Click **OK** to acknowledge the prompt.

Setting the Default Printer

The default printer is the device where Windows 9X submits all print jobs unless specifically instructed to do otherwise. If only one printer is installed on a computer, Windows 9X automatically makes it the default printer. If more than one printer is installed, the first printer installed is the default printer. Recognizing the default printer is easy. The default printer icon displays a small black circle with a check mark in the upper-left corner. Any printer installed after the first printer will not become the default printer unless the person installing the print device instructs Windows 9X to make the new printer the default printer.

Changing the default printer

1. From the Windows 98 Control Panel, double-click on the **Printers** icon. The Printers dialog appears.

2. Right-click on the printer that will become the new default printer. A menu appears.

3. Select the **Set as Default** option. Windows 98 places a check mark to the left of the option to show that it has been selected.

4. From this point on, Windows 98 will submit all print jobs to this printer unless instructed to do otherwise from within an application.

Working with Printers

After a print job has been submitted to a print device, a user can manage it from the printer's print queue. Individual print jobs can be paused or purged. In addition, Windows 9X provides the capability to manage the print device on a global scale with pause and purge options.

Managing a Printer

A printer's queue can be managed with a set of commands available on the Printer menu that affect the entire print queue. These commands are presented in Table 14.2.

Table 14.2 Printer Menu Commands

Command	Description
Pause Printing	Pauses all print activity on this printer. Selecting this option a second time resumes the print activity.
Set As Default	Sets the printer as the default printer.
Purge Print Documents	Deletes all print jobs from the print queue without printing them.
Properties	Presents the printer's Properties dialog.

Pausing the print device causes all print activity to stop. Print jobs that are currently printing will halt printing. Spooled print jobs will remain spooled. Print jobs currently spooling will complete, and new print jobs will be accepted and spooled but will not print. No activity will occur on the print device until it is unpaused.

Pausing print activity

1. From the Windows 98 Control Panel, double-click on the **Printers** icon. The Printers dialog appears.

2. Right-click on the printer that will become the new default printer. A menu appears.

3. Select the **Pause Printing** option.

Purging all print jobs on a printer's print queue deletes all printing, spooled, and spooling print jobs. Print jobs that arrive after the purge command has been completed will process normally.

SEE ALSO

➤ *For more information on how spooling works on Windows operating systems, see page 149.*

Purging all print jobs

1. From the Windows 98 Control Panel, double-click on the **Printers** icon. The Printers dialog appears.

2. Right-click on the printer. A menu appears.

How Windows Manages Your Print Jobs

Spooling is a process that Windows operating systems use to receive print jobs and save them as files on the hard drive, where they wait their turn before being submitted to the print device.

3. Select the **Purge Print Documents** option. Windows 98 deletes all print jobs currently printing, spooled, or spooling.

Managing individual print jobs requires selecting a specific job and then clicking on the Document menu. The two options available are Pause Printing and Cancel Printing. Pause printing halts the printing of the selected print job. After a job is halted, it can be canceled or deleted via the Cancel Printing option. Selecting a print job and clicking on Pause Printing places a check mark to the left of the Pause Printing option. To unpause a print job, simply select it and click on Pause Printing a second time. The check mark is removed.

Paused jobs remain in the print queue until they are canceled out of the queue or are unpaused. If new print jobs enter the queue while this job is still paused, the new jobs print normally.

Figure 14.5 shows two print jobs in a printer's print queue. The information provided in this dialog includes the name of the print job, its status, its progress, and the date and time it originated.

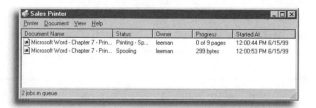

The status of the first print job is printing, which means that the print device is currently printing the print job. The status of the second print job is spooling, which means that the computer is currently spooling or passing the print job into the printer queue. After the first job has been printed, Windows 9X deletes it and begins to print the second print job.

Configuring a Printer

Like other hardware devices, Windows 9X provides a host of configuration tabs for controlling print-device performance and functionality.

These tabs are maintained on the printer's Properties page. Because printers have different features, the Printer Properties dialog where they are listed might look different for each printer. Although some printers have more options than other printers, there are some settings that most printers have in common, as shown in Table 14.3.

Table 14.3   Common Printer Configuration Options

Tab	Description
General	Provides for supplying a description of the printer and adding separator pages between print jobs.
Details	Provides for managing printer ports and controlling various time-out parameters.
Sharing	Provides for sharing the printer with other network computers.
Paper	Provides for selection of the type of paper to be used in the printer, and controls its basic layout and media quality.
Graphics	Provides for controlling graphic resolution, dithering quality, and the intensity of darkness.

Printer hardware vendors often create new drivers for their printers and make them available for download from their Web sites. Installing a new driver for a printer might result in changes in available settings on the printer's Properties dialog. Typically, this means that the vendor has added additional control and functionality for the print device.

Drag and Drop

An alternative to opening a program and then using it to access and print a file is *drag and drop*. For example, you could print a file on a local drive by simply dragging it over on top of the icon representing the destination print device and dropping it. However, drag-and-drop printing works only if the document is printable and if an application is associated with it.

Dragging and dropping print jobs

1. Using either **My Computer** or **Windows Explorer**, locate the file to be printed.

2. Open the **Printers** dialog to display available print devices.

3. Click on the desired file; continue to hold down the left mouse button while dragging the pointer on top of the selected print device, and then release the left mouse button. The application associated with the document might open for a moment during

Practical Dragging and Dropping

To make drag and drop a more feasible option, shortcuts can be created and placed on the Windows desktop for the destination print device. Users need only drag files to the desktop instead of opening the Printers dialog each time a print operation is required.

the print process before closing again. Windows 98 proceeds to print the document.

Windows 9X Administration

Windows 95 and Windows 98 share a rich set of network administration tools, including these:

- Selection of multiple network logon modes
- Net Watcher
- Remote administration
- System Policy Editor
- User profiles

Selecting a Logon Mode

When Windows 9X is first installed, the user is given the opportunity to set up an initial user ID and password. If the user chooses, these two fields can be left blank. This being the case, Windows will not prompt the user to log on in the future. This situation works fine when one person uses the computer. If *user profiles* are established, Windows 9X creates a user profile to store information unique to each user of the computer.

Establishing user profiles allows individual users to make changes to the system that are then automatically saved in their own unique profile. These changes will not affect other users, whose system customization will be saved in their own user profiles.

SEE ALSO
➤ *For more information on establishing user profiles, see page 443.*

Windows 95 and Windows 98 both support the following logon modes:

- Windows Logon (default for standalone computers)
- Client for Microsoft Networks

In addition, Windows 98 provides the Windows Family Logon.

Setting up Windows Logon Client as the primary network logon

1. Access the Network dialog by right-clicking on the **Network Neighborhood** icon and selecting **Properties**.

2. Make sure that the **Configuration** tab is selected.

3. From the Primary Network Logon drop-down list, select the **Windows Logon** option, and click **OK**.

4. When prompted, click **Yes** to restart the computer.

The Windows logon dialog appears after the computer restarts, as shown in Figure 14.6. This logon mode logs the user on to Windows 9X and allows network access but does not display an error message if the computer is unable to connect to the network. This logon mode is appropriate if the computer is not connected to a network.

FIGURE 14.6
The Windows logon dialog is the default option on Windows 9X computers that operate as standalone computers.

For Microsoft peer networks, the Client for Microsoft Networks is an appropriate logon client.

Setting the Client for Microsoft Networks as the primary network client

1. Access the Network dialog by right-clicking on the **Network Neighborhood** icon and selecting **Properties**.

2. Make sure that the **Configuration** tab is selected.

3. From the Primary Network Logon list, select the **Client for Microsoft Networks** option, and click **OK**.

4. When prompted, click **Yes** to restart the computer.

The Client for Microsoft Networks logon dialog appears after the reboot, as shown in Figure 14.7.

Windows 98 offers the Microsoft Family Logon as an alternative to the Client for Microsoft Networks. It displays a list of user IDs defined on the computer and allows a user to select a username from the list. The user then needs to supply only a valid password.

FIGURE 14.7
The Client for Microsoft Networks facilitates access to network resources on Microsoft networks.

The primary advantage of this client is that it saves the user some keystrokes when he or she is logging on to the computer. Otherwise, it provides the exact same function as the Client for Microsoft Networks. The one disadvantage of this client is that it publishes a list of user accounts stored on the local computer. This provides an intruder with half the information required to impersonate network users. If network users also have accounts on Windows 2000 and NT computers and their user IDs and passwords are the same, then a hacker who guesses a user's password can gain access to all resources to which the user has been assigned permissions.

Setting the Microsoft Family Logon as the primary network logon

1. Access the Network dialog by right-clicking on the **Network Neighborhood** icon and selecting **Properties**.

2. Be sure that the **Configuration** tab is selected.

3. From the Primary Network Logon list, select the **Microsoft Family Logon** option, and click **OK**.

4. When prompted, click **Yes** to restart the computer.

The logon dialog that appears after the reboot is shown in Figure 14.8.

FIGURE 14.8
The Microsoft Family Logon displays a list of users for selection.

Remote Administration

Remote administration allows control over a network computer's file system and printers from other computers located on the network.

When this support is not in place, the only way to manage shared resources on a computer on the network is to log on locally. Windows 9X offers remote administration as a means of allowing trusted users to administer shared resources from their own computers.

Configuring remote access

1. From the Windows Control Panel, double-click on the **Passwords** icon. The Passwords Properties dialog appears.

2. Select the **Remote Administration** tab, as shown in Figure 14.9.

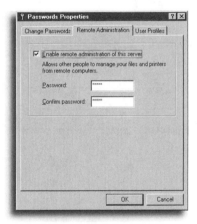

FIGURE 14.9
Remote administration of a computer is configured from the Password utility located in the Windows Control Panel.

3. Select **Enable Remote Administration of This Server**.

4. Type a password in the **Password** field.

5. Enter the password again in the **Confirm Password** field.

6. Click **OK**.

The computer is now ready to support remote administration. Under the covers, Windows creates a hidden share named ADMIN$ and applies the provided password to it.

Any user who knows the password specified to allow remote administration on a computer can access shares on the computer. A special share is created for every hard disk on the computer. This allows for complete remote access and control of the file system of the remote computer.

Bypassing the Logon Client

Windows 9X users can bypass the logon client by clicking **Cancel** when prompted to log on. This allows users to access local resources. However, access to network resources will be denied. This feature of Windows 9X is very different from the security model used on Windows 2000 and Windows NT operating systems, in which the user is denied access to any resource, local or network, unless a proper logon sequence has been completed.

Starting a remote administration session

1. From **Network Neighborhood**, find and select a computer that allows remote administration.

2. Right-click on the computer and select **Properties**.

3. Select the **Tools** tab, as shown in Figure 14.10.

FIGURE 14.10
Starting a remote administration session on a network computer.

4. Click on the **Administer** button.

5. At the prompt, provide the password of the ADMIN$ share, and click **OK**. A dialog displaying all shared resources on the remote computer appears.

After supplying the password, the administrator is given access to the remote computer's file system. The available resources on the remote system appear.

Administering remote network resources

1. Right-click on a resource and select **Properties**. The resource's Properties dialog is displayed.

2. Select the **Shared As** option.

3. Provide a **Share Name** and **Comment**.

4. Under **Access Type**, select one of the three available security options.

5. Enter a password if security is required, and click **OK**.

Finding and Managing Shared Resources on the Network

On Windows 9X operating systems there are multiple ways of finding resources, including these:

- Network Neighborhood
- Windows Explorer
- Mapping shared drives to local drive letters
- Using the UNC of a device or folder

Network Neighborhood

Network Neighborhood provides a window for viewing all shared resources over the network. When Network Neighborhood is first displayed, it presents an icon representing the local computer, an icon representing the entire network, and icons for every currently active computer that is a member of the local computer's workgroup.

Only resources that have been shared on network computers can be viewed through Network Neighborhood.

Using Network Neighborhood to access shared drives and folders

1. From the Windows desktop, double-click on **Network Neighborhood**. A dialog appears, as shown in Figure 14.11.

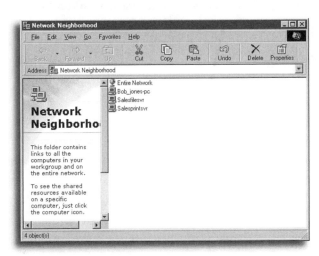

FIGURE 14.11
Accessing a shared resource using Network Neighborhood.

2. If the desired resource is the local computer's workgroup, skip to step 3. Otherwise, locate the workgroup of the machine that

431

owns the desired resource by double-clicking on the **Entire Network** icon and then double-clicking on the workgroup.

3. Find the computer where the shared resource is located. Double-click on the icon for the computer.

4. All resources shared by the selected computer are displayed except for the hidden shares. Double-click on a resource to open it if it's a file or start it if it's a program.

Windows Explorer

Windows Explorer is a utility commonly used for accessing a computer's resources. However, it also includes a link to Network Neighborhood.

Accessing shared drives and folders using Windows Explorer

1. Select **Start**, **Programs**, and then **Windows Explorer**.

2. Locate **Network Neighborhood** in the left window pane, and click on the plus sign just to the left of it, as shown in Figure 14.12.

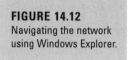

FIGURE 14.12
Navigating the network using Windows Explorer.

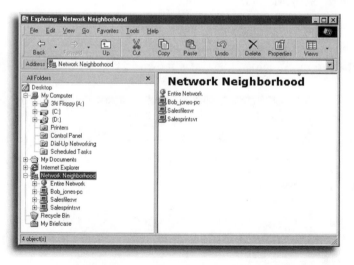

3. You are presented with a view of the local computer's workgroup and an icon representing the entire network. Use Windows Explorer to navigate the network using the same techniques that are used to navigate the local computer.

4. After you've selected a network computer, all resources shared by the computer will be displayed in the right window pane.

Double-click on a resource to open it if it's a file or start it if it's a program.

Mapping Shared Drives to Local Drive Letters

Mapping to a local drive letter is the process of locating a network drive or folder and assigning an unused driver letter between A and Z to that resource. When mapped, the resource appears as if it's a local resource and can be accessed like any local drive.

There are two reasons for mapping drives:

- The first reason is convenience. For example, if regular access is required to a network folder, mapping a letter to the drive might prove valuable. After the drive is mapped, the icon representing the drive can be dragged to the desktop, where it can be easily located and accessed.

- The second reason for mapping a network drive is that many older programs, such as legacy Windows 3.1 programs, are not aware of the network and can work only with local resources. Mapping network resources to local drive letters makes the network device appear as if it's hanging directly off the local computer.

Mapping a drive from Windows Explorer

1. From Windows Explorer, select **Map Network Drive** from the **Tools** menu. A dialog similar to the one shown in Figure 14.13 appears.

FIGURE 14.13
Mapping a network drive using Windows Explorer.

2. The Map Network Drive dialog provides a list of available drive letters that can be assigned to the network resource specified in the Path field.

3. Select a drive letter from the **Drive** drop-down box.

4. Enter a shared resource's path in the **Path** text box using the UNC convention.

5. To retain this mapping across system reboots, select the **Reconnect at Logon** option. Click **OK**.

In the My Computer dialog you see an icon for the mapped drive that looks like a regular drive icon with a network cable attached under it.

Mapping a drive from Network Neighborhood

1. Open **Network Neighborhood** by double-clicking on its icon on the Windows desktop.

2. Navigate down to the desired computer and select it. The computer's shared resources appear.

3. Select a shared resource, and then select the **Map Network Drive** option under the **File** menu. The Map Network Drive dialog appears.

4. To make the drive mapping permanent, select the **Reconnect at Logon** option; otherwise, the drive mapping will last only until the mapping is broken or the user logs off. Select a drive letter and click **OK**.

Mapping a Drive from the MS-DOS Prompt

Drive mapping can be created from the MS-DOS command prompt with the NET USE command. The NET USE command supports the Universal Naming Convention, or UNC. Here's the syntax of the UNC:

`\\computername\sharename\path`

SEE ALSO

➤ *For more information on the* NET USE *command, see page 504.*

Computername is the name of the computer on the network that owns the shared resource. *Sharename* is the name of the shared resource, and *path* is the path of the resource on the networked computer. For example, to address a shared drive on a computer named SalesFileSvr whose local hard drive is shared with a share name of C, the UNC would be `\\SalesFileSvr\C`.

Mapping a drive from the DOS prompt

1. Open a Windows MS-DOS window.

2. Type a command similar to NET USE F: `\\SalesFileSvr\C`, and press Enter.

3. If the shared resource is not password-protected, the command is complete.

4. If the shared resource is password-protected, the system prompts for a password. Type the password and press Enter. If the correct password is provided, the mapping process is complete and the mapped drive is ready for use. The next time the user logs on to the computer, a prompt appears, asking the user to supply the password for the mapped resource.

5. Supply the password for the shared resource. Selecting **S**ave **This Password in Your Password List** allows Windows to remember the password for this shared device so that you will not be prompted to supply it in the future. Click **OK**. If the password changes in the future, a new prompt will appear, asking for the password.

In the future when the user logs on to the computer, a prompt will appear, stating that Windows is connecting to the mapped resource. After a moment the prompt will disappear. Pressing **Cancel** will prevent the mapping from occurring.

Broken Mappings

If a network computer is unavailable, any drive mappings to drives or folders on that computer display as broken links. If the network resource is not available when the computer boots up, a prompt similar to the one shown in Figure 14.14 appears for every currently broken drive mapping.

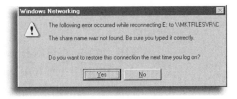

FIGURE 14.14
A command prompt notifies when Windows fails to reconnect to a mapped drive.

To keep the current drive mapping, click on the **Y**es button. Clicking on the **No** button permanently disconnects the drive. From the My Computer dialog, a broken drive mapping appears as a network drive icon with a red × on it.

Disconnecting a Mapped Drive

There are many ways to disconnect a drive mapping in Windows 9X, including disconnecting from the My Computer dialog.

Disconnecting a drive mapping from the My Computer dialog

1. Open the **My Computer** dialog.

2. Right-click on the mapped drive.

3. Select **Disconnect Drive Mapping**.

To disconnect the mapped drive from the MS-DOS command prompt, issue the following command:

```
NET USE \\computername\sharename\path /DELETE
```

System Policy Editor

The System Policy Editor helps create and enforce computer and user policies. Policies control what a user can do on a computer. Policies can be established for users, computers, or both.

Installing the System Policy Editor

1. Double-click on the **Add/Remove Programs** icon in the Windows Control Panel.

2. Select the **Windows Setup** tab.

3. Click on the **Have Disk** button.

4. Insert the Windows 98 CD-ROM and click the **Browse** button. Navigate to `\tools\reskit\netadmin\poledit` and click **OK**. Click **OK** a second time.

5. Select the **System Policy Editor** and then click on the **Install** button.

6. Click **OK** on the Add/Remove Programs properties dialog when the install process has finished.

7. Click **OK** to close the Add/Remove Programs dialog.

After it is installed, the System Policy Editor is located in **Start**, **Programs**, **Accessories**, **System Tools**, **System Policy Editor**. Establishing policies is a relatively straightforward process. For example, use the following steps to enable a logon banner on the local computer.

Creating a computer policy

1. Select **Open Registry** from the **File** menu.

2. Double-click on the **Local Computer** icon. The local computer's Properties dialog appears, as shown in Figure 14.15.

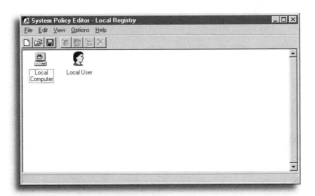

FIGURE 14.15
The System Policy Editor allows an administrator to create policies that govern local computer and user actions.

3. Double-click on **Windows 98 Network**.

4. Double-click on **Logon**.

5. Select **Logon Banner**. The fields in the Settings for Logon Banner area become enabled.

6. Enter the caption that will be displayed in the logon banner prompt, as well as the message to be displayed in the text field, as shown in Figure 14.16. Click **OK**.

FIGURE 14.16
Establishing a logon banner that warns individuals not to log on to the computer unless authorized.

7. Close the System Policy Editor. When prompted to save changes, click **Yes**.

8. Shut down and restart the computer to test the new policy. When the computer restarts, a dialog similar to the one shown in Figure 14.17 is displayed. Click **OK** to dismiss it, and continue logging on to the computer.

FIGURE 14.17
Windows 98 displays the logon banner before allowing a user to log on to the computer.

Net Watcher

Net Watcher is one of many utilities that, even though it's on the Windows 9X CD-ROM, does not install with the standard Windows 9X install. There are two ways to install this utility. The first is to select a custom install during installation of Windows 9X. The second method is to use the Add/Remove Programs utility in the Windows Control Panel.

Net Watcher enables a user to perform the following activities on other Windows 9X computers on the network from a single computer:

- View network users currently accessing a specific computer's resources
- Disconnect a user from a given network resource
- Enable or disable shared resources

Before a remote computer can be managed from the Net Watcher utility, the remote computer must meet the following requirements:

- File and printer sharing services must be installed and enabled
- Remote administration must be enabled

SEE ALSO

➤ *For more information on installing file and print services, see page 387.*

Connecting to a remote computer with Net Watcher

1. Start the Net Watcher utility by selecting **Start**, **Programs**, **Accessories**, **System Tools**, and then **Net Watcher**.

2. Click on **Select Server** on the **Administer** menu. The Select Server prompt appears.

3. Type the name of the computer to be managed in the **Name** field, and click **OK**.

4. When prompted, type the remote administration password required by the remote computer.

The Net Watcher utility is available on Windows 95, Windows 98, and Windows for Workgroups. It provides three views:

- Connections to This Server
- Shared Folders and Printers
- Files Open by Other Users

Connections to This Server

This view provides a look at who is connected to the computer, as shown in Figure 14.18. Information presented in the left pane includes the user, computer, number of shares accessed by user, number of files opened by user, amount of time users have been connected, and amount of time users have been idle on the system. The right pane displays the shares that the currently selected user is accessing.

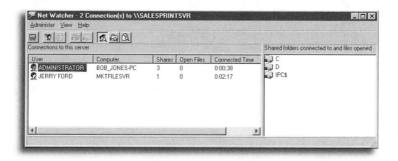

FIGURE 14.18
The Connections to This Server view provides a view of which shared resources users are accessing on a network computer.

Shared Folders and Printers

To see shared folders on a computer that other people are using, select the By Shared Folders option. The left pane displays the name of shared resources, their share names, the type of access allowed, and comment information. The right pane displays the names of any computers connected to the selected shares, as well as any files that are being accessed. Administrators can add, modify, or disable a shared resource from this dialog.

Creating a shared resource on a remote computer

1. Start Net Watcher.

2. Click on the **Administer** menu and then click on the **Select Server** option.

3. Enter the name of the network computer where the resource resides, and click **OK**.

4. Enter the remote administration password for the local machine when prompted.

5. Click on the **View** menu and select the **By Shared Folders** option, as shown in Figure 14.19.

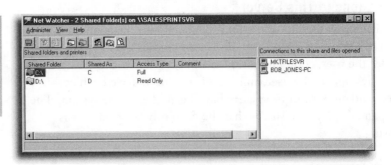

FIGURE 14.19
The Shared Folders and Printers view provides a view of shared folders on a given computer.

6. Click on the **Administer** menu and select the **Add Shared Folder** option.

7. Type the path to the resource, or click on the **Browse** button and use it to navigate to the location of the resource.

8. Click **OK**. A dialog windows appears for configuring the share parameters.

9. Click on the **Shared As** option and modify any default parameters as desired.

10. Click **OK** to complete the process.

Files Open by Other Users

To see files on your computer that other people are using, click **By Open Files** on the **View** menu. This view displays the name of opened files, the shares that are being used to access the files, the computer accessing the files, and the mode or type of access being used, as shown in Figure 14.20.

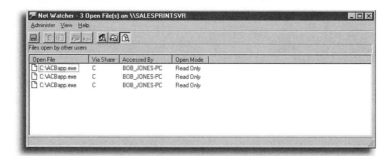

FIGURE 14.20
The Files Open by Other Users view provides a look at which files are being accessed on a computer.

Logon and Logoff

When a computer is booted, the selected login client appears. To log on to the network, a user must provide both a username and a password and then click **OK**. If the user does not require network access, the **Cancel** button can be clicked, as shown in Figure 14.21. This allows the user access to local computer resources.

FIGURE 14.21
The Client for Microsoft Networks provides logon access to the network.

After a user has logged on to either the network or the local computer and has completed working, it is appropriate for the user to log off. This does not require the user to perform a system shutdown. If the computer is shared by multiple users or is accessed often during a day, it might be preferable to simply log off and leave the system running.

Logging off Windows 9X

1. From the desktop, click on the **Start** button and then select **Log Off** *XXXX*, where *XXXX* is the logon name of the current user.

2. Windows 9X prompts for confirmation of the logoff request. To complete the logoff process click **Yes**. Windows closes all currently active applications. The currently selected Primary Network Logon appears.

Changing a Password

Users should also be instructed to change their passwords on a regular basis. If a user's password has been compromised, the account will be secured the next time the password is changed.

The Passwords utility located in the Windows Control Panel allows users to change their passwords.

Changing passwords

1. From the Windows Control Panel, double-click on the **Passwords** icon.

2. Select the **Change Passwords** tab.

3. The Passwords Properties dialog appears, as shown in Figure 14.22. Click on the **Change Windows Password** button to produce the Change Windows Password dialog.

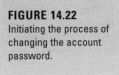

FIGURE 14.22
Initiating the process of changing the account password.

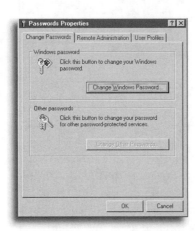

4. Enter the current password and press the **Tab** key.

5. Enter a new password and press the **Tab** key.

6. Enter the new password a second time and click **OK**.

7. Windows displays a confirmation prompt. Click **OK** when prompted to acknowledge that the password has been successfully changed.

User Profiles

User profiles support individual configuration of system settings user by user. When multiple users share the same computer, they can log on to that computer with a unique user ID and password, and Windows 9X will establish a profile for that user. This is where any customization is stored. For example, users can select their own preferred screen savers, choose a desktop background, and set up shortcuts on the desktop. Because these configuration changes are stored in individual profiles, they do not affect other users. Each time a user logs on to the computer, Windows loads any user-defined customizations stored in his profile.

These are the types of things stored in user profiles:

- Windows desktop settings
- Network settings, including mapped drives and defined printers
- Windows applications settings for applications that support per-user customization
- Shortcuts
- Changes made to the Start menu and Programs folder

Establishing User Profiles

User profiles allow multiple users to share the same Windows 9X computer and customize the system to suit their own needs without affecting other users. By default, Windows 9X sets up a computer so that all users of the computer share the same preferences and desktop settings.

Configuring user profiles

1. From the Windows Control Panel double-click on the **Passwords** icon.

2. Select the **User Profiles** tab, as shown in Figure 14.23.

3. Click on **Users Can Customize Their Preferences and Desktop Settings**. Windows switches to your personal settings when you log on. The two options under User Profile Settings now become available:

    - Include Desktop Icons and Neighborhood Contents in User Settings

443

■ Include <u>S</u>tart Menu and Program Groups in User Settings

The first option allows any customizations made by the user to the desktop to be saved in his or her profile. The second option adds customization of the Start menu and the Program menu.

4. Select the desired options and click **OK**.

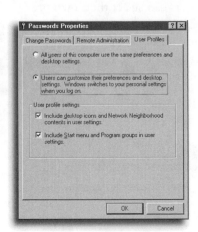

FIGURE 14.23
Windows 9X facilitates the sharing of a single computer by multiple users by allowing the establishment of individual user profiles.

When activated, the computer prompts for a user ID and password. After receiving the user ID and password, Windows looks to see whether the user has logged on to this computer before. If that is the case, the user's previously saved profile is loaded. If this is the first time the user has logged on to the computer, a new profile will be created for that user.

User profiles are stored in the directory where Windows was installed. For most computers this is `C:\Windows\Profiles`. Under the `Profiles` directory is a directory for every user who has logged on to the computer since user profiles were enabled. Each user profile is stored as the user's username. For example, the profile for a user whose username is Roberta would be `C:\Windows\Profile\Roberta`.

Enabling Multiuser Settings

When multiple users share the same computer, it is usually appropriate to set up a user account for each user. User accounts can be created in one of two ways. The first way is to enter a new username and password when prompted to log on to the computer. A unique user profile is automatically set up.

Creating a new user account at login

1. When prompted to log on to the system, enter a new user ID and password.

2. Windows asks for confirmation of the new password. Enter the password again where indicated.

3. Windows informs you that this is the first time this user has accessed this computer and asks for permission to establish a new user profile. Click **Yes** if you will be using this computer again in the future.

The second alternative is to use the Users utility, which is available on Windows 98 computers, to create new user accounts. It allows user accounts to be set up in advance in an organized manner.

The first time this utility is executed, a series of dialogs steps the user through the process of setting up an account and enables the multiple-user profiles feature.

Creating user accounts with the Users utility

1. Double-click on the **Users** icon on the Windows 98 Control Panel. The Enable Multi-user Settings dialog appears. Click **Next** to continue. The Add User dialog appears, as shown in Figure 14.24.

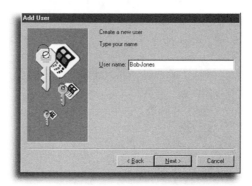

FIGURE 14.24
The User Name field will contain the account name of a user who will be using the computer.

2. Type the name of the new user account in the **User Name** field. This is the information that will be entered in the User Name field of one of the logon clients. Click **Next** to continue. The Enter New Password dialog appears.

3. Every user should have a password. This password must be entered two times to ensure that typing mistakes do not occur, as

445

shown in Figure 14.25. After entering a password in both fields, click **Next**. The Personalized Items Settings dialog appears next.

4. This dialog determines which of the available settings the user can customize. Any combination of the options provided in the Items section can be selected. The available options allow users to customize their Desktop folder and Documents menu, Start menu, and Favorites folder, as well as download Web pages.

5. The last two options on the dialog are mutually exclusive:

   ■ Create Copies of the Current Items and Their Content

   ■ Create New Items to Save Disk Space

6. Select the desired options, as shown in Figure 14.26, and click **Next** to continue. The Enable Multi-user Settings dialog appears.

7. Windows informs the user that the account-setup process has been completed. Click **Finish**.

8. Windows 98 copies the current settings to create a new profile for the newly created user account and then prompts the user to restart the computer. Click **Yes**.

The next time the user opens the Users utility, the dialog shown in Figure 14.27 will appear. All currently defined user accounts are displayed. New user accounts can be created with the New User button, which results in a series of dialogs similar to those shown in Figures 14.24 through 14.27. Selecting an account and clicking the Delete button deletes an existing account. An existing user account can be used as a template for creating a new account. Doing this requires selecting an account and clicking on the Make a Copy button. Windows displays a series of dialogs. A username and password must be provided, but Windows, using information gathered from the selected user's profile, automatically fills in the rest of the dialogs. The Settings for Selected User section provides the capability for changing a user's password and modifying profile configuration settings.

FIGURE 14.27
The User Settings dialog provides the capability to perform account maintenance.

chapter

15

Windows NT Workstation 4.0

Overview of Windows NT 4.0

Windows NT 4.0 is a high-end, multipurpose, 32-bit operating system complete with integrated networking support. Windows NT supports the NTFS file system, making it very secure. Until the arrival of Windows 2000, it was Microsoft's flagship operating system for corporate computing. It features support for multiple processors, multitasking and multithreading, RAID, and advanced memory management.

Workstation Versus Server

Windows NT 4.0 is delivered in two flavors, NT Server and NT Workstation:

- NT Workstation is designed to provide client functionality on a Microsoft Windows domain, provide peer functionality on a Windows peer network, or function as a standalone workstation. Microsoft targets this operating system as a desktop operating system for all businesses, both big and small.

- NT Server is designed to provide advanced server functionality. This includes file and print services, as well as support for applications. It provides all the functionality of Windows NT Workstation along with support for many advanced client-server functions. Microsoft targets this operating system as a competitor for Novell's NetWare, IBM's OS/2 Server, and various UNIX systems. It is intended to provide support for powerful network applications and network computers such as Windows NT Workstation 4.0.

Table 15.1 provides a comparison between Windows NT Workstation and Server.

Table 15.1 Comparison of Windows NT Workstation and Server

Category	Windows NT Workstation	Windows NT Server
Security	NTFS	NTFS
Remote access	1 inbound session	256 inbound sessions

Category	Windows NT Workstation	Windows NT Server
Performance	Optimized to provide client and peer services	Optimized to provide client-server services
Number of networks	10	Unlimited Connections
Administration	Decentralized (on peer networks)	Centralized

Workstation Versus Windows 9X

Windows NT Workstation requires more hardware resources than Windows 98 or 95. Microsoft's minimum hardware requirements for Windows NT Workstation are listed in Table 15.2.

Table 15.2 Official Microsoft Hardware Requirements for Windows NT Workstation 4.0

Resource	Requirement
CPU	80486 chip running at a minimum of 33MHz
Memory	12MB (16MB recommended)
Hard drive	127MB
CD-ROM	Optional if access is provided to a network CD-ROM or shared drive

SEE ALSO

➤ *For more information on determining the proper hardware requirements for Windows operating systems, see page 26.*

Windows 95 and Windows 98 are two other operating systems offered by Microsoft. Both are marketed as home and low-end corporate desktops. Windows NT Workstation 4.0 differs from these operating systems in many ways.

Windows 95 and Windows 98 require substantially fewer hardware resources. In addition, both will outperform Windows NT Workstation on a computer that just meets the minimum requirments of NT Workstation. However, on a computer with more generous resources, NT Workstation will run rings around these operating systems.

Table 15.3 summarizes many of the differences in the Windows 95, Windows 98, and Windows NT 4.0 operating systems.

Beware Minimum Requirements

Installing Windows NT Workstation 4.0 on a computer whose hardware just meets Microsoft's minimum stated hardware requirements will result in unacceptable performance. A more realistic minimum requirement would be a Pentium-class machine with 16MB of memory, a 400MB hard drive, and a 4-speed CD-ROM. For truly good performance, having 32MB and a 1GB hardware is recommended.

Table 15.3 Operating System Comparison

Category	Windows 95	Windows 98	Windows NT Workstation
Peer networking	Yes	Yes	Yes
Remote access	Yes	Yes	Yes
Support for MS-DOS	Yes	Yes	Not guaranteed
Security	Share	Share	Share and NTFS
Plug and Play	Yes	Yes	No
Support for legacy	Yes	Yes	Not guaranteed

Supported File Systems

In addition to the file allocation table, or FAT, file system used by MS-DOS–based operating systems and the virtual file allocation table, or VFAT, file system introduced by Windows 95, Windows NT introduces support for the new technology file system, or NTFS. NTFS is a secure file system that supports partitions as large as 16 exabytes. It provides file compression, fault tolerance, and support for long filenames up to 256 characters.

SEE ALSO

➤ *For more information about the advantages of NTFS, see page 197.*

NT Security Model

Windows NT Workstation is substantially more secure than Windows 95 or 98. Unlike Windows 95 or 98, one cannot simply gain access to a Windows NT Workstation by clicking Cancel at the logon prompt. Nor can one create a new user account by typing a new account name at the logon prompt. User accounts have to be created by a user with administrative privileges, and users must log on to the computer to gain access to its resources or to the network.

Like Windows 2000, Windows NT 4.0 supports NTFS. NTFS provides a high level of system security by assigning access permissions to users or groups for each object. As part of the logon process, Windows creates an access token for the user that contains the System ID assigned to the user's account and any Group IDs assigned to groups to which the user belongs.

Security is applied to individual objects. Everything in Windows NT is an object. For example, files, directories, drives, and printers are all objects. Every object maintains an *Access Control List*, or *ACL*, that Windows NT uses to decide whether a user may access the object. The ACL is composed of a series of *Access Control Entries*, or *ACEs*.

The system uses the token to determine when a user can access a given resource by comparing the user's access token to the Access Control List assigned to each object.

For example, a file with a filename of File1 might have an ACL that grants Read access to a security ID or SID belonging to a user named Bob, Read access to a user named Sue, Change access to a Group ID belonging to the Sales group, and No Access for a Group ID belonging to the Marketing group, as depicted in Table 15.4.

User Identification

A *SID* (*Security Identifier*) is a unique number that the system uses to identify accounts. The system actually refers to the SID and not to a user's account name when authenticating user credentials at login.

Table 15.4   A Sample of ACE Entries in an ACL

User/Group	Permission
Bob	Read
Sue	Read
Sales	Change
Marketing	No Access

If Bob is a member of the Marketing group, he will be unable to access the file.

Windows NT first examines all the access permissions assigned to a user (including group memberships) looking for an explicit No Access permission. If No Access is specified, the user cannot access the file. If Windows NT does not find a No Access permission, it checks again to see whether the user should be given access. Using the preceding example, Sue and all members of the Sales group have Change access to the file, and all members of the Marketing group (including Bob) are denied access.

Logoff and Logon

Windows NT 4.0 depends on the username and password to identify and authenticate users. After the user enters a valid username and password, Windows NT authenticates the user account information by searching its local security database for a matching username and then comparing passwords. After a positive match, Windows NT creates an access token for the user and completes the logon.

After a user has logged on and completed working, it is appropriate for the user to log off. Users can log off of Windows NT using one of two methods. The most common option is to use the Log Off option located on the Shut Down Windows dialog.

Logging off using the Shut Down dialog box

1. Select **Start** and then **Sh<u>u</u>t Down**. The Shut Down Windows dialog appears.

2. Select the **<u>C</u>lose all programs and logon as a different user?** option.

3. Click **<u>Y</u>es**. Windows displays a prompt stating that the Ctrl+Alt+Delete keys must be pressed to initiate a new login.

The second way to log off is through the Windows NT Security dialog, as described in the next section.

The Security Dialog

One particularly useful security feature in Windows NT Workstation 4.0 is the Security dialog. After logging on to a Windows NT computer, the user can access this dialog by pressing Ctrl+Alt+Delete. The name of the computer and the currently logged-on user is displayed. Six options are available, as outlined in Table 15.5.

Table 15.5 Windows NT Security Dialog Options

Option	Description
Lock Workstation	Provides a fast way for a user to secure the computer without logging off completely. This option is typically used when the user needs to step away from the computer for a few minutes.
Log Off	Provides a fast way for the user to log off the computer and shut down all running applications. Windows NT continues to operate and waits for the next user to log on.

Option	Description
Shut Down	Instructs Windows NT to display a dialog that allows the user to shut down the computer.
Change Password	Presents a dialog allowing the user to change his current password.
Task Manager	Launches the Task Manager utility. This utility displays real-time information about the performance of the computer and allows the user to terminate a program that has stopped responding.
Cancel	Instructs Windows NT to close the Security dialog.

Networking Windows NT

Network setup and configuration on Windows NT Workstation computer is performed using the Network dialog, which is located on the Windows NT Control Panel. The Network dialog consists of a series of property sheets, as outlined in Table 15.6.

Table 15.6 Windows NT 4.0 Network Property Sheets

Tab	Description
Identification	Contains settings that identify the computer to the network and assign workgroup membership.
Services	Provides the ability to view, add, delete, and configure network services on the computer.
Protocols	Provides the ability to view, add, delete, and configure network protocols on the computer.
Adapters	Provides the ability to view, add, remove, and configure network adapters on the computer.
Bindings	Provides the ability to activate, deactivate, and prioritize networking binding for services, protocols, and adapters.

SEE ALSO

➤ *To learn more about the Windows 2000 Add/Remove Programs utility, see page 118.*

Accessing the Network dialog

1. From the Windows NT **Control Panel**, click on **Start**, **Settings**, and then **Control Panel**.

Identifying Windows 2000 Computers

The Identification property sheet provides the same functions as the Network Identification sheet on the System Properties dialog in Windows 2000. Unlike with the Windows 2000 System Properties dialog, Windows NT 4.0 does not provide the Network Identification Wizard to assist the administrator in making changes.

Windows 2000 Services Are Installed Differently

The Services property sheet allows the administrator to install any of more than a dozen available Windows NT services (including Client services). On Windows 2000 only a few services and clients are installed from the Local Area Connection Properties dialog. The rest are installed from the Add/Remove Programs utility using the Windows Components Wizard.

2. Double-click on the **Network** icon in the Control Panel.

or

1. From the Windows NT desktop, right-click on the **Network Neighborhood** icon.

2. Select **Properties** from the pop-up menu that appears.

SEE ALSO

➤ *For more information about administrative accounts and privileges, see page 477.*

Naming Your Computer or Workgroup

Every computer must have a name. This name should be unique throughout the network. On a peer network every NT Workstation is assigned membership in a workgroup.

Naming a computer or workgroup

1. Open the Network dialog and select the **Identification** tab, as shown in Figure 15.1. The current name and workgroup assigned to the computer are displayed.

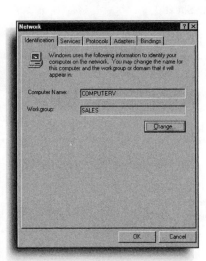

2. Click **Change** to modify these settings.

3. To rename the computer, type a new name in the **Computer Name** field, as shown in Figure 15.2. The Workgroup field becomes grayed out because these two fields are mutually exclusive. Click **OK**.

Locating Protocols

The Protocols property sheet allows the administrator to install any of seven protocols. On Windows 2000 only a few protocols are installed from the Local Area Connection Properties dialog. The rest are installed either from the Add/Remove Programs utility using the Windows Components Wizard or by the Network Connection Wizard when configuring network connections such as a Virtual Private Network connection.

FIGURE 15.1
The Identification tab on the Network dialog displays the computer name and workgroup membership.

Administrative Privileges Required

Making changes to Network settings on Windows NT Workstation requires administrative account privileges. A user without administrative privileges will not be able to make changes to the computer.

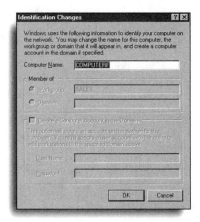

FIGURE 15.2
If the computer name is changed, the Workgroup field becomes unavailable.

4. Windows NT displays a prompt informing the user that the computer must be restarted before the new name will take effect. Click **OK**.

5. To change the workgroup membership for the computer, click on the **Change** button.

6. Select the **Workgroup** option. Type a new workgroup name in the **Workgroup** field and click **OK**.

7. A prompt appears, notifying the user that the computer has joined the workgroup. Click **OK**.

8. Click **Close** on the Identification tab.

9. Click **Yes** when prompted to restart the computer so that the changes can take effect.

The Domain option applies to Windows NT Server–based networks and does not apply to peer networking.

SEE ALSO

➤ *To learn more about Windows NT domains, see page 495.*

Managing Services

Windows NT Workstation is a very modular operating system. NT provides a great deal of flexibility and allows each workstation to be optimized to perform specific tasks. Windows 95 and 98 computers, by contrast, offer very few options for customizing a computer to perform a specific role on the network. By default, Windows NT Workstation loads a default set of services during its installation that provides it with a general network client capability. With the addition and removal of services, a computer's role on the network can be made more specific. Services are managed from the Services tab on the Windows NT Properties dialog.

Viewing network services on an NT Workstation

1. From the Network dialog select the **Services** tab. A list of currently installed services is displayed, as shown in Figure 15.3.

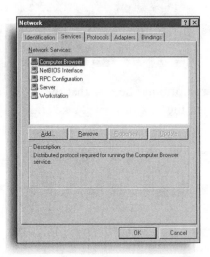

FIGURE 15.3
The Services property sheet on the Network dialog lists all installed services.

2. A list of installed services appears in the Network Services area of the Services property sheet. The Description area provides an explanation of the currently selected service. Click **OK** to close the dialog.

Installing a service

1. Click on the **Add** button on the Services tab of the Network dialog. The Select Network Services dialog appears and displays a list of available services.

2. Select a service and click **OK**. If the Windows NT Workstation CD-ROM is not already loaded in the CD-ROM drive, Windows NT will ask for it. Insert the CD-ROM and click on **Continue**. Windows proceeds to copy the files required to install the service.

3. Depending on the selected services, Windows NT might require some configuration information from the administrator. Click **Close** when you have returned to the Network dialog.

Available Services

The list of available services displayed on the Select Network Services dialog for Windows NT Server is more extensive. Microsoft included services with NT Workstation that provide workstation operations. These same services are available on Windows NT Server, but the server version also includes other services specifically designed to support server activities.

4. Windows NT might require a restart of the computer before the new service can be used. Click **Yes** if prompted to restart the computer.

Anytime a new service is added from the Windows NT CD-ROM, the most recent service pack that has been installed on the computer should be reapplied. Windows NT service packs contain updates and fixes of files that the Windows NT operating system comprises. However, installing a service from the Windows NT CD-ROM usually results in the files that were updated by the service pack getting replaced with the buggy older files. Reinstalling the service pack ensures that the most recent files are in place.

Removing a Service

Any service that is not going to be used should be removed. This allows Windows NT to redistribute any resources that would otherwise have been allocated to the unused service and helps ensure a better-performing computer.

Removing a service

1. To remove a service, select it from the available list on the Network dialog, and click on the **Remove** button.

2. Windows displays a prompt requesting confirmation before removing the service. Click **Yes** to remove the service.

3. Click **Close** on the Network properties dialog.

4. Windows NT requires a restart of the computer. Click **Yes** when prompted.

Configuring a Service

Most Windows NT services can be configured to allow an administrator to further refine their performance or to provide information required to allow the service to run. Services are configured when they are installed. However, as new hardware and software are added to and removed from the computer, there might be a need to reconfigure a service. For example, if a new modem was installed on the computer, the RAS service should be configured to work with it.

459

You Can't Do That from Here

Not every service is configurable. If, after a service is selected, the Properties button is grayed out, the service cannot be configured. For example, the Server and Workstation services cannot be configured because Microsoft has already fine-tuned them. Other services such as the Remote Access Service require specification of certain parameters, such as the identification of an installed modem and the appropriate dialing options.

NWLink?

NWLink is the Windows NT term that refers to its implementation of the IPX/SPX protocol.

Configuring a service

1. To configure a service, select it from the list of services on the Services tab of the Network dialog, and click on the **Properties** button. A configuration dialog for the selected service appears.

2. Make the desired changes and click **OK**.

3. Click on **Close**.

4. A restart of the computer might be required. If prompted, click **Yes** to restart the computer.

Network Protocols

Like every other operating system, Windows NT Workstation depends on protocols to facilitate communications with the network. Windows NT supports the following protocols:

- TCP/IP
- NWLink
- NetBEUI

Viewing Protocols

Protocols are managed from the Protocols tab on the Windows NT Properties dialog.

To view the installed network protocols, open the Network dialog and select the **Protocols** sheet. A list of installed protocols is displayed, as shown in Figure 15.4. Click **OK** to close the dialog.

FIGURE 15.4
The Protocols sheet on the Network dialog lists all installed protocols.

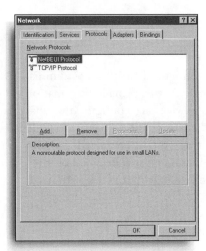

Adding a Protocol

Windows NT provides various protocols that support network communication:

- The NetBEUI, NWLink, and TCP/IP LAN protocols
- The PPTP protocol for building a VPN
- The AppleTalk protocol, which provides support for Apple computers
- The DLC protocol, which supports network printers and mainframe communications

SEE ALSO

➤ *For more information on LAN protocols, see page 524.*
➤ *For more information on the DLC protocol, see page 535.*
➤ *For more information on the PPTP protocol, see page 536.*

Adding a protocol

1. To add a protocol click on the **Add** button on the Protocols tab of the Network dialog. The Select Network Protocol dialog appears and displays a list of available protocols.

2. Select a protocol and click **OK**. If the Windows NT Workstation CD-ROM is not already loaded in the CD-ROM driver, Windows NT will ask for it. Insert the CD-ROM and click on **Continue**. Windows proceeds to copy the files required to install the protocol.

3. Depending on the protocol selected, Windows NT might require some configuration information.

4. Click **Close** on the Network dialog. Windows NT proceeds to set up the appropriate set of network bindings.

5. Windows NT requires a restart of the computer before the new service can be used. Click **Yes** when prompted to restart the computer.

> **Reinstall Service Packs**
>
> Anytime a new protocol is added from the Windows NT CD-ROM, the most recent service pack that has been installed on the computer should be reapplied.

Removing a Protocol

Just as with unused services and clients, any unused protocol should be removed from the computer. This allows Windows NT to free up and redistribute its resources and helps ensure a better-performing computer.

Removing a protocol

1. To remove a protocol, select it from the available list on the Network dialog, and click on the **Remove** button.

2. Windows displays a prompt requesting confirmation before removing the protocol. Click **Yes** to remove the protocol.

3. Windows NT removes any existing bindings against the protocol. Click **Close** after making any necessary changes.

4. Windows NT requires a restart of the computer. Click **Yes** when prompted.

Configuring a Protocol

For a computer to communicate over a network, at least one common protocol needs to be installed and configured on every computer. Some protocols, such as NetBEUI, require no configuration after installation. Others, such as TCP/IP, require configuration. Protocol configuration occurs when the protocol is first installed, but as changes in the network occur, configuration changes might be required.

Configuring a protocol

1. To configure a protocol, select it from the list of protocols on the Network dialog, and click on the **Properties** button. A configuration dialog for the selected protocol appears (see Figure 15.5).

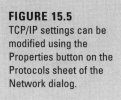

FIGURE 15.5
TCP/IP settings can be modified using the Properties button on the Protocols sheet of the Network dialog.

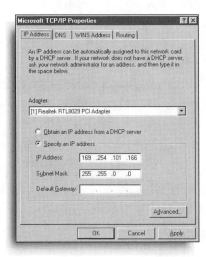

2. Make the desired changes and click **Apply** and then **OK**.

3. Click **OK** when you have returned to the Network dialog.

4. A restart of the computer might be required. If prompted, click **Yes** to restart the computer.

Network Interface Cards

Like every other computer attached to the network, a Windows NT Workstation computer requires a NIC. NICs are installed and managed from the Adapters tab on the Network dialog. If the NIC was already installed when Windows NT Workstation was installed, the card should have been identified and installed. However, if this is not the case, a manual installation of the card will be required.

Adding a NIC

1. Access the Network dialog and select the **Adapters** property sheet. Any currently installed NICs are displayed in the Network Adapters area of the dialog.

2. Click on the **Add** button. The Select Network Adapter dialog appears and displays a list of adapters. To install an adapter from this list, select the adapter card and click **OK**. Supply the Windows NT CD-ROM when requested. Windows NT might display a dialog of configuration settings. Usually, the default settings listed on the dialog are correct and should be accepted.

3. Restart the computer.

To remove a NIC, select it from the available list on the Network dialog, and click on the **Remove** button. Windows displays a prompt, requesting confirmation before removing the card.

To configure a NIC, select it from the available list on the Network dialog, and click on the **Properties** button. The properties dialog for the selected adapter appears. Make the desired changes and click **OK**. A restart of the computer might be required.

Bindings

A binding is the connection of a protocol or service to a NIC. Binding to a NIC allows the service or protocol to use it. Multiple services and protocols can be bound to the same card or to many different cards. By default, Windows NT binds a service or protocol to every NIC when installed. Each bound resource adds additional overhead. Part of optimizing a Windows NT Workstation computer's network configuration consists of reviewing and disabling unnecessary bindings or changing the order in which they are checked by Windows NT.

Current bindings can be viewed or changed from the Bindings tab on the Network dialog. NIC bindings can be viewed in a few ways:

- By services
- By protocols
- By adapters

The default view is by services. Each view can be expanded to show greater detail when the plus signs to the left of listed objects are clicked. This results in a treelike view of bindings. From here, bindings can be disabled and enabled. In addition, they can be prioritized using the Move Up and Move Down buttons. Bindings are processed in the order listed on the dialog. It is best to put the most frequently used binding on top because this reduces connection time.

Windows NT Application Performance

For a Windows NT computer to operate efficiently on the network, it is important that it be configured according to the role that it is assigned to perform. Windows NT automatically adjusts the priority of running jobs based on what the user is doing by raising the priority assigned to foreground processes.

This approach speeds up response time for the local user. Windows NT reduces the priority of applications running in the background. Windows NT automatically manages this priority-adjustment process for applications, and it also assigns resources to services to ensure that they can provide their services. Adjusting application performance, therefore, affects applications and not background services. However, if the applications being executed are network applications such as a database that is started and operated in the background, manually adjusting priorities can increase performance.

An application's priority can be changed in three ways in Windows NT:

- Configure the manner in which Windows NT handles all applications.

- Start an individual job with a specific priority from the command line.

- Change a running job's priority using the Task Manager utility.

Configuring the performance for all applications

1. From the Windows NT Control Panel, double-click on the **System** icon. The System Properties dialog appears.

2. Select the **Performance** tab.

3. Move the slider bar in the Application Performance section to the right to provide foreground applications with the best performance, move it to the middle to reduce the amount of attention given to foreground applications, and move it to the left to assign an equal priority to all applications.

4. Click **Apply** and then **OK**.

Using the Start command, users can run individual applications with different priorities. This allows more important applications to receive more system resources. The three levels of priorities are shown in Table 15.7.

Configuring VM and Performance in Windows 9X and 2000

Both virtual memory and application performance can be configured from the Systems utility on a Windows 2000 computer in the same manner as Windows NT.

Windows 9X computers are configured as either desktop computers or network servers.

Table 15.7 The Three Levels of Application Priorities

Priority	Description
Low	Starts an application with a lower than normal priority.
Normal	Starts an application with the same level of priority as other applications.
High	Starts an application at a higher-than-normal priority.

The following example demonstrates how to start an application with different priorities. This example uses Notepad.

Starting an application with different priorities

1. Select **Start**, **Programs**, and then **Command Prompt**.

2. Type `start /low notepad` and press Enter. The Notepad application appears.

3. Type `start /high notepad` and press Enter. A second instance of the Notepad application starts.

4. Work with both instances of Notepad and observe the different levels of response provided by each instance.

Altering a running application's priority

1. Press **Ctrl+Alt+Delete**. The Windows NT Security dialog appears.

2. Select **Task Manager**. The Task Manager utility appears.

3. Select the **Applications** tab.

4. Select the application and then select **Update Speed** from the **View** menu.

5. Select **High**, **Normal**, or **Low**.

Another configuration setting that can improve system performance is virtual memory. Virtual memory is an operating-system technique that uses a preset portion of a local hard drive to augment conventional memory. When a computer begins to run low on conventional memory, the operating system begins to transfer pages of data stored in memory from memory to a special file known as the paging file located on a local hard disk. This frees up memory, which is then made available to hold other data. If the operating system or an application requires data that has been moved onto the paging file, the operating system moves other data from memory to the paging file to make room and then retrieves that required data from the paging file and places it back into memory.

The more conventional memory a computer has, the less virtual memory will be required and the faster a computer will operate. Windows NT assumes control of virtual memory by default. However, several adjustments can be made that might improve performance. The process of configuring virtual memory is the same for both Windows NT Workstation 4.0 and Windows 2000 Pro.

SEE ALSO

➤ *To learn more about managing virtual memory and changing its settings, see page 108.*

Installing a Printer

The Windows NT print process operates in essentially the same manner as the Windows 2000 print process. Likewise, the process of installing a printer on a Windows NT Workstation 4.0 computer is very similar to the process of installing one under Windows 2000 Pro.

Printers are installed with the Add Printer Wizard, which is started from the Add Printer icon on the Windows Control Panel. After a printer, either local or network, has been installed, an iconic representation appears in this panel. Right-clicking on a printer's icon and then selecting Properties allows the printer to be configured.

SEE ALSO

➤ *To learn how Windows 2000 manages the print process, see page 146.*

Installing a local printer

1. Select **Start**, **Settings**, and then **Printers**. The Printers Panel appears.

2. Double-click on the **Add Printer** icon. The Add Printer Wizard starts.

3. Select **My Computer** and click **Next**.

4. Select the parallel port where the printer has been attached from the **Available ports** list, and click **Next**.

5. Select the manufacturer of the printer from the **Manufacturers** list. Select the Printer model from the **Printers** list. Click **Next**.

6. Supply a name for the printer up to 31 characters long in the **Printer Name** field, and click **Next**.

7. To set up the printer as a network share, select the **Shared** option and type a name for the printer in the **Share Name** field. Otherwise, select **Not Shared**. Click **Next**.

8. Select **Yes** to print a test page and then click **Finish**.

9. When prompted, supply the Windows NT Workstation 4.0 CD-ROM.

Managing Shared Resources

Windows NT Workstation can share printers, folders, and entire drives. Printers can be configured as network shares during their installation or from the Sharing tab on their Properties dialog. Windows NT also offers the same printing features as Windows 2000, such as establishing printer pools and managing printers by assigning priorities to printers. Folders and drives can be shared anytime after the installation of the operating system and can be protected using both share and NTFS security.

Sharing a Printer

All print management is performed from the Printers panel. Print sharing is established individually for each printer from the Sharing tab on the printer's property sheet.

Sharing a printer

1. Select **Start**, **Settings**, and then **Printers**. The Printers panel appears.

2. Right-click on a printer icon in the Printer panel, and select **Sharing** from the menu that appears.

3. Select the **Shared** option, as shown in Figure 15.6.

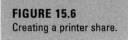
FIGURE 15.6
Creating a printer share.

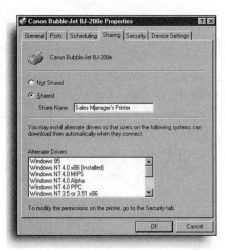

4. Type a name for the printer in the **Share Name** field, and click **OK**.

5. If the name assigned to the printer is longer than eight characters, Windows NT displays a prompt warning that MS-DOS applications will be unable to access the printer. Click **Yes**.

Share security does not apply to printers under Windows NT 4.0. If NTFS has been installed as the computer's file system, NTFS security can be applied from the Permissions button on the Security tab of the Printers Properties dialog. From here, security is applied to users and groups in the same manner as on Windows 2000.

Drive and Folder Sharing

Drive and folder security under Windows NT is performed from the Sharing and Security tabs on the Properties dialog on each object. If NTFS has been installed as the file system, both share and NTFS security will be available. The process of applying both share and NTFS security on a Windows NT computer is very similar to the manner in which it is done on Windows NT 2000.

Windows NT Management

Windows NT provides an abundance of administrative tools that an administrator will find helpful when managing the network. One such tool, the Task Manager utility, is started from the Windows taskbar. The rest are located in either the Windows Control Panel or the Administrative Tools menu:

Control Panel Utilities	**Administrative Tools**
■ Server	■ Event Viewer
■ Services	■ User Manager
	■ Performance Monitor
	■ Remote Access Admin
	■ Windows NT Diagnostics

Task Manager

The Task Manager is a great tool for network administrators. It provides quick access to various useful pieces of troubleshooting information. It can be used to monitor CPU and memory usage, change application priorities, and terminate nonresponsive programs.

Accessing the Task Manager utility requires either right-clicking on the taskbar and selecting **Task Manager** or pressing **Ctrl+Alt+Delete** and selecting **Task List**. The Task Manager provides three tabs for viewing current system information in the following categories:

- Applications
- Processes
- Performance

Figures 15.7 and 15.8 show the Applications and Processes tabs, respectively.

FIGURE 15.7
The Applications tab provides a view of all active applications and their statuses.

FIGURE 15.8
The Processes tab provides a view of all active processes and their statuses.

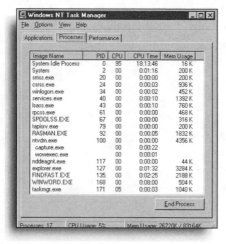

The Applications tab presents a view of all active programs or tasks and provides the ability to terminate or switch to a selected program. In addition, a new program can be started by selecting the New Task button and providing a program's name and path. The Processes tab displays information about every process currently active on the computer and allows the administrator to terminate processes. The Performance tab displays graphic information about a computer's CPU and memory usage.

Terminating an Application

The Task Manager is a useful tool for troubleshooting slow system performance and shutting down applications that have stopped responding. Applications that become nonresponsive leave the users unable to continue working. The solution is to use the Task Manager to stop and restart the application.

Terminating an application via the Task Manager

1. Right-click on the taskbar and select **Task Manager**.

2. Click on the **Applications** tab.

3. Select the offending application and click **End Task**.

Server

The Server utility provides a tool for viewing network users as they access local computer resources. It provides the same basic functionality as the Windows 2000 Shared Folders snap-in. This utility has three available views:

- Shares
- Sessions
- Open Files

SEE ALSO
➤ To learn more about the Shared Folders snap-in, see page 312.

Running the server utility

1. Double-click on the **Server** icon on the Windows NT Control Panel. The Server dialog appears, as shown in Figure 15.9.

What's in a Process?

Processes include applications, application components, and system background processes.

Monitoring Computer Performance

The Task Manager can be used to get a quick look at CPU and memory status when network users complain about slow response. If the CPU stays over 80% busy for long periods, it might be time to either upgrade the CPU or move some of the workload to another computer. If memory is constantly maximized and the hard drive is constantly thrashing, a memory upgrade may be in order.

Oust Them If You Must...

Administrators need to occasionally perform maintenance on network computers. This usually means that network users should not be permitted access to this box during this time. The server manager can be used to look for open network sessions and to forcefully terminate them if the connected network users cannot be located.

FIGURE 15.9
The Server utility provides the ability to monitor and control access to resources on the computer.

The information provided by this display is summarized in Table 15.8.

Shared Folders Snap-In

The Shared Folders snap-in in Windows 2000 Pro provides that operating system with similar control over shared resources. In addition, the snap-in provides the ability to create new shares for both local and network computers. Windows 9X operating systems provide similar functionality with the Net Watcher utility.

Table 15.8 Summary Information Provided by the Server Utility

Category	Description
Sessions	Displays the number of connected network computers.
Open Files	Displays the number of files being accessed by network users.
File Locks	Displays the number of files currently locked by network users.
Open Named Pipes	Displays the number of open named pipes. A pipe is a means of supporting communication with other network computers.

The Server utility provides three views of the current status of shared local resources: Users view, Shares view, and In Use view.

Users View

The Users view lists all network users currently accessing local shared resources, as shown in Figure 15.10. The bottom portion of the dialog shows all the resources being accessed by the currently selected user. The Disconnect button enables an administrator to disconnect a selected user from the computer. The Disconnect All button terminates all user sessions.

Shares View

The Shares view lists all currently shared resources on the computer, as demonstrated in Figure 15.11. The bottom portion of the dialog displays all network users currently connected to the selected resource. The Disconnect and Disconnect All buttons allow the administrator to terminate network users' sessions with local resources.

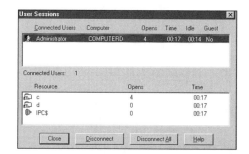

FIGURE 15.10
The Users view on the Server utility.

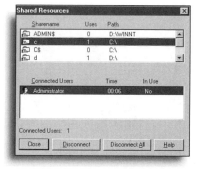

FIGURE 15.11
The Shares view on the Server utility.

Don't Disconnect Users Without Notice

When disconnecting network users' sessions to the local computer, any unsaved work will be lost. It is advisable to contact users before disconnecting them.

In Use View

The In Use view lists the resources opened by network users, as demonstrated in Figure 15.12. The Close Resource and Close All Resources buttons enable an administrator to terminate network user access.

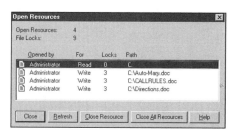

FIGURE 15.12
The In Use view on the Server utility.

Services

Like Windows 2000 Pro, Windows NT Workstation 4.0 is a modular operating system and provides many of its features in the form of services. A service is a part of the operating system that performs a given function. Services add to the core functionality provided by the base operating system and other services. Table 15.9 lists the network services that Windows NT Workstation 4.0 installs by default.

Table 15.9 Default Network Services

Service	Description
Computer Browser	Supports network browsing.
NetBIOS Interface	A software interface that supports Windows networking.
RPC Configuration	Supports programs by facilitating remote program execution.
Server	Manages file and printer services for remotely connected computers.
Workstation	Manages connections with network computers.

By adding, removing, and configuring services, administrators can limit or provide functionality on the computer. Services are added, removed, and configured through the Network utility on the Windows NT Control Panel. The Services utility located on the Windows NT Control Panel provides the ability to start and stop services, as well as to configure how they are handled when the computer boots up.

The Services utility displays a list of every installed service on the computer, including each service's current status and Startup configuration, as demonstrated in Figure 15.13.

A service can have a few statuses:

- Started
- Paused
- Stopped

Services Snap-In

The Services snap-in provides Windows 2000 Pro with similar control over services.

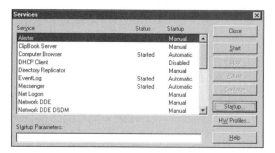

FIGURE 15.13
The Services utility provides control over service status and startup.

Services can also be started and stopped from the command line with the NET Start and NET Stop commands.

SEE ALSO

➤ *For more information about working with Net commands to control services, see page 504.*

Changing the Status of a Service

Sometimes, a service on a Windows NT computer stops operating and must be stopped and started to restore normal operations. For example, a Windows NT computer that shares its printer might stop submitting print jobs to the print device. If everything appears to be in order, sometimes stopping and starting the spooler service restores printing and saves the administrator from having to reboot the computer. This provides a minimal disruption and does not affect network users who might be accessing other resources on the computer.

Changing the status of a service

1. Double-click on the **Services** icon on the Windows NT Control Panel.

2. Select a service.

3. Select the **S**tart, S**t**op, **P**ause, or **C**ontinue button.

The Startup column displays the action Windows NT takes on a service when the computer is started. A startup type of Automatic means that the service is automatically started when the computer is started. A startup type of Manual means that the service is not automatically started but can be started from the Services utility. A startup type of Disabled prevents the service from being started.

Changing Service Startup

Not all services are needed all the time. This can be especially true when third-party applications install their own services. Windows

Ramifications of Stopping a Service

Many services depend on other services. Therefore, stopping one service might affect other services. For example, the Alerter service, which notifies selected users or computers when administrative alerts occur, depends on the Messenger service. Stopping the Messenger service will therefore affect the Alerter service.

Pausing a Service Might Be Less Disruptive

Sometimes, stopping a service is too abrupt an action. For example, stopping the Server service immediately disconnects any network users from the computer and might cause a loss of work. Pausing the service prevents any new network users from connecting to the computer while allowing currently logged-on users to continue. The administrator can then contact these users and ask them to complete their work and disconnect.

NT allows administrators to control when and how services are started.

Changing service startup

1. Double-click on the **Services** icon on the Windows NT Control Panel.
2. Select a service.

FIGURE 15.14
Modifying a service's startup mode.

3. Click on the **Startup** button. A dialog similar to the one shown in Figure 15.14 appears.
4. Under the Startup Type section, select one of the following options:

Automatic	The service will start at system startup.
Manual	The service will not automatically start but can be manually started by administrators.
Disabled	The service will not start and cannot be started.

5. Click **OK**.
6. Click **Close**.

Using the Event Viewer to Troubleshoot Problems with Services

Sometimes, services fail to start at system startup. Windows displays an error message when this occurs. Use the Windows NT Event Viewer to search the system log for more information about the cause of the problem.

Event Viewer

Like Windows 2000 Pro, Windows NT Workstation 4.0 records information about system events in logs. For example, an event record is written to the system log if a service fails to start upon system initialization. Windows NT logs event information in three different logs, as shown in Table 15.10.

Table 15.10   Event Logs

Log Name	Description
System	Contains event records for operating-system and software-driver events.
Security	Contains audit information as specified by the audit policy.
Application	Contains events records generated by Windows applications.

A utility called the Event Viewer is used to view and manage event logs.

Starting the Event Viewer

1. Select **Start**, **Programs**, **Administrative Tools**, and then **Event Viewer**. The Event Viewer appears.

2. By default, the System log is displayed. To select a different log for viewing, select it from the **Log** menu.

3. When done viewing logs, click on **Exit** on the **Log** menu to close the Event Viewer.

Different priorities are assigned to events as they are written to the log. The priorities appear on the far-left side of the Event Viewer and provide a visual means of immediately locating more critical events. A description of event priorities is provided in Table 15.11.

Table 15.11   Event Logs

Alert Category	Alert Icon
Information	Blue I
Alert	Yellow exclamation mark
Critical	Red stop sign

User Manager

The User Manager utility provides an interface for performing the following functions on a Windows NT Workstation:

- Creating and managing user accounts

Event Viewer Provides the Same Functionality

The Windows 2000 Event Viewer snap-in provides the operating system with similar control over event logs. Windows for Workgroups also supports a simpler version of the Event Viewer that provides substantially less functionality. There is no similar tool in Windows 9X operating systems.

- Creating and managing group accounts
- Creating and managing an account policy
- Administering user rights
- Establishing an audit policy

SEE ALSO
➤ *For more information on the basics of creating and managing group accounts, see page 189.*
➤ *For more information on the basics of creating and managing account, user rights, and audit policies, see page 189.*

Creating User Accounts

Windows NT uses user accounts to identify and authenticate users. No one can access the computer without access to a valid user account and its associated password. Administrators create user accounts and assign them appropriate access permissions to control the level of access permitted to users.

Creating a user account

1. Select **Start**, **Programs**, **Administrative Tools**, and then **User Manager**. The User Manager dialog appears, as shown in Figure 15.15.

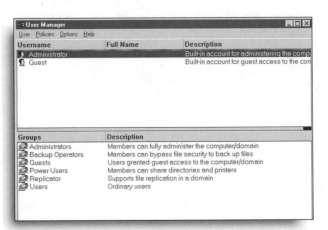

2. Select **New User** from the **User** menu. The New User dialog appears, as shown in Figure 15.16.

Local Users and Groups Provides the Same Functionality for Windows 2000

On a Windows 2000 Pro computer, the Local Users and Groups snap-in provides that operating system with similar tools for managing user and group accounts.

A User Account Is Needed for Each Computer

A user account must be created on every Windows NT computer that its associated user will need to access.

FIGURE 15.15
The User Manager utility is Windows NT Workstation's account management tool.

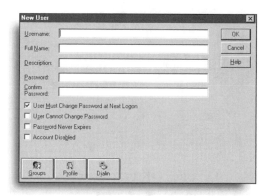

FIGURE 15.16
Adding a new user
account.

3. Type entries into the **Username**, **Full Name**, and **Description** fields for the new user account.

4. Type a password for the new account in the **Password** and **Confirm Password** fields.

5. **User Must Change Password at Next Logon** is selected by default. This ensures that no one other than the user will know the user's password after the first time the user logs on to the computer.

6. If this is an account to be shared by multiple users, you might want to select **User Cannot Change Password** to prevent the user from changing the password for the account and preventing other users from using the account.

7. Select **Password Never Expires** to override the Password Expires In X Days entry on the Account Policy.

8. Select **Account Disabled** to place the user account in a disabled state. This option can be cleared later to enable the account.

9. Click on the **Groups** button to assign the account group memberships. The Group Memberships dialog appears, as shown in Figure 15.17.

10. By default, all new user accounts are added to the Users group. Use the **Add** and **Remove** buttons to change group membership, and click **OK**.

11. Click on the **Profile** button to establish profile information. Click **OK** when done.

12. Click on the **Dialin** button to configure the account for remote access. Select the appropriate dial-in options and click **OK**.

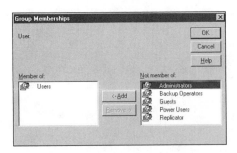

FIGURE 15.17
Selecting group membership

13. Click **OK** to create the account. The new account now appears in the list of users' accounts on the local computer.

Creating Group Accounts

Windows NT provides for the establishment of groups as a means of managing large numbers of users. For example, if a network has 30 users, an administrator could create several groups and add the users to these groups and then manage security at a group level. Any changes made to group accounts affect all members' user accounts.

Windows NT Workstation 4.0 provides a set of default groups, as shown in Table 15.12.

Table 15.12 Built-In Group Accounts

Group	Description
Administrators	Provides member accounts with Administrative privileges.
Backup Operators	Provides member accounts with the capability to backup and restore files.
Guests	Provides member accounts with limited access capabilities.
Power Users	Provides member accounts with advanced capabilities, including the capability to share printers, drives, and folders.
Replicator	Supports file replication on a domain network and is not used on a peer network.
Users	Provides member accounts with normal network rights and permissions.

Creating New Local Group Accounts

In addition to the default set of group accounts described in the preceding section, administrators can create new ones that further refine the access levels required by the company.

Creating a group account

1. Select **Start**, **Programs**, **Administrative Tools**, and then **User Manager**. The User Manager dialog appears.

2. Select **New Local Group** from the **User** menu. The New Local Group dialog appears, as shown in Figure 15.18.

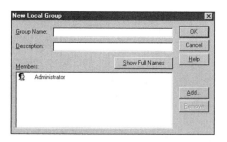

FIGURE 15.18
Creating a new local group.

Group Accounts Are Needed on Each Computer

Like user accounts, a group account must be created on every Windows NT computer on which its member accounts are located.

3. Type a name for the group in the **Group Name** field and an option description in the **Description** field.

4. Click **Add** to add user accounts as members of the group. The Add Users and Groups dialog appears, as shown in Figure 15.19.

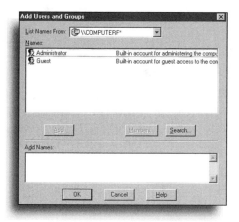

FIGURE 15.19
Adding a user account to a new group.

5. Select a user from the **Names** section and click on **Add**. Repeat this step as many times as necessary, and then click **OK**.

6. Click **OK** to close the New Local Group dialog.

Deleting an Account

When an account is no longer needed, it should be deleted. This eliminates unnecessary clutter and confusion. Because of the nature of peer networking, the account needs to be deleted on every computer on which it was created.

Deleting an account

1. Select **Start**, **Programs**, **Administrative Tools**, and then **User Manager**. The User Manager dialog appears.

2. Select a user or group account, and then select **Delete** from the **User** menu.

3. If a user account was selected, Windows NT displays a prompt informing the administrator that after the account is deleted the access assigned to the account is lost and cannot be retrieved by re-creation of the account. Click **OK**.

4. Click **Yes** when prompted for confirmation.

Establishing Policies

Policies are a tool for enforcing advanced security on Windows NT. Policies are established from the User Manager utility. Windows NT policies include the following:

- Account
- User Rights
- Audit

Account Policy

An account policy governs the use of passwords by network users by enforcing a set of preconfigured standards designed to help ensure network security.

An account policy is a set of rules Windows NT enforces on the creation of user passwords and the management of user accounts. Password policy is established locally on each Windows NT computer. This policy is used to enforce certain rules over passwords, such as a minimum length, maximum age, and uniqueness requirements.

The available password policy settings and their default values are listed in Table 15.13.

Table 15.13 Available Password Policy Entries on Windows NT Workstation

Description	Default Setting
Maximum Password Age	Expires in 42 Days
Minimum Password Age	Allows Changes Immediately
Minimum Password Length	Permits Blank Password
Password Uniqueness	Do Not Keep Password History
Account Lockout/No Account Lockout	No Account Lockout
User Must Logon To Change Password	Not Selected

Group Policies Snap-In

Policies are set with the Group Policies snap-in on Windows 2000 Pro computers. Windows 9X operating systems provide support for policies using the System Policy utility.

Establishing an account policy

1. Select **Start**, **Programs**, **Administrative Tools**, and then **User Manager**. The User Manager dialog appears.

2. Select **Account** from the **Policies** menu. The Account Policy dialog appears, as shown in Figure 15.20.

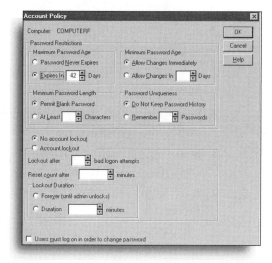

FIGURE 15.20
Establishing an account policy.

3. Select the desired policy options and click **OK**.

Setting User Rights Policies

A rights policy manages the rights assigned to user and group accounts. A right provides the capability to perform a specified action on the system. Users without an assigned right cannot perform its associated actions. Rights are global in that they apply to the entire computer, as opposed to permissions, which are applied to individual objects.

Two sets of rights are available on a Windows NT computer: basic rights and advanced rights. Advanced rights are related to programming issues and are not involved in typical computer administration.

A list of the basic user rights is shown here:

- Access this computer from the network
- Back up files and directories
- Change the system time
- Force shutdown from a remote system
- Load and unload device drivers
- Log on locally
- Manage auditing and the security log
- Restore files and directories
- Shut down the system
- Take ownership of files or other objects

Setting a user rights policy

1. Select **Start**, **Programs**, **Administrative Tools**, and then **User Manager**. The User Manager dialog appears.

2. Select **User Rights** from the **Policies** menu. The User Rights Policy dialog appears.

3. Select a right from the **Right** drop-down list. A list of all users and groups assigned this right appears in the **Grant To** area.

4. Use the **Add** and **Remove** buttons to add or remove users and groups for this right.

5. Click **OK**.

Setting Audit Policies

An audit policy controls which Windows NT events are recorded in the security log. A computer's audit policy is established from the User Manager utility.

Setting an audit policy

1. Select **Start**, **Programs**, **Administrative Tools**, and then **User Manager**. The User Manager dialog appears.

2. Select **<u>A</u>udit** from the **<u>P</u>olicies** menu. The Audit Policy dialog
   appears, as shown in Figure 15.21.

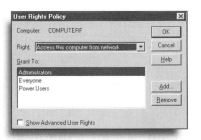

FIGURE 15.21
Establishing an audit policy.

3. Select **<u>A</u>udit These Events.** The remaining portions of the dialog are enabled.

4. Select the types of success and failure events to be audited, and
   click **OK**.

Performance Monitor

The Performance Monitor utility is a graphical tool for viewing and
collecting performance data on network computers. Key system
components are viewed objects. Each object has an associated group
of counters that provide data about that specific aspect of the object.
Data is viewed as a graphic chart or report and can be archived and
retrieved for later review.

Using Performance Monitor, an administrator can monitor a computer's performance and look for problems such as poor performance
or insufficient hardware resources.

Monitoring system performance

1. Select **Start**, **<u>P</u>rograms**, **Administrative Tools**, and then
   Performance Monitor.

2. Select the **<u>A</u>dd to Chart** option from the **<u>E</u>dit** menu. The Add
   to Chart dialog appears.

3. Type the name of the computer you want to monitor in the
   <u>C</u>omputer field.

4. Select the type of object you want to monitor from the **O<u>b</u>ject**
   drop-down list.

5. Select a counter from the available list for that object in the
   Coun<u>t</u>ers list.

6. Select a specific instance for the selected counter in the **Instance** list.

7. Click **Add**. To add additional counters repeat the preceding steps. When done, click **Done**.

Refer to Windows NT's online help for more information on working with Performance Monitor.

SEE ALSO

➤ *For more information on working with Performance Monitor, see page 320.*

Windows NT Diagnostics

The Windows NT Diagnostics utility displays information about the status of the computer. Information is categorized and displayed in a series of nine tabs, as shown in Table 15.14.

System Information in Windows 2000

The Windows 2000 System Information snap-in provides information about a computer's system configuration. This includes information about software, hardware, and other system components. Windows 98 provides similar information with the Microsoft System Information utility.

Table 15.14 Windows NT Diagnostics Categories

Tab	Description
Version	Provides information about the current version of Windows NT.
System	Provides information about the CPU, motherboard, and BIOS.
Display	Provides information about the video card and its current settings.
Drives	Shows a list of all drives on the computer categorized by type.
Memory	Shows the total amount of memory on the computer and its current usage, including information about the paging file.
Services	Provides a list of services or devices and their current status.
Resources	Provides lists showing the allocation of the following types of resources: IRQ, I/O Port, DMA, Memory, and Devices.
Environment	Shows the current status of system and user variables.
Network	Provides information about the current network status.

Summary and detail reports can be printed or saved for the currently selected tab or for all tabs. This allows administrators to archive system information for the computer and retrieve it in the future for troubleshooting.

SEE ALSO

➤ *For more information on the Windows 2000 System Information snap-in, see page 309.*

Creating a file or printed report

1. Select **Start**, **Programs**, **Administrative Tools**, and then **Windows NT Diagnostics**. The Windows NT Diagnostics dialog appears, as shown in Figure 15.22.

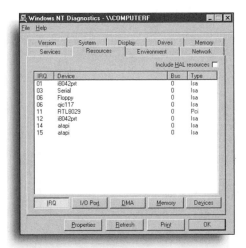

FIGURE 15.22
The Resources sheet on the Windows NT Diagnostics dialog.

2. Select **Save Report** from the **File** menu to save a report as a file, or select **Print Report** to submit a report to a print device. The Create Report dialog appears.

3. Select either **Current** tab or **All Tabs** to specify the information to be presented.

4. Select either **Summary** or **Complete** to determine the content of the report.

5. Select either **File** or **Default Printer** to determine the destination of the report. If File was selected, specify the location where the report should be stored when prompted, and click **Save**.

Upgrading Your Peer Network

So You've Outgrown Your Peer Network

When the network consists of fewer than 10 computers, peer networking provides a very effective solution. As the network grows beyond this size, however, peer network administration begins to grow cumbersome while network performance declines.

Peer networks provide most of the functionality provided by server-based networks. The one lagging exception is the lack of strong centralized security. There are two other differences:

- Peer networks are not capable of scaling beyond 10 computers.
- Peer computers don't provide the same level of performance as their server counterparts.

If your peer network is lacking in speed or functionality, one idea (other than resorting to a client-server networking model) is to introduce dedicated peer servers. Users do not log on to dedicated peer computers to perform their daily work as they would in a server-based environment. Instead, these machines are devoted exclusively to the task of providing services such as email, print, or file services to other workstations on the network.

A dedicated peer computer allows computers in a peer network to focus all their resources on providing network services. This option reduces the number of available peer computers available to network users but can be used to improve the delivery of network services by dedicated resources and remove some of the workload that would otherwise have been performed on other peer computers.

If dedicated computers still do not provide a robust enough level of performance or you find your network growing well beyond 10 computers, you will need to change to the client-server networking model. However, the migration to the client-server model comes with a price tag—as well as a sharper learning curve. At a minimum, the following components must be purchased:

- A copy of a network operating system, or NOS, with sufficient licenses to provide access to all users
- A computer with sufficient hardware to serve as the primary network server

- One or more additional computers to act as backup to the primary computer and to balance the workload

- Additional NIC cards and cabling

Planning and implementing a client-server network requires a great deal more technical skill and experience than is required for a peer network. Whereas one or two company employees might manage a peer network as a part-time activity, client-server networks typically require at least one experienced full-time network administrator.

Many companies look for employees with several years of hands-on experience and for administrators who possess the Microsoft Certified Systems Engineer, or MCSE, certification. To achieve this certification, network administrators must study and pass a series of six computer-based exams demonstrating their knowledge with Windows NT Server; a major operating system such as Windows 95, 98, or NT Workstation; and networking in general. Of course, vendors of other operating systems offer similar certifications for networking professionals who support their respective network operating systems.

Several excellent network operating systems are available on the market today, such as Novell's NetWare, IBM's OS/2 Warp Server, and Microsoft's Windows NT Server. Although each NOS provides its own distinctive strategy for NOS implementation, all provide the same core set of networking services. The rest of this chapter focuses on using Windows 2000 Server as the NOS model.

According to Microsoft, the data shown in Table 16.1 represents the minimum requirements for supporting Windows 2000 Server.

Table 16.1   Microsoft's Minimum Hardware Requirements for Running NT Server

Resource	Minimum Requirement
CPU	Pentium 166MHz
Memory	64MB (128MB recommended)
Hard drive	685MB

Want to Learn More?

Que offers a fine assortment of study guides that will prepare you for the rigors of MCSE certification. If you decide that becoming an MCSE is a viable career option, I suggest picking up copies of the following books at your local bookstore:

- *MCSE Microsoft Windows NT Server Exam Guide, Second Edition,* ISBN 0-7897-2264-X

- *MCSE Microsoft Windows NT Workstation Exam Guide, Second Edition,* ISBN 0-7897-2262-3

- *MCSE Microsoft Windows NT Server in the Enterprise Exam Guide, Second Edition,* ISBN 0-7897-2263-1

- MCSE Networking Essentials Exam Guide, Second Edition, ISBN 0-7897-2265-8

- *MCSE Core Certification Exam Guide 6-in-1,* ISBN 0-7897-2259-3

Windows Operating Systems' Functionality

All Windows operating systems starting with Windows for Workgroups are capable of participating on a network. They also have the capability of providing services. However, these operating systems are not all equal, as demonstrated in Figure 16.1.

FIGURE 16.1
Windows operating-system functionality has increased with each new generation of operating system.

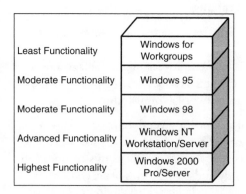

Least Functionality	Windows for Workgroups
Moderate Functionality	Windows 95
Moderate Functionality	Windows 98
Advanced Functionality	Windows NT Workstation/Server
Highest Functionality	Windows 2000 Pro/Server

As one would expect, not all Windows operating systems are equally equipped to perform the role required by a network server:

- Windows for Workgroups, as the oldest network operating system, offers the least functionality.

- Windows 95 and 98, though primarily targeted as client workstations, possess a moderate level of functionality suitable for performance as a dedicated peer server. The workstation version is targeted at high-end, powerful client workstations.

- Windows NT Workstation 4.0 has been Microsoft's flagship operating system for high-end users and corporate desktops for many years. It features advanced security and a high level of integration with Windows NT domain networks.

- Windows 2000 Pro represents the latest advancement in the evolution of Windows NT. When supported with appropriate hardware, it is the best-performing Windows client. Its capability to perform the role of a dedicated server is equally superior to that of other Windows clients. Windows 2000 Server and Windows NT Server, though normally thought of as members of a server-based network, are capable of membership on a peer network. Their natural role is that of a dedicated server in an NT domain. As such, they are the best suited of all the Microsoft operating systems for providing services to other network clients.

A quick review of the evolution of the Microsoft operating system might help in understanding the role of each operating system.

Microsoft's first operating system was MS-DOS, or DOS. DOS is a command-line operating system in which users communicate with the operating system by typing commands at the DOS command prompt, which is normally represented by a drive letter in the form of c:>. There have been many versions of DOS, and DOS is still a very commonly used operating system today. Typing the command VER, short for version, at the Windows 95 command prompt will show the user that MS-DOS Version 7 is running.

Next, Microsoft developed its Windows operating system. This added a graphical user environment on top of the DOS operating system. This version of Windows, however, did not provide network support. To network a computer running the DOS/Windows combination required the installation of additional software. Various versions of Windows were created, culminating in Windows for Workgroups. Windows for Workgroups introduced 32-bit integrated network support into the operating system. This made the first Microsoft peer network possible. At the end of 1995, Microsoft released Windows 95, and it immediately became the fastest selling operating system of all times. In early 1998, Microsoft introduced Windows 98.

Although the evolution of Windows 98 from the early MS-DOS operating system is probably well-known to most computer users, the history behind Windows 2000 is not.

Microsoft worked very closely with IBM in the early 1980s to develop its MS-DOS operating system in support of the IBM personal computer. Sales of both were strong. Both companies recognized the need to develop a more powerful operating system.

The two companies jointly developed OS/2 as a next-generation operating system. However, user acceptance of OS/2 never reached the level of acceptance that Windows achieved. It required substantial hardware resources for its day and was seen by many as a very complex operating system. Eventually, IBM and Microsoft decided to go their separate ways with both parties sharing rights to the new jointly developed operating system. IBM, however, retained exclusive rights to the OS/2 name and continued to develop the NOS independently, eventually evolving it into OS/2 Warp Server. Microsoft continued working on its version as well, eventually producing Windows NT Server. The first significant release was NT version 3.1, which was followed by version 3.5, version 3.51, and version 4.0.

Don't Bet the Farm on Microsoft's Minimums

Microsoft's minimum requirements are just that, minimum requirements. A computer that just meets these requirements will not make a good network server. Supporting a network of more than 20 computers requires a server with a better processor. A minimum of 64MB of memory will result in slow server response time and generally poor performance on all but the smallest networks. An upgrade to 128MB will provide a substantial performance boost but might still result in excessive swap-file usage, especially if the server performs additional roles such as print and file services. Many network administrators consider 128MB of memory a minimal starting requirement. The minimum hard-drive requirement provides just enough storage space to install and run NT Server. However, it leaves no room for installing other software and fails to provide additional space for storing data files, print spooling, or database services. A better minimum requirement would be considered to be 2GB.

Microsoft began working on Windows NT 5.0 but before releasing it decided to change its name to Windows 2000.

Both of Microsoft's current network operating systems evolved from a common starting point but have arrived as very different and distinct systems, as shown in Figure 16.2. Windows 98 provides strong support for MD-DOS and Windows 3.1 legacy software and hardware. Windows NT, on the other hand, does not guarantee backward compatibility with older versions of software and hardware. By limiting its supported hardware platform and releasing itself from the promise of 100 percent backward compatibility, it has been able to redesign the entire operating system from the ground up. Windows 98 is marketed as a home-computer and network-client operating system. Windows 2000 Pro is marketed as a corporate desktop and Windows NT Server as a high-end network operating system. Both operating systems have overlapping capabilities. For example, Windows 2000 now provides Plug and Play technology previously available only on Windows 95 and 98.

More About DOS

Detailed coverage of DOS is outside the scope of this book. If you'd like to brush up on your DOS skills, I recommend *Special Edition Using MS-DOS 6.22, Second Edition*, published by Que.

FIGURE 16.2
The evolution of Microsoft Windows operating systems.

Peer Workgroups

Peer networks are appropriate for small businesses, which require connectivity for 2 to 10 computers plus peripherals. Often, peer networks can be satisfactorily secured by lock and key. This negates the networks' lack of advanced security. These networks are organized using the workgroup model shown in Figure 16.3.

FIGURE 16.3
The Windows workgroup is an organization model for logically grouping computers that commonly share resources.

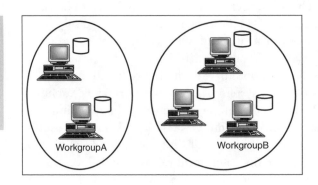

On peer networks, workgroups allow network computers to be logically grouped. Figure 16.3 shows a peer network consisting of five computers, organized into two workgroups. Workgroups do not provide security, so each computer must maintains its own security database.

Peer networks have a growth limitation. If a small business finds itself growing into a larger company, the demands on the network will eventually grow beyond the network's capacity. The decentralized nature of the peer network will lead to administrative overload as more and more computers are added to the network. Every time a new computer is added to the peer network, the burden of applying and administering security increases. Eventually, it might become impossible to protect every computer using the lock-and-key method.

The next evolutionary step is usually to move on to a Windows 2000 Server domain network. This network offers a significantly more advanced security model and can grow from just a few workstations to many hundreds and eventually evolve into a network of thousands of computers in a multidomain network.

The Windows Domain

A Windows 2000 Server–based network supplants the workgroup with the *domain model*. Workgroups, however, can and do still exist within the domain. A domain is a group of computers that share a centralized directory database. At the heart of the domain are the domain controllers. Domain controllers contain a complete copy of all user and computer account information for the entire domain. This information is stored in security databases that are located on the domain controllers. The domain controllers automatically synchronize all account information. This allows these servers to back each other up and efficiently share the workload. When users try to log on, their usernames and password credentials are automatically passed onto one of the domain controllers for authentication. Individual computers are then relieved of the burden of maintaining their security database. As Figure 16.4 shows, the workgroup modem is still supported within the domain as a means of organizing computers. Figure 16.4 presents an overview of a Microsoft domain network.

> **Defining a Workgroup**
>
> The primary organizational model in a peer network is the workgroup. A workgroup is a logical grouping of computers. For example, a company might choose to create workgroups based on departments. Members of the sales department would be added to a group called the Sales workgroup. Computers in the bookkeeping department might be organized into a Bookkeeping workgroup. Workgroups are only organizational tools. They do not have anything to do with security. A member of the Bookkeeping workgroup can still see all the resources in other workgroups. Being a member of a workgroup simply makes finding shared resources in that particular workgroup easier.

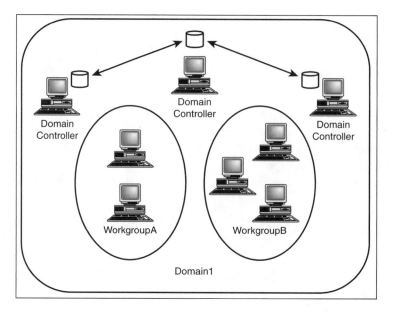

A user is permitted onto the network only if the directory database maintained on the domain controllers has an entry for the user. In addition to the domain controllers, other Windows 2000 servers can be installed as standalone servers. Standalone servers are installations of Windows 2000 Server that are not designated as domain controllers. In other words, they do not contain a copy of the directory database. Standalone servers are dedicated machines that exist to provide a service such as email, print, or file services to other clients on the network. Computers running other Windows operating systems such as Windows 95, Windows 98, and Windows for Workgroups can be added to the domain. This is accomplished by simple parameter changes in their workstation settings that inform the workstations of the name of the domain they are to join.

Before any user can log on to the domain and access network resources, a domain controller must authenticate the user. A domain is a grouping of computers that share a single security account database. Therefore, domains can be administered from one central location or computer. Users log on to the domain instead of a single computer. When logged on, users can access any resources for which their account has been given permission.

Windows 2000 Pro and Windows 2000 Server computers must have accounts established in the domain. If the Windows 2000 computers are not defined in the directory database on the domain controllers, users will not be able to use that machine on the network. This tight security makes using Windows 2000 Server and Windows 2000 Professional operating systems a stronger security model than using Windows 9X, for which the only requirement is a valid username.

The domain provides for a single user logon. This allows domain members to access any resource for which they have been assigned permission after logging on to the domain. All account information is stored in the directory database, which is replicated among the domain controllers.

Computer Account Required

Windows NT Server and Windows NT Workstation computers also require a computer account before they can access the domain.

Setting Up a Windows Domain Network

The actual establishment of a Windows 2000 domain is very involved and is best covered in its own book. However, a generalized synopsis follows:

- Purchase a copy of Windows 2000 Server with the appropriate license support for the number of users the network will support.

- Acquire hardware to support the domain controller computers that will be supporting the network. At least two domain controllers are recommended for redundancy and workload balancing. This hardware should meet the requirements identified earlier in Table 16.1.

- On the computers specified to serve as domain controllers, install Windows 2000 Server as a domain controller.

- Create accounts for every user who will use the network.

- Create a computer account for any Windows 2000 or Windows NT computer that will operate on the network.

- Visit each computeron the network and configure it to join the new domain.

part

V

APPENDIXES

Appendix

A

Net Commands

Introduction

Windows operating systems' network resources are easily managed using the graphical user interface. Windows also provides a host of commands you can execute from the MS-DOS command prompt that enable you to manage networking resources. Windows for Workgroups, Windows 95, and Windows 98 Net commands provide essentially the same features and functionality. Windows NT Workstation and Windows 2000 Pro provide the same core set of capabilities and add some additional features.

Windows for Workgroups Net Commands

Windows for Workgroups Net commands provide the same basic functionality as their Windows 95 and 98 counterparts. Table A.1 gives an overview of each of these commands. Just as with Windows 95 and 98, you can get more information about a specific Microsoft Windows for Workgroups Net command by typing the command name followed by /?. For example, type NET VIEW /?.

Table A.1   Windows for Workgroups Net Commands

Command	Description
NET	Loads the pop-up interface into memory and displays it on your screen.
NET CONFIG	Displays your current workgroup settings.
NET DIAG	Runs the Microsoft Network Diagnostics program to display diagnostic information about your network.
NET HELP	Provides information about commands and error messages.
NET INIT	Loads protocol and network-adapter drivers without binding them to Protocol Manager.
NET LOGOFF	Breaks the connection between your computer and the shared resources to which it is connected.
NET LOGON	Identifies you as a member of a workgroup and reestablishes your persistent connections.
NET PASSWORD	Changes your logon password.
NET PRINT	Displays information about print queues and controls print jobs.
NET START	Starts services or loads the pop-up interface.
NET STOP	Stops services or unloads the pop-up interface.

Command	Description
NET TIME	Displays the time on or synchronizes your computer's clock with the clock on a Microsoft Windows for Workgroups, Windows NT, or LAN Manager time server.
NET USE	Connects to or disconnects from a shared resource or displays information about connections.
NET VER	Displays the type and version number of the workgroup redirector you are using.
NET VIEW	Displays a list of computers that share resources or a list of shared resources on a specific computer.

Windows 95 and 98 Net Commands

Windows 98 and 95 provide various networking commands that can be executed from the command line. The following tables provide an overview of each command. These commands can be executed in place of those made available through the Windows point-and-click graphic interface. However, not all commands are available in the normal Windows mode of operation. Some Net commands can be executed only if the computer is restarted in the MS-DOS mode.

A summary of the Net commands available from the MS-DOS prompt running within the Windows graphical interface is shown in Table A.2.

Table A.2 Windows 98 and Windows 95 Net Commands

Command	Description
NET CONFIG	Displays your current workgroup settings.
NET DIAG	Runs the Microsoft Network Diagnostics program to display diagnostic information about your network.
NET HELP	Provides information about commands and error messages.
NET PRINT	Displays information about print queues and controls print jobs.
NET TIME	Displays the time or synchronizes your computer's clock with the clock on a Microsoft Windows for Workgroups, Windows NT, Windows 95, or NetWare time server.
NET USE	Connects to or disconnects from a shared resource, or displays information about connections.

continues...

Table A.2 Continued	
Command	Description
NET VER	Displays the type and version number of the workgroup redirector you are using.
NET VIEW	Displays a list of computers that share resources or a list of shared resources on a specific computer.

A summary of Net commands available only if the computer has been started using the MS-DOS mode is provided in Table A.3.

Table A.3 Windows 98 and Windows 95 Net Commands (MS-DOS Mode Only)	
Command	Description
NET INIT	Loads protocol and network-adapter drivers without binding them to Protocol Manager.
NET LOGOFF	Breaks the connection between your computer and the shared resources to which it is connected.
NET LOGON	Identifies you as a member of a workgroup.
NET PASSWORD	Changes your logon password.
NET START	Starts services.
NET STOP	Stops services.

To start a Windows 9X computer in MS-DOS mode

1. Click **Start** and then select **Shut Down**.

2. Select the **Restart in MS-DOS Mode** option and click **OK**.

For more information about a specific Microsoft Windows 98 Net command, type the command name followed by /?. For example, type NET VIEW /?.

Windows NT Workstation 4.0 Net Commands

Windows NT Workstation provides an extensive set of commands for administering and controlling its networking environment. Use Windows NT Help to get additional detailed information on the available Net commands and their functions.

To use Help to learn more about Windows NT Net commands

1. Click **Start** and then select **Help**.

2. Select the **Find** tab and type NET in the **Type the Word(s) You Want to Find** field; then press Enter.

3. Select **net** in the **Select Some Matching Words to Narrow Your Search** list. Select **Command Index** in the **Click a Topic, Then Click Display** list, and click the **Display** button. A dialog similar to the one shown in Figure A.1 will appear.

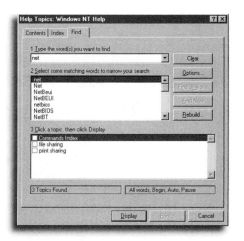

FIGURE A.1
Windows NT Workstation's Help provides detailed information on the available Net commands.

4. Scroll down to the **N** category. A complete list of Net commands is listed, as shown in Figure A.2. Select any command to learn more about it.

FIGURE A.2
Windows NT provides detailed information about all supported Net commands.

Windows 2000 Professional Net Commands

Windows 2000 Pro expands on Windows NT's set of commands available for administering and controlling its networking environment. Windows 2000 Pro Help provides detailed information on the available Net commands and their functions.

To use Help to learn more about Windows 2000 Net commands

1. Click **Start** and then select **Help**.

2. Select the **Search** tab and type Windows 2000 Command Reference Main Page in the **Type in the Keyword to Find** field; then press Enter.

3. Select **Windows 2000 Command Reference Main Page**. A list of Windows 2000 commands appears in the right pane, as shown in Figure A.3. Scroll down until you find the Net commands.

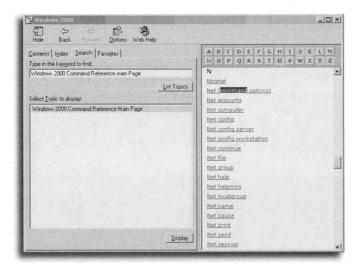

FIGURE A.3
Windows 2000 Professional's Help provides detailed information on the available Net commands.

4. Select any command to learn more about it.

Appendix

B

OSI Model and IEEE Standards

The OSI Model

This appendix presents an overview of the Open Systems Interconnection, or OSI, reference model. The OSI is a theoretical model developed in 1983 by the International Standards Organization. An understanding of this networking model is not a prerequisite to implementing or administering a peer network. This appendix reviews the OSI model because it provides an excellent overview of how modern networks communicate and manage network traffic. The intention is to provide additional insight into what is occurring behind the scenes and help broaden your understanding of how networks operate.

The OSI model consists of seven layers, as shown in Figure B.1. Each layer provides a specific set of network functionality. Each layer provides services to the layers above it and depends on services on the layers below it.

FIGURE B.1
The OSI model.

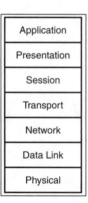

| Application |
| Presentation |
| Session |
| Transport |
| Network |
| Data Link |
| Physical |

The OSI model outlines the passage of data between computers on a network. As a user interacts with a network-aware application, data is passed from the application to the operating system to the NIC driver to the NIC card over the network cabling until it reaches its destination, and then the reverse process occurs on the receiving computer.

As defined by the OSI model, data enters at the Application layer, where it is processed and embedded into a layer-specific wrapper before it is passed on to the next-lower layer. This process continues until the Physical layer receives the packet of data and sends it out over the wire. This process is depicted in Figure B.2. The communication that occurs between the layers is accomplished through an interface.

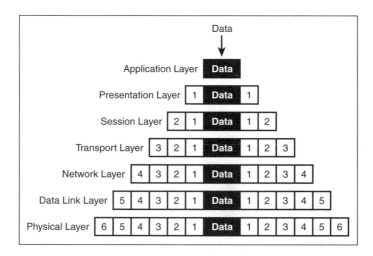

FIGURE B.2
Each layer processes the data and wraps it with layer-specific information before passing it on to the next layer.

At each layer of the OSI model, the information passed down to it from the above layer is processed and wrapped with layer-specific data. This layer-specific information can be interpreted only by the same layer on the receiving computer.

The rules that the layers use to communicate with corresponding layers on destination computers is done via a protocol. On the receiving computer an unwrapping process occurs as the packet travels up the protocol stack (starting with the Physical layer), with each layer unwrapping its portion of the data packet before passing the remainder up to the next layer in the stack. This process is illustrated in Figure B.3.

The OSI model provides a conceptual framework. Actual network implementation does not fully conform to the specifications of the OSI model. Some implementations combine multiple functional layers into a single layer or divide a single OSI layer into multiple layers. However, the OSI model is accepted as an excellent comparative model for examining today's modern network implementations.

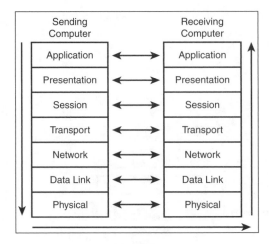

FIGURE B.3
Data passes down the protocol stack on the first computer, is passed across the wire, and then travels up the protocol stack on the receiving computer.

The OSI Layers

The OSI model is divided into seven layers, each of which provides its own distinctive features.

Application Layer

The Application layer of the OSI model

- Allows applications to access network services.
- Supports applications by offering file transfer, messaging, and database access.
- Represents the layer at which applications can access the network.
- Provides services that directly support network applications.

Presentation Layer

The Presentation layer of the OSI model

- Translates application data, via the transmitting side, into a format that can be sent over the network.
- Translates the application data, via the receiving side, back into its original format.
- Is the level at which the redirector operates.

- Manages security by providing functions including data encryption and compression.

Session Layer

The Session layer

- Creates a session between two computers to allow communication to occur.
- Places checkpoints in the data stream that are used to ensure synchronization of the data stream between the two workstations.
- Only data, after the last successful checkpoint, ever has to be resent when errors occur.
- Determines how long each workstation gets to transmit and when transmission occurs.

Transport Layer

The Transport layer

- Ensures that data passed onto the higher levels is error free.
- Ensures proper sequencing of data packets.
- Packages data that is to be sent efficiently by breaking long messages into smaller packets when necessary. On the receiving end, it collects the packets to rebuild the original message.
- Sends acknowledgment messages.

Network Layer

The Network layer

- Handles message addressing.
- Translates logical addresses into physical addresses.
- Routes packets from source to destination.
- Handles networking problems such as congestion.

Data Link Layer

The Data Link layer

- Establishes a logical link.

- Manages frame sequencing and traffic control.

- Relies on acknowledgment from its counterpart to ensure that frames are received.

- Retransmits any frame that is not acknowledged.

- Adds error-correction information. A Cyclical Redundancy Checksum (CRC) distinctly identifies the contents of the frame. The receiving Data Link layer recalculates the CRC to ensure that they match (that is, that the data received is the same as what was sent).

- Translates the data packets of the uppers layers into bit streams to be sent over the wire or converts the received bit streams into packets before sending them up to the next layer.

Physical Layer

The Physical layer

- Defines methods that transfer the bit stream of data across the network and defines which transmission technique is used to send the data over the wire.

- Defines the interface to the network cable.

- Carries signals to receiving computers.

- Defines cabling type.

- Defines how the cable is attached to the NIC.

- Defines pin configurations.

- Deals with transmission speed and encoding of data.

The Microsoft Network Model

As has already been stated, modern networks do not completely adhere to the OSI model. The functions carried out at various layers of the OSI model might be located in different layers in other network models or might be combined with other functions.

Regardless, all networking models can be mapped back to the OSI model for comparative purposes.

Figure B.4 provides some practical context for comparing the OSI model to the Microsoft networking model. The first two layers of the model correspond to network hardware. Included here are the network cabling, NICs, terminators, and so on.

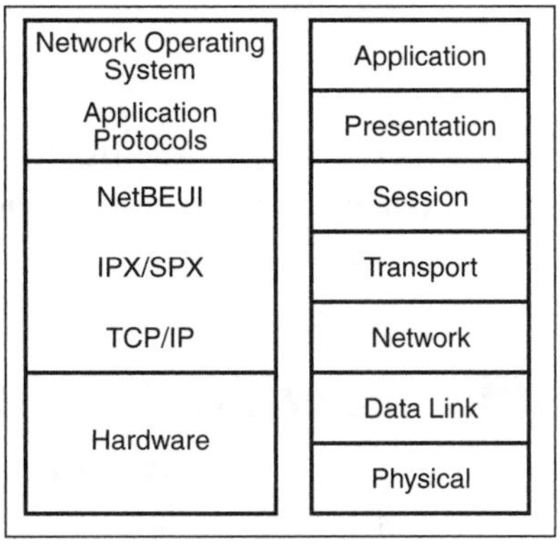

Network Operating System	Application
Application Protocols	Presentation
NetBEUI	Session
IPX/SPX	Transport
TCP/IP	Network
Hardware	Data Link
	Physical

FIGURE B.4
Comparative roles of the OSI model.

SEE ALSO

➤ *To learn more about the Microsoft networking model, see page 520.*

The next three layers include network communication protocols. Microsoft networking has three primary protocols: NetBEUI, IPX/SPX, and TCP/IP.

SEE ALSO

➤ *To learn more about NetBEUI, IXP/SPX, or TCP/IP, see page 524.*

The top two layers in the OSI model include the network operating system, client portions of the network operating system, and application protocols such as File and Print services.

SEE ALSO

➤ *For more information about network clients, see page 76.*

➤ *For more information about File and Print services, see page 78.*

The IEEE 802 Model

No review of networking communications would be complete without the mention of the IEEE 802 networking standards. The Institute of Electrical and Electronics Engineers, or IEEE, is a standards body dedicated to the creation and refinement of network and communications standards.

The IEEE developed a family of LAN standards, which details precise specifications for many different network architectures. Most modern networks conform to these models' specifications. Unlike the OSI model, the IEEE model defines sets of standards that can actually be implemented and hence are both practical and theoretical models.

IEEE Network Models

As a reference, Table B.1 summarizes the series of IEEE network models. This table is provided to give you an overview of the 802 networking standards and to point you in the right direction should you want to do more research on a particular network standard. Visit the IEEE Web site at http://www.ieee.com to learn more about the IEEE and its 802 standards.

IEEE 802.3 specifies the CSMA/CD (Ethernet) standard that most of today's networks use. The IEEE 802.4 specifies a token-passing BUS network. The IEEE 802.5 specifies a token-passing ring network. Token-passing ring networks, while still present in older networks, are less prominent today. Almost all new networks, especially smaller ones, are based on the IEEE 802.3 model.

Table B.1 IEEE Standards

Standard	Description
802.1	Internetworking—deals with the upper five layers of the OSI model
802.2	Logical Link Control
802.3	Carriers Sense with Multiple Access and Collision Detection (Ethernet)
802.u	Fast Ethernet
802.4	Token Passing Bus
802.5	Token Passing Ring

Standard	Description
802.6	Metropolitan Area Network (MAN)
802.7	Broadband
802.8	Fiber-Optic
802.9	Integrated Voice/Data Networking
802.10	Networking Security
802.11	Wireless Networking with Carrier Sense Multiple Access/Collision Avoidance
802.12	100BaseVG-AnyLAN—Demand Priority Access

Appendix

C

Protocols

Overview of Windows Supported Protocols

This appendix is designed to serve as a technical reference. It goes beyond the hands-on coverage provided in the rest of the book to present a more detailed look at networking protocols.

A *network protocol* is an agreed-on set of rules and procedures for communicating and exchanging data over a network. The Microsoft Windows networking model combines clients, services, and multiple layers of protocols, as shown in Figure C.1.

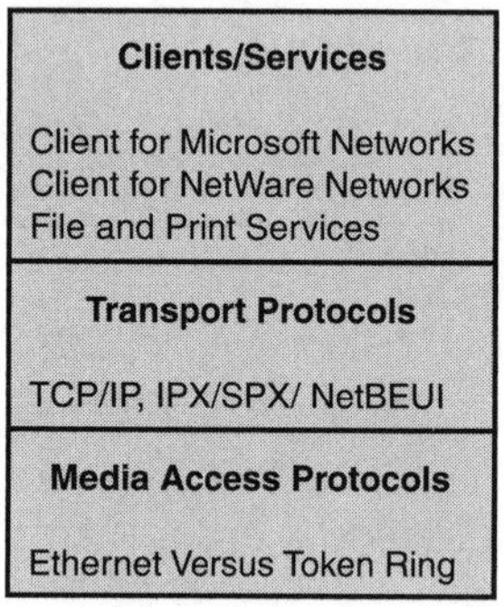

FIGURE C.1
The Microsoft networking model consists of three layers.

Clients/Services
Client for Microsoft Networks Client for NetWare Networks File and Print Services
Transport Protocols
TCP/IP, IPX/SPX/ NetBEUI
Media Access Protocols
Ethernet Versus Token Ring

Figure C.1 presents the Microsoft networking model introduced in Appendix B, "OSI Model and IEEE Standards," at a more detailed level by specifying examples of member components that exist at each of the three levels.

SEE ALSO

➤ *To learn more about the Microsoft Networking model, see page 514.*

Adding TCP/IP to Windows for Workgroups

Windows for Workgroups does not include support for TCP/IP out of the box. However, Microsoft provides an update at its Web site, which adds TCP/IP support.

At the lowest level are media access protocols. For Microsoft networks this usually means either Ethernet or Token-Ring. These are hardware-level protocols that manage how network traffic traverses the network. This includes determining how network devices will exchange information and how lost or corrupted transmissions will be handled.

The next layer of protocols is the transport protocols. Windows operating systems include support for multiple transport protocols, the most common of which are TCP/IP, IPX/SPX, and NetBEUI. These are software protocols that control data packets' formation and speed. All networked computers must run at least one common protocol to establish communications.

On a small peer network, NetBEUI is often a preferred protocol because it is easy to install and is optimized for small networks. In addition, Windows computers can run multiple protocols in parallel.

For example, a computer must have NetBEUI and TCP/IP installed, with the NetBEUI protocol bound to the computer NIC to provide network communication, and the TCP/IP protocol bound to a modem to provide dial-up access to the Internet. However, each additional protocol that is installed on a computer introduces additional overhead.

Part of the process of optimizing a computer involves removing any unnecessary protocols and unbinding protocols from network devices where they are not required. For example, Windows 2000, NT, and 9X operating systems automatically bind every protocol installed on a computer to the modem when one is installed. If the modem will be used only for connecting to the Internet, the NetBEUI should be unbound from the modem.

SEE ALSO

➤ *To learn more about managing protocol bindings, see page 534.*

Client and server software operates at the highest level. Installing a service on a computer allows it to share either file or print resources with the rest of the network. Installing a network client provides a computer with the capability to access services provided by network servers.

Selecting a Network Access Method

Access methods are hardware protocols. All computers on a network use the same access methods. In most cases the access method of choice is Ethernet. The access method used by a computer is determined by the type of network adapter card installed and is configured when the card's software driver is installed.

Features of Ethernet

On an Ethernet network there is no central controlling point. All nodes have an equal opportunity to access the network. When a computer has some data to transmit, the data is automatically broken down into discrete frames, and the individual frames are then sent

Ethernet Roots

Ethernet was invented in late 1972 by Xerox. The first Ethernet network operated at 2.94Mbps and connected Xerox personal computers.

out on the network. Every computer on the network receives a copy of every frame, but only the destination computer accepts the frame. All other computers simply discard any packets not addressed to them. Today's Ethernet networks transmit at either 10Mbps or 100Mbps, although faster Ethernet technologies are now emerging. One exception is HomePNA-based networks that combine Ethernet with a 1Mbps transmission rate.

SEE ALSO

➤ *For more information on HomePNA networks, see page 559.*

SEE ALSO

➤ *To read more about Ethernet, see page 12.*

The composition of an Ethernet frame is presented in Figure C.2 and is described here:

- The preamble is used to synchronize transmissions so that if the data to be sent must be broken down into multiple frames, the receiving computer knows the order in which to reassemble them.

- The next section is the start frame delimiter, or SFD. The SFD is an eight-bit pattern, which is always 10101011.

- The destination address identifies the computer's target to receive the data.

- The source address identifies the sending computer.

- The frame length section identifies the length of the entire frame.

- The next component of the frame contains the actual data to be transmitted. It must be divisible by 8. If the data is not evenly divisible by 8, padding is added.

- Finally, the frame check sequence, or FCS, contains *cyclic redundancy check*, or *CRC*, data that enables error detection. The value of the CRC is computed after the packet is created. The receiving computer recalculates the CRC for each frame it receives and compares its calculation to the value stored in the FCS. If the two values match, the data is assumed to have arrived intact. Otherwise, the data is assumed to have been corrupted and is discarded.

Preamble	Start Frame Deliminator	Destination Address	Source Address	Frame Length	Data and Padding	Frame Check Sequence
56 bits	8 bits	16/48 bits	16/48 bits	16 bits	576 to 12,208 bits	32 bits

FIGURE C.2
A diagram of an Ethernet frame.

The Token-Ring Alternative

IBM invented Token-Ring in the 1970s. It uses a physical star topology with a logical ring topology. A Token-Ring network passes an electronic signal around the network ring in one direction from computer to computer until the signal is returned to the computer that sent it. When a computer has the signal or packet, it is allowed to transmit its data over the network. After it is done or its time expires, it passes the packet on to the next computer, which then is given an opportunity to transmit any data it might have before it, in turn, passes the packet on.

SEE ALSO

➤ *To read more about Token-Ring, see page 30.*

Every computer on the network is guaranteed an equal chance to transmit. A device multiple access unit, or MAU, is a type of hub used on Token-Ring networks which ensures that the token moves around the network. The token-passing feature allows Token-Ring networks to degrade gracefully over time, whereas CSMA/CD-based networks can experience a rapid decline when the practical limitation of the number of computers it can support is reached.

Token-Ring networks are very reliable. However, they have been largely displaced in recent years by Ethernet. Token-Ring hardware is also considerably more expensive than Ethernet hardware. Thus, Token-Ring networks are typically used only in specialized situations in which high availability is required. Token-Ring networks operate at either 4Mbps or 16Mbps, although 100Mbps technology is being introduced.

Understanding MAC Addresses

Every network card has a unique *Media Access Control*, or *MAC*, number burned into it. Network card manufacturers register with the

IEEE and receive a range of unique addresses they can assign to their NICs. These addresses are 48 bits long. The first 24 bits identify the manufacturer of the card, and the last 24 bits identify the card's unique address. The various transport protocols use their own addressing scheme in conjunction with the MAC addresses to locate and communicate with networked devices.

For example, communications on a TCP/IP network are achieved when a source computer successfully determines the MAC address of a destination computer. If two computers named ComputerA and ComputerB want to transmit and receive data, each computer broadcasts on the network the IP address of the destination computer. Part of the broadcast includes information on the IP address of the sending computer, the sending computer's MAC address, and the IP address of the destination computer.

Every computer on the network inspects the broadcast frame, and based on the destination computer IP address, either accepts or rejects it. Only the destination computer processes the broadcast message. It in turn sends an acknowledgment message back to the original sending computer using the sending computer's specific MAC address.

The information sent back includes the MAC address of the destination computer. After both computers have completed this initial exchange of information, transmission of additional data can occur.

Selecting a Transport Protocol

Windows operating systems support three transport protocols. These protocols are NetBEUI, IPX/SPX, and TCP/IP. Each protocol enables the routing of data over the network, but they have distinct differences that make them incompatible with one another. Using a binding process, Windows operating systems support running any combination of these protocols concurrently over the same NIC.

NetBEUI: The Simplest Protocol

NetBIOS Extended User Interface, or *NetBEUI*, is the simplest of the protocols to implement and requires no configuration after it is installed. IBM created it in 1985 for small department-sized networks. It does not support the routing of data between interconnected networks, as does IPX/SPX and TCP/IP. It is ideal for networks of 20 to 200 computers in which IP connectivity to the Internet is not required. NetBEUI is a completely self-tuning protocol and is optimized for operation on small networks, making it a good choice for such networks.

SEE ALSO

➤ *For more information on the NetBEUI protocol, see page 71.*

SEE ALSO

➤ *For instruction on how to install a protocol, see page 87.*

NetBEUI is considered a busy protocol because it uses network *broadcasts* for many network activities, such as name resolution. Broadcast data is sent to every computer on the network. This results in increased workload on the network, as well as on every computer that has to examine the data packet.

As long as the network is kept within the 200-node limit, however, NetBEUI should provide faster performance than either IPX/SPX or TCP/IP. But if too many computers are added to the network, performance will degrade quickly. NetBEUI is therefore not well suited for medium-sized and large networks.

NetBEUI uses NetBIOS names and broadcasting in conjunction with MAC addresses to locate computers on the network. Each computer is identified by its NetBIOS name.

SEE ALSO

➤ *For instruction on changing a computer's name, see page 101.*

When NetBEUI was developed in the mid-1980s, memory was sparse and programs had to live together in the 640KB lower memory area. As a result, it requires very little memory overhead. NetBEUI is a self-configuring protocol and requires no administration. For small networks, such as peer networks, NetBEUI is usually the best protocol. However, with the advent of the capability of Windows 2000 and Windows 98 to self-configure their IP addresses, TCP/IP now rivals NetBEUI's simplicity for peer networking.

NetBEUI supports two kinds of network transmissions, connectionless and connection-oriented. When using connectionless communications, NetBEUI sends data packets across the network to the destination computer without taking steps to ensure that the message

Configuring TCP/IP in Other Windows Flavors

Windows NT 4.0, Windows for Workgroups, and Windows 95 operating systems do not provide support for dynamic self-configuration of TCP/IP settings. These systems require manual configuration unless either a DHCP server is available or the network has been configured to take advantage of Windows 2000 modem sharing, in which case the computer that provides the modem proxy service can provide dynamic TCP/IP configuration assignments.

is successfully received. For example, NetBEUI uses this form of communications to perform name resolution. On the other hand, with connection-oriented communications, both the sending and the destination computers establish a communications session before transmitting any data and automatically retransmit any lost or corrupted data. For example, NetBEUI uses connection-oriented transmission when processing commands such as NET USE and NET PRINT.

SEE ALSO

➤ *For more information on working with Net commands, see page 501.*

Novell's IPX/SPX Protocol

Internetwork packet exchange/sequential packet exchange, or *IPX/SPX*, is a combination of protocols, or a protocol stack, developed by Novell based on the Xerox XNS protocol.

IPX/SPX is a routable protocol, which means that it can transport data packets between connected networks using IPX-enabled routers.

SEE ALSO

➤ *For more information on the IPX/SPX protocol, see page 71.*

What Are Routers?

A *router* is a device or computer that supports connections to multiple physical networks. The router receives data packets from each network segment and forwards them on to the appropriate destination network.

IPX is a connectionless protocol, meaning that there are no built-in mechanisms for ensuring that data packets reach their intended destination. There is no attempt to sequence data or determine whether it is successfully received. SPX is a connection-oriented protocol that establishes a logical session between two network devices before transmitting any data and then uses IPX for transport. If SPX detects that any data is lost or corrupted, it retransmits the missing data.

IPX/SPX has always been the default protocol on NetWare networks. However, with the release of NetWare 5, Novell has made IP the default protocol, though IPX/SPX is still supported. IPX/SPX is commonly associated with NetWare networks, but Microsoft Windows 2000 peer network can be established using this protocol.

Whereas NetBEUI uses NetBIOS names to locate computers on the network, IPX uses a combination of an automatically assigned IPX network address and the burned-in Media Access Control address on the network adapter card to identify computers on the network. This means that both protocols automatically handle network addressing issues.

IPX/SPX is somewhat slower than NetBEUI and requires a little more setup, but it provides routing and high speed when compared to TCP/IP. It is a good choice for a peer network if direct access to the Internet is not required and if there is a need to connect to network segments using a router. A disadvantage of IPX/SPX is that there is no mechanism for centrally managing computer network addresses to ensure unique network addressing.

Microsoft's implementation of the IPX/SPX protocol provides the following features:

- Ease of setup
- Support for routing
- High speed
- Automatic detection of data frame type and network address
- Connection to NetWare servers

Communicating with TCP/IP

Internet Protocol, or *IP*, is a connectionless protocol used on the Internet and in medium- to large-scale networks. However, it is becoming common to find it being used on smaller networks as well. Compared to NetBEUI and IPX/SPX it is a high-maintenance protocol. IP provides roughly the same functionality as IPX on a NetWare network. It requires up-front planning and administration. *Transmission Control Protocol*, or *TCP*, is a connection-oriented protocol that creates a logical session between communicating devices and ensures that lost or corrupted data packets are retransmitted. TCP depends on IP as its delivery mechanism.

Although TCP and IP together are only two protocols, the term TCP/IP has come to refer to a suite of protocols that support and depend on TCP and IP.

TCP/IP was originally designed as a WAN protocol but has moved into the LAN arena as well. TCP/IP's origins can be traced back to 1969 when the Department of Defense began its ARPAnet network. The *ARPAnet* network was designed to survive a nuclear war and provide consistent network services even if large portions of the network were damaged or destroyed.

SEE ALSO

➤ *For more information on the TCP/IP protocol, see page 72.*

IPX/SPX on Windows 2000 and NT

On Windows 2000 Pro and Windows Workstation 4.0, IPX/SPX is implemented as the NWLINK IPX/SPX protocol.

TCP/IP provides many benefits, including these:

- Internet connectivity
- Routability across interconnected network segments
- Support for automatic configuration on larger networks
- Support for many common utilities such as PING and IPCONFIG

TCP/IP has become a universal protocol. Unlike NetBEUI, which is found only on Microsoft networks, or IPX/SPX, which belongs to Novell, no one company owns the rights to TCP/IP. An international body manages it, and anyone has the opportunity to contribute to its development. From its early requirement to be able to support network operations on a network, which might or might not be fully intact, it has developed a robust routability capability. This allows TCP/IP to provide network communications over large networks of any size, including the Internet.

TCP/IP scales well to large networks, where it is usually the protocol of choice. Even Novell, in its new NetWare 5.X version, has opted to make TCP/IP its default protocol over its own IPX/SPX protocol.

The performance of TCP/IP is typically less than that of NetBEUI and IPX/SPX on smaller networks. TCP/IP requires the most configuration during setup. TCP/IP is the default protocol for Windows 2000 and Windows 98 and is automatically installed during the network adapter installation process.

Internet Address Classifications

There are five classes of Internet addresses. Of these, only three are used for assigning IP addresses: classes A, B, and C. Each IP address belongs to a specific class and includes both network and host information.

Each host or computer is identified with a uniquely assigned IP address. The IP address identifies the computer's location on the network. There are two parts to every IP address: the network ID and the host ID. The network ID specifies whether the computer is located on the same physical network segment, whereas the host ID identifies an individual computer. Each host ID must be unique within its network segment. On a small peer network, all computers are located on the same physical network. Therefore, the network ID portion of the address is the same for every computer on the network, and only the host ID portion is unique.

For example, for a class B address of 169.254.111.123, the network-address portion of the IP number is 169.254, and the host-address portion is 111.123. All computers on this same network share the same network address of 169.254.0.0, and each is assigned an IP address whose host address portion is unique.

Static or Dynamic Addressing

An IP address can be assigned either statically or dynamically. Statically defined addresses are added by being manually keyed into the TCP/IP Properties dialog, as shown in Figure C.3.

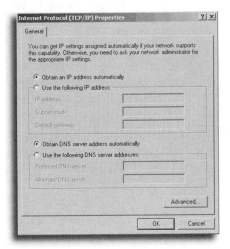

FIGURE C.3
TCP/IP configuration is performed using the TCP/IP Properties dialog.

Selecting **Use the Following IP Address** enables the IP Address and the Subnet Mask fields to be specified for the local computer. The *subnet mask* complements the IP address and is used by TCP/IP when determining the location of other computers on the network. The default subnet masks for class A, B, and C networks are shown in Table C.1. Each IP class has its own default subnet mask, which is used by every computer on the network.

Table C.1	Default Subnet Masks for Class A, B, and C Networks
Class	Default Subnet Mask
Class A	255.0.0.0
Class B	255.255.0.0
Class C	255.255.255.0

Thus, a computer assigned a class B address of 131.111.7.27 has a subnet mask of 255.255.0.0.

On large networks that include Windows 2000 Server or Windows NT Server 4.0, a DHCP server might be available. The Dynamic Host Configuration Protocol, or DHCP, provides an IP address to a computer requesting one. Other IP information can be provided as well, including subnet mask, default gateway, and DNS server settings. Selecting **Obtain an IP Address Automatically** instructs the computer to look for a DHCP server when it is started. A small Windows peer network will not have a Windows DHCP server, so IP address and subnet mask information must be manually assigned.

Learning More About the InterNIC

Visit http://inter-nic.net to learn more about this organization and how it operates.

Many companies have computer networks and connect their networks directly to the Internet. Because of the requirement that every IP address be unique, there is a single organization known as the InterNIC that controls the assignment of IP addresses. Larger telecommunications companies and Internet providers acquire large blocks of IP addresses, which they then sell, or lease to customers. Today, virtually all the IP address classes have been distributed. Internet Service Providers such as America Online provide connection services to their customers by assigning or leasing an IP address to a customer who dials in. When the customer disconnects, the IP address is returned to the pool of available IP addresses. Because not all of AOL's customers require access to the Internet at the same time, the assignment of a permanent IP address to every customer is not required. Instead, an IP address can be dynamically assigned to each dialed-in computer as required.

In most cases, peer network administrators do not need to be concerned about purchasing a range of IP addresses. Instead, they can use the 169.254.0.0 network address. This network address has not been assigned to anyone on the Internet. It has been set aside for use by networks that do not have direct connection to the Internet. This network provides for a total of 65,534 IP addresses that range from 169.254.0.1 to 169.254.255.254.

Because networks using the 169.254.0.0 network address do not have direct access to the Internet, there is no chance that their network addresses will conflict with someone else's assigned IP address. This does not mean that computers on the network cannot access the Internet. Network computers can connect to the Internet with an attached modem and a defined dial-up adapter. The dial-up adapter can be assigned, either dynamically or statically, a valid Internet IP address. Another option is to establish a network computer with a modem as a proxy server, as demonstrated in Figure C.4.

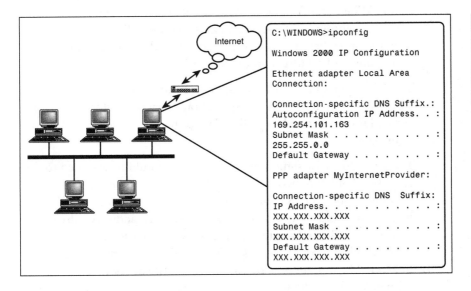

FIGURE C.4
A dual-homed computer providing proxy access to the Internet.

Computers that are connected to two networks at the same time are dual-homed. Windows operating systems automatically keep both connections isolated from one another in that the side connected to the Internet is unaware of the local NIC and its assigned IP address. This is demonstrated by the results of the IPCONFIG command on a computer that is dual-homed, as shown in Figure C.4.

In this example, a Windows 2000 proxy server receives requests from local network computers that it routes out to the Internet using its Internet IP address. When responses are returned to the proxy server, they are received using the Internet IP connection. Windows 2000 then passes the Internet data on to the network computer that requested it using the network computer's private IP address. At no

531

point in this process are private network addresses revealed to the Internet.

One new feature incorporated into Windows 2000 and Windows 98 is the capability of these operating systems to automatically assign themselves temporary IP addresses when they boot up. This feature is designed for small networks that do not have a DHCP server. Windows 2000 and 98 automatically create a class B network address of 169.254.0.0. The subnet mask also is automatically assigned. Because this is a class B network, the subnet mask is 255.255.0.0.

To enable this feature, each computer must have the **Obtain an IP Address Automatically** option selected in the TCP/IP Properties dialog. When each Windows 2000 and 98 computer boots up, it will attempt to automatically locate an available DHCP server on the network, and when it fails to locate one, it will automatically assign itself a unique IP address on the network.

The advantage of automatic IP address configuration is that it decreases the administration required on every computer where it is in use. However, it adds a small delay to the startup process of each computer.

The IP addresses assigned to the computer should be assigned to the same 169.254.0.0 network with the 255.255.0.0 subnet mask. Windows 2000 and 98 computers that support automatic IP address assignment avoid assigning to themselves any IP addresses already allocated to other computers on the network, provided that the computers owning those IP addresses are running when the Windows 2000 and 98 computers boot up. However, IP address conflicts can occur if Windows 2000 and 98 computers dynamically assign themselves IP addresses that have been assigned to other computers that are currently shut down. When the other computer is started, it will detect the IP address conflict and will not be able to join the network. For this reason, assigning static IP addresses might be preferable.

Table C.2 shows the number of networks available in each of the three classes of IP addresses, as well as the number of host computer IP addresses that can be assigned to each network. The last entry in the table shows the range of network IDs available in each class. For example, the first octet in a class B network must be in the 128 to 223 range. By examining the first octet in an IP address, one can

What About Windows 95, Windows NT, and Windows for Workgroups?

Manual IP assignment is required on any computer on the network having Windows for Workgroups, Windows 95, or Windows NT installed.

determine the default network. Using this information with the data provided in Table C.1, the default subnet mask can be determined.

Table C.2 Available Networks and Hosts by Class

Class	# of Networks	# of Hosts Per Network	Range of Network IDs
Class A	126	16,777,214	1–126
Class B	16,384	65,534	128–223
Class C	2,097,152	254	192–223

IPCONFIG = WINIPCFG

The IPCOFIG command is not supported by the Windows 9X operating systems. These two operating systems provide the WINIPCFG command, which provides the same functionality.

PING and IPCONFIG are two common commands used to view TCP/IP status and troubleshoot problems. The PING command provides the capability to poll the status of another TCP/IP computer from a command prompt. The following example shows a successful attempt to ping a computer whose IP address is 169.254.111.111. A successful PING indicates that connectivity exists between the two computers and that the target computer is operational. A computer can also be pinged using its name if it is known. The output of a sample PING command is shown here:

```
C:\WINDOWS>ping 169.254.111.111
Pinging 169.254.111.111 with 32 bytes of data:
Reply from 169.254.111.111: bytes=32 time=1ms TTL=32
Reply from 169.254.111.111: bytes=32 time=1ms TTL=32
Reply from 169.254.111.111: bytes=32 time=1ms TTL=32
Reply from 169.254.111.111: bytes=32 time=1ms TTL=32
Ping statistics for 169.254.111.111:
Packets: Sent = 4, Received = 4, Lost = 0 (0% loss),
Approximate round trip times in milli-seconds:
Minimum = 1ms, Maximum =  1ms, Average =  1ms
```

The IPCONFIG command provides the capability to view a computer's current IP address and subnet mask. This is useful on computers that use Windows 2000's capability to automatically assign dynamic IP addresses.

The output of an IPCONFIG command is shown next. In this example, the computer where the command was issued had one NIC and a dial-up adapter for an installed modem. The top portion of the command results displays IP information for the local network. The bottom portion shows IP settings assigned by the ISP that provided the Internet connection.

```
C:\WINDOWS>ipconfig
Windows 2000 IP Configuration
Ethernet adapter Local Area Connection:
        Connection-specific DNS Suffix  . :
        Autoconfiguration IP Address. . . : 169.254.101.163
        Subnet Mask . . . . . . . . . . . : 255.255.0.0
        Default Gateway . . . . . . . . . : 169.254.0.1
PPP adapter MyInternetProvider:
        Connection-specific DNS Suffix  . :
        IP Address. . . . . . . . . . . . : 152.172.248.212
        Subnet Mask . . . . . . . . . . . : 255.248.0.0
        Default Gateway . . . . . . . . . : 152.172.248.212
```

Configuring Protocols' Bindings for NICs and Dial-Up Connections

Binding and unbinding protocols from NICs and dial-up connections are performed separately. For example, on a Windows 2000 computer, configuring the bindings for a NIC requires selecting the NIC from the Local Area Network Connection Properties dialog and then selecting or clearing available protocols, as shown in Figure C.5.

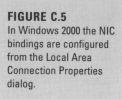

FIGURE C.5
In Windows 2000 the NIC bindings are configured from the Local Area Connection Properties dialog.

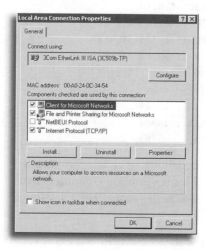

Dial-up connections are configured on a connection-by-connection basis. For example, on a Windows 2000 computer, dial-up connections are managed from the Networking property sheet for the selected dial-up connection by the selecting or clearing of available protocols in the same manner as is done for NIC protocols, as shown in Figure C.6.

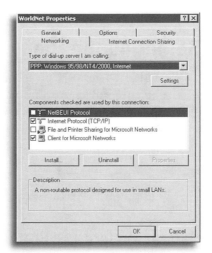

FIGURE C.6
NIC bindings are configured individually for each dial-up connection.

Protecting a Local Resource from Internet Hackers

Figure C.6 shows that the File and Printer Sharing for Microsoft Networks has been cleared for the dial-up connections. Windows 2000 automatically clears this option. If this were an Internet connection, selecting this option would allow people on the Internet to access local resources provided that they had an account on the local computer. Hackers could use this opening to attack your computer by trying to guess at user accounts and passwords. Windows 98 warns users if file and print services are bound to a dial-up connection and offers to disable this. Windows 95 and Windows NT 4.0 do not issue any warning messages.

Using DLC to Support Network Printing

The DLC protocol provides the capability to connect to IBM mainframe computers when TCP/IP connectivity is not available. It provides the capability to communicate with System Network Architecture, or SNA, which is the protocol used on IBM mainframes. DLC is not a routable protocol. It is not capable of supporting peer network communications. The Client for Microsoft Networks cannot use DLC as a transport protocol.

DLC also provides the capability to communicate with Hewlett-Packard laser printers that are connected directly to the network, as opposed to being connected to a parallel port on a computer. This type of printer has its own built-in network adapter card. This protocol is installed on a single computer that will function as the print server for the network. No other computers on the network require this protocol. This protocol allows the print server to locate and communicate with the printer. The DLC protocol allows the computer to connect directly to the printer using the network rather than a physical port. After the DLC protocol is installed, the printer is added via the printer wizard. After the printer is installed, the print server can share it with other computers using a common transport protocol such as NetBEUI.

Selecting the Right WAN Protocols

Wide area network protocols or *line protocols* take transport protocols and encapsulate them into a format capable of traveling over a dial-up connection. Windows operating systems support many types of WAN protocols, including these:

- SLIP
- PPP
- PPTP

Serial Line Internet Protocol (SLIP)

Serial Line Internet Protocol, or SLIP, is the oldest of the available WAN protocols. It is designed to communicate with UNIX servers using TCP/IP over serial connections. SLIP cannot support other protocols. In recent years, SLIP has been largely replaced with the PPP and PPTP protocols. It has a greater overhead than PPP and does not provide for connection authentication. Slip performs no error checking, security, or flow control. Windows computers can act as SLIP clients but cannot accept inbound SLIP traffic.

Point-to-Point Protocol (PPP)

Point-to-Point Protocol, or PPP, is a common protocol used for Internet access and remote WAN communications on Windows networks. PPP supports TCP/IP for Internet communications. It can also support NetBEUI and IPX/SPX for remote communications. PPP supports dynamic assignment of an IP address. It requires less overhead than SLIP, is faster, and provides basic error checking.

Point-to-Point Tunneling Protocol (PPTP)

Point-to-Point Tunneling Protocol, or PPTP, provides support for creating virtual networks over the Internet with secure connections. PPP supports dynamic IP assignment. PPP supports the transport of network protocols such as TCP/IP, NetBEUI, and IPX/SPX. PPP performs the same essential function as Ethernet does over a hardware LAN connection.

Understanding NIC Bindings

Windows operating systems support multiple protocols over a single NIC, as well as binding a single protocol across multiple NICs. Microsoft makes this work by introducing an additional layer of software between the NIC driver supplied by the card manufacturer and the various transport protocols. This layer of software, called the NDIS interface, is depicted in Figure C.7.

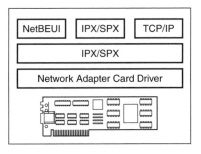

FIGURE C.7
The NDIS interface supports binding multiple protocols over a single network interface card.

In 1988, 3Com and Microsoft co-developed the NDIS standard defining an interface for NIC driver programmers. Previously, programmers had to create a custom driver for each supported protocol the network adapter would support. The NDIS interface removes this responsibility from the programmer by creating a standard software interface. With NDIS the programmer can write a single driver designed to work with the NDIS interface without being concerned with the transport level protocols. This interface also allows the transport protocol to operate without any knowledge of the NIC.

Binding is the process by which the NIC driver establishes communications with specified transport protocols through the NDIS interface.

Appendix

D

Networking Cabling Specifications

Introduction

This appendix provides supplemental information about network cabling. The information presented here is not essential to the successful implementation of your peer network. It does, however, provide a more complete discussion of cabling specifications than was presented earlier in the book, and it will help you if you need to make your own network cables or repair existing cable.

SEE ALSO

➤ *To read more about network cabling, see page 37.*

This appendix identifies the standards governing the use of coaxial and twisted-pair cable. In addition, it provides an overview of the wiring specification for regular twisted-pair cable, as well as a special type of twisted-pair cable known as a crossover cable that facilitates the direct connection of two computers. This information will provide the do-it-yourself administrator with everything required to crimp or create custom cables.

This appendix ends with a discussion of serial and parallel cable support for Direct Cable Connection between two computers.

Coaxial Cable

10BASE-2, or ThinNet, is a specific type of coaxial cable designed to support network traffic. Though not often used to build networks today, it is found in older networks and temporary networks. It has specific guidelines that must be followed for the network to operate properly. Table D.1 lists some of these standards. Failure to follow these standards results in unpredictable network performance.

Table D.1 10BASE-2/ThinNet Cable Standards

Specification	Maximum Setting
Maximum length of a segment	185 meters
Maximum number of segments	5
Maximum number of populated segments	3
Maximum number of devices per segment	30 nodes
Maximum total extended length	925 meters

SEE ALSO
➤ *For more information about coaxial cabling, see page 39.*

Twisted-Pair Cable

10BASE-T twisted-pair cabling is the most common type of cabling used in building small networks today. It consists of four pairs of wires, each twisted around the others. Twisted-pair cable consists of one solid and one striped wire of the same color. Like coaxial cable, it has its own set of standards that must be adhered to in order to ensure correct network performance. These standards are presented in Table D.2.

Table D.2   10BASE-T Cable Standards

Specification	Maximum Setting
Maximum length of a segment	100 meters
Maximum number of segments	1,024
Maximum number of populated segments	1,024
Maximum number of devices per segment	2 nodes
Maximum number of nodes per network	1,024
Maximum number of daisy-chained hubs	4

SEE ALSO
➤ *For more information about twisted-pair cabling, see page 41.*

Standard RJ-45 Twisted-Pair Cable

RJ-45 twisted-pair cable is the *de facto* standard for twisted-pair network implementations. It supports data transmission rates up to 100Mbps. It is wired as shown in Figure D.1. RJ-45 twisted-pair cables are wired in a straight-through manner, meaning that the wire connected to a pin number on one side is connected to the corresponding pin number on the other side.

Table D.3 specifies the wiring layout for a standard RJ-45 twisted-pair cable.

FIGURE D.1
RJ-45 twisted-pair wiring specification.

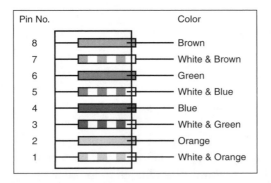

Pin No.   Color

8 — Brown
7 — White & Brown
6 — Green
5 — White & Blue
4 — Blue
3 — White & Green
2 — Orange
1 — White & Orange

Table D.3   Standard RJ-45 Wire Assignments

Pin Assignment	Color Wire
1	White and orange
2	Orange
3	White and green
4	Blue
5	White and blue
6	Green
7	White and brown
8	Brown

Figure D.2 illustrates the pin layout of both ends of a standard RJ-45 twisted-pair cable.

FIGURE D.2
RJ-45 twisted-pair pin assignments.

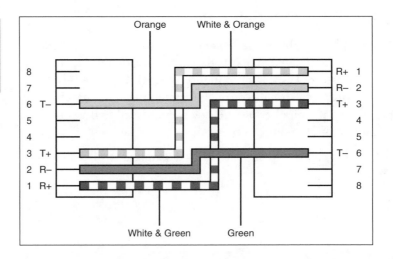

Crossover Cable

Crossover cables are used to support the direct network connection of two computers without an intervening hub. There are currently two standards for wiring a crossover cable: T568A and T568B. Only two pairs of wires are used in crossover cables. The only difference between the two cable standards is that the solid and striped wires are crossed or reversed, as shown in Figure D.3, Figure D.4, Table D.4, and Table D.5.

T568A RJ-45 Crossover Cable

The T586A standard is the newer standard for crossover cabling. It uses the green and orange solid and striped wires. The other two pairs of wires, if present, are ignored. The green and orange wires are used to transmit and receive data, as shown in Figure D.3 and explained in Table D.4.

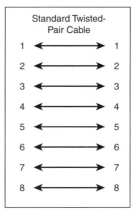

Standard Twisted-Pair Cable

FIGURE D.3
RJ-45 T568A twisted-pair crossover wiring specification.

Table D.4   T568A Twisted-Pair Crossover Wiring Assignments

Side 1 Pin Assignments	Wire Color	Side 2 Pin Assignments	Wire Color
1	White and orange	1	White and green
2	Orange	2	Green
3	White and green	3	White and orange

continues...

Table D.4 Continued

Side 1 Pin Assignments	Wire Color	Side 2 Pin Assignments	Wire Color
4		4	
5		5	
6	Green	6	Orange
7		7	
8		8	

T568B RJ-45 Crossover Cable

The T568B standard reverses the green and orange wires, as shown in Figure D.4 and Table D.5.

FIGURE D.4
RJ-45 T568B twisted-pair crossover wiring specification.

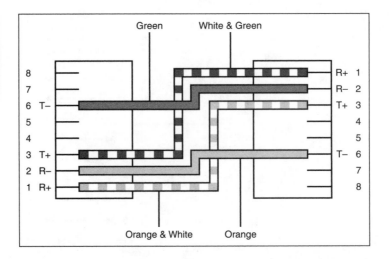

Table D.5 T568B Twisted-Pair Crossover Wiring Assignments

Side 1 Pin Assignments	Wire Color	Side 2 Pin Assignments	Wire Color
1	White and green	1	White and orange
2	Green	2	Orange
3	White and orange	3	White and green
4		4	
5		5	
6	Orange	6	Green

Side 1 Pin Assignments	Wire Color	Side 2 Pin Assignments	Wire Color
7		7	
8		8	

Figure D.5 illustrates the pin layout of both ends of crossover cable.

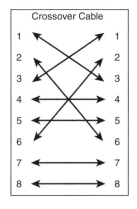

FIGURE D.5
Crossover wiring pin assignments.

Direct Cable Connection Cabling

A direct cable connection is a network connection between two computers using an infrared or cable connection. Cable communications are supported by serial or parallel cables as depicted in Figure D.6. However, these cables are configured with special pinouts. These cables are usually sold and advertised as PC-to-PC cables and are wired as shown in Tables D.6 and D.7.

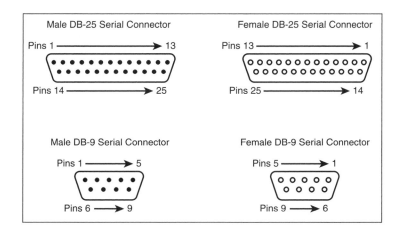

FIGURE D.6
DB-9 and DB-24 pin connectors.

PART V

APPENDIX D Networking Cabling Specifications

SEE ALSO

➤ *To learn more about how to set up a DCC connection, see page 549.*

Table D.6 Pin Connections for Serial Cables

9-pin	9-pin	25-pin	25-pin	9-pin	25-pin
pin 5	pin 5	pin 7	pin 7	pin 5	pin 7
pin 3	pin 2	pin 2	pin 3	pin 3	pin 3
pin 7	pin 8	pin 4	pin 5	pin 7	pin 5
pin 1 & 6 pin 4	pin 6	pin 20	pin 1 & 6 pin 20		
pin 2	pin 3	pin 3	pin 2	pin 2	pin 2
pin 8	pin 7	pin 5	pin 4	pin 8	pin 4
pin 4	pin 1 & 6	pin 20	pin 6	pin 4	pin 6

Table D.7 Pin Connections for Bidirectional Parallel Cables

25-pin	25-pin
pin 2	pin 15
pin 3	pin 13
pin 4	pin 12
pin 5	pin 10
pin 6	pin 11
pin 15	pin 2
pin 13	pin 3
pin 12	pin 4
pin 10	pin 5
pin 11	pin 6
pin 25	pin 25

Appendix

E

Direct Cable Connections

Overview

Direct Cable Connection, or *DCC*, provides network communications between two computers connected by a serial, parallel, or infrared link (see Figure E.1). DCC provides a means for establishing a simple network connection between two computers without implementing an Ethernet or Token-Ring solution. If one of the computers is connected to a network, it can provide access to network resources by acting as a *gateway*.

Following are some important points regarding DCC:

- DCC is a good option for establishing temporary network connections.

- The connection is established using a dedicated port.

- Available ports include serial, parallel, and infrared.

- These ports were never intended to support sustained network operations.

- The data transfer rates over these ports are substantially less than traditional network solutions such as Ethernet or Token-Ring.

- Because DCC establishes a network connection, basic networking features such as file and printer sharing are supported.

- DCC makes file transfers easier for people who use a laptop computer with their desktop PC.

- With DCC one computer is set up as a host or server. The other computer is set up as a guest or client.

- If the host computer is attached to a network, it can act as a gateway and provide access for the guest.

- In Windows 2000, DCC supports NetBEUI, IPX/SPX, and TCP/IP protocols.

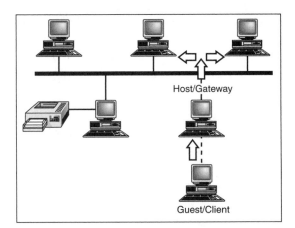

FIGURE E.1
Using DCC to connect a computer to a Windows 2000 Peer Network.

Direct Cable Connectivity

If you choose to establish a DCC using a serial connection, you will need a null-modem cable or a regular modem cable with a null-modem adapter attached to one end.

DCC can provide data transfer rates up to 11.5Kbps over serial connections, depending on the supporting hardware. If your computer is less than four years old, it probably has a 16550 universal asynchronous receiver-transmitter (UART) chip and can provide the 11.5Kbps data transfer rate. However, older computers that do not have this chip are limited to a transfer rate of 2Kbps over serial connections.

Running DDC over a parallel port provides the fastest performance. Windows supports parallel DCC connections over either *standard parallel ports* or *enhanced capabilities ports*, or *ECP*.

Standard parallel ports include unidirectional four-bit and bidirectional eight-bit ports. They are found in computers built before 1995. There are two types:

- Four-bit ports provide 40–60Kbps transmission rates.
- Eight-bit ports provide 80–120Kbps transmission rates.

Enhanced Capabilities ports provide transmission rated at 1Mbps and faster.

The parallel cables that support DCC are generally sold and advertised as PC-to-PC parallel cables. There are three types:

- *Standard or Basic four-bit cable*: Supports 40–70Kbps data transfer rates.

- *Extended Capabilities port (ECP) cable*: Works only when both computers support ECP-enabled parallel ports.

- *Universal Cable Module (UCM) cable*: Senses the type of parallel port present and adjusts itself accordingly. On a bidirectional parallel port, it can provide 80–120 Kbps data transfer rates. On an EPP or ECP port, it can provide 500Kbps to 2Mbps data transfer rates. This cable provides the best overall performance and allows connections between computers with different port types.

Architecture

The primary difference between networking over a LAN with Ethernet or Token-Ring and using DCC to connect two computers is that DCC supports only two connections and depends on the Point-to-Point Protocol, or PPP, to move data packets over the communications medium, as shown in Figure E.2. PPP is a line or WAN protocol.

FIGURE E.2
Direct Cable Connection *architecture.*

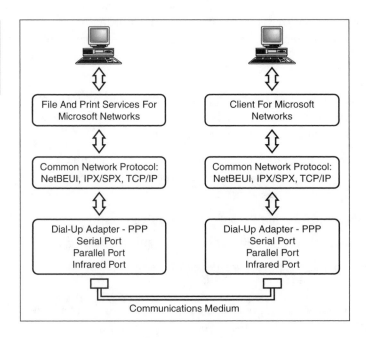

SEE ALSO

➤ *For more information on the Point-to-Point Protocol, see page 245.*

➤ *For more information on the Point-to-Point Protocol, see page 282.*

➤ *For additional information on the Point-to-Point Protocol, see page 536.*

Installation

Three steps are involved in getting a DCC network session up and running. The first step is the establishment of the DCC communication medium. This is usually a PC-to-PC parallel or serial cable, although infrared communication is supported. The second and third steps involve the configuration of DCC on both computers. One acts as the DCC server or host computer. The other acts as the DCC client or guest computer. The rest of this appendix demonstrates how to establish a DCC network session between two Windows 2000 Pro computers.

Setting up the host side of the connection

1. Right-click on the **My Network Places** icon on the Windows 2000 desktop, and select **Properties** from the menu that appears. The Network and Dial-Up Connections dialog appears.

2. Double-click on the **Make New Connection** icon. The Network Connection Wizard starts. Click **Next**.

3. Select **Connect Directly to Another Computer** and click on **Next**, as shown in Figure E.3.

> **DCCs Between Different Operating Systems**
>
> As long as two computers support a common protocol, a DCC network connection can be established between them even if they are running different Windows operating systems. For example, a Windows 98 guest can connect to a Windows 2000 Pro DCC host and vice versa using a serial, parallel, or Infrared connection. The only exception is that a DCC session with a Windows NT 4.0 computer requires a serial connection.

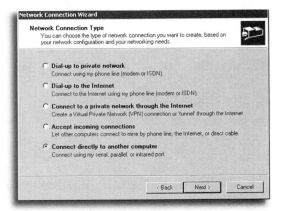

FIGURE E.3
The Network Connection Wizard.

4. To set up the DCC server computer, select **Host**, as shown in Figure E.4. Click **Next**.

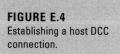

FIGURE E.4
Establishing a host DCC connection.

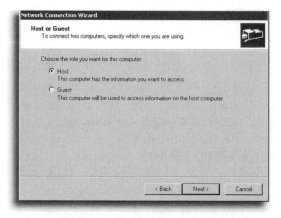

5. Select the appropriate connection medium from the **Device for This Connection** drop-down list, as shown in Figure E.5. Typical choices include Direct Parallel, Communications Ports (serial ports), and Infrared Ports, if such a device is available. Click **Next**.

FIGURE E.5
Selection of a communications port.

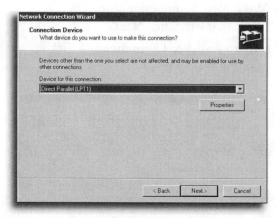

6. Windows displays a list of all defined user accounts on the computer. Select the users who will be permitted to connect to the host computer using this connection, as shown in Figure E.6. Click **Next**.

FIGURE E.6
Selecting users who will be permitted to access the host computer through a DCC connection.

7. Click **Finish**.

An icon representing the Host connection is created in the Network and Dial-Up Connections dialog. The host computer then begins to monitor the assigned port for a request for a connection from a guest computer.

Setting up the guest side of the connection

1. Right-click on the **My Network Places** icon on the Windows 2000 desktop, and select **Properties** from the menu that appears. The Network and Dial-Up Connections dialog appears.

2. Double-click on the **Make New Connection** icon. The Network Connection Wizard starts; click on **Next**.

3. Select **Connect Directly to Another Computer**, as shown previously in Figure E.3. Click **Next**.

4. To set up the DCC client computer, select **Guest** and click **Next**.

5. Select the appropriate connection medium from the **Select a Device** drop-down list, and click **Next**.

6. To allow other users on this computer to use this connection, select **For All Users**. Otherwise, select **Only for Myself**. Click **Next**.

7. Click **Finish**.

An icon representing the Guest connection is created in the Network and Dial-Up Connections dialog. A connection request is automatically initiated on the guest computer.

DCC Is Limited to a Serial Connection in NT 4.0

DCC is limited to a serial connection on Windows NT 4.0 and is referred to as *Dial-Up Networking Serial Cable Between 2 PCs* in Windows NT. Installing it from the Modem utility requires initiating the manual installation of a modem, selecting the Dial-Up Networking Serial Cable Between 2 PCs option, and following the instructions presented.

Installing DCC in Windows 9X

On Windows 95 and 98, DCC must first be installed using the Add/Remove utility in the Windows Control Panel. After installation, you can configure it by selecting Programs, Accessories, Communications, and then Direct Cable Communication. A wizard then guides you through the installation of either a DCC client or a host.

The Life of a DCC Network Session

After the host and guest computers have been configured, a network session can be established between them. After the host computer is configured, it begins monitoring the assigned port. It is up to the user at the guest computer to initiate a session.

Starting a DCC session

1. On the guest computer, right-click on the **My Network Places** icon on the Windows 2000 desktop, and select **Properties** from the menu that appears. The Network and Dial-Up Connections dialog appears.

2. Double-click on the icon representing the guest DCC connection. The Connect Direct Connection dialog appears.

3. Type the username and associated password of an account that has been set up on the host computer to use a DCC connection, as shown in Figure E.7. Click **Connect**.

FIGURE E.7
Initiating a DCC session from a guest computer.

4. The guest computer attempts to contact the host computer. When the host computer acknowledges the connection request, the guest computer passes the username and password to the host. The prompt shown in Figure E.8 appears.

FIGURE E.8
The username and password credentials are exchanged.

5. Next, a prompt appears on the guest computer indicating that the host is registering the guest computer on the network, as shown in Figure E.9.

FIGURE E.9
The host computer registers the guest computer on the network.

6. Next, a prompt appears, showing that the credentials presented by the user have been authenticated, as shown in Figure E.10.

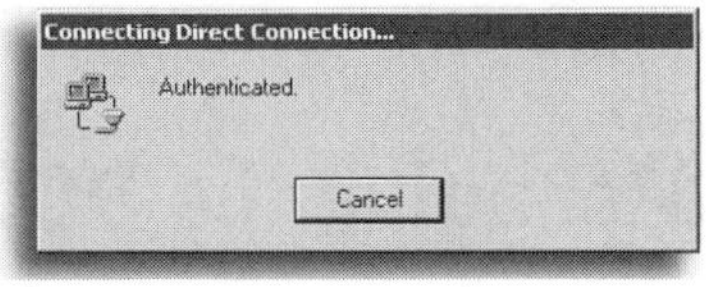

FIGURE E.10
Authentication has been completed.

7. Finally, the dialog shown in Figure E.11 appears, stating that the connection is complete. To prevent this dialog from appearing in the future, the **Do Not Display This Message Again** option must be cleared. Click **OK**.

FIGURE E.11
Windows 2000 completes the establishment of the DCC session.

After a DCC connection has been established, an icon representing the active connection appears in the system tray on the taskbar of both computers. Double-clicking on the icon brings up a dialog that provides general session information and the capability to terminate the session from either computer by use of the Disconnect button.

When the DCC session is established, network applications such as custom Microsoft Management Consoles can be executed as shown in Figure E.12. Here, a custom MMC has been configured to manage user and group accounts on both the guest and the host computer.

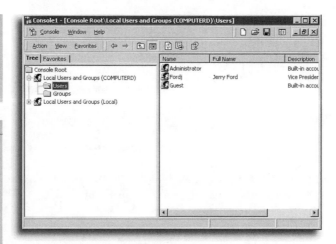

FIGURE E.12
Using a custom MMC to manage the remote computer on a DCC session.

Initiating DCC with a Dial-Up Networking Entry

DCC connections are initiated by the creation of a dial-up networking entry in the Dial-Up Networking phone book. To do this, double-click on the **My Computer** icon, double-click on the **Dial-Up Networking** icon, and click **Add**. Do not provide a phone number when prompted. After the connection definition has been created, click on **Dial** to initiate a connection.

Initiating a DCC Guest

On Windows 9X computers, a DCC guest is initiated by the selection of **Start**, **Programs**, **Accessories**, **Communications**, and then **Direct Cable Connection**. When the DCC dialog appears, click on **Connect**. If the DDC host computer is a Windows 9X computer, the DDC program must be started and must be monitoring activity. To do this, select **Start**, **Programs**, **Accessories**, **Communications**, and then **Direct Cable Connection**. When the DCC dialog appears, click **Listen**.

Managing the DCC Gateway

By default, Windows 2000 sets up any computer with a Host DCC connection as a network *gateway*. This enables the users at the guest computer to access both host and network resources to which the user has access permissions. This gateway function can be disabled, thus limiting the guest computer to host resources.

Configuring a DCC gateway

1. On a host computer, right-click on the **My Network Places** icon on the Windows 2000 desktop, and select **Properties** from the menu that appears. The Network and Dial-Up Connections dialog appears.

2. Right-click on the icon representing the DCC connection and select **Properties**. The Properties dialog for the DCC connection appears.

3. Select the **Networking** tab, as shown in Figure E.13.

4. Clear any protocols that should not be supported by the DCC connection. For each remaining protocol, select it and click on **Properties**. The selected protocol's Properties dialog appears. To disable the gateway support, clear the **Allow Callers to**

Access My Local Area Network option, as shown in Figure E.14. Click **OK**.

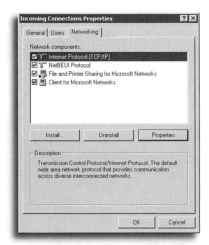

FIGURE E.13
Selecting protocols to be supported by the connection.

DCC in Windows 9X and NT?

Windows 95 and Windows 98 both offer full support for DCC. However, Windows NT supports only a serial connection.

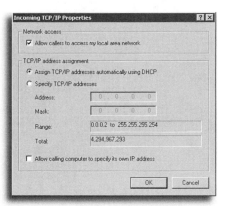

FIGURE E.14
Configuring DCC gateway access.

Load NetBEUI

If the host computer is unable to provide a gateway to its network, try loading NetBEUI on all involved computers.

5. Click **OK** to close the Properties dialog for the DCC connection.

Appendix

F

HomePNA

Overview of HomePNA Networks

The first quarter of 1999 saw the emergence of a new type of networking aimed at the nontechnical home user. This new market is led by the *Home Phoneline Networking Alliance*, or *HomePNA*. HomePNA was established to build a standard for networks using existing telephone wiring, as demonstrated in Figure F.1. HomePNA founding members include 3Com, IBM, Intel, AT&T Wireless, Compaq, Hewlett-Packard Company, AMD, Epigram, Lucent Technologies, Tut Systems, and Rockwell Semiconductor Systems.

FIGURE F.1
HomePNA networks use existing telephone wires in homes and offices to connect computers.

HomePNA recognizes that many households do not deploy networks for many reasons, including these:

- Complexity involved in administering modern networks.
- Costs required to set up a network (cabling, hub, labor, and so on).
- Difficulty in running network cabling.

To overcome these constraints, HomePNA networks attempt to address the following objectives:

- To work over existing home wiring using RJ-11 modular phone jacks.
- To provide easy installation with Plug and Play technology.
- To provide a low-cost network solution.
- To support existing cable lengths (capable of serving homes up to 10,000 square feet).
- To provide high-speed data transmission rates.
- To provide for future growth to higher data rates with backward compatibility.
- To establish secure networks.
- To operate alongside existing systems such as telephones, answering machines, and fax machines.

- To impose zero interference with existing systems operating on the phone line.

HomePNA objectives are complicated by the fact that telephone wiring in homes is not intended to support networking and differs greatly from house to house. The older the home, the greater the chances that existing wiring will produce more signal noise. HomePNA must accommodate these varied conditions.

HomePNA networks must be able to support three types of communications over a single wire. This is accomplished using a technique known as *Frequency Division Multiplexing*, or *FDM*. FDM works by assigning different frequencies to each type of service that shares access to the phone line. These are the three types of communications handled by HomePNA networks:

- Voice communication

- Internet access

- Network traffic

By operating at different frequency levels, each signal can coexist without interfering with the other signals. This permits continuous network operation while regular telephone services, such as voice communications and fax machines, are being used.

Multiple manufacturers have already brought HomePNA network products to the marketplace. A partial list of product offerings is shown in Table F.1.

Table F.1 A Sampling of HomePNA Products

HomePNA Network Name	Manufacturers
HomeLink Phoneline Network in a box	www.linksys.com
Boca HAN	www.bocaresearch.com
Diamond HomeFree	www.diamonmm.com
ActionTec ActionLink	www.actiontec.com
Zoom	www.zoomtel.com
i.Share KoJack	www.artisoft.com
Home PC Link	www.bestdata.com

HomePNA manufacturers sell starter kits for establishing two-computer networks. Additional computers can be added to the network with the purchase of single-computer HomePNA expansion kits. A typical HomePNA networking kit includes the following:

- Two HomePNA network adapter cards.
- Proxy software allowing multiple computers on the network to access the Internet using one modem.
- Two RJ-11 telephone cables.

Current HomePNA networks provide support for up to 25 networked computers (see Figure F.2). After the network has been set up, support for printer and disk resource sharing is achieved using standard Windows networking services and client software. HomePNA manufacturers provide an installation wizard to step the user through the setup process. All the current HomePNA networks support Windows 95 and 98. Most also support Windows NT or are planning to provide Windows NT support. Windows 2000 support will soon be on its way. One vendor's kit even includes a 56K modem.

Each manufacturer also supplies some sort of proxy support for providing shared Internet access over the network. Proxy software typically includes built-in firewall protection. A *firewall* protects the network by denying outside access to the network. Proxy software allows multiple computers to access the Internet simultaneously using one dial-up connection. This provides multiple advantages, including these:

- Eliminates the need for extra phone lines for every computer requiring Internet access.
- Eliminates the need to purchase additional modems.
- Allows all users to share a single Internet account.
- Provides simultaneous access to the Internet.

HomePNA networks provide up to a 1Mbps transmission rate over an Ethernet network. This rate is 20 times faster than the fastest modems but only 10% of the speed of regular 10Mbps Ethernet. Although 1Mbps might not be sufficient for small businesses' network requirements, it should be sufficient for home use. HomePNA manufacturers provide network adapter cards that include a pass-through port facilitating a telephone connection (see Figure F.3).

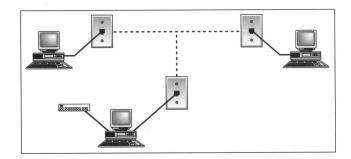

FIGURE F.2
HomePNA networks offer a proxy service and automatically select and configure a network computer to provide access to the Internet.

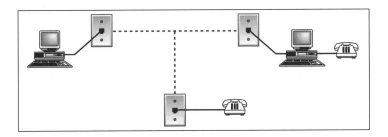

FIGURE F.3
HomePNA allows both regular phone service and network services to coexist on a wire.

HomePNA networks offer many advantages for home computer owners:

- No hub or additional wiring required.
- Fast and easy installation.
- Requires little technical experience or knowledge.
- Modem sharing eliminates the need for multiple personal Internet accounts.
- Uninterrupted phone service.

The primary disadvantage of a HomePNA network is the limited bandwidth capacity of the current standard. This limitation is currently being addressed, and a new 10Mbps standard is being proposed.

Bargain Hunting

Combining shared Internet access with free email accounts offered by companies such as Yahoo or Hotmail provides a very inexpensive Internet solution. It eliminates the need for each family member to pay for an individual Internet account.

Identifying HomePNA Network Features

HomePNA networks provide the same basic services found in standard 10Mbps Ethernet networks, such as file and print sharing. In addition, other features are found on HomePNA networks, including these:

- Automatic detection of a network computer with installed modems.
- Automatic selection of the computer best suited to serve as the network gateway using proxy software.
- Support for ISDN, ADSL, V.90, 56K, or V.34 modems.
- Automatic IP assignment.
- Support for many popular Internet applications, such as browsers and email.
- Built-in firewall capabilities.

HomePNA NIC features vary by vendor but typically include link, activity, and collision LED indicators.

HomePNA-compliant networks run over home-grade copper telephone cabling using RJ-11 cables to connect computers to wall outlets. Despite the fact that home phone cabling was never intended to support network traffic, HomePNA networks provide transmission rates up to 1Mbps and allow as many as 25 computers to be connected.

HomePNA works without interfering with devices currently operating over phone lines. This includes support for regular telephone service (POTS) and digital subscriber lines (xDSL) (see Figure F.4).

Some HomePNA manufacturers are shipping NICs that provide support for standard 10BASE-T Ethernet networks. These cards have the obvious advantage of providing a direct means of expanding from a 1Mbps HomePNA network to a full 10Mbps Ethernet-based network.

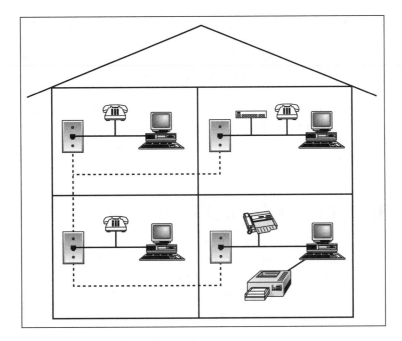

FIGURE F.4
HomePNA networks can connect up to 25 computers over existing phone lines without interfering with existing phone services.

Reviewing Required Hardware

Typical HomePNA network offerings require computers equipped with Pentium-class processors. Different manufacturers' HomePNA kits have different minimum hardware requirements. These are the typical minimum hardware requirements:

- Pentium 100
- 16MB of memory
- CD-ROM
- An open PCI card slot
- 7MB to 40MB free hard-drive space
- Windows 95, 98, or NT
- A modem for Internet access

Initial pricing is around $100 to $150 for a two-network kit, with additional cards costing between $50 and $80 each.

HomePNA hardware requirements preclude the capability to include older computers such as 386 or 486 machines.

Windows for Workgroups is also currently not supported. Machines with less than 16MB or no available PCI expansion slots are not good candidates for HomePNA networking. If the network must connect older or underpowered computers, HomePNA will not be able to support them. This will necessitate setting up a traditional standard Ethernet network running at 10Mbps or 100Mbps. Standard Ethernet networks are capable of supporting computers with older operating systems or fewer hard resources than a HomePNA network can accommodate.

Installing a HomePNA Network

One of the objectives of HomePNA networking is simplicity of installation and setup. This means that the network owner does not need any special technical skills. The installation process is straight-forward, as outlined here:

1. Install a HomePNA-compliant NIC in an open expansion slot.

2. Use the provided RJ-11 telephone cable to attach the computer to an available telephone outlet.

3. Power up the computer and allow Plug and Play to install the network adapter card.

4. Execute the vendor-provided installation wizard.

Examining the Future of HomePNA

The current standard for HomePNA networks is 1Mbps. Many vendors of HomePNA networks are including dual-port network adapter cards that support both an RJ-11 and an RJ-45 connection. This enables the owner of the network to eventually convert to a standard 10Mbps Ethernet network by replacing telephone cabling with RJ-45 cables and a network hub (see Figure F.5).

However, HomePNA is already examining the means of introducing 10Mbps networking over standard home wiring without the need to convert to a traditional Ethernet network. This will allow the home network owner to continue to use existing wiring and removes the requirement of replacing the RJ-11 cabling with RJ-45 and purchasing a hub.

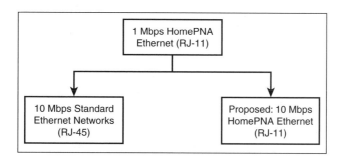

FIGURE F.5
There are two expansion paths from the current HomePNA standard.

GLOSSARY

10BASE-2   Also known as ThinNet cable. It is typically used to implement a bus network. This cable supports up to 10Mbps baseband transmission rates over a distance of 185 meters.

10BASE-5   Also known as ThickNet. It is an older cabling technology not commonly found in modern networks. It is thicker than 10BASE-2 and requires special tools to attach it to network devices. This cable supports up to 10Mbps baseband transmission rates over a distance of 500 meters.

10BASE-T   A twisted-pair network cable typically used to implement a star network. This cable supports up to 10Mbps baseband transmission rates over a distance of 100 meters.

56K LAN modem   A special type of modem that includes built-in support for multiple concurrent users. This device is typically connected to the network with its built-in Ethernet interface and might provide multiple communication ports for direct connection.

100BASE-T4   A 100Mbps Ethernet specification that supports transmission over CAT 3, 4, or 5 cable.

Access methods   Low-level hardware protocols such as Ethernet and Token-Ring used by all computers on the network.

Access token   An access token is created as a part of the Windows NT logon process. It contains the System ID assigned to the user's account, as well as the Group IDs of any assigned group accounts of which the user is a member. The operating system uses the token to determine when a user can access a given resource.

Account   An account is established to identify a user to the computer. Account information includes a username, password, and description.

Account lockout   An account lockout occurs either when a user mistypes his or her password more times than allowed by the system's security policy or when an administrator locks the account. Until the account lockout is removed, the account cannot be used to log on to the computer.

Account policy   A policy that establishes security rules that govern the activity of users' accounts on the computer. Options include the capability to establish thresholds for account lockouts, minimum password ages, password histories, and minimum password lengths.

ACE (Access Control Entry) A component of the Access Control List on a Windows NT computer. It contains a list of access permissions for users and groups that have been assigned to it.

ACL (Access Control List)   Every object on a Windows NT computer maintains an Access Control List, or ACL, that the operating system uses to decide whether a user may access the object. The ACL is composed of a series of Access Control Entries, or ACEs.

Active hub   A hub that regenerates all received electrical signals and sends them on to every connected network device.

Adapter   A peripheral card that is usually mounted inside a computer's case that provides a connection with a system bus. A network adapter card is an example of an adapter that provides physical connectivity between a computer and a network.

Administrators   Individuals charged with the responsibility of configuring and maintaining a computer network.

ADSL (Asymmetric Digital Subscriber Line)   A network communications technology that supports communications over standard telephone lines without interrupting regular telephone services. The *A* in *ADSL* stands for "asymmetric," which means that it is a technology that allows greater bandwidth for receiving data than for transmitting it. ADSL is capable of supporting download rates of up to 6Mbps and upload rates of up to 1Mbps.

Analog router   A device similar to a LAN modem. It provides multiple 56K modems that are combined into a single logical bandwidth to provide faster transmission rates.

AppleTalk   A peer networking protocol used by Apple computers to create small networks.

Application response   A measurement of how quickly the operating system responds to the local user. Windows 2000 provides the capability to tune applications from the System Properties dialog.

Arpanet (Advanced Research Projects Agency Network)   A project of the United States Department of Defense back in the 1960s that eventually led to the creation of the Internet. The network was designed to survive a nuclear attack and continue to provide reliable services.

Audit   The process of logging event information on a computer. Windows 2000 provides three audit logs for storing system, security, and application information.

Barrel connector   A special connector that can join two pieces of coax cable to form a single cable.

Baseband   A type of data transmission in which the entire bandwidth of the communications channel is dedicated to transmitting a single bit stream.

Binding   The process of setting up protocols, services, and network adapters to work with one another. A protocol that is bound to an adapter can use that adapter for transmitting data. Similarly, a service that is bound to a protocol can use that protocol to communicate over the network.

BIOS (Basic Input/Output System)   Software stored in read-only memory on a computer's motherboard that contains the bootstrap process that starts the computer when powered on.

Bit   The smallest unit of data that can be manipulated by a computer.

BNC connector   Connects to the ends of the coax cable and provides connection to BNC T connectors and terminators. It is also referred to as a bayonet or a stab-and-twist connector.

BNC T connector   A connector that attaches a computer to a coaxial-cable network connection.

BPS (Bits Per Second)   A measure of transmission speed commonly used to gauge modem throughput.

Broadband   A type of data transmission in which the available bandwidth of the communications channel is divided into multiple communications channels, each of which is capable of transmitting a bit stream.

Broadcast   A data packet or frame that is sent to every computer on the network.

Brownout   The sudden loss or reduction of electrical power that results in rebooting computer equipment and that might cause damage to sensitive computer equipment.

Browsing   The act of using a utility such as the Network Neighborhood to navigate a computer or network and to view or access computer resources.

Bus   A network topology in which all computers are connected to a single trunk or line of cabling. Computers are connected to the line with BNC connectors. Both ends of the line must be terminated with terminators. Bus networks are commonly implemented using ThinNet or 10BASE-2 cabling.

Cable modem   Provides modem services over a shared cable connection. Depending on the number of active users on the cable, transmission rates up to 1Mbps can be achieved. Today many ISP cable providers limit the connection bandwidth to 122Kbps.

Cable type   The type of cabling used to support network traffic. Typically, either twisted-pair or coaxial cable is the choice for peer networks.

Cache   A portion of the local memory used to store information retrieved from the hard drive that provides for faster retrieval of data.

CAT3   Standard voice-grade wiring found in many of today's homes and office buildings. Though seldom used for computer networks, it can support 10Mbps Ethernet data transmissions.

CAT5   The most common twisted-pair cable used in modern networks. It supports 10Mbps and 100Mbps networking.

Client   A computer that uses information or services provided by network servers.

Client for Microsoft Networks Software that enables a Windows computer to access resources shared by other computers on the network.

Coaxial Cable   A copper-based cable used in building networks that is capable of supporting 10Mbps data transmissions.

Collision   Occurs when two computers attempt to transmit at the same time on an Ethernet network.

Combo card   Also known as a hybrid card, it supports multiple interfaces. For example, a combo network card may support either coaxial or twisted-pair cabling.

Computer networking   A means for interconnecting computer equipment to support communication, data exchange, and device sharing. Computer networks provide a communication medium for sending and receiving information in the form of text, audio, and video from device to device at enormous speeds.

Concentrator   See *hub*.

CRC (Cyclical Redundancy Checksum)   A component of a network packet or frame that enables error detection. The value of the CRC is computed after the packet is created and added to the end of the packet. The receiving computer recalculates the CRC for each frame it receives and compares its calculation to the value stored at the end of the frame. If the two values match, the data is assumed to have arrived intact.

Crossover cable   A special type of twisted-pair cable in which the transmit and receive wires are reversed to allow two computers to establish a small network without an intervening hub.

Crosstalk   A quality of wire-based communications in which the electric signals of nearby wires tend to interfere with one another.

CSMA/CD (Carrier Sense Multiple Access with Collision Detection) An access method employed by Ethernet networks. This is a competitive method in which every computer with data to send on the network competes for access to the line. Before transmitting over the wire, the computer first listens to find out whether another device is currently transmitting. When no other devices are transmitting, the computer assumes that it is free to send its data on the wire. If another network device is currently using the network, the computer waits for a random period before repeating this process. After the network is free, the computer can transmit its data. The computer then listens to the wire after transmitting its data to ensure that no collisions occur.

DCC (Direct Cable Connection) A Windows utility that provides temporary networking connectivity between two computers using a special PC-to-PC parallel or serial cable or infrared connection.

Demodulation   The process a modem uses to convert analog signals back into digital signals after receiving them over a telephone line.

Dial-Up Networking (DUN)   The sharing of resources over a telephone communications link using a remote network connection.

DIP-switches   A series of switches located on older motherboard and adapter cards that are used to provide configuration information by toggling individual switches to off and on positions.

Disk quota   A preset limit on the amount of storage space a user can consume on a computer.

DMA (Direct Memory Access) DMA assignments provide a NIC with direct access to a limited portion of system memory that can be accessed without relying on the CPU.

Domain   A collection of clients and servers that are managed as an organizational unit with a centralized security database.

Drag and drop   The selection of one or more files which are then moved to a new location and dropped there.

DSL (Digital Subscriber Lines)   A technology provided by some local telephone companies that supports high-speed data transportation over standard telephone lines.

ECP (Enhanced Capabilities Ports)   Parallel ports that support connection of parallel print devices and communication using Direct Cable Connection with 1Mbps transmission rates.

EMI (Electromagnetic Interference)   An outside source that interferes with electrical signals traveling over a network wire. Sources of EMI include fluorescent lighting and electrical generators.

ERD (Emergency Repair Disk)   A disk containing critical system files and configuration information that can be used to repair deleted or corrupted files on the Windows 2000 computer from which it was created.

Ethernet   A low-level access method protocol that operates on the premise that all workstations can transmit network data as long as the network is not busy at the moment when the computer is ready to retransmit.

External print server   A device with its own processor and memory that is attached directly to the network and provides a port connection for a parallel printer.

FAT (File Allocation Table)   The original file system used by IBM PCs. This file system lacks the advanced security features supported by NTFS. FAT filenames are up to eight characters with a period and a three-character extension. Each file entry also contains a date and time stamp and attribute information such as read-only and hidden.

FAT32   The latest version of the FAT file system. It supports smaller cluster sizes to provide more efficient use of hard-drive storage. It also provides support for long filenames up to 255 characters, including spaces and multiple periods.

Firewall   A piece of hardware or software that protects the network by controlling outside access to the network.

FMD (Frequency Modulation Distribution)   A method of allowing multiple types of communication to occur over a single communication medium by assigning a different frequency range to each technology.

Gateway   A device or piece of software that provides shared access to another computer or network.

Home Phoneline Networking Alliance   An organization dedicated to leading the development of HomePNA networks. HomePNA founding members include 3Com, IBM, Intel, AT&T Wireless, Compaq, Hewlett-Packard Company, AMD, Epigram, Lucent Technologies, Tut Systems, and Rockwell Semiconductor Systems.

HomePNA   A home-based networking solution provided by third-party companies. HomePNA networks operate using existing home telephone wiring to connect Windows 95, 98, and NT computers.

Home run cabling   A cabling technique used on star networks to connect network devices to the hub.

Each cable connects a single device to the hub.

Hub   A device that provides connectivity on a star network.

Hybrid card   A card that supports multiple interfaces. For example, a combo network card could support both coaxial and twisted-pair cabling.

Internet   A public worldwide network based on the TCP/IP protocol suite.

Internet Explorer   Microsoft's Internet browser that permits navigation of Internet, local network, and computer resources.

Internet hub   A network hub that provides for the connection of external modems to allow it to provide shared access to the Internet.

Intranet   A private network built using the same standards and protocols that support the Internet.

I/O port address   A location on an adapter card that identifies the addresses where the data being manipulated by the card will be stored.

IP (Internet Protocol)   A connectionless protocol in the TCP/IP protocol suite that is responsible for addressing and sending information over a TCP/IP network.

IP address   A unique address on a TCP/IP network assigned to an individual device, such as a computer or network printer. It is composed of the network address and the host address.

IPSec (IP Security Protocol) A protocol that supports the establishment of virtual private networks by tunneling or encapsulating NetBEUI, IPX/SPX, and TCP/IP traffic.

IPv6   The next-generation Internet protocol that will replace the current IPv4 protocol. It is a 128-bit addressing system that will resolve the current shortage of IP addresses associated with the 32-bit IPv4 protocol.

IPX/SPX (Internetwork Packet Exchange/Sequential Packet Exchange)   A protocol stack developed by Novell based on the Xerox XNS protocol. It is the default protocol on all NetWare version 4.x and earlier network operation systems. It is a routable protocol typically used on Microsoft networks to allow computers to connect to NetWare servers.

IRQ (Interrupt Request)   A communications channel assigned to peripheral devices used to communicate with the CPU. Personal computers have 16 IRQs available, numbered 0–15.

ISA (Industry Standard Architecture)   The original bus architecture used on IBM PCs. Originally an 8-bit architecture, it was later expanded to 16 bits.

ISDN modem   A device that provides modem-like services. It requires an ISDN communication line that is leased from a local telecommunications carrier.

ISDN LAN modem   A special type of ISDN modem that also provides gateway Internet services to other computers. It provides the services of both a hub and an ISDN modem on the network.

ISP (Internet Service Provider)   A company that provides access to the Internet as a subscriber service.

Jumper   A small grouping of pins that stick up on the motherboard and adapter cards that provide configuration information.

L2TP (Layer-2 Tunneling Protocol)   A protocol that supports the establishment of virtual private networks by tunneling or encapsulating NetBEUI, IPX/SPX, and TCP/IP traffic. Similar to the PPTP protocol except that it does not require IP connectivity. It can operate over frame relay, ATM, IP, and X.25 networks.

LAN (Local Area Network)   A network that occupies a small area such as a small office, floor, or building.

Legacy cards   Older hardware that does not support Plug and Play and must be manually configured.

Line conditioner   A device that conditions the flow of electrical current to attached computer devices.

Line protocols   See *wide area network protocols*.

Local printer   A print device that is connected to a port on the computer.

Low-level protocol communication   See *access methods*.

MAC (Medial Access Control)   A 48-bit number burned into every NIC card that uniquely identifies the card. The first 24 bits identify the manufacturer of the card, and the last 24 bits identify the card's unique address.

MAN (Metropolitan Area Network)   A network that spans a city or other similar metropolitan area.

MMC (Microsoft Management Console)   A tool that provides a standardized interface for working with administrative tools known as snap-ins.

Modem   A device that converts digital signals (modulation) used by the computer into analog signals so that they can be transported over standard-grade telephone wire. The receiving modem converts (demodulation) signals back into a digital format.

Modulation   The process a modem uses to convert digital signals into analog signals for transmission over telephone lines.

MSDN (Microsoft's Developer Network)   A Microsoft Internet Web site at http://msdn.microsoft.com dedicated to providing technical information to IT professionals.

NetBEUI (NetBIOS Extended User Interface)   A protocol stack designed for small department-sized networks up to 50 computers. It is supported exclusively by Microsoft and IBM-based networks.

Network adapter   See *network interface card*.

Network aware application   An application that is able to recognize and work with network resources. This includes such functionality as being able to browse and open files in network shares.

Network card   See *(NIC) network interface card*.

Network drive   A hard drive or folder that is shared over the network.

Network operating system   An operating system used on network servers such as Windows 2000 Server or Novell's NetWare. Operating systems such as Windows 2000 Professional have network operating system software integrated into them.

Network printer   A printer that is available to computers on the network.

NIC (Network Interface Card)   An adapter card that connects a computer to a network.

NTFS (New Technology File System)   A secure Windows file system that provides support for hard-drive partitions up to 16 exabytes. It supports advanced features such as file compression, fault tolerance schemes, transaction tracking, and NTFS security.

NTFS security   A security system that assigns permissions to users and groups on a resource-by-resource basis and then uses Access Control Lists and access tokens to protect access to these resources.

NWLink   The name given to Microsoft's IPX/SPX implementation on Windows NT operating systems.

Outlook Express   Microsoft Windows 2000 Professional's built-in email client.

Passive hub   A hub that acts as a simple pass-through device and does not increase the strength of electrical signals as they are sent to every connected network device.

PCI (Peripheral Connection Interface)   A 32-bit bus specification designed by Intel designed to provide optimum support on Pentium-based computers.

Peer print server   A computer on a peer network that makes a locally attached printer available on the network.

Plug and Play   A computer standard supported by Microsoft and

577

many hardware vendors in which peripheral devices are designed to allow the operating system to discover and configure them during system startup.

Plug and Play BIOS   A BIOS capable of detecting and configuring hardware during system boot. It then passes this information to the operating system after the operating systems starts.

PPP (Point-to-Point Protocol)   A wide area network, or WAN, protocol typically used to establish dial-up connections to the Internet. It supports the transmission or encapsulation of multiple protocols, including TCP/IP, IPX/SPX, and NetBEUI.

PPTP (Point-to-Point Tunneling Protocol)   A secure protocol that supports the establishment of a Virtual Private Network over public and private IP networks. It supports the transport or encapsulation of NetBEUI, IPX/SPX, and TCP/IP.

Print device   In Windows terminology this is the physical printer, whereas the software driver for the print device is known as the printer.

Print driver   A software module that extends the operating system's control over a print device.

Print Queue Manager   A component of the Windows 2000 Print Subsystem that manages the process of receiving, spooling, and submitting print jobs to a print device.

Print server   The computer that provides and manages the print queue for a network printer.

Printer   In Windows terminology this is the software driver for the print device, whereas the physical printer is know as the print device.

Protocol   An agreed-on set of rules and procedures for communicating and exchanging data over a network. Examples of local area network protocols include TCP/IP, NetBEUI, and IPX/SPX.

Protocol access method   The lowest level of network protocols. The two most appropriate for small networks are Ethernet and Token-Ring.

Proxy server   A computer with a NIC and a modem that provides shared modem access to network computers.

PWL (Password-List)   A file where Windows for Workgroups stores passwords used by the user when accessing network resources. Windows for Workgroups later can transparently supply passwords from this list to gain access without prompting the user to supply the password.

RAS (Remote Access Service)   A Windows NT service that supports dial-up networking.

Redirector   A software component that intercepts requests for resources and determines whether the targeted resource is located on the local computer. If it is a request for a local resource, the request is allowed to proceed normally. Otherwise, the request is redirected out over the network. The Client for Microsoft Networks performs redirection on a Microsoft network.

Registry   A special database that contains system operating-system and configuration information.

Remote access   The capability to use a modem and a regular phone line to dial into a computer or network and access shared resources.

Remote control   A third-party software application that provides the capability for one computer to connect to another and monitor or gain control over the remote computer's mouse and keyboard, and to view all output displayed on the remote computer monitor.

Resource-level security   See *NTFS security*.

RJ-45   A modular jack used to connect twisted-pair cabling used in networks.

Router   A network device that connects two or more network segments into a single logical network. A router can also translate data packets from one access method to another, thus allowing a Token-Ring network to be connected to an Ethernet network.

Share   A driver, folder, or printer that has been made available to network users.

SLIP (Serial Line Internet Protocol)   An older protocol used to connect with UNIX servers. Windows operating systems support the capability to act as a SLIP client but do not provide SLIP server capability. SLIP is an outdated protocol seldom used today.

Snap-in   An administrative tool that can be added to a Microsoft Management Console. Examples of snap-ins include the Event Viewer, Services, Shared Folders, and Local Users and Groups snap-ins.

Sneaker Net   A network in which one shares data by copying it onto portable media such as floppy disks and carrying it to other users.

Spooling   The process of storing a print job in a temporary file on a local hard drive, where it waits until its turn to print.

Standard parallel ports Unidirectional four-bit and bidirectional eight-bit ports found in computers built before 1995 that support connection to a parallel printer and communication using Direct Cable Connection.

Star   A network topology in which all nodes are connected to a central hub or concentrator. Physically, the network is laid out in a star formation with the hub at the center. Network nodes are connected back to the hub, which manages all network traffic. Locally, the network is managed within the hub like a bus in that every node still receives all network traffic that passes through the hub.

STP (Shielded Twisted-Pair) A form of twisted-pair cabling in which an extra layer of cabling is added to further insulate networking wiring in an effort to protect against electro-magnetic interference. STP was the first type of twisted-pair cabling used in networks. However, in recent years unshielded twisted-pair has become the new standard. An STP cable run is limited to a maximum of 100 meters from hub to workstation.

Subnet mask A value used in con-junction with a computer's IP address to determine the location of other computers on the network.

Surge protector A device that is similar to a power strip but adds pro-tection from surges in the electrical current.

System root folder The location of the folder where Windows's system files are stored. By default, this is `c:\WINNT` on Windows 2000 computers.

TCP (Transmission Control Protocol) A session-oriented pro-tocol that is part of the TCP/IP pro-tocol suite. TCP depends on IP for packet delivery but adds an extra layer of control to ensure reliable delivery.

TCP/IP (Transmission Control Protocol/Internet Protocol) A protocol suite that supports networks of enormous size. It is the protocol of the Internet and is the protocol of choice on larger networks. TCP/IP is known for its complexity, reliability, and capability to support routed networks.

Terminator A small device that fits onto the end of a bus network to pre-vent the transmitted data from being reflected back down the bus after it has reached the end of the cable segment.

Token A signal used on Token-Ring networks to manage how and when individual computers can trans-mit network data. Only the computer currently assigned the token can transmit.

Token-Ring A star-based network topology that operates as a logical ring. A device known as a Multiple Access Unit, or MAU, serves as a central hub or concentrator for the network. A token is passed around the network in one direction. A com-puter can transmit data over the net-work only when it has possession of the token. When the computer's time has expired or when it has no more data to transmit, the token is passed on to the next computer on the ring.

Topology The logical and physical design of a network. A topology describes how the network communication medium is to be configured and how data is transmitted. The three most common topologies are the bus, star, and ring.

Twisted-pair cable   A twisted-pair cable consists of two or more pairs of copper wire. Two types of twisted-pair cables are used in modern networks, shielded and unshielded. Twisted-pair is typically used to support star networks.

UNIX   An operating system typically found on larger computers known as minicomputers. TCP/IP was invented for use on UNIX servers.

UPS (uninterruptible power supply) A device that provides the same services as a line conditioner, with the added benefit that it can supply temporary power to attached devices during lapses in electrical current. Some UPS devices can instruct the computer to safely shut down in the event that the loss of electrical current continues beyond the UPS's capability to supply it.

User account   A collection of information about a user on a network. Every user on the network must have a user account. Among the information stored in each user account are the username and password. A user can access the network only from a valid account.

User profile   A unique profile established for each user of a com-

puter that allows the user to customize his or her own computing environment without affecting other users.

Username   The name assigned to a network user account. A user is required to present the username along with its associated password before gaining access to the network.

UTP (Unshielded Twisted-Pair) A network cable that consists of multiple pairs of twisted wires in a simple plastic-covered casing. The twisted-pair cable used on modern networks consists of two to four pairs of wires connected to an RJ-45 modular jack.

Virtual memory   A technique that allows the operating system to augment physical memory by allowing a portion of the local hard drive to provide virtual memory. The portion of the hard drive set aside is known as the page file or swap file.

VPN (Virtual Private Network) A secure network that operates over a public or private network. VPNs are best known as a means for allowing companies to establish a WAN using the Internet.

WAN (Wide Area Network)   A network consisting of multiple local area networks connected in an area larger in size than a city or other metropolitan area. Communications links are usually established over lines leased from long-distance carriers.

Wide area network protocols
Line protocols used to support transport protocols and encapsulate them into a format capable of traveling over a dial-up connection.

Windows 3.1   The last version of Windows not to include integrated networking support.

Windows 3.11   See *Windows for Workgroups*.

Windows 9X   A generic term used to describe features that both Windows 95 and Windows 98 have in common.

Windows 95   Microsoft's successor to Windows for Workgroups. It features integrated 32-bit network support and was the first operating system to introduce Plug and Play. It supports peer networks of up to 10 computers.

Windows 98   Microsoft's successor to Windows 95. It further refined network support, provided an integrated Internet shell, and included support for the Universal Serial Bus hardware. Like Windows 95, it supports peer networks of up to 10 computers.

Windows 2000 Professional
Microsoft's most recent workstation operating system evolving from Windows NT technology. Originally named Windows NT Workstation 5.0, this operating system provides many new features, including Plug

and Play support, modem proxy services, the Windows 98 interface, improved VPN capabilities, and support for the Universal Serial Bus.

Windows 2000 Server   Microsoft's most recent network server operating system evolving from Windows NT technology. It was originally named Windows NT Server 5.0.

Windows for Workgroups
Microsoft's first operating system to incorporate integrated network support. It is still used on many computers in homes and offices all over the world.

Windows NT 4.0   A high-end 32-bit Microsoft operating system that is sold in two formats: Windows NT 4.0 Workstation and Windows NT 4.0 Server.

Workgroup   An organization model used on peer and domain networks that logically groups computers.

Workgroup Add-On for Windows
A software upgrade that converts a Windows 3.1 installation to a Windows 3.11 installation.

Workstation   A windows NT term referring to a computer running either Windows NT Workstation 4.0 or Windows 2000 Professional.

INDEX

X-Y-Z